THE
ELIZABETH
RIVER

THE
ELIZABETH
RIVER

AMY WATERS YARSINSKE

Charleston · London

History
PRESS

Published by The History Press
Charleston, SC 29403
www.historypress.net

Front cover: Artist Robert Postle contributed this rendering of the Elizabeth from The Hermitage Foundation Museum property to The Living River art exhibition in 2002. *Courtesy of Robert Postle, www.bobpostle.com.*

First published 2007

Manufactured in the United Kingdom

ISBN 978.1.59629.207.9

Library of Congress CIP data applied for.

CONTENTS

PREFACE

In 1619 those who had discovered and mapped the Elizabeth River personified this key body of water—in its beautiful and protected natural harbor, alive with possibilities—with a name. For over two hundred years inhabitants and visitors to the Elizabeth's riverbanks called her by this name; there is much correspondence and original documentation cited herein that demonstrably tells us of her significance, referencing her by name. But there would come a time when the population that sprung up quickly along the Elizabeth River and its tributaries stopped mentioning the princess by her given name. Just prior to the American Civil War the river's stewards were scant and the majority of references to this important place had become impersonal—and often inaccurate—in their description. The river would change dramatically in the century in which she was referenced as "the Norfolk harbor," "the harbor," "the channel" or "the river" by those living on and taking from the Elizabeth; she no longer had a "face." Despite the best efforts of chroniclers from far-flung places, who made the river a geographic point of reference in innumerable stories, the name "Elizabeth" had been relegated to official government documents and nautical charts. Norfolk newspaper columnist Jack Dorsey wrote in November 1977 that the joys of remembering the Elizabeth were more pleasant at that time than the reality of inspecting her polluted waters. Since the mid-1970s, the river's stewards have returned—and so has that personification of the river that those who named her nearly four hundred years ago intended.

Ralph Lane's map of explorations from Roanoke in 1585–86 exists in several forms wrought by engraver Theodor de Bry, the first appearing in 1588 and 1590. This map figuratively broke ground that had heretofore never been seen—the coastal area from Chesapeake Bay to the Neuse River. For the first time the name Chesepiooc Sinus, Lane's spelling of the bay, and the land between the Chesapeake Bay and Albemarle Sound, including all of Lower Tidewater, was called by the Indian name of Weapemiooc. Lane's

In 1619 those who had discovered and mapped the Elizabeth River personified this key body of water— in its beautiful and protected natural harbor, alive with possibilities—with a name.

John White, a member of the company sent by Sir Walter Raleigh to establish an English colony on Roanoke Island in 1585, went at least twice to the Carolina coast in the 1580s. There he produced a series of drawings of the everyday life of the Native American populations. White also compiled this map of the North Carolina coast from Cape Lookout to the mouth of the Chesapeake Bay, based on the British explorations of 1585–86, which was subsequently engraved by Theodor de Bry and published in 1590. *Courtesy of the Library of Congress Geography and Map Division.*

explorations had not extended far enough north to show the peninsula of Hampton Roads. A manuscript map made by gunner Robert Tindall in June 1608, the first detailed map of the land and water courses from the Virginia Capes up the river above Jamestown, shows the location of Cape Henneri (later spelled Cape Henry), Point Comfort and Chechotanke, also called Kecoughtan. The map, however, is not accurate regarding Indian settlements south of Hampton Roads; Nassamonge, an alternative spelling for Nansemond, and Oriskeyek, also called Warrosquyoacke, were both placed too far to the east. The map that Captain John Smith made in 1612, based on his explorations of the same period, is one of the most important maps of Virginia and Maryland, and was reproduced and published in many versions. The 1624 version of the map appeared in Smith's *Generall Historie of Virginia*, which also contained another map of particular interest. The second map was based on and covered the same territory as that of Lane's travels in 1585–86, and was dotted with English place names that have not survived and never came to be used by the early colonists. But the most interesting part of the 1624 map is its title *Ould Virginia*, which was indicative of the custom that grew, after the Jamestown settlement, of distinguishing between the area from Hampton Roads south and that to the north. Most of what is today geographically designated Lower Tidewater was in "Ould Virginia," through which runs its most important body of water—the Elizabeth River.

There would be other interesting maps of this quarter, but only three others will be noted here. There was a map published in Florence, Italy, in 1646 titled *Virginia Vecchia e Nuova*—Virginia Old and New—which has three unusual features. Land between the Chesapeake and Delaware

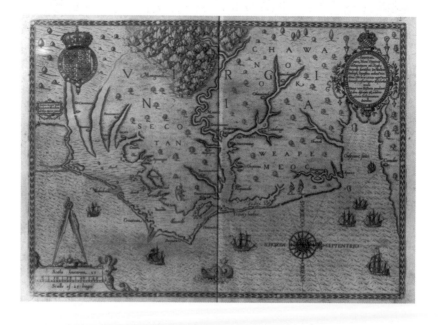

Bays was designated Virginia Orientale, while that to the west and south of the Chesapeake was Virginia Occidentale. The Atlantic Ocean was labeled Mare di Virginia. In 1651 John Farrer, an official of the Virginia Company in England, produced a map called *Ould Virginia and New*, which also displayed some unusual features. The most unusual of these are the term Rawliana for the territory south of the Chesapeake, and the designation Carolana at the upper reaches of the Roanoke, Chowan and Meherrin Rivers. The *Map of Virginia and Maryland* by Augustine Herrman was published in 1673 and is the most interesting of all. Herrman, a native of Bohemia, was the first naturalized citizen of Maryland by order of Cecil Calvert, Second Lord Baltimore. He produced the most accurate map of the Chesapeake Bay, for which he was famous during his lifetime. Herrman's map shows Lower Norfolk, Cape Henry, Willoughby's Point, Seawell's (also Sewell's) Point, Elizabeth River, Lynnhaven River, Tanner's Creek, Nansemond River and its branches, Isle of Wight and its Pagan River, Elizabeth City and the Hampton River and Warwick, showing the Warwick River. Herrman's map was wrought before the formation of Princess Anne and Southampton Counties.

Throughout this account of the river's past and present, the correct, original references and spellings of place names will be used, examples of which include Seawell's Point, today misspelled Sewell's Point, and Tanner's Creek, which has been aggrandized by the name Lafayette River. The Lafayette River is not a river unto itself; it is a large tributary of the Elizabeth

Based on a three-month exploratory survey by boat in the summer of 1608 under the direction of Captain John Smith (ca. 1580–1631), this map is the earliest published of the entire Chesapeake Bay region, inclusive of the Elizabeth River and its watershed. It not only shows the location of Jamestown, the first English settlement in the region, but also the location of Indian villages along the bay and its numerous tributaries. The map is oriented with west at the top, drawing attention to the approaching ships from England at the bottom of the sheet. This engraved version of the Smith map was published in *Virginia, Discovered and Discribed by Captayn John Smith*, sixth state, by William Hole of London, and dates to 1624. *Courtesy of the Library of Congress Geography and Map Division.*

The map that Captain John Smith made in 1612, based on his explorations of the same period, is one of the most important maps of Virginia and Maryland, and was reproduced and published in many versions.

River and, as such, was properly named Tanner's Creek by early settlers. This body of water has a rich history and legacy in Lower Tidewater; in so many words, this storied creek earned its name and will be referenced accordingly throughout this volume.

It is worth noting here that Virginia was the name originally given to all the northern part of the continent of America, and as grants were made to other colonies, their names served only to distinguish them as various parts of Virginia until the colonies became familiar to the citizens of their English homeland. Virginia historian Robert Beverley wrote around 1703 that in the course of time the name came to apply only to the land on the Chesapeake, both Virginia and Maryland. In Beverley's time Virginia implied the territory bounded on the south by North Carolina; on the north by the Potomac River, which divided it from Maryland; on the east by the Main Ocean, also called the Virginia Sea; and on the west and northwest by the California Sea.

Eastern Virginia is part of the Great Coastal Plain, which extends from New York to the Rio Grande. Early explorers and cartographers included in their maps the portion of the Great Coastal Plain known geographically as the Norfolk quadrangle, which embraces the region lying between the parallels 36°30' and 37° north latitude and the meridians 75°30' and 76°30' west longitude. The geographic divisions within the Norfolk quadrangle include low level plain, the Great Dismal Swamp ("the Dismal Swamp"), tide marsh and sand dunes. The Elizabeth River and its watershed fall geographically within the bounds of the Norfolk quadrangle, the principal feature of which is a very level terrace elevated from ten to twenty feet above

In 1651 John Farrer, an official of the Virginia Company in England, produced a map called Ould Virginia and New, which also displayed some unusual features. The most unusual of these are the term "Rawliana" for the territory south of the Chesapeake, and the designation "Carolana" at the upper reaches of the Roanoke, Chowan and Meherrin Rivers. Courtesy of the Library of Congress Geography and Map Division.

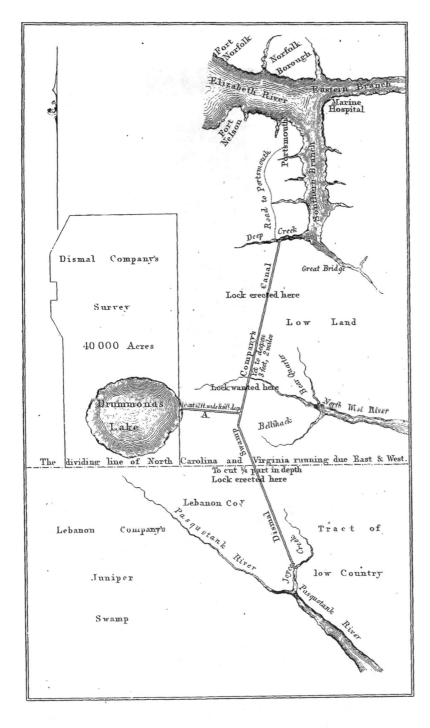

Virginia was the name originally given to all the northern part of the continent of America, and as grants were made to other colonies, their names served only to distinguish them as various parts of Virginia until the colonies became familiar to the citizens of their English homeland. Virginia historian Robert Beverley wrote around 1703 that in the course of time the name came to apply only to the land on the Chesapeake, both Virginia and Maryland. In Beverley's time Virginia implied the territory bounded on the south by North Carolina; on the north by the Potomac River, which divided it from Maryland; on the east by the Main Ocean, also called the Virginia Sea; and on the west and northwest by the California Sea.

This plat of the Great Dismal Swamp, included in United States Senate documents (10th Congress, 1st session) and dated April 6, 1808, illustrates clearly the "dividing line" that William Byrd had first surveyed in 1728. *Courtesy of the Library of Congress.*

The Elizabeth River and its watershed fall geographically within the bounds of the Norfolk quadrangle, the principal feature of which is a very level terrace elevated from ten to twenty feet above sea level and intersected by extensive tidewater areas and a few shallow valleys of freshwater streams. On this plain to the west is the Dismal Swamp, where the Elizabeth begins, and to the north and east, along the bay and ocean shores, there are sand dunes, which at one time had a height of up to seventy feet or more.

sea level and intersected by extensive tidewater areas and a few shallow valleys of freshwater streams. On this plain to the west is the Dismal Swamp, where the Elizabeth begins, and to the north and east, along the bay and ocean shores, there are sand dunes, which at one time had a height of up to seventy feet or more. The plain is crossed transversely by a shallow trough that is occupied on the north by the estuarine channel of the Elizabeth River and its Southern Branch. In the middle of the depression, from North Landing to Great Bridge, there is a swamp through which the Albemarle and Chesapeake Canal was excavated. The plain is trenched by a number of valleys reaching tide water in their lower portions. Of these, the Nansemond River, the Eastern and Western Branches of the Elizabeth River, Tanner's Creek, Mason's Creek, Little Creek, Lynnhaven River and Broad Bay flow to the north into the James River and then the Chesapeake Bay; and the Northwest River and its smaller branches, together with the North Landing River, flow southward into Currituck Sound. Portions of these plains in the eastern and northern parts of the quadrangle have traditionally been well drained, owing to the sandy soil, but a large area in the southwestern part of the plain, with imperfect drainage, is occupied by the Dismal Swamp. A small detached area of the swamp is known as the Green Sea, bounded loosely by the Dismal Swamp Canal to the west, Great Bridge to the north, the Northwest River to the south and the community of Hickory to the east. The Green Sea was originally part of the main swamp, but the Dismal Swamp Canal, which traverses the eastern portion of the area from north to south, drained the intervening region. The canal sustains the water level and

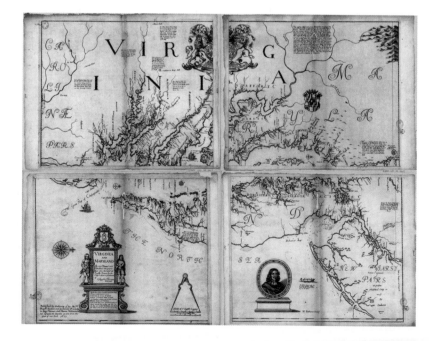

Map of Virginia and Maryland, by Augustine Herrman, published in 1673. Courtesy of the Library of Congress Geography and Map Division.

the resulting swamp conditions to the west, but reclaimed from inundation a zone of considerable width to the east—the Green Sea—an area that is further drained by the branch ditch known as the Herring Canal.

Swamp flora at the turn of the twentieth century was characterized by a profusion of bald cypress, juniper, black gum and extensive canebrakes. The swamps in the Elizabeth's watershed lie in shallow basins in the surface of the general terrace of the Norfolk region. The basins filled the general level of the surrounding country with vegetal accumulations, which had, by United States Geological Survey figures taken in 1900, thickness of about twenty feet. In excavations also taken about this time for a gate on the feeder about half a mile east of Lake Drummond there were exposed ten feet of peat filled with roots and tree trunks, lying on eight feet of clear peat that merged with the overlying beds, and this, in turn, was underlain by fossiliferous sand of the late Neocene age. The thickness of the swamp deposits decreases toward the periphery of the swamp area, but the geological survey noted that their study at the turn of the twentieth century was incomplete; so few excavations had been made along the border zone that the conditions of thinning were not known. The basin of the Dismal Swamp, which will be discussed further in this volume, owes its origin to an extensive depression in the surface of the Columbia formation.

The coastal plain represents two different levels of geological development. After it had risen above sea level to greater height than it is today, the land mass was cut by streams, then sank again, allowing the seas to fill valleys. This is the origin of what were later called rias, or drowned valleys, such as the Potomac, Rappahannock, York and James Rivers. The Chesapeake Bay is but the ria of the Susquehanna River, the longest river on America's East

This soil map was issued by the United States Department of Agriculture, Bureau of Soils, in 1903 from surveys conducted by Jesse Erwin Lapham. At the center of the map are the Elizabeth River and its Eastern, Southern and Western Branches, as well as Tanner's Creek, the river's expansive tributary to the north. *Courtesy of the author.*

PREFACE

A small detached area of the swamp is known as the Green Sea, bounded loosely by the Dismal Swamp Canal to the west, Great Bridge to the north, the Northwest River to the south and the community of Hickory to the east. The Green Sea was originally part of the main swamp, but the Dismal Swamp Canal, which traverses the eastern portion of the area from north to south, drained the intervening region.

Coast. The eight major rivers flowing into the bay include the aforementioned Susquehanna, Rappahannock, York and James Rivers, but also the Potomac, Patapsco, Choptank and Patuxent Rivers.

Geologically, too, the area encompassed by the Elizabeth River watershed has a particularly rich sedimentary record worth mention. The geologic deposits of the Norfolk quadrangle, of which the watershed remains a critical cog, are composed of sandy loams, sands, clays, marls, peat and muck. They are in greater part of sedimentary origin, but some of the sands are Aeolian, and the marsh accumulations have been aided and augmented by plant growth. The general surface formation is a sheet of sandy loam of no great thickness. This is underlain by an extensive series of coastal plain deposits lying on a floor of the crystalline rocks that constitute the surface of the Piedmont region to the west, but which slope far below sea level in their extension eastward under the coastal plain. The rocks of the coastal plain consist of broad sheets of sands, gravels, clays, diatomaceous earth, marls and glauconitic sands composed in a succession of formations that dip very gently to the southeast. They rise above sea level in regular succession westward and northward, and in the Norfolk region have an aggregate thickness over 2,300 feet, ranging from early Cretaceous to late Pleistocene. The Pleistocene formations are the only ones seen at the surface in the Norfolk quadrangle, but the Neocene, Eocene and Cretaceous formations have been explored by well borings.

Sedimentary deposits of the coastal plain are divided into two groups: one corresponds more or less with those formations in the process of deposition in the estuaries and along the shores in the immediate vicinity; the other corresponds closely to offshore sediments known from soundings to be deposited more deeply in submerged portions of the quadrangle. In general the shore and estuarine deposits overlie those of the second group, and are thus known to be younger. The younger layer records modifications in geography due to changes in altitude of the land and, moreover, displays

Oystermen once proliferated Norfolk waters tonging for oysters. This was a familiar scene along the Elizabeth River's main stem and tributaries. The picture shown here was taken about 1905. *Courtesy of the author.*

This scene in the Dismal Swamp was taken by Harry C. Mann for the Jamestown Official Photographic Corporation, ca. 1906. *Courtesy of the Library of Congress Prints and Photographs Division.*

certain distinctive characteristics indicating the climate of the periods during which it was laid down. The older formations contain abundant remains of marine organisms, preserved as fossils, and thus these deposits are records of periods during which the land stood lower and the sea consequently extended farther inland than at present. Interestingly, in a well at Lambert's Point, Norfolk, about 1900, borings at depths of 563 to 610 feet yielded marine Cretaceous fossils, including *Exogyra costata* Say and the following additional species: *Astarte octolirata* Gabb, *Ostrea plumosa* Morton, *Gouldia decemnaria* Conrad, *Gryphæa vesicularis* Lam., *Liopistha* (*Cymella*) *bella* Conrad, *Corbula* sp., *Modiolus* sp. and *Beculites*. The marine Cretaceous deposits in this area and other locations in Norfolk were believed then to be at least 65 feet thick, possibly greater. Just beneath the covering of Columbia and alluvial formations in the Norfolk region there is a thin layer of marls and sands of the Pliocene age. They do not outcrop at the surface, but over time were reached by many wells, which uncovered the strata in places excavated for the canals in the Dismal Swamp. In most localities encompassed in the Elizabeth River watershed, there are large numbers of shells, many identical with living or relatively recent forms, with others of the late Neocene age intermixed with them. These deposits were extensively exposed by the Dismal Swamp Canal excavations, notably at three points: one on the main canal, four miles south of Wallaceton; another on the feeder from Lake Drummond, about halfway between the lake and the main canal; and the other on the main canal in the vicinity of Lilly, North Carolina. According to L. Woolman of the Philadelphia Academy of Natural Sciences, who published his findings in 1898, among the fossils collected from these beds were *Area limula* Conrad, *Cæcum cooperi* Smith, *Corbula contraeta* Say (*numerotus*), *Meretrix convexa* Say, *Tellina tenera* Say and *Ostrea virginica* (the Eastern, also American, oyster).

In some of the clays containing these shells Woolman noted that there were also diatoms in abundance, comprising many species ranging from Miocene

The western margin of the Dismal Swamp, showing overflow during the wet season, was photographed about 1900 and made part of a Norfolk folio produced by the Department of the Interior, United States Geological Survey, two years later. *Courtesy of the author.*

to the present, a few never observed in Miocene beds and several that were supposed to belong to Miocene exclusively. At Great Bridge Pliocene beds were exposed by the excavations of the Albemarle and Chesapeake Canal, which yielded a few fossils, and on the Jericho Canal southeast of Suffolk the same beds yielded a large number of distinctive Pliocene forms. It was evident, even then, from the widespread occurrence of the fossils that the entire area of the Norfolk quadrangle is underlain by Pliocene deposits, except the deep channel extending down the James River and out to the ocean through the Chesapeake Bay.

The entire land area of the Norfolk quadrangle is covered by a thin sheet of loam and sand called the Columbia formation, the surface of which constitutes the wide, low plain so characteristic of the region. The formation was laid down along the coast in a belt that, in the region, extended back to the base of the highlands along the west side of the Dismal Swamp. The thickness of the Columbia formation is usually from twenty to fifty-five feet, and in the greater part of the area its base is slightly below tidewater level. The surface on which it lies is known to be somewhat irregular or gently rolling. The Columbia formation is cut through by the deeper valleys, notably those of the James, Elizabeth and Nansemond Rivers, Hampton Roads and Chesapeake Bay. Under the surface of the Columbia formation a relatively uniform character is presented throughout, but there are some local variations, and there is also a considerable range in thickness. Large boulders were found occasionally enclosed in finer material, and their occurrence could be explained only by the hypothesis that they were transported

The Wood Towing Company tug *Atlas* was photographed by H.D. Vollmer in 1935 as it passed under the old Berkley Bridge. Wood Towing was in business from 1920 to 1951. A number of historic tugs remained in service into the mid-1950s. Several of these tugs participated in some of the most exciting events in history, among them the *Salvor*, which eventually met her fate at the bottom of Smith's Creek—today, The Hague—in the 1930s. The *Salvor* had laid a transatlantic cable for the Western Union Telegraph Company in the first part of her career, and later was used for treasure salvage off Cape Henry. The *Dauntless* was a blockade runner during the Spanish-American War, and was aptly nicknamed the "Phantom Ship" due to her quickness. The *Dauntless*, renamed the *Restless*, worked the Elizabeth River for many years, not a terrible end for the vessel that carried the first news of Theodore Roosevelt's capture of San Juan Hill back to the United States. Wood Towing Company had the distinction of owning the oldest tug in service on the Elizabeth, and the fourth oldest in the United States—the *Venture*. The *Venture* had been built in 1863 in Philadelphia and named the *Grace Titus*. Soon after the tug came into service, she was bought by the Commonwealth of Virginia and renamed *Virginia*, a name that she carried through the end of the Civil War. Captain Joseph M. Clark bought the *Virginia* after the war and gave her the name *Venture*. Wood Towing later bought the *Venture* to haul barges between Norfolk and Suffolk. *Courtesy of the author.*

by floating ice. A very instructive series of borings was made in the late nineteenth century by the Norfolk City Water Department in an area east of the city, which passed through the Columbia deposits to the marl of the underlying Chesapeake formation.

Under the greater portion of the area of the Norfolk quadrangle the coarser basal beds of the Columbia formation contain considerable water. This was the source of hundreds of shallow private wells scattered over the region and a portion of the city supplies for Norfolk and Portsmouth. The water is low in mineral constituents, but contains a moderate amount of organic matter. Unfortunately, observed Nelson Horatio Darton of the United States Geological Survey in his June 1901 report, it was also subject to surface contamination, owing to the imperfect protection afforded by the relatively permeable sandy loam under which it lies. Where wells were near sources of pollution, Darton noted, "they are soon contaminated, and probably throughout the region there is some seepage of surface water containing malarial germs, drainage of manured fields, and so on." It was Darton's finding that, in this region, it was prudent to locate sinking wells as far as possible from stables, cesspools or ponds of stagnant water. While Norfolk drew its water from ponds east of the city, during the period of Darton's study it was also drawing water from wells driven into the Columbia formation. Portsmouth was supplied by a series of shallow-driven wells. At Money Point, five miles south of Norfolk, a five-inch well was sunk to a depth of 562 feet, and furnished a good supply of slightly ferruginous water that rose 10 feet above tide level. Its source of supply was low in the Chesapeake formation, in sand under an 8-foot bed of rock. Another well, about a half-mile southwest, was sunk 450 feet and yielded saltwater. During the same period, at Kempsville, in the region at the head of the Eastern Branch of the Elizabeth River, the water was generally brackish or hard in shallow wells. Fairly good water was obtained, however, from wells driven at a depth of 80 feet. Owing to some hard stratum at that depth at Kempsville, no deeper-driven wells were considered practical at that time. Wells in the North Landing area varied from 10 to 14 feet in depth. On the wide, flat area around Hickory, there were numerous wells from 10 to 15 feet deep, all of which obtained good supplies of excellent water in sand and gravel, in places overlain by sandy clay. In the region about Fentress, wells from 10 to 15 feet in depth obtained satisfactory water supplies. In the vicinity of Cornland, southwest of the Green Sea, wells were from 8 to 12 feet deep, the deeper ones usually furnishing a satisfactory volume of water. There were actually wells driven 36 to 45 feet at Cornland from which cool water was drawn in great abundance, though slightly mineralized. In the settlement of Benefit, east of Cornland, plenty of water was obtained in wells 10 to 12 feet deep. Farther north, at Grassfield, the wells were 8 to 10 feet deep on the lower lands, but yielded poor water; on the higher slopes to the south, however, wells 12 to 14 feet deep furnished good water. About Gilmerton wells averaged 8 to 10 feet deep, but a few had been sunk from 20 to 80 feet. On the peninsula north of the city of Norfolk, roughly about Tanner's Creek, the wells were dug 8 to 10 feet deep. The quality of water for human consumption was of great importance at this time—well over a century ago—when so much was still being discovered about the geographical and geological underpinnings of the Elizabeth River watershed.

Smaller rivers and creeks in Lower Tidewater are tidal bodies of water, subject to the rhythms of the moon, with no current other than what is caused by the ebb and flow of the tide. The coastal plain consists of beaches, saltwater and brackish marshes, freshwater swamps and forests. The region straddles an environmental borderland marking the southernmost extent of many northern species and the most northerly limit of many southern plants and animals. The Elizabeth River and its branches, including Tanner's Creek, are tidal waters—estuaries—just as the Chesapeake Bay is an estuary. The Elizabeth River drains into the James River, one of the eight major tributaries of the Chesapeake Bay. The river's watershed also, importantly, includes brackish Lake Drummond in the Great Dismal Swamp, where the river is born and to which much attention is given herein. The Elizabeth's watershed also includes rainwater runoff from surrounding urban areas.

Estuaries such as the Elizabeth River are defined as semi-coastal bodies of water that have a measurable salinity gradient from its freshwater drainage to its ocean entrance. The brackish quality of an estuary varies according to its sources, proximity to the ocean and to the seasons. The Elizabeth River and Chesapeake Bay each have very different scales and shoreline topographies. Estuary ecology changes constantly. Aside from twice-daily shifting of the tides, there is a sectional layer of water. Due to the higher density of saltwater, salinity is generally higher at greater depths, thus the river is the least saline at its source. As the salinity gradient shifts between the main stem and the river's mouth, the communities of plants and animals found in the waters and wetlands change accordingly. There are five major Chesapeake Bay communities. Wetland types are defined by the primary plant communities of which they are composed. Marshes can exist as freshwater, brackish or saltwater and are dominated by grasses and reeds. Swamps tend to exist farther inland and farther down the chain of salinity succession, although it is worth noting here that the Great Dismal Swamp is not a "normal" swamp. Swamps contain shrubs and tress as well as forbs; these plants gradually replace marsh grasses. Submersed grassbeds consist of only about ten major species that are known as submerged aquatic vegetation and include wild celery, common waterweed, pondweed, eelgrass and sea lettuce. Plankton is the key in this food chain. These organisms float near the surface of the water and include zooplankton or copepods, bacteria and jellyfish. Nekton are free swimming aquatic life such as fish, crustaceans and other invertebrates.

The Elizabeth River is often characterized as one of the nation's most polluted waterways. Yet many of its headwater areas, some of which are fed by the waters of the Great Dismal Swamp, offer relatively untrammeled marshes and backwaters where boating, fishing and crabbing are still popular.

Early settlers called raccoons "apes."

Smith's Creek, a portion of which was dubbed The Hague by Norfolk Company promoters, is a small tidal branch of the Eastern Branch of the Elizabeth River. Its shorter end skirts the filled-in land on which the Norfolk Museum of Arts and Sciences, later renamed The Chrysler Museum of Art, was constructed in the early 1930s, while the other end comes up to Olney Road facing Stockley Gardens at the Stone Park. Children in a rowboat (right) gaze toward Frank J. Conway, photographer, in this ca. 1920 photograph of The Hague on a hot summer's day. The view is looking toward Olney Road. The large cedar shake structure behind the two sailboat masts is the Ghent Club. Note the trolley passing down Olney. *Courtesy of the author.*

Residing in the bottom sediments, the benthos group includes algae, bacteria and ciliates. The Elizabeth River's wetland areas are generally brackish marshes. Cordgrass, narrow-leaved cattail, switchgrass and common reed are the dominant vegetation.

Endemic species of the Chesapeake Bay that are particular to the Elizabeth River are cited in Christopher White's *Chesapeake Bay: Nature of the Estuary.* White noted that freshwater wetlands and waters are home to broad-leaved cattail; river bulrush; tall grasses, including wild rice and Walter's millet; smartweeds and tearthumbs. At the edge are found red maple and common alder; in the realm of transition and succession (sometimes high tide), minnows; amphibians and reptiles, including various frogs such as the northern spring peeper, upland chorus frog, northern cricket frog, green frog, southern leopard frog and northern water snake; birds such as the blue heron, great egret, marsh ducks, rails, coots, sandpipers, allies and other birds; and mammals such as raccoons—which the early settlers called apes—voles and muskrat. In fresh water, White noted invertebrates like grass shrimp, river snail, fingernail clam and freshwater mussels and fishes that dominated, such as the American eel and yellow perch. The brackish marshes are full of big cordgrass, narrow-leaved cattail, olney three square, tall grasses, shorter grasses, herbaceous plants, shrubs and sedges; reptiles and amphibians, namely the green tree frog, turtles and water snakes; birds like herons and egrets, swans, geese, ducks, Canada goose, snow goose and many species of ducks and other birds; and mammals commonly seen, including raccoon, marsh rice rat and muskrat. Estuarine brackish water is rich in invertebrates such as the common clam worm, seaweed snail, brackish water clam and blue crabs. The salt marsh has plants of which only two species are predominant: saltmarsh cordgrass and saltmeadow cordgrass; invertebrates include marsh insects such as the mosquito and deer fly, crustaceans and mollusks, the most common of which are marsh crab, saltmarsh snails and Atlantic ribbed mussel; reptiles; birds that amaze and captivate, including the

herons and egrets, ibises, gulls and terns, sandpipers and allies, plovers, birds of prey and passerine birds; and aforementioned mammals—and then some. In the salt shallows fishes include bay anchovy; mummichong or killfishes; juvenile fishes, which are generally sandbar shark, black sea bass, bluefish, silver perch, spotted sea trout, Atlantic croaker and summer flounder; other foragers that encompass needlefish, lined seahorse and northern pipefish. The shallows also include waders and water birds; of particular interest are the double-crested cormorant, snowy egret, common tern, pied-billed grebe, American coot and American black duck.

Since the early seventeenth century, when Captain John Smith sailed past on his way to Jamestown, Virginia's Elizabeth River has undergone dramatic changes. In the past century, development of a bustling industrial economy attracted to the banks of the Elizabeth an assortment of commercial and military facilities all dependent on the river for transportation. The Elizabeth River is the major deep-water port for Virginia, home of the largest naval base in the world and a link to the Atlantic Intracoastal Waterway and the Great Dismal Swamp. The relentless dredging required to improve navigation has made the Elizabeth twice as deep as it once was but only two-thirds as broad. Many areas of wetlands and shoal water have disappeared. Today the Elizabeth River is an imposing wall of industrial plants; freighters carrying break bulk and containerized and bulk cargo, liquid cargo tankers, passenger ships and military vessels that line both sides of the river's main channel. Fertilizer and pesticide plants, creosote and cement factories, shipyards and drydocks, oil terminals and coal-loading operations make the Elizabeth a living, working river. The Western Branch is the exception; it is primarily residential use that defines the margins of the land where the river rolls to the shore. The Elizabeth River is often characterized as one of the nation's most polluted waterways. Yet many of its headwater areas, some of which are fed by the waters of the Great Dismal Swamp, offer relatively untrammeled marshes and backwaters where boating, fishing and crabbing are still popular.

Europeans first settled along the banks of the Elizabeth River and its tributaries in the 1600s, from Norfolk on the east bank to Portsmouth and Gosport on the west. Smaller communities sprung up in and around established towns, and many of those are discussed in this volume. There were certainly major springboards to development on the Elizabeth, from the ready supply of timber to the many shipyards that populated the river's main stem and tributaries. The Norfolk Naval Shipyard was a great catalyst for growth and the beginning of the United States Navy's footprint in Norfolk waters. It has the distinction of being the oldest shipyard that is a United States Navy shipyard; it dates to November 1, 1767, and includes construction of two Continental navy ships and service as a leased federal

The Eastern Branch of the Elizabeth River headwaters at a dam in the Kempsville section of Virginia Beach, then curves through Kempsville, meanders by Chesapeake and ends in Norfolk, where it meets the main stem of the Elizabeth, mother water of not only the Eastern but also the Western and Southern Branches. The river is nearly hidden altogether in many places in Virginia Beach. There is, however, the Elizabeth River Nature and Canoe Trail off the Carolanne Farms Neighborhood Park, where Challedon Drive and Gainsborough Road meet.

yard beginning on May 27, 1794. It was bought by the federal government on June 15, 1801. Purchase of the first site for a United States Navy shipyard, the Washington Navy Yard, was completed on October 2, 1799. The growth of early industries along the river triggered moderate periods of population gain, but in truth Norfolk's population of 14,524 in 1790 spiraled downward until 1820. The intervening years had been checkered by continued tensions—and another war—with Great Britain. The first railroad was completed in 1834, and the first track laid from Portsmouth to Suffolk was only the beginning. Railroads soon began to link the port's maritime transportation capability to inland areas.

By 1900 dredging for navigation was already well underway, reaching its peak during World War II. As recently as 1957 much of this dredged material was deposited directly into the water at Hampton Roads or the Chesapeake Bay, perhaps as much as forty million cubic yards. Since that time, with the growth of South Hampton Roads and its port facilities showing no signs of slowing down, dredged material has been deposited at the United States Army Corps of Engineers' Craney Island Disposal Facility, where, because of contaminants in the sediment, special handling and disposal procedures have been developed.

The Virginia blue crab (*Callinectes sapidus*) supports one of the largest fisheries in the Chesapeake Bay and remains plentiful in the Elizabeth River and its tributaries. This image of Chesapeake Bay blue crabs being picked for market was taken about 1905. *Courtesy of the Library of Congress Prints and Photographs Division.*

The Elizabeth River watershed encompasses roughly 300 square miles within the cities of Chesapeake, Norfolk, Portsmouth and Virginia Beach, and is inclusive of the Great Dismal Swamp. Virginia Beach, once an isolated beach town, is now Virginia's largest city with over 425,000 residents. The Elizabeth's watershed covers 9,600 acres, or 5 percent, of Virginia Beach. This 5 percent includes nearly 600 acres of open water. A decade before, in 1990, the population of Virginia Beach living within the watershed was 50,000; however, another 260,000 lived within 5 miles of the Elizabeth River. There are thirteen Virginia Beach city parks and fourteen schools in the river's watershed.

Virginia Beach's portion of the Elizabeth River—the Eastern Branch—was once a route for shallow-water vessels from colonial times to the early 1900s. These ships would pull into port at Kempe's Landing to load and unload cargo. Over time eroding land from area farms filled the channels, reducing their depth, and urban development in the latter half of the twentieth century furthered that erosion. The Eastern Branch of the river in Virginia Beach is today very shallow, with numerous mud flats along its banks at low tide. As more people are attracted to South Hampton Roads, it seems reasonable to expect the demand for enhancing recreational opportunities and the aesthetic value of the Elizabeth River will exponentially increase, but so, too, will demands on the Elizabeth's ecosystem.

It is significant that, as the importance of the Elizabeth River's place in American history is documented, the ravages of time on a working river are appreciated. There is no doubt that Lower Tidewater (also South Hampton Roads) owes its existence and growth to the Elizabeth River, the canal system connecting North Carolina to Virginia and the Atlantic Intracoastal Waterway. The river's power, its inextricable role as the lifeblood that runs through our communities, has been fueled by the maritime industry, mills and processing plants and the military. But even eighteenth-century inhabitants of the Elizabeth River watershed knew that the river was becoming polluted to the point of making people sick. In 1983 the United States Environmental Protection Agency (EPA) Chesapeake Bay Program identified the Elizabeth River as one of the most highly polluted bodies of water in the entire Bay watershed. Heavy metals and organic compounds have contaminated bottom sediments and made the Elizabeth River a toxic hot spot. Substantive concentrations of metals such as lead, copper, zinc and mercury have been detected in the Elizabeth River at levels two to ten times as great as those found mid-Bay or in the Potomac River to the north. Over three hundred different organic compounds have been identified in Elizabeth River sediments. Research reveals that contaminated sediments are to blame for a lack of diversity of life in the sediments. Poor flushing characteristics of the tidal river, exacerbated by dredging navigation channels, indicate that sediments and toxics are trapped there.

The river's power, its inextricable role as the lifeblood that runs through our communities, has been fueled by the maritime industry, mills and processing plants and the military. But even eighteenth-century inhabitants of the Elizabeth River watershed knew that the river was becoming polluted to the point of making people sick.

Oily wastes and creosote dumped in the river are sources of polynuclear or polycyclic aromatic hydrocarbons—a family of chemicals sometimes called PNAs or PAHs. These compounds have been strongly correlated with fish disorders in the Elizabeth River, including skin lesions, cataracts and fin rot. Other sources of PNAs include industrial processes, petroleum spills, urban runoff, sewage effluent and combustion of fossil fuels. Polychlorinated biphenyls (PCBs), another family of toxic chemicals, have also been detected in significant quantity in the Elizabeth River and recent research has shown that these toxic substances bioaccumulate or are retained and concentrate in the tissues of crabs, fish and other aquatic life.

Three designated Superfund sites are located along the river: one a source of lead, the second of creosote and pentachlorophenol (PCP) and the third of storage, assembly and testing of naval gun ammunition. According to the Virginia State Water Control Board, there are many inactive industrial sites that have contaminated soil, groundwater and surface water, and which contribute to the problems of the Elizabeth River. Using EPA data, the Hampton Roads Planning District Commission estimated that there could be anywhere between 1,200 and 4,300 underground storage tanks in Southeastern Virginia, with many located in the Elizabeth River basin. Interestingly, while the data is now outdated, a 1988 EPA report examined 649 potentially hazardous waste sites in Southeastern Virginia and on closer examination, 377 sites, both government-owned and private, were considered potential Superfund sites. Of these, 316 or 84 percent were located in the Elizabeth River basin, and it is remarkable, as observed, that the number of potential sites increases closer to the river. There are other contributors to the Elizabeth River's water quality problems, which will be discussed in a later chapter, but the Virginia Institute of Marine Science (VIMS) has been monitoring tributlyltin (TBT), an extremely toxic antifoulant in marine paint, since 2000 and found TBT to be the most serious problem in the water column of the river.

While this volume covers centuries of the Elizabeth River's history, geographical and geological context and her rich biodiversity, she is a living body of water. Those who named her also opened a tablet in which human history with this enduring, beautiful princess is recorded everyday. Today there is much to be gleaned from the river's strengths. As you read through *The Elizabeth River*, remember that this remarkable river is your river. From the Great Bridge Lock to the Norfolk Naval Station, the importance of the Elizabeth River is ever-present in our everyday lives. Since man came to live on her shores, she has been a river with a story.

INTRODUCTION

News correspondent Charles Kuralt once wrote that rivers run through our history and folklore, and link us as a people. Kuralt's "The Magic of Rivers" remains a poignant reminder, in his words, that rivers "nourish and refresh us and provide a home for dazzling varieties of fish and wildlife and trees and plants of every sort. We are a nation rich in rivers." During one of his *On the Road with Charles Kuralt* segments Kuralt remarked that "America is a great story, and there is a river on every page of it." He could not have been more on target in that pointed observation of the intertwining of our history and that of rivers flowing through our communities. America is much about her rivers. Virginians have cited having access to places of natural beauty, such as mountains and rivers, as the number one reason they value living in the commonwealth of Virginia, according to the Virginia Environmental Endowment. The broad Elizabeth, the dominant natural feature of Hampton Roads's south side, is still beautiful and teeming with wildlife and waterfowl. In fact, it is this mother water—the great Elizabeth—that has inspired the revitalization of the downtowns of Norfolk and Portsmouth over the past thirty years. Upscale condominiums, festival marketplaces, parks, high-rise offices, museums and a baseball stadium reminiscent of Baltimore's Camden Yards are all strategically placed to maximize lovely views of the Elizabeth. Harborfest, with hundreds of thousands pouring in for a riverside party each June, began around the splendor of tall ships through the mists on the Elizabeth River.

A greater gift still of the river is her service as a world-class harbor. Our port cities owe their populations to the river for attracting the world's largest naval base, the world's largest coal-exporting facility and, from before the Revolutionary War, other maritime trade that made Hampton Roads an international center for ship repair and waterborne foreign commerce. The river's commercial vitality continues to increase.

INTRODUCTION

Many years ago it was my intention to write this book chronicling the history of Virginia's Elizabeth River, which has held court for centuries over our nation's history. So struck by the beauty and vitality of this broad expanse of water, and tethered to its edge by personal experience and family history, I wondered what could be written that would adequately convey the river's story? What story did she have to tell? The Elizabeth, after all, is not a big, winding river. The Elizabeth is only two or three miles long. Its tributaries are longer than the Elizabeth itself. At one end, toward Norfolk and Portsmouth, are the Western, Eastern and Southern Branches, and Tanner's Creek, known today by another name—the Lafayette River. Toward Newport News the Elizabeth River joins Hampton Roads. But as one observer wrote a few years ago, the Elizabeth is the only river in the United States named after a woman—and it is all mouth. The Elizabeth's glistening waters have greeted me as they have innumerable voyagers, making it my river in a way that told me deep down that I was home. Some of my best times have been spent on this storied river, taking in vibrant scenes—a river alive, that has endured centuries and still harbors one of the most diverse ecosystems I have ever encountered.

The river's story is our story. The Elizabeth has sustained all who have lived along her riverbanks and tributaries for centuries, prompting Alf J. and Ramona H. Mapp to write that "the life rhythm of the Indians was literally synchronized with the rise and fall of tides of the Chesapeake and its tributaries," an observation of people's use of this vital body of water and its key tributaries that rings familiar of the relationship of people and

"DAR DAY IS, AN MO TER CUM."
Scene in Norfolk Harbor. (From a local painting.)

This scene on the Elizabeth River was painted by an unknown artist in the late nineteenth century. Courtesy of the author.

the river even today. Several years ago, in the fall of 1993, *Virginian-Pilot* columnist Guy Friddell asked ninety-year-old Leland Thomas what the river meant to him. Thomas fell in love with the Elizabeth River when his father, Andrew Tilden Thomas, took him fishing at age two in 1905. "I don't know why he waited so long," Thomas wrote later of that first fishing trip and his river. "I have wanted to say something about this small river for a long time," the Portsmouth native recounted. "It has touched the lives of more West Norfolk people for a longer time than any other body of water nearby, even than the mighty Atlantic Ocean." That first morning he went fishing with his father, Thomas remembered that they set out before breakfast in a sixteen-foot skiff to catch the first incoming tide that brought the fish—"or so Papa would say. But that day the fish never heard Papa. We fished 'til about two o'clock in the afternoon, and I was very, very hungry." Having caught nothing, Thomas's father rowed to Craney Island, where Captain Frank Ashberry protected oyster beds. All Captain Ashberry had left from breakfast was cold bread, cooked atop the stove, and black molasses. "That was my first experience learning that when you are hungry, anything will taste good," Thomas recounted.

News correspondent Charles Kuralt once said, "America is a great story, and there is a river on every page of it."

But the Elizabeth also fed more West Norfolk families than all the area's food stores put together, Thomas would observe, including those run by Parsons, Blanchard, Davis, Ayers and Adolph Bloom. "Between West Norfolk and Craney Island was Love's Creek, so muddy you could walk its length barefooted at low tide and catch all the fish bait you could use in a day's fishing: hard and soft shell crabs, alewives, and gudgeons." At high tide Love's Creek offered two swimming holes where most West Norfolk boys learned to swim before daring to try the Elizabeth River, Thomas remembered. "On the first high tide of the day following the first low tide, most families who had a boat went fishing in the Elizabeth for such varieties as croakers, trout, spot, perch, black Wills, butters and hogs, including the unwanted toads and eels." He also noted that at night, with a rod and reel, fishing off the West Norfolk Bridge under a light yielded a catch of large trout and rockfish. "So many were chasing alewives and fish bait drawn by the light, that I have dipped the big fish up with a shrimp net," he recalled. "The Elizabeth River floats the United States Navy's battleships and carriers, but the fish have gone. Where to, I wonder." The Elizabeth was where Leland Thomas and his boyhood friends learned to swim, fish, catch crabs and wade in mud up to their knees that stuck so tight to their feet it would pull off their shoes, if they had shoes to wear.

Stories like Thomas's give us an affective portrait of the Elizabeth. The story of people seeking use of the Elizabeth over the course of her lengthy history, much of it before humans ever knew and named her, is conveyed best by what we have learned of her secrets and what has been recorded since humans first came to live on her shores. At The Elizabeth

River Project conference, "Elizabeth River Visions," held on October 22, 1993, at the Norfolk Waterside Marriott, former United States Senator William B. Spong Jr. of Virginia told attendees that it was easy to observe that in many respects the history of our nation is intertwined with the history of the Elizabeth River. He cited examples. In September 1608, scarcely eighteen months after Jamestown had been settled, Spong told his audience, Captain John Smith and twelve sailors in a long boat crossed Hampton Roads and entered what today is known as the Elizabeth River. They went six or seven miles, so the records show, and they made two observations of some significance. First, Smith and his crew saw traces of previous habitation, but along this trip on the Elizabeth they did not see any Indians; and second, they documented the large fir and pine trees on the banks of the river.

A view of West Norfolk, ca. 1895, showing the West Norfolk Lumber Company. Courtesy of the author.

It would be a number of years before the first record of someone seeking use of the Elizabeth River appeared, observed Spong. A man named John Wood petitioned the London Company for land to build a shipyard on the banks of the Elizabeth River, and the same year,

VIEW AT WEST NORFOLK, WEST NORFOLK LUMBER CO.

1620, about the time the Pilgrims were settling Plymouth Rock, William Tucker petitioned for several acres of land at Seawell's Point (today spelled Sewell's Point), now the site of the Norfolk Naval Station. A site for Norfolk on the Elizabeth River was purchased and laid out as a town in 1680, and on the other side of the Elizabeth a man named Captain William Carver had petitioned and patented for the land there on which now stands the city of Portsmouth. Carver was not politically adept, joining Bacon's Rebellion, which failed. He was rewarded for his efforts by being hanged at the Chesapeake Bay.

Carver's land was given to a man named Colonel William Crawford in 1716, and it was Crawford who laid out Portsmouth as a town. The first settlers in the two towns had come across the James River and Hampton Roads to settle in what became Princess Anne and Lower Norfolk Counties. As shipping, shipbuilding and commerce developed, three-quarters of the town lots in Norfolk and Portsmouth were occupied by those employed in some type of maritime endeavor. The Virginia House of Burgesses established Elizabeth River Parish and the site of its first house of worship was located near the present site of Saint Paul's Episcopal Church.

The seventeenth century also saw the creation, in 1636, of the first known public utility in America when Captain Adam Thorowgood (also spelled Thoroughgood) established the first ferry service. While key bridges were later constructed over streams and small tributaries of the Elizabeth, the interim solution—ferries—gave birth to a form of transportation that endured into modern times. The first ferry in Lower Norfolk County began as Thorowgood's private enterprise. He set up his ferry operation at the convergence of the Eastern and Southern Branches of the Elizabeth River between Norfolk and Portsmouth. This ferry was a basic skiff handled by Thorowgood's slaves; however, the captain's operation was so popular that within a few short months the county took over the business, supporting it with a public levy as it did other community services—and the number of rowboats grew. The ferry continued to be run from the same location until 1952, when it was dubbed too antiquated a mode of transportation to handle the people and automobiles that tried to clamor aboard Thorowgood's modern progeny. The birth of bridge-tunnels rendered automobile ferries obsolete.

As Norfolk and Portsmouth grew on either side of the Elizabeth River, Scot merchants, shrewd, frugal, canny and knowledgeable of trade by sea, emerged as the most affluent and influential group in the area. These merchants were Tories and as the American Revolution fast approached they were loyal to the British Crown. One of these Scotsmen, Andrew Sprowle, started his business in Norfolk and moved across the river to Portsmouth, purchasing one of William Crawford's lots fronting the Elizabeth River. Here, on this strategic plot of land, Crawford established

The Elizabeth is only two or three miles long. Its tributaries are longer than the Elizabeth itself. At one end, toward Norfolk and Portsmouth, are the Western, Eastern and Southern Branches, and Tanner's Creek, known today by another name—the Lafayette River.

a private mercantile business. In time he would buy all of the land south of Portsmouth on the Elizabeth's Southern Branch, where he built a shipyard. He named the community Gosport, very similar to Portsmouth, England. Sprowle's Gosport shipyard eventually became today's Norfolk Naval Shipyard.

In Sprowle's day, his Gosport shipyard serviced not only private watercraft, but the British fleet as well. When the American Revolution began, Sprowle had a friend in the colonial governor of Virginia, John Murray, Lord Dunmore. When Dunmore fled Williamsburg he headed for Gosport, where Sprowle gave him quarters under the protection of numerous British ships at the yard. Dunmore occupied Norfolk. He took over most of the region, using Gosport as his headquarters. Then, learning that the American Patriots were descending on the towns of Norfolk and Portsmouth from Williamsburg and from the west, he went out to meet them at what is today known as Great Bridge, in the city of Chesapeake. A tremendous battle was fought there; among the soldiers who engaged the British was a very young John Marshall, later to become the first chief justice of the Supreme Court in the new American republic. The Americans prevailed at the battle of Great Bridge and Dunmore fled back into Norfolk in great disarray and disgrace.

As retribution for his defeat at Great Bridge, Dunmore burnt Norfolk to the ground on January 1, 1776. There has been ongoing argument for years about who actually set Norfolk afire. In his inimitable style, Spong offered this composite of events: the guns from Dunmore's ships laid low the waterfront and about 32 of the 1,200 houses in Norfolk. The remainder of the houses, over 1,000 in number, were burned either by American Patriots who were angry with their resident Scottish Americans and wanted to get even with them for siding with the crown, or, perhaps, by those of a military bent, who did not want the British to have Norfolk as a center from which to sail. With Norfolk burned to the ground, Dunmore retreated again to the other side of the river, and this time he occupied a position on Hospital Point, where he quartered his remaining troops and about 1,500 Tories who assembled to flee with him. Dunmore could not maintain a presence at Hospital Point for very long, and soon they all boarded ships and departed for Mathews County, Virginia, where Dunmore was again defeated and the Tories and Scot merchants dispersed back to London, Bermuda or on to Nova Scotia. Andrew Sprowle died at the battle fought in Mathews County.

"Now we, today, regard Thomas Jefferson, and we should, as one of the greatest Americans," said Spong in his October 1993 address. "And he was, but he had his bad moments." Jefferson's "bad times" came largely during his time as governor of Virginia, when he seemed completely incapable, Spong observed, of keeping British vessels out of the Elizabeth River during the American Revolution. Despite a number of warnings, Jefferson did very little, and as a result, three different British expeditions sailed into the Elizabeth River and landed at Portsmouth. Norfolk, which had been burned to the ground, had nothing to offer the British at that time and was thus never considered a point of destination for British vessels. The first expedition was in 1779, the second in 1780 and the third in 1781, commanded by Benedict Arnold, who had switched sides, betraying the colonists' fight for freedom from the British Crown. The British sent Arnold to Portsmouth to join up with Lord Charles Cornwallis, coming from the south, to take over the Virginia colony. Cornwallis met the force that had been under Arnold around Petersburg, Virginia, and after some time, this force withdrew to Portsmouth.

Cornwallis did not like Portsmouth, observed Spong, but he liked it better than anything else the British had encountered. He subsequently had to choose between setting up at Old Point Comfort or going to Yorktown. He went to Yorktown, and the result there proved Cornwallis's demise. He was headquartered on the Elizabeth, and then left in 1781 to

The entrance to the Albemarle and Chesapeake Canal at Great Bridge, photographed about 1895. *Courtesy of the author.*

ENTRANCE TO ALBERMARLE AND CHESAPEAKE CANAL AT GREAT BRIDGE.

meet his fate at Yorktown. After the Revolution ended, the Scots returned to the area almost immediately. With Norfolk destroyed, Scotsmen went to Portsmouth, and the people of Portsmouth, with their usual good judgment, as Spong noted, ran them out of town. Portsmouth's citizens would not permit the Scots to settle there, so they came over and rebuilt Norfolk. Patriots had been starving out in Princess Anne and Lower Norfolk Counties, but the Scots in a relatively short period of time got Norfolk and its surrounding counties thriving again.

The trade that sprung up along the banks of the Elizabeth River by 1801 was remarkable. There were so many ships in the harbor that the

The *Thomas W. Lawson* visited Norfolk waters in 1906. The ship represented the ultimate in colossus schooners. The only seven-masted schooner ever built, the *Lawson* had been designed by B.B. Crowninshield and named for Thomas W. Lawson, an eccentric Boston stock investor who had made a fortune as a bear on Wall Street. Built in Quincy, Massachusetts, by the Fore River Ship and Engine Company, the schooner was launched in May 1902. Each of the *Lawson*'s masts weighed 3 tons. Her carrying capacity was 8,100 tons, but only had a length-to-breadth ratio of eight to one, out of sync with the weight displacement in her rigging.

About a year after this picture was taken, in 1907, the steel-hulled schooner was converted to a fourteen-compartment oil tanker by the Sun Oil Company. Despite tremendous sail capability, her first transatlantic trip bearing a full load of oil took nearly six weeks to reach the English Channel. On reaching the channel the *Lawson* ran aground on the Scilly Islands and lost all but two of her crew of seventeen to unforgiving waters. The schooner's maiden ocean crossing was also her last. *Courtesy of the author.*

ferry boats had trouble going back and forth across the river. Millions of dollars in foreign commerce was taking place, and in their euphoria, town leaders on both sides of the water believed it was prosperity that would last forever. War between Great Britain and France, the Napoleonic Wars, soon threatened trade between Norfolk and the West Indies. French privateers began attacking American vessels and taking them over. The British, believing there were British seamen aboard American ships who had deserted his majesty's navy, began boarding American ships and taking British seamen off, while impressing others into service in the British fleet. "Then Jefferson—and this was a bad day for my hero," Spong said, "his solution to all of this, and to the French and British War, was to declare an embargo which stopped all shipping in and out of this port anyway, and killed what would have been a very profitable trade." The war between France and Great Britain was eventually settled, but the impressments of seamen and other disagreements between the British and Americans gave rise to another conflict.

The thirty-six-gun frigate USS *Chesapeake*, which had been built at the Gosport Navy Yard, went out from the Elizabeth bound for a deployment to the Mediterranean Sea to become the flagship of her squadron. About twelve miles from Cape Henry she was confronted by the fifty-gun British frigate *Leopard*, which demanded to search the American warship. When the American commander refused, the *Leopard* fired on the *Chesapeake*, stopped her, wounded some of her crew and took four sailors off, three of them Americans and one British. The great *Chesapeake*, gravely wounded, limped back into the Elizabeth River to the embarrassment of the nation. The *Chesapeake*'s commander was Commodore James Barron, who had earlier been accused by the legendary naval hero Stephen Decatur of failing to face up to the British. From this rebuke came Barron's call for a duel with Decatur to settle the insult. Barron shot and killed Decatur. Barron would go on to live a long life in Norfolk and, on his death, was interred in Trinity churchyard in Portsmouth.

As a result of the *Chesapeake-Leopard* affair another war began and, in 1813, four years after their encounter, a British squadron showed up in the Elizabeth River, intent on landing a tremendous force at Craney Island. Troops from Portsmouth and Norfolk went out to meet them, and the result was a resounding defeat of British forces. American troops had been prepared to meet the British with guns on Hospital Point and at Fort Norfolk, but the British, in truth, were defeated before they ever got that far up the river. Craney Island was a pivotal turning point on the road to American victory in its second war with Great Britain.

There were a number of other events affecting the Elizabeth River that occurred after the War of 1812 and during the balance of the nineteenth century. In October 1820 the USS *Delaware* was launched

"When the wetlands really come back," Charles Kuralt said, unveiling The Elizabeth River Project's Watershed Action Plan on June 20, 1996, "when the forest returns to the shore, when healthy fish and clams and oysters find a home in the southern reaches of the river again, and the sun rises off the Atlantic in the morning to reflect itself in the serene, pure waters of the Elizabeth River, our children and grandchildren will know that we had them in mind."

at the Gosport Navy Yard. It was the first of a large number of battleships constructed at the yard. Andrew Sprowle's private yard had become a federal shipyard in 1801.

In 1805 the Dismal Swamp Canal was finally opened after several years of construction. It did not enhance foreign trade, but eventually provided an easier method of coastal trade from North Carolina to the cities of the North. The Norfolk newspapers had written: "The canal is invaluable. It has staved off ruin. But it will take more than a ditch through the Albemarle Sound to make Norfolk a second New York." In 1859 a second canal, the Albemarle and Chesapeake, was opened.

In June 1833, after six years of construction, the first stone dry dock in America was opened at the Gosport Navy Yard. In June 1855 the steamer *Ben Franklin*, en route from Saint Thomas to New York, entered the Elizabeth River for repairs at Gosport. Yellow fever mosquitoes were in the hold. Within days there was an epidemic that killed over three thousand people in Norfolk and Portsmouth. In January 1857, the temperature dropped to nine degrees below zero and the Elizabeth River froze over. Horses and pedestrians could cross with ease from Norfolk to Portsmouth and from Portsmouth to Norfolk.

The ports had never reached the potential that many had foreseen in the nineteenth century. The canals leading into the Elizabeth River were too narrow; the railroads running out of Baltimore, Philadelphia and New York had developed rapidly, due to superior transportation connections. While Norfolk's port had been largely thwarted by Richmond interests, the frustration of those seeking to develop the port were such that resolutions were drawn reviving a century-old theme that the towns on the Elizabeth River should become a part of the state of North Carolina.

As the American Civil War approached, both Norfolk and Portsmouth elected delegates to the Secession Convention who wanted Virginia to remain in the Union. But Abraham Lincoln's announcement that he would start a war to preserve the Union moved the Virginia convention to secede. In April 1861 the Gosport Navy Yard was the largest navy yard in the United States, and one of the largest in the world. Union forces were determined to deny Federal ships in the Gosport yard to Confederate forces. The Confederates began sending troops into Norfolk and William Mahone, who had built the precursor railroads that eventually became today's Norfolk Southern Corporation, was a son of the South and one of her generals. He had perhaps four regiments moved into Norfolk overnight on receiving word that Virginia seceded. He rode them into town on rail cars, standing up, then had them lie down and ride back out of town, then back in again standing up—repeating the procedure so that no one could get an accurate count of their actual numbers. The lookout in the crow's nest of the *Delaware*, berthed at the navy yard, watched this coming and going troop movement all night, reporting to Washington that the Confederates had ten to twenty thousand troops moved into the city of Norfolk under the cover of darkness. The lookout had mistakenly counted the same eight hundred Confederate troops, going in standing up and coming out, laying down, many times over. Mahone had pulled off a marvelous ruse.

The man in charge of the navy yard, Commodore Charles S. McCauley, panicked at the possibility of twenty thousand Confederates and burned the yard, despite having assured the Confederates under a flag of truce that eleven large United States Navy ships would not leave the harbor. Among the vessels burned was the frigate *Merrimack*. The *Merrimack*, a wooden vessel, was brought up by the Confederates on taking possession of the yard and fitted into the world's first ironclad. A year later, in March 1862, the *Merrimack*, renamed the CSS *Virginia*, went out into Hampton Roads and was in the process of destroying the Federal fleet when the USS *Monitor* appeared and engaged her. The famous battle that took place in Hampton Roads could be seen by onlookers from the mouth of the Elizabeth.

The battle of the ironclads was a standoff. The *Virginia*'s effectiveness was limited to what it could do in the protected waters of the Elizabeth

The United States Coast Guard training ship *Eagle* is shown on the Elizabeth River in July 1974. The young men and women of the United States Coast Guard Academy get their first taste of life at sea aboard this vessel. The *Eagle*, with her twenty thousand square feet of sails, was built in 1936 as the *Horst Wessel*, a training ship for the German navy. She was acquired by the United States at the end of World War II. The *Eagle* has been a frequent visitor to Norfolk waters since the early 1970s. *Courtesy of the author.*

River and Hampton Roads. It was not seaworthy and could not have ventured out to sea. As the ironclads fought in "the Roads," Roanoke Island fell to Union forces, a Federal maneuver that outflanked the city of Norfolk. It meant that Norfolk was sitting in an exposed position to be taken by the Union army at any time. The Confederates withdrew from the city and, as a result, the Norfolk harbor was blockaded during the war as well as occupied by Union troops.

While former Senator Spong had proffered only a few key events pertaining to the Elizabeth River's rich history, his observation that the history of the nation is tied so closely to the history of the Elizabeth River holds true. Sprowle's private shipyard has become the oldest, largest and best naval shipyard in the United States. Seawell's Point, first purchased back in 1620, has become the site of the world's largest naval base. Hospital Point is the site of the oldest naval hospital.

Aside from the military buildup that has taken place, Mahone's railroad coming into Norfolk, its expansion fought so vigorously by forces at work in Richmond, has become penultimately important in Norfolk, and is today the Norfolk Southern Corporation. The port facilities have been developed, with terminals on all sides of the river, including the largest coal facility in the world.

Concluding his remarks all those years ago, Spong observed that he had talked much about the river's past and his audience was present to discuss its future: "How economic development, which has had so much of a struggle throughout the centuries to come to any fruition, and how the necessary military structure can be maintained, and at the same time the river maintained, is a tremendous challenge." While the Elizabeth River lost the voice of an articulate, passionate spokesperson with Spong's death on October 8, 1997, his spirit and advocacy continue, as do those of Charles Kuralt, whose words on behalf of the Elizabeth were a further wake-up call that rivers that are the lifeblood of our nation must be saved; Kuralt died on Independence Day 1997. In his "The Goodliest Land," the keynote address at the Scenic America's National Conference held in Baltimore, Maryland, on May 12, less than two months before his death, Kuralt acknowledged how hard so many people had worked on the Chesapeake Bay and how determined they were and how daunting the task of bay restoration had been since the effort was initiated. "I believe we are going to see this Bay come back because so many people love it," he said. "I think the extravagantly polluted Elizabeth River down at the other end of the Bay is going to be revived because so many people want to do so and have banded together…to do so." For Kuralt, like so many of the rest of us, the land that English explorers Captains Philip Amadas and Arthur Barlowe first saw over four hundred years ago was truly "the goodliest land under the cope of Heaven," a viable river for generations to come. "When the wetlands really come back," Kuralt had said nearly a year earlier, in June 1996 with the debut of the Elizabeth River Project's Watershed Action Plan, "when the forest returns to the shore, when healthy fish and clams and oysters find a home in the southern reaches of the river again, and the sun rises off the Atlantic in the morning to reflect itself in the serene, pure waters of the Elizabeth River, our children and grandchildren will know that we had them in mind."

CHAPTER ONE
BEFORE THE WHITE MAN

There are innumerable romanticized accounts of Captain John Smith and his Indian princess, Pocahontas, but most of those stories are just that—stories. It is far easier to picture native people swiftly paddling their light canoes over the deep and quiet waters of the Elizabeth River and its tributaries. Upon these shores they held their councils, and "as the sun wheeled on his broad disk behind the western hills," or "as the moonbeams melted over the verge of the evening cloud," they gazed intently upon nature's beauties as they were dispersed liberally around them, and admired nature for the wildness, untouched, unaltered as it then was by the otherwise ever-changing and self-appropriating hand of civilization. The native people's council fires drove back the darkness of the deep midnight to the gloomy recesses of the forest, and lighted up the adjacent shores. William S. Forrest, a nineteenth-century historian fascinated by those whose presence was felt here long before the white man, observed that the plough may, in after times, turn up their stone calumets, and the railroad excavation reveal their moldering skeletons, but their forms, their characters, their rugged virtues and fight for existence in the face of European settlement, might be known for all time only by the vivid accounts of those white men or the canvas of an adventurous artist. To Forrest, here lived and loved another race of people. "Beneath the same sun that rolls over your head," he wrote in 1853, "the Indian hunter pursued the panting deer;—gazing on the same moon that smiles on you, the Indian lover wooed his dusky mate." Here, too, he noted, they worshipped, and from them came fervent prayers to the Great Spirit, who had not written his laws for them on tablets of stone, but had traced them in the depths of their hearts. The child of Nature knew not the God of Revelation, but the God of the Universe he acknowledged in everything around him. "He beheld him," wrote Forrest, "in the star that sank in beauty behind his lonely dwelling; in the sacred orb that flamed on him from his midday throne; in the flower that snapped in the morning breeze; in the lofty pine that defied a thousand whirlwinds; in the timid warbler that never left its native grove; in the fearless eagle whose untired pinion was wet in clouds; in the worm that crawled at his feet; and in his own matchless form, glowing with a spark of that light to whose mysterious source he bent in humble, though blind, adoration." To Forrest's chagrin, these native peoples live on only in the songs and chronicles of their exterminators.

But life before the white man began long before the time when European explorers and settlers began documenting their encounters with the Elizabeth's native people. The late Pleistocene geologic period—the end of the Ice Age—set the stage for the first human activity in the eastern United States. Glacial melting as the result of climatic warming and the introduction of new animal and plant species is significant to the nomadic people of the Paleo-Indian period.

The late archaeologist Floyd Painter spent decades excavating the Hampton Roads area, documenting four distinct periods, from nomadic to post-European contact: Paleo-Indian, Archaic and Woodland, and ending with European settlement in North America. The Paleo-Indian period, beginning some 13,000 years ago and ending in 8000 BP (before present), indicates that the landmass surrounding the Elizabeth River and its tributaries was very different than it appeared to Europeans in the sixteenth and seventeenth centuries. In the Paleo-Indian period nomadic hunters may have sought diverse wildlife and vegetation in the marshes, which are thought to have extended at that time farther out—as much as ninety miles—into the present-day Chesapeake Bay. Rich marshland is still present in the topography of the Elizabeth and its tributaries. These indigenous, nomadic hunters also hunted up small tributaries and along the riverbanks. Archaeologists, including Painter, found evidence

Archaeologist Floyd Painter documented four aboriginal archaeological periods at the Great Neck site. The Paleo-Indian period, depicted in this 1986 drawing by Painter, followed Archaic Man and was approximately 13,000 to 10,000 years before present (BP), following on the heels of the Ice Age nomadic hunters who migrated to Great Neck. *Courtesy of Deborah R. Painter.*

of prehistoric hunting sites on upland ridge settings such as floodplain terraces and benches, many of them overlooking minor tributaries and broader interior bays and bodies of water.

For many years archaeologists and historians subscribed to the notion that Paleo-Indians hunted Pleistocene megafauna, including mammoths and mastodons, but these megafauna were extinct from eastern woodlands and marshes by the time nomadic hunters arrived on the scene. Archaeological evidence indicates Paleo-Indians hunted native species of deer, rabbits and boar, for example, as a primary source of game.

The Paleo-Indian populations identified in southeast Virginia, primarily by Painter and archeologist James G. Pritchard, were quite mobile and preferred to hunt in what archaeologists dubbed "low relief environments." The best examples of such environments were located in present-day Virginia Beach, which at the time of Painter's and Pritchard's excavations had not yet been developed to the point of disturbing or destroying Native American settlement sites. Norfolk and Portsmouth had been subject to continuous development since the 1600s, making excavations far more difficult. Today, the Eastern Branch is very shallow, with many mud flats along its banks at low tide. Pritchard, a contemporary and friend of Painter's, found Paleo-Indian fluted point tips, gravers and scrapers at the Quail Spring site in the Great Neck area of Virginia Beach, while Painter, also working at the Great Neck site, discovered important Paleolithic artifacts. While certainly closer to the Lynnhaven River than the Elizabeth, their research, documented in publications through the early 1960s, provided critical understanding of how the Paleo-Indians lived in sync with the rivers in southeast Virginia, importantly including the Elizabeth, with a 9,600-acre watershed stretching across about 5 percent of the city of Virginia Beach in proximity of the areas excavated by the two archaeologists.

As the temperatures of the seasons could be felt warmer and colder along the coastal plain in the period of Archaic Man (10,000–3000 BP), a broader range of food choices enabled humans to migrate seasonally, thus leaving more permanent imprints on the land. Seasonal sites have been found indicating Archaic Man not only hunted and fished, but also did so with more advanced tools and weapons than their precursors. They attached bannerstones, ground and perforated stones used as counterweights, on their hunting spears. Ben C. McCary, in his article about bannerstone usage for the Archaeological Society of Virginia, wrote that bannerstones were excavated from sites at Dam Neck, Kempsville, Back Bay and Lynnhaven Inlet. Bannerstones were indicative of the development of increasingly specialized bone and lithic tools that began to appear in the Middle Archaic Period (8000–5000 BP). Some of these ground-stone tools were used to process plants. During this period, Archaic Man established transitory camps later uncovered in the most

By the Middle Woodland period (2000–1000 BP) the Native American population was growing and there is evidence that horticulture, especially the cultivation of corn, beans, pumpkin and tobacco, was on the rise. During this period tribes were tied strongly to village life.

This engraving of a twenty-three-year-old Virginia Algonquian man by etcher Wenceslaus Hollar (1607–1677) illustrates typical head necklace and ornaments, but also facial markings. The etching was published in 1645. *Courtesy of the Library of Congress Prints and Photographs Division.*

likely places—fringes of floodplains, interior waterways and higher ground. Archaic Man also fashioned soapstone tools.

The transition from Late Archaic (5000–3000 BP) to Early Woodland (3000–2000 BP) is demarcated by advances in technology as Late Archaic Man shifted settlement patterns from inland waterways and upland riverine settings. The transitional natives were more mobile and relied on fishing more than their ancestors. One of the marked differences between cultures in this transitional period is the technology of handling and storing food. Soapstone and steatite bowls indicative of Late Archaic Man were precursors of ceramics that begin to appear in Lower Tidewater archaeological digs of the Early Woodland period. The development of more sophisticated vessels to contain or prepare foods is indicative of an emerging sedentary lifestyle.

There were several important Early to Late Woodland period (3000–500 BP) sites excavated in Lower Tidewater in the twentieth century. This key period covers Native American culture before European contact, when the population "intensified" and permanent villages cropped up along rivers and creeks, including the Elizabeth, which were the main transportation and communication routes. Native American woodland paths account for the beginnings of several major roadsteads in Lower Tidewater. Indigenous tribes began to cultivate crops but continued to hunt and fish. Deer, though not as plentiful in Virginia as they are today, were hunted along with smaller game, but what the Native Americans could glean from the river and bay—from sturgeon and herring in cold months to oysters,

A scallop pot from the Chesapeake site, uncovered and photographed by Floyd Painter in January 1980. *Courtesy of Deborah R. Painter.*

commonly as large in size as a man's foot—provided important sources of food. Subsistence strategy shifted as villagers dug storage pits and produced ceramics fashioned from sand, shell and crushed rock temper that exhibited a cord- or net-pressed exterior. Native Americans also fashioned substantive bows and arrows to hunt game in this period.

By the Middle Woodland period (2000–1000 BP) the Native American population was growing and there is evidence that horticulture, especially the cultivation of corn, beans, pumpkin and tobacco, was on the rise. During this period tribes were tied strongly to village life. The village became the focal point of foray and procurement activities. Pottery was decorated with rather simple designs, but the application of the designs reflected the use of fabrics and native materials to impress the various pieces. Carved pieces demonstrated a vast array of utility. By the Late Woodland period there is a more complex culture of sedentism. Native Americans of this culture dug postholes for longhouses or circular house structures, constructed storage pits, conducted burials and left behind organic remains of food products. Archaeologists working on significant Late Woodland sites in what is today part of Virginia Beach found seasonal and temporary camps, hamlets and villages typical of Virginia's coastal tribes of that period. One of the "giveaways" or strongest predictors in the siting of Late Woodland period villages is fertile soil. The Algonquian chiefdoms, to which Native Americans of Lower Tidewater belonged, used slash-and-burn agriculture in the cultivation of their crops, especially that of corn. The Native Americans of this period lived within highly stratified societies, with a chief or king who possessed absolute power over the life and death of his people. With a descending layering of power, priests had power over military matters and were able to will the confederations and alliances of Indians to mobilize over matters of war. Emergent contact with Europeans effectually increased tribal priests' power, enabling them to incorporate and organize large political organizations, called confederations.

The earliest definite record of a Native American settlement on land now occupied by Norfolk was set down by Captain Arthur Barlowe, a member of Sir Walter Raleigh's first expedition in 1584 to what is now known as the Outer Banks of North Carolina. Barlowe recorded that the main town of the Chesapeake, the Late Woodland tribe then occupying what is now the cities of Norfolk, Portsmouth, Chesapeake and Virginia Beach, was Skicoak. Later, in 1585–86, Ralph Lane, the governor of Raleigh's first Roanoke Island colony, mentioned that aside from Skicoak the Chesapeake also had two additional towns—Apasus and Chesepiooc—both near the Chesapeake Bay in what is now Virginia Beach. The towns are shown on the first printed map of the North Carolina and Virginia coastal area, engraved in 1590 by Theodor de Bry

The earliest definite record of a Native American settlement on land now occupied by Norfolk was set down by Captain Arthur Barlowe, a member of Sir Walter Raleigh's first expedition in 1584 to what is now known as the Outer Banks of North Carolina. Barlowe recorded that the main town of the Chesapeake, the Late Woodland tribe then occupying what is now the cities of Norfolk, Portsmouth, Chesapeake and Virginia Beach, was Skicoak.

from watercolor maps drawn by John White during Lane's northward explorations from Roanoke Island that breached the Chesapeake's hunting grounds. The Chesapeake were named for the bay that washed gently against the boundary of their tribal lands.

The best example of Late Woodland period villages is found along the Long Creek Midden on Great Neck Creek and Lynnhaven Inlet, in the vicinity of another Lower Tidewater river—the Lynnhaven—but it is certainly typical of Native Americans' life along the Elizabeth River as well. Archaeologist Floyd Painter wrote that there was no more ideal geographic location or ecological location for man's habitation in prehistoric times on the central Atlantic seaboard than the village that once stood along the Long Creek Midden. "The midden," wrote Painter, "represents the permanent habitation on site of a large population who no doubt had lived on and near the area for perhaps three thousand years or more." In Painter's opinion the culture evolved in that three-thousand-year span at or near the midden, but was influenced by other groups, to varying degrees, from the north, south and west. But the influence of other cultures upon the tribes of the Long Creek Midden enhanced the course of their development, improving upon their traits and practices. Painter's findings indicate the people of Long Creek Midden were coastal Algonquian living in "an ideal environment" and "who attained the highest stage of cultural development ever [achieved] by aboriginal inhabitants of the Central Atlantic Coast."

But the Long Creek Midden was only a sliver of the Great Neck site consisting of hundreds of acres of that area and adjacent Bay Island, which separates Long Creek and Great Neck. The Long Creek Midden was untouched when Painter began his excavations there in the 1960s. He found evidence of inhabitants of the Early, Middle and Late Woodland periods. Describing the midden as "one to three feet in depth and on a stretch of sand from one to ten feet in depth, most of this sand piled up by earth moving and dredging activities in recent years, and also accumulated by wind action [marching dunes]," Painter noted that the search for Late Woodland pottery in the upper layer of the midden proved fruitful. He also investigated the two deepest layers for debris from the Early and Middle Woodland periods, aware that the inhabitants of this place discarded their everyday items on the floor of the village.

The oldest pottery Painter discovered in the deepest layer of the midden was "thick, grit tempered, [fishing] net impressed and made of red clay. These pots are made in the form of a deep, almost perfect concave [shape]," he wrote later. Above the net-decorated pottery, he found thick, grit-tempered, cord-marked ware made from yellow clay. The sides of the pots he pulled from this layer were convex, but maintained a "sharp conical base." The Middle Woodland layer contained large quantities of grit-tempered, fabric-impressed potsherds of medium thickness fashioned out of yellow and tan clay. The pots were straight- or slightly convex-sided, and the bottoms, according to Painter's reports, had a more round appearance containing a conical tip or base. The fabric used to press the face finish had to have been coarse. But in the upper or top level of the midden, the fabric imprints become finer and the clay is thinner and orange in color. Pots in the upper midden had round bases or bottoms. The designs on the pots were ingenious, "far surpassing anything produced by the contiguous cultures along the Central Atlantic Coast," observed Painter.

During excavations of the Long Creek Midden and its surrounding digs, the only alien pottery uncovered was a single shard of Savannah Creek Check Stamped pottery located on the greater Great Neck site. This shard originated very late from South Carolina, Georgia and Florida, and was a surprise to find in the Long Creek Midden area. Long Creek Midden ceramics, in Painter's estimation, lacked only fiber and steatite-

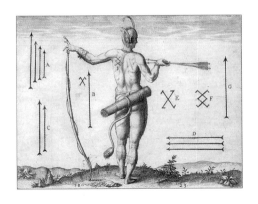

The tribal groups of Virginia, of Algonquian origin, used symbols, particularly body tattoos, to denote affiliations and status within their respective groups. This Theodor de Bry engraving, likely from a John White watercolor (though there has not been found a White match to this work), is from *Admiranda Narratio fida tamen, de Commodius et Incolarum Ritibus Virginiae*, published in Frankfurt in 1590, with text from Thomas Hariot. The translation of this title is *A Briefe and True Report of the New Found Land of Virginia*.

The engraving shown here, titled "The Marckes of sundrye of the Cheif mene of Virginia," was plate number twenty-three. The long title of the book was *A Briefe and True Report of the New Found Land of Virginia: of the Commodities and of the Nature and Manners of the Naturall Inhabitants : Discouered bÿ the English Colonÿ There Seated by Sir Richard Greinuile Knight In the ÿeere 1585 : Which Remained Vnder the Gouernment of Twelue Monethes, At the Speciall Charge and Direction of the Honourable Sir Walter Raleigh Knight Lord Warden of the Stanneries Who therein Hath Beene Fauoured and Authorised bÿ Her Maiestie and Her Letters Patents / This Fore Booke Is Made in English by Thomas Hariot seruant to the Aboue-Named Sir Walter, a Member of the Colonÿ, and There Imploÿed in Discouering. Courtesy of the Library of Congress Rare Book and Special Collections Division.*

temper in representing a complete sample of central Atlantic coast pottery types. Painter continued his archaeological work at the Long Creek Midden with the rumble of nearby bulldozers ringing in his ears. A boat marina was being built on one portion of the midden while some of the most expensive homes in the area were built on another. Despite the angst of losing the site to development, Painter saw it this way: "It is fitting that this site, so long the home of [Lower] Tidewater's aboriginal inhabitants should continue to function as a homesite and a safe harbor for small boats." And, he continued, "may the noise, the odors and ugliness of industry and commerce never blot out the beauty and tranquility of this well-chosen spot for man's habitation."

Floyd Painter excavated Late Woodland remains—specifically Chesapeake—at the Great Neck site again in the late 1970s and early 1980s under the auspices of the Virginia Department of Historic Resources (VDHR). The excavation could not tie any of the remains to known chieftains or tribal members, but it did document a Chesapeake village site, possibly known as Chesepiooc, based on available historical documents that trace the tribe's history to the fifteenth century. There were shell-tempered Townsend and Roanoke ceramics that indicated the village site was continuously occupied by the same culture from the Late Woodland period until sometime in 1635, when the site was abandoned as an English settlement, according to the VDHR. The burial sites Painter uncovered all appeared to have originated in this time frame.

The Chesapeake did not long enjoy their way of life after Barlowe's and Lane's reports to Raleigh had been written. Historical documents indicate that by 1607 the Chesapeake had joined, but also incurred heavy losses from, the powerful Powhatan Confederacy. William Strachey's *The Historie of Travaile into Virginia Britanica*, published in 1612, reported that the Chesapeake were wiped out by Powhatan, chief of the Peninsula-based Powhatan Confederacy, some time before the arrival of the English at Jamestown in 1607. Powhatan reportedly eliminated the Chesapeake because his priests had warned him that "from the Chesapeake Bay a nation would arise, which should dissolve and give end to his empire." The last mention of them as a tribe in historical records is in 1627, indicating an English plan to attack the Chesapeake and some of the other coastal tribes. The tribe does not have lineal descendants, having been wiped out as a people sometime in this period by disease and attrition, though some Chesapeake were allied with the Nansemond tribe in the sixteenth and early seventeenth centuries. During key months in 1981 and 1982 the remains of seven Chesapeake were recovered from the site, including funerary objects such as tobacco residue, three copper pendants and one copper bead. Five additional sets of remains were recovered shortly thereafter, including one infant and the previously disturbed remains of at

William Strachey's The Historie of Travaile into Virginia Britanica, *published in 1612, reported that the Chesapeake were wiped out by Powhatan, chief of the Peninsula-based Powhatan Confederacy, some time before the arrival of the English at Jamestown in 1607. Powhatan reportedly eliminated the Chesapeake because his priests had warned him that "from the Chesapeake Bay a nation would arise, which should dissolve and give end to his empire."*

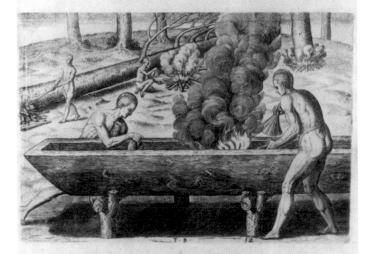

Lintrium conficiendorum ratio. XII.

IsA est in VIRGINIA cymbas fabricandi ratio: nam, cum ferreis instrumentis aut aliis nostris similibus careant, eas tamen parare nerunt nostris non minus commodas ad nauigandum quo lubet per flumina & adpiscandum. Primum arbore aliqua crassa & alta delecta, pro cymba quam parare volunt magnitudine, ignem circa eius radices summa tellure in ambitu struunt ex arborum musco bene resiccato, & ligni assulis paulatim ignem excitantes, ne flamma altius ascendat, & arboris longitudinem minuat. Pane adusta & ruinam minante arbore, nouum suscitant ignem, quem flagrare sinunt donec arbor sponte cadat. Adustis deinde arboris fastigio & ramis, vt truncus iustam longitudinem retineat, tignis transuersis supra furcas positis imponunt, ea altitudine vt commode laborare possint, tunc cortice conchis quibusdam adempto, integriorem trunci partem pro cymba inferiore parte seruant, in altera parte ignem secundum trunci longitudinem struunt, praeterquam extremis, quod satis adustum illis videtur, restincto igne conchis scabunt, & nouo suscitato igne denuo adurunt, atque ita deinceps pergunt, subinde ventes & scabentes, donec cymba necessarium alueum nacta sit. Sic Domini spiritus rudibus hominibus sug gerit rationem, qua res in suum vsum necessarias conficere queant.

B 4

This Theodor de Bry engraving from a John White watercolor was plate number twelve in *Admiranda Narratio fida tamen, de Commodius et Incolarum Ritibus Virginiae*, published in Frankfurt, 1590. In this engraving, originally titled "The manner of makinge their boates," Hariot's caption detailed the manner of construction. A large tree, suitable for the size of canoe being built, was felled by burning through its base by means of controlled fire. The branches were burnt off, the trunk shortened to an appropriate length, also by burning. The trunk section was then raised to a convenient height on poles laid across forked posts, and the bark removed with shell scrapers. The log was then hollowed out by burning, quenching the fire and removing the charred wood with shell scrapers, repeating this process until the hollowing was done. *Courtesy of the Library of Congress Rare Book and Special Collections Division.*

least four individuals (labeled a "trophy" burial by Painter). The roughly one hundred associated funerary objects were shell disc beads found with the infant.

Between the Late Woodland and early European settlement periods—the latter indicating permanent settlement—Europeans began to explore the Chesapeake Bay area, including the Elizabeth River and its expansive watershed. The Spanish sailed past the bay, landing at Cape Fear, North Carolina, and Chincoteague, Virginia, in 1524, but did not discover the beauty within its reaches or the Native Americans who lived there, dotting the bay and its interior rivers. The first English expedition was dispatched under the auspices of Sir Walter Raleigh. Raleigh's men explored between Cape Henry and Cape Lookout during the heat of July and August 1584 under the command of Captains Philip Amadas and Arthur Barlowe. Barlowe conveyed his observations to Raleigh, providing a first glimpse of the area's topography and people, including the complex political divisions of the Algonquian tribes who occupied the land from the Atlantic Ocean to the Elizabeth River. The hierarchy of the Native Americans, who spoke the Powhatan dialect of the Algonquian language but did not defer to Powhatan's chiefdom, were divided into five provinces or kingdoms—Weapemiooc, Chawanook, Secotan, Pomeiooc and Newsiooc—each ruled by a chief or king. To defy Powhatan was to defy the most powerful chieftain in the Chesapeake Bay area. He dominated more than thirty

Trophy burials were uncovered on the Riding Ring site along with those of revered chieftains and Chesapeake families. Floyd Painter photographed this trophy burial pit on May 26, 1979. Courtesy of Deborah R. Painter.

Algonquian-speaking tribes—as many as thirty thousand strong by some estimates—but he ruled personally only six of these tribes: the Powhatan, Arohatock, Appamattuck, Pamunkey, Youghtanund and Mattaponi. He conquered others; Raphael Semmes wrote in his 1937 volume *Captains and Mariners of Early Maryland* that Powhatan had amassed so many tribes that he required eight interpreters to converse with his own subjects. The English called the land "Virginia" even then, but the Powhatan Algonquians knew it as Wingandacoa (another name for the land of Secotan).

This Theodor de Bry engraving, after a watercolor by Jacques Le Moyne de Morgues, was published as part of de Bry's work *Brevis narratio eorvm qvæ in Florida Americæ provincial Gallis acciderunt*, published in Frankfurt, 1591. In this volume, de Bry tells the story of the French attempt to colonize Fort Caroline, now Florida, before the settlement was destroyed by the Spanish, using Le Moyne de Morgues's paintings to render his engravings. The engraving, though illustrative of a tribal group in Florida, remains an excellent depiction of celebratory gatherings after battle with an enemy. Chief Holata Outina is the chieftain standing in the foreground with French soldiers. Trophies from the fight are staked around the circle, including the enemy's arms, legs and headdress pieces. *Courtesy of the Library of Congress Rare Book and Special Collections Division.*

Wingina ruled Secotan from Pomeiooc, its capital, but his land was on the mainland across from Roanoke Island and a respectable distance southwest of Pamlico Sound. The familial relationships of the Algonquian brought tribes in what is today Northeastern North Carolina closer to those in Lower Tidewater. Secotan covered the ground between the Albemarle Sound and the Roanoke River on the north, and Pamlico River on the south, including its islands or banks to the east. To the north of Albemarle Sound lay the land of Weapemiooc, bordering on the Atlantic Ocean and extending toward the southern shore of the Chesapeake Bay. Barlowe did not name this province nor did he have a great appreciation for Native American hierarchy—in other words, he did not know the names and importance of key chieftains, only that Weapemiooc was the

Queen Elizabeth I (1533–1603) is shown in this view as a young princess, ca. 1545. Though the river is not named for her, it was Queen Elizabeth I who expanded English influence in the New World. *Courtesy of the author.*

most important kingdom with the most notable capital—Skicoak. The Indians living in the kingdom of Weapemiooc fashioned their arrows from the small canes or reeds they fished from the marshes. They initially tipped them with sharp shells or fish teeth, later evolving to more substantive stone points that have been well documented. Of Skicoak, Barlowe stated only that he and seven others went twenty miles up a river called Occam, which led toward the city of Skicoak. Since Skicoak was about where Norfolk is today, the river that Barlowe referenced leading toward it may have been the Chowan River or Currituck Sound. Barlowe's journey was likely the closest approach of any English detachment to the Elizabeth River watershed during the 1584 expedition made to Lower Tidewater. From Barlowe's writings, it is readily apparent that he had heard of Skicoak from the Indians encountered on this trip, who confirmed for him that it was six days' journey away and was the greatest city in the area, requiring more than an hour for a man to walk around it.

Early Europeans also observed, importantly, that the Native Americans were expert boat builders, making them capable of crossing large bodies of water. The Indians' ability to carve, burn and hew out large boats or "canowes," as Smith called them in his writings, was noticed clearly by John White in 1585 and, later, in Thomas Hariot's narrative, *A Briefe and True Report of the New Found Land of Virginia*, dated 1588, and in Theodor de Bry's subsequent compilation of his engravings from White's paintings and Hariot's narrative in 1590. "The manner of makinge their boats in Virginia is very wonderfull," wrote Hariot, "for whereas they want Instruments of yorn, or other like vuto ours, yet they knowe how to make them as handsomely, to saile with whear they liste in their Riuers, and to fishe with all, as ours."

Raleigh launched a second expedition to Virginia almost exactly one year later, in June 1585, and remained ashore at Roanoke for nearly a year. The expedition was led by Raleigh's kinsman, Sir Richard Grenville, with Captain Ralph Lane as deputy general and Captain Amadas (from the previous expedition) as "admiral" in charge of the new venture. Lane wrote a complete account of the land and inhabitants he encountered on this journey. Thomas Hariot, another member of Lane's party, wrote a spirited narrative of the expedition, mentioned above, accompanied by John White's map, engraved by Theodor de Bry. The map subsequently proved an excellent source for locating Indian sites in Virginia between the Chesapeake Bay and Neuse River, located in North Carolina, but it also confirmed Barlowe's earlier accounts of the new land. In the interim, White returned to Roanoke in 1587 as "governor of Virginia" at the head of a company of colonists who later earned the legendary name the "Lost Colony." White's report to Raleigh mentions names that are all too familiar—the island of Croatan, the Bay of Chesapiok, the inlet of Hatorask (Hatteras) and the island of Roanoke.

The first English expedition was dispatched under the auspices of Sir Walter Raleigh. Raleigh's men explored between Cape Henry and Cape Lookout during the heat of July and August 1584 under the command of Captains Philip Amadas and Arthur Barlowe. Barlowe conveyed his observations to Raleigh, providing a first glimpse of the area's topography and people, including the complex political divisions of the Algonquian tribes who occupied the land from the Atlantic Ocean to the Elizabeth River.

Interestingly, Lane's account of the second expedition elaborated further on Skicoak. Lane reported that he received information in March 1586 from Menatonon, Chawanook chief, that he could travel three days' journey up the Chawanook (now Chowan) River, thence overland in a northeasterly direction "to a certain King's country whose province lieth upon the sea, but his place of greatest strength is an island situate, as he [Menatonon] described it to me, in a bay, the water round about the island very deep." The original site of Norfolk, broken up by creeks and swampland, was, before being filled in, almost an island. The "very deep" water that Menatonon mentioned is relative. The waters of the Elizabeth River would be "deep" by comparison to shoal water or inland creeks. It was claimed, too, that the king to the north possessed a great quantity of white and black pearls, with which he and his followers adorned themselves. Menatonon reportedly gave Lane a strand of these pearls, unfortunately lost later on the return trip to England. Lane, impressed by what he heard from Menatonon, wanted to look for the land of Skicoak, but this exploration did not take place. Lane set sail on Sir Francis Drake's ships bound for his native land on June 19, 1586.

There is no particular mention in these early narratives of Powhatan's confederacy north of Chawanook and Weapemiooc. While he is not mentioned at this pivotal juncture in the early colonization attempts in the New World, Powhatan is later credited with a role in the demise of the Lost Colony—but there is no proof of this. Significantly, the only tribe mentioned by explorers at Roanoke is the Chesapeake, with villages at Skicoak, Apasus and Chesepiooc (according to the Lane map of 1585), the latter in the vicinity of London Bridge; all located in what were later Lower Norfolk and Princess Anne Counties. The first real look at Native American inhabitants of these counties comes from three primary sources: Captain Gabriel Archer's account of 1607; map explorations made in May 1607 and February–March 1607–08 and drawn by Robert Tindall in 1608; and Captain John Smith's account of his explorations in 1608, first published (with the Smith map) in 1612.

Skicoak, the most important of the Chesepiooc's towns and mentioned in the Barlowe and Lane accounts, was later described by late nineteenth- and early to mid-twentieth-century historians to be the site chosen for Norfolk Town, on the north side of the Elizabeth River where its Eastern and Southern Branches flow together. Later, however, some twentieth-century historians and archaeologists adjusted the location of Skicoak farther down the Elizabeth River, perhaps in a location between Fort Norfolk and Lambert's Point toward Hampton Roads, a theory supported by an intriguing article in the *Virginian-Pilot* dated April 13, 1905, and titled "Hundreds of skeletons dug up" with the subtitle "Mound of Indian graves excavated at Sewell's Point and remains of red men exposed to view." While improving the grounds of the Pine Beach Hotel at Seawell's

Point, workmen discovered an Indian burial mound reportedly containing hundreds of well-preserved skeletons. Further investigation showed that the bodies had been buried two or three deep in a wide circle and that arrowheads and other Indian artifacts were scattered among the bones. But the initial discovery was only the beginning. The man charged with the Pine Beach Hotel beautification project estimated that thousands of other, similar burials remained uncovered. Nothing was done, however, to follow up on what the workers found. This burial place, and conceivably the site of Skicoak, were obliterated either by the western part of the Norfolk Naval Station or by private development.

It is on Smith's map of 1612 that the name Skicoak appears for the last time, demarcated by a "king's house" on the site he called Chesepiooc, on or near the site of the burial mound discovered in 1905. After the Chesapeake were reportedly massacred between 1590 and 1607, Powhatan

The English made their first attempt to colonize the vast land they called Virginia from Roanoke Island (left in this image) in 1584. The map, originally a watercolor by John White, was engraved by Theodor de Bry and published with Thomas Hariot's narrative in *Admiranda Narratio fida tamen, de Commodius et Incolarum Ritibus Virginiae*, published in Frankfurt in 1590. *Courtesy of the Library of Congress Rare Book and Special Collections Division.*

populated what is now Norfolk with warriors of his own whom he trusted, although they continued to be known as Chesapeake. In more recent times it has been suggested that Skicoak was located at the juncture of Indian River and the Western Branch of the Elizabeth River; this site would place Skicoak in the modern city of Chesapeake. Another study suggests that Skicoak was on the Southern Branch of the river, generally near present-day Great Bridge. Skicoak's location, or that of any significant Chesapeake tribal settlement, is best understood by models of Indian behavior forwarded by noted anthropology scholars studying the Algonquian along the Great Coastal Plain. Helen C. Rountree has suggested that boats of fifty feet, such as those constructed by Indians from large trees, could not be kept on open bodies of water, as they would be subject to damage from storms and floods, nor would such vessels be left in the water permanently, only to become waterlogged. Such conditions would dictate that a harbor safe from high tides, storms and flooding was preferable; a body of water such as a small creek that afforded protection for large boats or "canowes" would have been an important consideration. Another part of the profile could conceivably be two Indian villages located on both sides of a river at the point where the river narrows. Such locations make natural land trails and over time were possibly incorporated as trading centers. Floyd Painter's findings from his excavations at Great Neck and other sites now located in the city of Virginia Beach largely support Rountree's model of Indian settlement and behavior. Small, protected creeks near large bodies of water best describe where most Indian settlements have been found in the Elizabeth River watershed; this is true of Painter's findings along the Lynnhaven and its tributaries as well. While probable that there had been Chesapeake settlements along the Western and Southern Branches of the Elizabeth River, scholars place it near the confluence of the James River and Chesapeake Bay—closer to accounts placing this very important town between Fort Norfolk and Seawell's Point. Fort Norfolk was built, in fact, at a point along the river called The Narrows.

Roanoke colonists purportedly visited Skicoak in the winter of 1586, according to David Beers Quinn's 1955 work on the Roanoke expeditions. In Arthur Barlowe's September 1584 account of the first exploration of the American coast, he wrote of extensive contact with Granganimo, brother of King Wingina, in the country of Wingandacoa, which the English later named "Virginia." King Wingina was observed to be greatly obeyed and his brothers and children reverenced. Visitation and trade between Wingina's people and Amadas's and Barlowe's parties was frequent. During one such visit, after the Indians had been several times aboard his ships, Barlowe noted that he and seven of his party went twenty miles "into the river that runneth toward the city of Skicoak, which river they called Occam, and the evening following we

Raphael Semmes wrote in his 1937 volume Captains and Mariners of Early Maryland *that Powhatan had amassed so many tribes that he required eight interpreters to converse with his own subjects.*

came to an island which they call Roanoke, distant from the harbour by which we entered seven leagues." Beyond the island of Roanoke there was the mainland, "and over against this island falleth into this spacious water the great river called Occam by the inhabitants, on which standeth a town called Pemeoke, and six days' journey further upon the same is situate their greatest city called Skicoak, which this people affirm to be very great. But the savages were never at it; only they speak of it by the report of their fathers and other men, whom they have heard affirm it to be above one day's journey about."

Powhatan made it clear to the Englishmen that the Chesapeake were not a confederacy, but "an Enemye generally to all these Kyngdomes." According to Lane's account, the Chesapeake flirted with danger by enjoining with the Mangoak (who may have been Iroquoian) in an alliance with Wingina, chief of Secotan, against the English. Okisko, chief of the Weapemiooc, refused to join the alliance, but "the rest of his province," probably Chesapeake, jumped ship and joined Powhatan. Chesapeake—and possibly some Nansamund (Powhatan's allies)—later attacked Smith's landing party at Cape Henry when they alighted on the beach on April 26, 1607.

But the Native Americans in Lower Tidewater also exhibited, for some, a metaphysical understanding of the universe and the role they were to play in it. Sir George Yeardley (the spelling of Yeardley was later changed to Yardley), an important member of the Virginia colony and later appointed royal governor of Virginia in April 1619, observed that the Indians believed in the resurrection of the body, and that when the body dies, the soul goes into a pleasant field to solace itself until the end of the world; then the soul is to return to the body again and they shall live together both happily and perpetually. King James I inferred from his friend George Yeardley's description that the gospel must have been known to Virginia's Indians, though it had been lost in its entirety, and only a fragment had been interpreted by the colony's indigenous people. Recorded by the early English settlers, not all has been lost. The Algonquian language was recorded as the English understood it. The best sources of their speech are in the works of Arthur Barlowe, published in 1584; Ralph Lane, 1585–86; Thomas Hariot, 1588; Gabriel Archer, 1608; John Smith, 1612; William Strachey, 1616; and Robert Beverley, 1705. There is also another of equal importance: Reverend Johannes Campanius, who lived from 1601 to 1683. Campanius was chaplain of the colony of New Sweden and translated Lutheran catechism into what he called the American-Virginian language for the purpose of converting the Delaware Indians to Christianity. Though completed in 1656, Campanius's work was not published for forty years. His use of the term "American-Virginian" was not incorrect. Virginia applied originally to all

This original 1840 print of Sir Walter Raleigh was first published by Dugdales England and Wales Delineated. Little is known about Raleigh's birth or childhood, other than that he was born about 1554 at Hayes Barton in Devonshire. In 1569 he was in France fighting for the Huguenots and three years later, in 1572, he arrived at Oriel College, Oxford. By 1575, he was at the Middle Temple, one of the Inns of Court. On March 25, 1584, he received a patent to lands discovered in the name of the Crown of England.

On April 27, 1584, an expedition commanded by Philip Amadas and Arthur Barlowe sailed from Plymouth with Simon Fernandez as pilot. They arrived off the coast of what is now North Carolina on July 13, 1584, took possession of the area in the name of the Queen, explored the region and returned to England with two young Indian men, Manteo and Wanchese. As a result of this

SIR WALTER RALEGH.

Engraved by R. Cooper, after Houbrahen.

expedition, Raleigh was knighted on January 6, 1585. Later that year Raleigh sent a colony to America under Sir Richard Grenville with Ralph Lane as its governor. The men in this colony, who included John White and Thomas Hariot, gathered a great deal of information and explored as far north as the Chesapeake Bay. But in 1586 they returned to England with Sir Francis Drake. Although disappointed by their return, Raleigh did not give up. In 1587 he sent a second colony, one including women and children, with John White as its governor. The disappearance of this colony sometime between John White's departure from Roanoke Island in August 1587 and his return in 1590 is one of the enduring mysteries of American history.

The Roanoke Island colonies, however, were not Sir Walter's only colonial interests. He continued his involvement in Ireland, and in 1585 he acquired a plantation in Munster, an area where land had been confiscated from rebels. Much of the land he held was in County Waterford and in County Cook, sites to which he sent colonists in 1587, the same year he sent the second colony to Roanoke Island. Among the colonists in Ireland were Thomas Hariot and perhaps some of the other men who had returned from the Ralph Lane colony. Sir Richard Grenville was also active in Ireland. An Irish rebellion at the end of the sixteenth century forced many of these colonists to return to England. *Courtesy of the author.*

that part of North America claimed by England. The Indians of Virginia's coastal plain, including those in what is now North Carolina, belonged to the eastern division of the Algonquian family and were linguistically close to their counterparts in Maryland and Delaware, and onward up the coast of New England. There are many words of interest, but only a few can be covered herein. Campanius stated that *rhenus* was the Algonquian word for "man" and *renappi* stood for "mankind." Some English chroniclers replaced the *r* with an *l*, largely because that is how they heard the sound of the letters as they were spoken. Two terms are particularly important to the story of the Elizabeth River: the words for "land" and "river." The word for "land," still used in Cree as *aski* and Fox as *acki*, also appears in tribe and land name combinations as the suffix *-ack*, *-ock*, *-ask* and *-iooc*. Variations of these are many, including Hatorask, Pasquenoke, Weapemiooc, Chawanook, Renapoak, Chesapeake and Weyanoke, just to name a few. Campanius mentioned *hacking*, a locative word meaning "on earth," when he translated the Lord's Prayer for his converts. The word for "river" was not used as frequently but was important nonetheless. Barlowe wrote that Currituck Sound was *Cipo*, which he said was "a great river" spilling into the Occam River (the combined Roanoke River and the Albemarle Sound). Campanius used *sippussing* for "stream," also likely a locative. The name Chesapeake had been etymologized *K'che*, for "chief"; *sepi*, "river"; and *ack*, "land"—translated this reads "land on a chief or principal river." The word "river" was applied by the Indians in a very broad sense. Skicoak, in existence before 1584, when it is first mentioned by the English, meant "land owned or ruled by Skyco." The Chawanook chief, Menatonon, had a son named Skyco in 1586, but the name of this important capital was likely derived from the boy's namesake.

Aside from their linguistic similarities, the Algonquian in Virginia also shared cultural ties with their brethren up the Atlantic coast. One observer noted that there was an unbroken chain of Algonquian tribes that linked the Virginia Indians northerly to the mouth of the Saint Lawrence River and thence westerly to the vast lands near the Great Lakes, still occupied by Algonquian tribal groups in the early seventeenth century. This fact, coupled with the absence of Algonquian tribes to the west and south of old and new Virginia, bears out that Virginia Algonquian came from the north in a later phase of migration of the tribes of Algonquian origin from their homes between the Great Lakes and Hudson Bay toward the west, east and south. Exactly when they arrived in Virginia is best understood through the work of archaeologists, such as Floyd Painter, and cultural anthropologists. The tribes of old southeast Virginia who resided within the bounds of the Elizabeth River watershed—the Chesapeake, Weapemiooc, Secotan and Chawanook—were Algonquian, as were tribes of the Powhatan Confederacy. The exception was the Mangoak

RALEIGH'S EXPEDITION AT ROANOKE.

This hand-colored engraving of Sir Walter Raleigh's expedition to Roanoke Island, North Carolina, was wrought by Lossing Barret for an unknown volume of American history in the early twentieth century. *Courtesy of the author*.

tribe who, like the Nottoway and Tuscarora, were Iroquoian. But more is known about them through the valuable work of archaeologists such as Floyd Painter and James Pritchard, who actually excavated the site of the Chesapeake Indian village of Apasus near Cape Henry and Lake Joyce in the mid-1950s. The village was pinpointed on the Lane map of 1585, but having it thoroughly excavated by Painter led to a new appreciation for the culture of a people now extinct from the earth.

Later, when the English arrived, Apasus was in close proximity to the mouth of the Lynnhaven River. On an island in Pleasure House Creek, later named Lake Joyce, early twentieth-century inhabitants of the area found an Indian settlement and burial mounds. A number of Native American relics were recovered in this vicinity in the early 1900s. About this time county residents also uncovered the Great Neck settlement farther up the river, which early settlers called "the Indian settlement," found on the Brooks farm. "It was probably here," wrote Benjamin Dey White, a judge in the Twenty-eighth Judicial Circuit and a local historian, in August 1924, "that [the English] found Indians roasting oysters. There have been evidences," he continued, "of other [Indian] settlements especially in the Pungo District, which district is said to have been named after an Indian chief."

The Chesapeake lived in towns and had town boundaries. As the "whites" invaded their shores, those boundaries would be tested—and eventually, their culture would succumb to the impact of European settlement. The first English expedition in 1584 has been largely assumed to have been the first opportunity of white men to become familiar with the Virginia coast and its inhabitants. But this is not necessarily true. The people of Secotan told Captain Barlowe of a shipwreck of some white men on their coast some twenty-six years earlier, which would have been 1558. This occurred on an island of the Outer Banks then called Wokokon, just to the southwest of the inlet now called Ocracoke. After being saved by the Indians, these white men remained on the island for three weeks, during which time they improvised a vessel by lashing together two Indian canoes, fitting them with masts to which they attached sails made of their own clothing and then attempted to make their departure. They were clearly unsuccessful, since the Indians spoke of the remains of their boats having been found shortly thereafter on another nearby island. Other than these rather ill-fated visitors, there was scant mention of other white men before the arrival of the English. Robert Beverley wrote in Book III of *The History and President State of Virginia*, published in 1705, that the Indians in this quarter had reason to lament the arrival of the Europeans, "by whose means they seem to have lost their Felicity, as well as their Innocence. The English have taken away a great part of their Country, and consequently," he observed, "made everything less plenty amongst them."

Wingina ruled Secotan from Pomeiooc, its capital, but his land was on the mainland across from Roanoke Island and a respectable distance southwest of Pamlico Sound. The familial relationships of the Algonquian brought tribes in what is today Northeastern North Carolina closer to those in Lower Tidewater.

Chapter Two
Explorers and Settlers

The potentiality of growing rich, to the point of avarice, drove European explorers to venture to new lands. The New World held great promise. The record of European exploration and settlement, no matter how brief, in some cases, goes back much further in time than permanent settlement by the English in 1607. In the mid-1930s the *Norwegian Historical Review* published an article by M. Meljde, one of Norway's most distinguished citizens of the twentieth century, stating that it was his belief that there had been a miscalculation from available data as to where Leif Ericson and his exploration party landed in North America, and that when accurately figured, Meljde was convinced Ericson's landing place was in Virginia—"in the Chesapeake Bay's southern incision," which exactly fit the description of the Elizabeth River. A later item relating to this matter plainly stated that Portsmouth and vicinity was Ericson's landing place. Meljde's article went on to note that both the astronomical and topographical descriptions of the Sagas brought Ericson southward to Virginia, farther south than prior historians believed Ericson's "Vinland" might be found. Historians up to the time Meljde published his work largely believed that Vinland was as far north as the Saint Lawrence River and Nova Scotia, believing that the Norsemen, with their small ships, could not or dared not sail farther south. But sailing from Greenland to Virginia was no longer for the Norsemen than sailing from western Norway to Gibraltar. Norwegian Viking ships went down to the Mediterranean long before the year 1000, and it was Meljde's belief that they could also pass along America's East Coast as far down as the latitude of Gibraltar. Meljde, who lived in London as Norway's press attaché in that city, convinced the English historian G.M. Gathorne-Hardy, author of *Norse Discoveries in America*, of the accuracy of his theories. Gathorne-Hardy then brought Meljde's material to M. Schroeter, a German professor of astronomy in Oslo, Norway, who found his calculations correct, as far as he could ascertain.

Lending support to Meljde's belief that Norsemen had made their way to what is today the west side of the Elizabeth River from Norfolk, it is worth noting that as late as September 1833 a coin was drawn up from a depth of nearly thirty feet by men boring for water. The coin was described as the size of an English shilling, oval in shape and unlike anything ever seen in the Norfolk area by its oldest resident. Although the coin had remained embedded far below the surface soil for what was then believed to have been many centuries, the figures on it were still plainly and distinctly marked, representing a warrior or hunter, and other characters, apparently of Roman origin. This may have had some bearing, according to early accounts, on the traditions associated with the visit of chieftain Madoc and the Northmen—the Vikings—hundreds of years before the discovery of the Americas by Christopher Columbus.

This Theodor de Bry engraving, entitled "Their manner of fishynge in Virginia" and after a John White watercolor, differs from White's rendering with respect to the crouching figures in the canoe. The figure to the right is a woman. The fish swimming beneath the water's surface, almost directly under the woman in the canoe, is a longnose gar. Aqua life in the water varies from turtles, stingrays and horseshoe crabs to snake-like creatures. There are many fish in the water. In the background are more canoes and Indians spearing fish. There is a brown pelican in flight in the top left corner of the engraving. The de Bry engraving was included as plate number thirteen in *Admiranda Narratio fida tamen, de Commodius et Incolarum Ritibus Virginiae*, published in Frankfurt, 1590. *Courtesy of the Library of Congress Rare Book and Special Collections Division.*

In the mid-1930s the Norwegian Historical Review *published an article by M. Meljde, one of Norway's most distinguished citizens of the twentieth century, stating that it was his belief that there had been a miscalculation from available data as to where Leif Ericson and his exploration party landed in North America, and that when accurately figured, Meljde was convinced Ericson's landing place was in Virginia—"in the Chesapeake Bay's southern incision," which exactly fit the description of the Elizabeth River.*

This strange coin, with many others of the same kind, might have been circulated by unknown aborigines, who ceased to exist before the Native Americans, as previously described, became tenants of the soil, and whose name has, as one nineteenth-century historian observed, "sunk into oblivion, with numberless unchronicled events, in the wide and deep ocean of the past." There is a tradition that has received scholarly attention that indicates that a Welsh voyage to America under Prince Madoc, tied largely to a period following the Icelandic voyages, did occur. This voyage by the son of Owen Gwyneth is said to have taken place in the year 1170, and is based on a Welsh chronicle of no authority, though it was widely debated by nineteenth-century historians, including Norfolk historian William S. Forrest.

In the early seventeenth century, particularly during the reign of James I, pride of birth largely prevailed in England—though it could have its downside. With the death of Queen Elizabeth I and the accession of James I (who held the title of James V in his native Scotland) in 1603, Sir Walter Raleigh's favored status was quickly eclipsed. Before the end of that year Raleigh would be tried, convicted, condemned to death, reprieved and imprisoned in the Tower of London. Due to Raleigh's conviction for a capital offense, all of his rights in the Virginia colony reverted to the British Crown, but when the Virginia Company charter was issued in 1606, many of the men who had been associated with Raleigh's previous attempts to establish a permanent English colony were named, including Sir Thomas Smith, Reverend Richard Hakluyt and Raleigh's own nephew, Raleigh Gilbert. Smith, Hakluyt and the others were expected to furnish the capital, according to early twentieth-century historian and scholar Conway Whittle Sams, who remarked that James I, a canny Scotsman, was desirous of the prestige and revenue that would be derived from a permanent colony, but not to the extent that he would finance the venture personally or by his government.

For our purposes, interest in the colonists who arrived in Virginia in 1607 is only to do with their activities in the area encompassed by the Elizabeth River and its expansive tributaries, but even this story requires explanation. The first journey to make a permanent settlement in Virginia set sail on a dreary day from Blackwall, England, on December 19, 1606, in three small ships—the *Susan Constant*, *Goodspeed* and the little pinnace *Discovery*—commanded by Captains Christopher Newport, Bartholomew Gosnold and John Ratcliff. The docks swarmed with sailors boarding these stalwart ships in that broad reach of the Thames. Newport, the expedition's ranking officer, was commander of the squadron. As the small fleet sailed down the river and disappeared into the mists and masts of the lower end of the Thames, they did not get far. The three ships were delayed at the Downs by inclement weather until the New Year, when the

The Algonquian village of Secotan, shown here, was located on the Pamlico River estuary, near today's North Carolina Outer Banks. Leading a life not unlike the tribal groups within the Elizabeth River watershed, the people of Secotan lived in permanent villages near today's North Carolina Outer Banks. Like the Northern Algonquian, they farmed collectively in the growing season and dispersed into family units to hunt during the colder months. The engraving, based on a drawing made by John White in the 1580s, shows careful management and use of the land. Crops include tobacco and pumpkins, corn in three stages of growth and sunflowers, while domesticated deer graze in the adjoining woods. The buildings include family units and storehouses for the surplus corn. The Secotan traded with other groups like the powerful Mandoag of the Piedmont area of North Carolina, who acted as middlemen in the copper trade. De Bry's engraving illustrates native structures, agriculture and spiritual life and was included as plate number twenty in *Admiranda Narratio fida tamen, de Commodius et Incolarum Ritibus Virginiae*, published in Frankfurt, 1590. *Courtesy of the Library of Congress Rare Book and Special Collections Division.*

Lending support to Meljde's belief that Norsemen had made their way to what is today the west side of the Elizabeth River from Norfolk, it is worth noting that as late as September 1833 a coin was drawn up from a depth of nearly thirty feet by men boring for water. The coin was described as the size of an English shilling, oval in shape.

squadron made haste to get to sea. The ships followed an established route to the Canaries and West Indies before turning north and heading up the coast. Approaching the Chesapeake Bay from the south as all those before them, Newport's small ships made landfall at four o'clock the morning of April 26, 1607, the third Sunday after Easter. Captain John Smith was not present for the first landing because he was being held in bondage aboard ship for having plotted a mutiny at sea. Reverend Robert Hunt, chaplain for the expedition, is often seen in depictions of the cross being planted at the place these settlers subsequently named Cape Henry, but he is not mentioned in Captain George Percy's account of events.

The natural beauty of Cape Henry impressed the English. The first sight they had of the Virginia coast were gigantic tree formations that stood like "cathedral aisles along the shore," according to Kathleen Eveleth Bruce, in her assessment of that first espying of the magnificent, untouched land that they would colonize in the name of James I. They observed "flowers of divers kinds and colors and goodly trees," but they, too, encountered warriors of the Chesapeake tribe who attacked the Englishmen under cover of darkness. "At night, when we were going aboard, there came the savages creeping upon all fours from the hills like bears, with their bows in their mouths, charged us very desperately in the faces, hurt Captain Gabrill Archer in both his hands, and a sailor in two places of the body very dangerous," wrote Percy, describing two of their party being wounded. But it was through Captain John Smith's later account that the name of the wounded sailor is learned: Mathew Morton. The English returned fire with harquebus shot and the Indians retired screaming into the woods.

The English encounter with the Chesapeake was brief but significant. Powhatan's priests had prophesied that from the Chesapeake Bay a nation would come that would dissolve and give end to his empire. The Indians were predisposed to dislike white faces before Newport's ships came into view, due largely to this prophecy and the fact that the English, like the Spanish before them, were perceived as marauders bent on taking possession of the land. Their fears were well founded. The English explorers' first night ashore, Newport opened the sealed orders with which he had been entrusted before sailing from Blackwall. Carefully opening his instructions, Newport learned the composition of the first council for the first colony in Virginia. There were seven names on the list: Captain Christopher Newport, Captain Bartholomew Gosnold, Captain John Ratcliff, Captain John Smith, Captain John Martin, Captain George Kendall and Captain Edward Maria Wingfield. The opening of their sealed orders on the Cape Henry shore automatically started the first permanent English colonial government in North America, thus the site of the first landing's significance was twofold in the establishment of Great

King James I is shown in this ca. 1840 engraving by W.J. Edwards, from scenes originally painted by Paul Vansomer. *Courtesy of the author.*

Britain's claim to Virginia. A cross was planted on the spot where the orders were opened, officially claiming the lands of the great colony of Virginia in the name of the British Crown.

The purpose of concealing the identity of the council until their arrival in Virginia was to prevent conflict between shipboard and land officers on the trip. English law governing the powers of an official council took effect once the box was opened, thus superseding Newport's authority as leader of his small squadron of ships. The quarreling and competitiveness of the seven men named to the first council became readily apparent in accounts of the voyage later published for the consumption of the British public, but also as these intrepid explorers settled into their roles at Jamestown. Captain John Smith had not come ashore with Newport, due to heated words he and others exchanged and that some took to be mutinous. Smith later cleared himself of any wrongdoing and was permitted to join his brethren on the council, though it was a close call with the gallows for the good captain—and one he would not soon forget.

On their second day, Captain Percy observed that the expeditionary party had gone about eight miles inland, likely east of Lynnhaven. To the west the English would have encountered the Indian village of Apasus, indicated on the John White map of 1585, but they must also have traversed a route that took them away from Chesepiooc, the

This depiction of the circular palisade of the Algonquian village of Pomeiooc was originally painted by John White, who accompanied the Roanoke voyages, and engraved by Theodor de Bry. The pond visible to the north of the palisade was used for drinking water. There is only a front entrance to the village in this view. The village of Pomeiooc was situated near Lake Mattamuskeet in present-day Hyde County, North Carolina. The de Bry engraving was included as plate number nineteen in Admiranda Narratio fida tamen, de Commodius et Incolarum Ritibus Virginiae, published in Frankfurt, 1590. Courtesy of the Library of Congress Rare Book and Special Collections Division.

Chesapeake's village on the west side of the river near present-day London Bridge. Percy's narrative of events indicates that they arrived at a place where the Chesapeake had made a great fire in which they were roasting oysters. "When they perceived our coming," wrote Percy, "they fled away to the mountains, and left many of the oysters in the fire. We ate some of the oysters, which were very large and delicate in taste." The mountains to which Percy refers were the Antaean tree-covered sand dunes that rose nearly a hundred feet high at Cape Henry. Percy was transfixed by the oysters and mussels, which he described as laying on the ground "as thick as stones; we opened some and found in many of them pearls." As they explored inland, Percy noted that they found "beautiful strawberries four times bigger and better than ours in England. All this march we could neither see savage nor town." They also found something else: a canoe fashioned from a single tree approximated to be about forty feet long. In later expeditions up the Elizabeth River, they would see more of these, but at the moment of this first discovery of a Chesapeake canoe, the English had never before seen any vessel like it.

The English had been clearly relieved to find land, despite the initial hostile encounter with the Chesapeake. Smith's map, based on the expedition's findings, shows Morton's Bay where Lynnhaven Inlet is today. Arguably, the first landing may have occurred at Lynnhaven Inlet or slightly to the east of it. On "the nine and twentieth day we sett up a crosse at Chesepiooc Bay and named the place Cape Henry," penned Percy. This was exactly two weeks before the landing and settlement of Jamestown on May 13, and when the first English name was formerly bestowed in New Virginia. Nine years after his exploration of Virginia, Captain John Smith wrote in his account that the English explorers named two otherwise nameless headlands for the sons of James I; these would be Capes Henry and Charles. Though the English were taken with the beauty of the Virginia shore, they would not settle there in 1607.

Interestingly, there was clear evidence of European settlement on the Chesapeake Bay in 1610 near what was later Ocean Park in Virginia Beach, but while the physical remains were compelling, the lack of archaeological and anthropological work at the site hobbles certainty. Digs at Ocean Park were moot after a point. There has been continuous development on the Ocean Park site since the late nineteenth century. Much of what might have been occupied by early European settlement is covered today by condominiums, restaurants and parking lots—and it has been that way for well over a century.

Captain Smith continued to explore Virginia. He made notes of his travels, including a map of Indian village sites in the Chesapeake Bay area. He documented the activities, dress and customs of many groups, particularly the Algonquian-speaking Indians of Lower Tidewater. Before the end of July 1608 Smith set out on his second exploration of Virginia waters. Though there is some uncertainty surrounding the story, it was likely about August, as Smith was returning to Cape Comfort, that his expedition ran into a violent thunderstorm that drove his party to take shelter until the weather passed. As the sky cleared, Smith made the decision to cross over Hampton Roads to the land of the Chesapeake and Nansemond down a narrow river—the Elizabeth. He observed that the river had a good channel, but with some shoal water at its entrance. Smith's explorers followed the river six or seven miles, according to the early accounts, and saw several fields in cultivation and some Indian lodges. The distance Smith traveled would have brought his expedition about as far as the 1585 location of Skicoak, the village that Smith had called Chesepiooc on his map. Smith's description, however, does not imply it was a village settlement that he observed on this trip. He does

This full-length, front and back view of an Algonquian chief by Theodor de Bry illustrates manner of dress, in particular, and a river scene in the background. Titled "A cheiff Lorde of Roanoac," the engraving was included as plate number seven in *Admiranda Narratio fida tamen, de Commodius et Incolarum Ritibus Virginiae*, published in Frankfurt, 1590. *Courtesy of the Library of Congress Rare Book and Special Collections Division.*

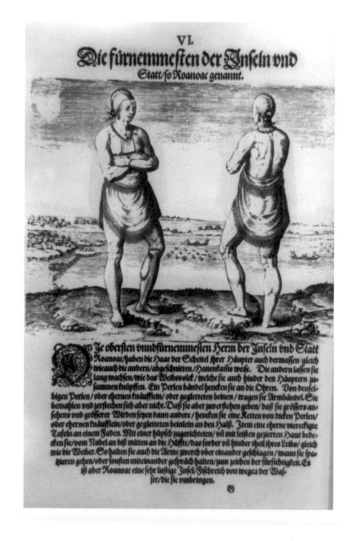

describe shores overgrown with tall pines and cedars, and this is where his observations—and journey—up the Elizabeth end. The Smith party returned to the river's mouth and followed the shore toward Nansemond, where they found many oyster beds. By September 7, 1608, Smith and his men returned to Jamestown.

The Elizabeth River had appeared on late sixteenth-century watercolor maps wrought in 1585 by John White, the grandfather of Virginia Dare, the first white child born in English America at what is today known as Roanoke Island, North Carolina. Later, when Captain John Smith published his *Map of Virginia with a Description of the Country* in London, the river, still unnamed, was depicted in far greater detail than it had appeared on White's earlier chart. While there is no definite, recorded date when the river was formally named, it was christened for Elizabeth Stuart, a daughter of James I and a sister of Prince Henry and Prince Charles, for whom the first colonists named the capes that guard the entrance to the Chesapeake Bay. Elizabeth City County, Virginia, was also named for her. It was one of the earliest settled parts of the Virginia colony and became a part of the present city of Hampton on July 1, 1952. The county was represented in the first legislative assembly at Jamestown in 1619 by Captain William Tucker and William Capps, still, at that time, under the name of Kecoughtan. A request was made, and granted, to change the county's name and on May 17, 1620, by order of the Jamestown council, "the ancient Borough of Kiccowtan hereafter shall be called Elizabeth City by the name of His Majesties most vertuous and renowned daughter." At that time the Kecoughtan delegation made it known that "they will be pleased to change the savage name of Kiccowtan, and to give that incorporation a new name." It is believed that it was during this time that the river was personified with a name.

During this period in which the Elizabeth River was believed officially designated by name, the Virginia colony was divided into four corporations, and the first General Assembly convened on July 30, 1619, composed of Governor Sir George Yeardley, the council and two burgesses from each corporation and from each of seven particular plantations—twenty-two burgesses in all. Burgesses from the corporations represented company plantations, but the others represented specific plantations that were situated within corporation bounds but not under their control. Only two Lower Tidewater locales were represented in the first General Assembly: the borough of Kecoughtan, renamed the corporation of Elizabeth City; and Captain Christopher Lawne's plantation, subsequently called Isle of Wight. The cities of Chesapeake, Norfolk and Virginia Beach were also included within the corporate bounds of Elizabeth City County by the time it was renamed. According to the census of 1624–25, there were 257 persons living in the county. One of these families was that of John

King James I chartered the Virginia Company of London in 1606 to establish a commercial venture in "Virginia," which included all lands in North America not occupied by the Spanish or French. The company founded the first permanent English settlement at Jamestown. Its records provide an invaluable resource for the early settlement of America.

Laydon, whose marriage to Ann Burras was the first to be performed at Jamestown. In 1635 there were 859 persons residing in Elizabeth City County, from whom many of the oldest families residing along the Elizabeth River's Eastern, Western and Southern Branches descended. Those living on the south side of Hampton Roads split from Elizabeth City County two years after the census, creating the Lower County of New Norfolk, which consists of today's cities of Chesapeake, Norfolk, Portsmouth and Virginia Beach. The Lower County of New Norfolk was formed with Captain Adam Thorowgood, a native of Norfolk, England, presiding as its first justice.

The English encounter with the Chesapeake was brief but significant. Powhatan's priests had prophesied that from the Chesapeake Bay a nation would come that would dissolve and give end to his empire.

Princess Elizabeth, for whom the river is named, was one of the most fascinating women of her time. Born at Falkland Palace, Frithshire, Scotland, on August 16, 1596, to King James VI of Scotland, Princess Elizabeth would later accompany her father to England when he succeeded Queen Elizabeth I, becoming James I of England. Soon after her arrival, young Elizabeth, her father's eldest daughter, gained the reputation as "the Queen of Hearts" for her beauty, sweet nature and ready wit. Sir Henry Wotton, one of the most celebrated courtiers of the princess's day, called her "Th' eclipse and glory of her kind." On December 27, 1612, Princess Elizabeth was betrothed to Frederick, Prince Palatine, later King Frederick V of Bohemia, also called Frederick the Winter King. To celebrate the betrothal, there was a magnificent celebration in the Palladian Banqueting Hall at Whitehall; the play put on for the occasion was William Shakespeare's *The Tempest*. The sea imagery in the play was derived from an account of the wreck of the *Sea Venture*, the flagship of Sir Thomas Gates and Sir George Somers on their ill-fated voyage to Virginia in 1609. An account of the wreck was published in London and caught the attention of Shakespeare, who used the details of the West Indian hurricane in the play's storm sequence.

Princess Elizabeth was married with much pomp and circumstance on St. Valentine's Day, 1613. Six years later she became the queen of Bohemia, though her husband did not retain his position among European royalty for long, exiled after a series of devastating defeats, the last in 1620 at White Mountain. Despite her many adversities, the princess remained popular as ever in her native England; she was rendered aid and money by many men and women who would give their lives to show acts of kindness to "the Queen of Hearts." The mother of thirteen children, Princess Elizabeth's most famous sons were Princes Rupert and Maurice, celebrated Cavaliers during the British civil war. Her daughter, Sophia, married into the House of Brunswick and became the mother of George I, the first Hanoverian king of England. Two years after the restoration of her nephew, Charles II, in 1662, Princess Elizabeth died in London. Five years after Princess Elizabeth died, out in the harbor, between what is now

Nobilis Matrona Pomeioocensis. VIII

IRCITER viginti ab ea insula miliaribus, proxime lacum PAGVIPPE, aliud est oppidum POMEIOOC nuncupatum, mari vicinum. Eius oppidi nobiliorum matronarum amictus paululis ab illarum quæ in ROANOAC vivunt, vestitu differt: nam capillos in nodum implexos gerunt, vt virgines iam dictæ, eodemque modo sunt punctæ, torque tamen crassiorum vnionum aut ærearum sphærularum, ossiculorumve perpolitorum quinquies aut sexies collum cingunt, in eo alterum brachium imponentes, altera manu cucurbitam suam quodam liquore plenam gerentes. Altius reliquis & sub pectore pelles duplicatas cingit, quæ anteriore parte ad genua vsque fere propendent, posteriore parte propemodum nuda. Pone sequuntur plerumque illarum filiolæ septennes aut octennes, coriaceo cingulo cinctæ, quod a tergo propendens sub natibus inter crura reducitur, & supra vmbilicum adstringitur, interposito ad pudenda tegenda arborum musco, exacto autem decennio, pellibus cinguntur vt reliqua. Pupis & tintinnabulis ex Anglia delatis, maxime delectantur.

This Theodor de Bry engraving, "A chieff Ladye of Pomeiooc," was printed as plate number eight in *Admiranda Narratio fida tamen, de Commodius et Incolarum Ritibus Virginiae,* published in Frankfurt, 1590. The woman's stance in the engraving differs from the original John White painting. In de Bry's interpretation, the girl is running toward her from the right, holding up in her right hand an English rattle, with a doll in her left. The figures are set against a landscape background that reveals shoal water with Algonquian men fishing from canoes. *Courtesy of the Library of Congress Rare Book and Special Collections Division.*

Norfolk and Portsmouth, there was a battle fought in 1667 between Dutch men-of-war and English merchant ships. The Dutch ships, after a stake in the river's rich harbor, were driven away, though any number of these vessels might have been carrying slaves to Virginia, just as the Dutch had brought them to the commonwealth in 1619.

Through the seventeenth century—and continuing well into the twentieth—the most effective means of travel around the complex system of tidal rivers and tributaries surrounding Hampton Roads, many of them flowing into small bays and inlets that recede into creeks and marshes, were ferries. The area's natural waterways cut deep into the land to the point that some places were accessible only via small skiffs. The first land grants on waterways were ceded to Captain Adam Thorowgood. Nearly

The Elizabeth River had appeared on late sixteenth-century watercolor maps wrought in 1585 by John White, the grandfather of Virginia Dare, the first white child born in English America at what is today known as Roanoke Island, North Carolina. Later, when Captain John Smith published his Map of Virginia with a Description of the Country *in London, the river, still unnamed, was depicted in far greater detail than it had appeared on White's earlier chart.*

all large landowners—even the majority of smaller ones—owned skiffs or shallops to navigate the shallows. Others depended on sailboats and larger rowboats to conduct daily business such as attending church or court, shopping at the market or visiting a friend. The navigable waterways also circumvented having contact with the Indians, who still made occasional raids on their English neighbors. After these raids tapered off, the English began to use interior roads.

Bridges were constructed over streams and small tributaries later, but the interim solution—ferries—gave birth to a form of transportation that endured into modern times. The first ferry in Lower Norfolk County began in 1636 as Captain Thorowgood's private enterprise. He set up his ferry operation at the convergence of the Eastern and Southern Branches of the Elizabeth River between Norfolk and Portsmouth. This ferry was a basic skiff handled by Thorowgood's slaves; however, the captain's operation was so successful that within a few months the county took over the business, supporting it with a public levy as it did other community services. The number of rowboats plying the Elizabeth increased, going between Norfolk and Portsmouth and West Norfolk. The ferry continued to be run from the same location until 1952, when it became too antiquated a mode of transportation to accommodate the people and vehicles that tried to clamor aboard Thorowgood's modern progeny. The birth of bridge-tunnels sped up vehicular traffic to and from one destination to another but also distanced people from a sense of intimate knowledge and appreciation of the river.

Thorowgood's ferry, though the first, was not the only ferry service in the county that plied the Elizabeth. The first three ferries traveled the Elizabeth River, Lynnhaven River and Tanner's Creek. The latter ferry ended at the foot of present-day Wythe Place, crossing Tanner's Creek to what is now Algonquin Park. The existence of these earliest ferry routes across the Elizabeth, Lynnhaven and Tanner's Creek has led to the presumption that there might have been an overland link between these points. In this respect there were known lines of communication between important points along the Lynnhaven and the Elizabeth, and the section between its Southern and Western Branches, also between the Elizabeth and the relatively populous territory at Seawell's Point, Mason's Creek and Willoughby's Point. These first inland roads were nothing more than woodland paths, old Indian trails that gradually became widened by passage of carts drawn by oxen or horse, and then commonly used by the area's planters—bridges did not come until later. There seems to have been no official designation of public roads until the Virginia General Assembly convened in March 1661–62 and passed a law requiring that a road be constructed and maintained to link Jamestown with every courthouse and parish church. There is yet another record that indicates

THE PORTRAICTUER OF CAPTAINE JOHN SMITH ADMIRALL OF NEW ENGLAND

These are the Lines that shew thy Face but those
That shew thy Grace and Glory, brighter bee
Thy Faire-Discoueries and Fowle-Overthrowes
Of Salvages, much Cwilliz'd by thee
Best shew thy Spirit and to it Glory Wyn
So, thou art Brasse without—but Golde within

Through the seventeenth century—and continuing well into the twentieth—the most effective means of travel around the complex system of tidal rivers and tributaries surrounding Hampton Roads, many of them flowing into small bays and inlets that recede into creeks and marshes, were ferries.

This portrait of Captain John Smith is from an original engraving by Simon van de Passe dated 1616. Van de Passe belonged to an illustrious family of Dutch engravers. He studied printmaking techniques under his father, Crispijn (1560–1643). After working several years for his father, Simon van de Passe moved to London (1613) and worked for publishers in that city for a period of around ten years. He was also employed by the famous miniature painter, Nicholas Hilliard, to create engravings after his paintings of the English royal family. After that date he moved first to Paris and then entered the service of the King of Denmark and became the engraver to the Danish royal family. In England, Simon van de Passe engraved some very famous portraits including those of King Charles I; Queen Anne; George Villiers, the Duke of Buckingham; Captain John Smith; and King James I. He also was commissioned to engrave the portraits of Philip III, king of Spain, and Christian IV, king of Denmark. *Courtesy of the author.*

that on August 17, 1668, James Wishard (also Wichard) was designated to repair roads in the Elizabeth River Parish on the Eastern Branch. Each of the most important ferry crossings—one on the Elizabeth and the other on the Lynnhaven—was in close proximity to a parish church, connecting the two points. The ferry crossing in Norfolk made its way from the town of Norfolk and eventually followed the course of East Princess Anne Road to the head of Broad Creek, where the creek divided into two branches, dammed to make Lakes Wright and Taylor, which the road crossed by two bridges called Moore's Bridges. This was most likely where the Cason Moore family resided, hence the name. The county courthouse was somewhere on Broad Creek. The road's main course from that point toward the Lynnhaven Ferry and Church has been long lost, but at one time it branched south toward Captain William Moseley's at Rolleston, Simon Hancock's at New Town and James Kempe's and Anthony Walke's at the head of the Eastern Branch, a route that can be traced even today. It is highly probable that the first road coming off this early road to Lynnhaven was one that turned northerly at what is now Fox Hall and, avoiding all the branches of Tanner's Creek and Mason's Creek, ultimately arrived at Seawell's Point. This is today's Sewell's Point Road, though its northern end is gone and part of it has been renamed Little Creek Road. Following the notion that courthouses and parish churches were close to these early roads, Sewell's Point Road was not far from the 1661 Tanner's Creek Chapel, which is discussed further herein.

The importance of these land and water routes of communication, their ties, in particular, to the world beyond the Elizabeth River reaches, could not have been more critical than in time of war, which will be discussed in another chapter of this volume. Portsmouth's Colonel William Crawford had facilitated ferry service from the Elizabeth River's western shore. When

This undivided back postcard, dating to 1907, depicts what has been called the first naval fight in Virginia, which took place in September 1608. The caption, extracted from The Generall Historie of Virginia *by Captain John Smith, book three, chapter 4, describes Smith in an open barge of three tons burthen, six gentlemen, including a surgeon and six soldiers, being attacked by eight "canowes" filled with warriors armed with bows and arrows in the Nansemond River. Sailing back to the bay, with their muskets, Smith and his men reportedly killed or drowned all the Indians save two or three who swam ashore. Smith's party destroyed or captured all "canowes," according to his account.* Courtesy of the author.

First Naval Fight in Virginia September 1608

Capt. John Smith in open barge of 3 tons burthen, 6 gentlemen including surgeon and 6 soldiers was attacked by eight "canowes" filled with warriors armed with bows and arrows in Nansemond river. Sailing back to the bay, with his muskets he killed or drowned all the Indians save 2 or 3 who swam ashore. He destroyed or captured all "canowes" and he had one wounded". The Historie of Virginia by Capt. John Smith, Book 3 Chap. 4.

Portsmouth farmers petitioned the Virginia General Assembly for a ferry in 1705 it was agreed that a point on Crawford's plantation would be the most suitable spot. Crawford provided land at the extreme eastern point of what was later North Street, where the Seaboard warehouses stood. When the committee undertook to raise the money to put the ferry into operation, Norfolk refused to subscribe its quota, seeing no benefit of investing in Portsmouth's ferry operation when it already had one of its own. Ferry operations antedated Portsmouth as a town by many years, but when the town was formally laid out, the Norfolk ferry docks ended up within its limits. On the Portsmouth side of the river the landing place of the ferry changed several times, first in 1834, when it was moved to the foot of High Street for the convenience of the newly established railroad. Then it was changed to a point on Water Street just north of High, but in later years the ferry took over the High Street wharf. The Norfolk ferry dock never changed locations, though it grew larger as land was added to it.

In the early days the ferry was operated by Colonel Crawford on the Portsmouth side of the river and he received six thousand pounds of tobacco for the use of his property. The year after the town of Portsmouth was incorporated, in 1753, the ferry was leased to Alexander Bruce and Francis Miller for about the same amount of tobacco. The first account of Portsmouth's ferry fleet is from the diary of a Frenchman in 1764. He wrote that there were three boats plying between Norfolk and Portsmouth. Twenty years later, in 1784, George Dyson was ferry keeper. The fleet

Algonquian men and women are shown dancing around a circle defined by posts with carved faces. Three Algonquian women stand together in the center of the circle. This scene was interpreted as part of dances performed during their feasts. The engraving, by Theodor de Bry, was after a watercolor by John White and included as plate number eighteen in *Admiranda Narratio fida tamen, de Commodius et Incolarum Ritibus Virginiae*, published in Frankfurt, 1590. *Courtesy of the Library of Congress Rare Book and Special Collections Division.*

The ferry dock on the Norfolk side of the river belonged to Norfolk County, though the Town, later City, of Norfolk tried several times to lay claim to it.

had expanded considerably since the unknown Frenchman wrote of them decades before. Rowboats had increased to five in number and there were two barges and a horse boat. Nothing further is known of ferry management in its earliest days. The cost of travel across the river about 1715, when Major Samuel Boush ran the ferries, was six pence for passengers or horses to cross. The fee was prescribed by the Virginia General Assembly. While individual rates were not documented at the end of the eighteenth century, it is known that the cost to use the ferry for one year was six dollars. Thomas J. Wertenbaker wrote that Isaac Weld, who visited Norfolk in 1795, found Virginia ferries "a most irksome piece of business. There is not one in six where the boats are good and well manned, and it is necessary," Weld recorded in his *Travels through North America*, "to employ great circumspection in order to guard against accidents." Weld had heard of numerous incidents of horses being drowned, killed or having their legs broken getting in and out of the boats.

The ferry dock on the Norfolk side of the river belonged to Norfolk County, though the Town, later City, of Norfolk tried several times to lay claim to it. The terminal was on the original fifty acres bought by Nicholas Wise in 1662, as the site for the future city. It was set aside for a public dock and used by the county in undisputed possession until 1811, when Norfolk refused to allow the ferry committee to repair it. On May 11 of that year the county court appointed commissioners to see to the repairing of the county wharf. The men appointed were all residents of Portsmouth: Tapley Webb, Jordan Merchant, Holt Wilson, Mordecai Cooke and William Pritchard. The committee was authorized to contract for the best material and to have all repairs made as required. Work on the dock began on August 13, and progressed for two days before the town sergeant of Norfolk, on the scene, ordered all repairs stopped by order of the borough court, which had empowered the sergeant to have everything erected on the wharf torn down. When the superintendent reported this threat to the commissioners, they told him to continue his work until stopped by force. The commissioners then went to Norfolk to watch what happened. In due time the sergeant returned with an armed guard bearing a new order. Despite all the hoopla, the ferry terminals were repaired and opened for business.

Thomas Rowland, of Norfolk, who lived to be ninety years of age, gave a description of the old team boats that were introduced by W.H. Wilson in 1820, while Wilson was lessee of the ferries. These were the first boats that could carry vehicles of any kind. Stables for the ferry horses stood where Macon House was built in 1853. "After some ten years of use on the ferry," Rowland recounted long ago, "these old, blind horses were turned over to the mud machine. I have an indistinct recollection of the old team ferry boats which were used between Norfolk and Portsmouth. My aunt, Mrs. Selina Dickson, lived on First Street, Gosport, on the corner opposite the officers' quarters." The team ferry boats were lighters with square ends. There was a circular pit on the deck; horses were used to operate the wheels, which were three or four feet in diameter, for propelling the vessel over the water. Steam-propelled ferry boats that followed the horse boats were of small dimensions, but amply filled demand. Rowland could not remember any shelter for passengers, and in fact accommodations for the traveler were scant aboard ferries in the 1820s; box-like rooms about six by twelve feet furnished passengers' only shelter from the weather. But despite relatively basic provisions, the Junior Military Company of Portsmouth, invited to a party at Deep Creek, took one of the team ferry boats run by Captain James Cornick to their event.

Night service aboard the ferries was done by Captain James Jarvis's small boats. His oarsmen were two black men, each with a wooden leg. There was a story that came down through the years that a man once applied to Jarvis for a place on his boats. The captain replied, "Yes, I will take you. Come, Bill, bring the bucksaw and saw this fellow's leg off." The applicant quickly disappeared. It was not until April 1898 that ferry boats ran all night. This change was made possible when Gill and Thomas

This Theodor de Bry engraving, after a 1564 watercolor by Jacques Le Moyne de Morgues, was published as part of de Bry's work *Brevis narratio eorvm qvæ in Florida Americæ provincial Gallis acciderunt* in Frankfurt in 1591, and would have been typical of Algonquian tribal farming practices within the Elizabeth River watershed. De Bry and Le Moyne show a division of agricultural labor between the sexes: the universally young and attractive Timucua women with incongruous blond and curly locks and modest moss skirts perform the less physically demanding task of planting the maize while the men, who are perhaps more realistically depicted, till the soil. The baskets and implements are all European types with the exception of the digging stick. Father Joseph Lafitau only slightly modified this same engraving for his 1724 account of the Iroquois, even though he described farming as being purely women's work. *Courtesy of the Library of Congress Rare Book and Special Collections Division.*

Daniel Tanner's creek has been called the Lafayette River since the late nineteenth century, when it seemed fashionable to commemorate the relationship of America to the Marquis de Lafayette, but this moniker has robbed this amazing waterway of its far more impressive place in the history of the Elizabeth—and American history.

leased the ferries and a profit was to be made in making the ferries available twenty-four hours a day.

By the early 1850s numerous complaints were received about the ferries. Passengers claimed that the ferries kept no schedule, ran only as long after dark as the superintendent permitted, took their time crossing the river and moreover did not have enough room on the boats for the crowds that boarded to cross. Added to these inconveniences, an order was given by the ferry superintendent requiring all boats to stop at Washington Point (Berkley) for passengers and freight. After much protest from Portsmouth's citizens, the order was withdrawn, but this was the beginning of ferry boats making the Berkley run. Complaints against the ferries put them on the road to improvement. The steering gear on the boats was removed to the upper deck, thus giving passengers more room below, but the boats were not nearly large enough. A two-cent fare was collected for each trip, reduced from the five-cent fare that had the public up in arms. The ferry at this time was making its owners about $20,000 a year, despite complaints. Profits would improve over time, with the exception of periods in which the federal government took over the ferries. The first time occurred when Portsmouth fell to the Union in 1862 and Federal troops took over the Norfolk County and Portsmouth ferries, and a second, memorable, occasion was during the First World War.

During the earliest days of the Civil War, just as Virginia seceded from the Union in April 1862, with uncertainty as to who would hold the Gosport Navy Yard, ferry boats were mounted with cannon, but there is no record that they were ever fired. After the Federals took Norfolk and Portsmouth, going between these two cities was not easy; the ferries were under the control of the Federals, who required that citizens have a passport issued by the provost marshal's office. To get a passport, citizens were subjected to all manner of questions and occasionally searched before the permit was issued. After the war, Portsmouth and Norfolk Counties made a claim against the federal government, through their legal counsel of James G. Holladay, for $100,000 in payment for the use of the ferry. Many years later the claim was paid, but the amount reduced to one-half the sum initially requested. From that time the ferries went on quietly serving the public, with little trouble, save a ferry boat that sunk in about fifteen minutes in the 1850s.

In the old days it was believed that being on the water was excellent therapy for sick babies. The ferry boats were a convenient platform for taking out infants. The decks were often crowded with nurses and babies, and in 1873 an order was issued by the ferry committee forbidding nurses to block the outside decks of the ferry with baby carriages; they were required to leave the carriages at the ferry house, where they would be

Harry C. Mann took this picture of Richard N. Brooke's full-length portrait of an anglicized Pocahontas, which was on display at the Jamestown Exposition, held in 1907. Pocahontas married wealthy planter John Rolfe and was known after her marriage to him as Rebecca Rolfe. Her father, Powhatan, king of the Powhatan Confederacy, called her Amonte, and her secret clan name was Matoaka. The artist of Pocahontas's painting, Richard Brooke, was born in Warrenton, Virginia, in 1847. He was educated at Virginia Military Institute, where he also taught from 1871 to 1872, before being named United States consul to LaRochelle, France. While in France, he continued to perfect his art. Interestingly, after 1881 Brooke devoted himself almost entirely to painting landscapes, though he did paint a number of famous figures in American history, such as John Marshall, first chief justice of the United States Supreme Court. *Courtesy of the author.*

watched closely until the nurses returned. But the ferries were so popular for baby outings that the ferry steamer *Manhasset* eventually had a latticed screened enclosure built on the roof where the nurses and babies could be made comfortable.

About 1910 the ferry schedule was changed from twenty- to ten-minute trips. This was achieved by running two boats. The law required the schedule to be kept; this was enforced by fining lessees if they failed to keep the ferries on schedule. The ferries were leased for about $100,000 a year. The greatest hardship on them was shortly after the United States entered World War I, when military traffic on the river nearly choked out the ferries completely. To add to the ferries' troubles, it was then that the federal government had taken over the ferries under less than favorable terms. The fare for passengers and vehicles doubled and despite the government's oversight, ferry owners were still required to make repairs. The ferries reverted back to their owners and lessees after the war, but in the mid-1930s, just before another world war, there was already discussion of laying tunnel tubes between Norfolk and Portsmouth, which one observer astutely said, "will be done in the course of time."

As has been observed over the course of the Elizabeth's history, her tributaries are longer than the river itself. Thus it is appropriate to conclude this chapter with a bit of background on lengthy, winding Tanner's Creek, named for Daniel Tanner, one of her earliest settlers. Though there are no surviving copies of early grants to him, a description of a subsequent grant issued to William Croutch by Tanner on November 21, 1637, described his association to the river in this manner: "In the great creek on the lefthand going into the mouth of the Elizabeth River about two miles on the north side from Daniel Tanner" lies the land of the aforesaid Croutch. A grant issued two years later mentioned land adjoining Daniel Tanner's. What became of Daniel Tanner was later found in Lower Norfolk County court records. A British document issued by William Stanley, mayor of the city of Canterbury, on August 10, 1654, and entered into the records of Lower Norfolk County court on January 1, 1654/55, documents the marriage of Daniel and Charity Tanner on November 26, 1614, as well as the birth of their son John, on October 14, 1627. Daniel died in December 1653, leaving no heirs to his property. The document filed by Stanley was likely part of the process required to dispose of John Tanner's land and personal effects. Daniel Tanner's creek has been called the Lafayette River since the late nineteenth century, when it seemed fashionable to commemorate the relationship of America to the Marquis de Lafayette, but this moniker has robbed this amazing waterway of its far more impressive place in the history of the Elizabeth—and American history.

CHAPTER THREE

COMMUNITIES TAKE HOLD

The seventeenth century was more than half over before communities began to take hold on the banks of the Elizabeth River, each defining its boundaries by water. The story of what would become the town of Norfolk began in 1662: two hundred acres of land, eventually occupied by the city of Norfolk, were sold by Lewis Vandermull to Nicholas Wise, a shipwright. On June 8, 1680, seventy-three years after the first permanent settlement in Virginia at Jamestown, an Act of Assembly was passed, directing the purchase of fifty acres of land for the establishment of the town of Norfolk. This was called an "Act for Cohabitation and Encouragement of Trade and Manufacture." Fifty acres of land were purchased by feoffees of several counties that were at that time formed, including fifty in Lower Norfolk County on Nicholas Wise's property, located at the entrance to the Eastern Branch of the Elizabeth River. A survey of the land was accomplished as ordered, and on October 19, 1680, John Ferebee was paid for his work. Precisely one year later, another payment was recorded to Ferebee for laying out the streets of the town. These aforementioned facts clearly demonstrate that the town of Norfolk was established by law in 1680, was surveyed almost immediately and ready to receive settlers before the end of 1681. It is thus contrary to historical facts that the city of Norfolk displays the date 1682, which is incorrect.

The discrepancy perhaps stems from the fact that it was not until August 16, 1682, that a legal settlement was reached regarding land purchased by trustees from Nicholas Wise's son, of the same name, a house carpenter of Elizabeth River Parish, in Lower Norfolk County. The grant was made "for and in consideration of the sum of ten thousand pounds of good merchantable tobacco and cask," to Captain William Robinson and Lieutenant Colonel Anthony Lawson, feoffees in trust for the county. The grant embraced all of the land on the river, from the eastern to the western end of Norfolk's Main Street, bounded on the north by Town Back Creek,

This is perhaps the earliest known photograph of Great Bridge Bridge, ca. 1895. The battle of Great Bridge came at an important juncture in the Revolutionary War and prevented the British occupation of much of the strategic ground between the bridge and the town of Norfolk. *Courtesy of the author.*

which, at that time, flowed from the river eastwardly nearly to old Church Street. Granby and Bank Streets crossed this creek, and where the old City Hall (now the MacArthur Memorial) stands, was then navigable for small craft and lighters. The greater portion of the land south of Main Street has since been added by filling up the river.

The old deed from Wise to the trustees set the location and boundary of the property as situated and lying in Elizabeth River Parish, on the north side of the river, bounded with the Elizabeth River on the south and west, to the north with a creek, and to the east with several stacks, running partly across an old field, and partly through some points of woodland, "it being a small nick of cleared ground and woodland." The deed concludes: "In the year of the reign of our sovereign lord, King Charles the Second, over England, Scotland, France, and Ireland, defender of the faith." This land was part of the two-hundred-acre tract that young Nicholas Wise had inherited from his father. The remaining one-hundred-fifty-acre tract afterward included in the limits of the town was bought by Charles Wilder, who sold it to William Porten, clerk of the county court, from whom it was purchased by Anthony Walke, some of whose descendants continued on as highly respected citizens of the city of Norfolk, but also Princess Anne County. Part of this tract, extending from Bermuda Street to Plume's Cove, including Fenchurch Street and the whole of Briggs' Point, remained in the Walke family for more than a century; some of the family's heirs subsequently became proprietors of portions of the old Walke family estate.

Those who had first laid out and settled in Norfolk Borough had chosen a location well suited to trade. The Chesapeake Bay, to the north, stretches two hundred miles though eastern Virginia and Maryland to the border of Pennsylvania. Just a few miles away are the mouths of the James and York Rivers; the Potomac can be reached, then and today, in a day. Norfolk historian Thomas J. Wertenbaker wrote in 1931 that it seemed certain to these early settlers that the products of the region drained by these great inland waterways would pour into Norfolk, there to be reshipped to foreign ports. But they would be initially quite disappointed as Norfolk did not become, at least at first, the port within the reaches of the Chesapeake Bay that her founding fathers had anticipated. Tobacco ships sailed from the James and York Rivers past the Virginia Capes and did not come down the Elizabeth. The reason was not so difficult to ascertain. Every plantation had its own wharf; seagoing ships tied up to these wharves, making it unnecessary to pick up their cargo at a point of reshipment. English merchant captains brought their ships from one river to another, creek to creek, dropping European commodities and luxuries unavailable in the Virginia colony. In return, English merchant crews loaded hogsheads of Sweetscented and Orinco tobacco—brown gold to the Europeans, who relished their tobacco from the New World. Norfolk and Portsmouth did not become large centers of trade until the 1720s, when ships became much larger and could no longer travel Virginia's winding rivers, some of which could not accommodate the drafts of these vessels, particularly loaded down with cargo.

The first mention of the name "Norfolk" in early land grant records was in April 1637. The first affirmation that Lower Norfolk County was operating independently is contained in Lower Norfolk County Records, *Book A.*

From 1680 a new commercial center had developed on the northern bank of the Elizabeth River, but the town of Norfolk remained subsidiary to the Port of Hampton (which was not the same as the town of Hampton), although by 1738 Norfolk had grown large enough to petition the Virginia Company's London council for the appointment of a deputy collector of customs to reside in the town and save the Norfolk people the trouble of making frequent trips across Hampton Roads for the necessary papers. Norfolk soon had the largest share of waterborne trade in the lower bay, but it had not yet become an independent port.

The fact that the Norfolk harbor was not a major point of destination for traders until the early eighteenth century belies the fact that trade on the Elizabeth River itself was quite extensive. Norfolk and Portsmouth, by virtue of their facing, strategic positions on the river, were the eventual beneficiaries of that trade. As trade increased for the communities along the Elizabeth, there was increased interest and activity in the ships that carried it, both in the river, its tributaries and creeks and over the oceans to foreign ports. Much is known of colonists on the east and west banks of the Elizabeth by virtue of the ships they owned and the goods they transported, both over land and water. During the colonial era Norfolk and Princess

Anne Counties did not produce large enough food crops to ship. Tobacco was not a crop that did well in the sandy soil that covers much of Lower Tidewater, and it would be nearly two centuries before the wealth from truck farming came to pass. Plantations had not yet become profitable. Captain John Smith, had he been alive to see the Elizabeth in the late 1600s, might have commented that it looked the same—the stately cypress, cedars and pines that populated the Elizabeth's shores were still there.

Fast forward to the closing decade of the eighteenth century and the trees remained—the richly forested banks of the Elizabeth were also a commodity. Edward Randolph, in his report to the British government, indicated that pitch, tar and turpentine were produced in large quantities on the branches of the Elizabeth River by poor men who constructed kilns. Turpentine was drained from the pines. There were no indentured servants or slaves to assist them, and their barrel output was low. Tar burners, as these men were known, set up their trade on navigable streams and inlets, all in close proximity to Norfolk. With a reasonable number of barrels produced, the tar burner loaded his cargo on a simple flat-bottomed boat, sometimes a shallop, raised his sail and headed for the town wharves to sell his tar, pitch or turpentine. The tar burners did their personal shopping

Land for Norfolk's Borough Church was originally set aside when Norfolk was surveyed in 1680 and its streets laid out a year later. The first chapel of ease was not built until after July 15, 1698, and was likely completed about 1700. The first Samuel Boush presented a London-manufactured silver chalice to "the parish church of Norfolk Towne" in March of that year. By 1738 the chapel of ease had become obsolete, and a year later, in 1739, Saint Paul's Episcopal Church was built. Harry C. Mann took this photograph of Saint Paul's about 1910. There were 265 grave markers in the churchyard when they were inventoried in 1902, but many had already disappeared. The oldest grave marker was located on the south side of the church and was documented in the survey. It was inscribed, "Here lies the body of Dorothy Farrell who deceased the 18th of January 1673." The presence of a seventeenth-century marker in the cemetery suggests that Farrell—and perhaps others—were reinterred on the site. *Courtesy of the author.*

among Norfolk's mercantile stores. A few of the early tar burners lived on properties with cypress, cedar and oak trees, from which they would add to their income by cutting planks and shingles. From Norfolk County records it is known that one-inch oak plank brought nearly six shillings per hundred feet, and cypress or juniper shingles nine shillings per thousand. It is also known from early records concerning the town of Norfolk that as early as 1697 Lewis Conner, one of Norfolk's first merchants, owned a ship and a brigantine. In 1717 Matthew Godfrey was purchasing barrels of tar from one of his Norfolk Town neighbors, Owen Jones, who was also a carpenter. About this time Godfrey owned the sloop *America*. A few years later, in 1723, Robert Tucker had one brigantine, three sloops and three flat-bottom boats; Tucker's brother John, in 1736, had three sloops and one shallop. That same year, Captain Nathaniel Tatem owned the ship *Caesar* and the sloop *Indian Creek*, but he also owned cartwheels, chains, axes, whipsaws and wedges—the tools required for cutting and hauling planks. About this time the sloop *Industry* was constructed in Norfolk, and the ship *Moseley*, named for Colonel Edward Moseley of Rolleston and New Town, was loading cargo at Norfolk bound for England.

Close proximity to the Dismal Swamp provided what early settlers believed was an endless supply of timber. The swamp, which stretched from the Southern Branch of the Elizabeth River to the Pasquotank River in North Carolina, was then an untouched natural wonder in which bears, wolves, wildcats, raccoons, opossum, deer and foxes ran freely under the boughs of expansive forests; countless species of birds, resident and migratory, sought shelter there, protected by the swampy environs that seemed altogether a natural barrier to human contact. Hunters and market gunners had not yet discovered the plethora of game in the Dismal Swamp. Early settlers took timber, at first, from the margins of the swamp. William Byrd II's *History of the Dividing Line* documented his visit to the swamp between Virginia and North Carolina. In it Byrd remarked that the local people got boards, shingles and other lumber out of the swamp in great abundance. He also observed that the swamp had been a free feeding ground for cattle and hogs. Livestock were branded by their owners to preclude confusion of ownership as the animals grazed openly. Cattle and hogs would eventually be slaughtered and the meat salted down as a preservative. Meat was sold at market in Norfolk, often alongside the tar burners' tar, pitch and turpentine, as well as plank and shingles.

Thomas Wertenbaker observed that Norfolk owed its first real growth to the geography of eastern North Carolina. The Tar Heel State's marshy topography and shore broken by innumerable bays, sounds and rivers worked well for inland trade but could not accommodate seagoing vessels. From Princess Anne County to Cape Lookout there were small inlets affected dramatically by shifting sandbars. North Carolina traders, out of

This pen-and-ink French map dated 1781 shows the area of Virginia from Williamsburg down to the Elizabeth River. Key towns such as Norfolk and Portsmouth are on the map, as well as the village of Great Bridge; all are clearly marked. *Courtesy of the Library of Congress Geography and Map Division.*

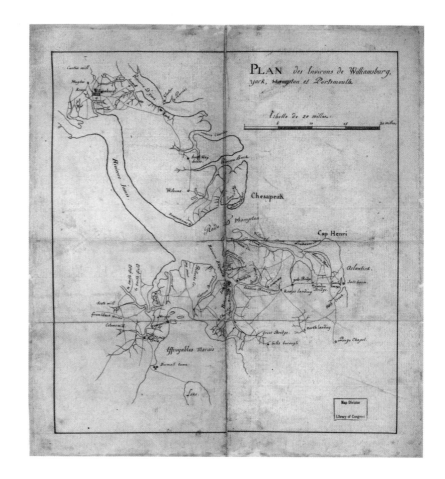

necessity, used an overland route to Norfolk or loaded their goods on small vessels and brought them around Cape Henry. From the time this trade route was first established, Norfolk and North Carolina struck a synergistic relationship that was mutually beneficial to both parties. There remained, too, many similarities between the lives of Virginia and North Carolina colonists. A trade route via the Atlantic Ocean was used often when roads were blocked, hard to find, washed out by creeks and rivers or choked with mud and debris. Like their counterparts in Norfolk and Portsmouth, North Carolina traders and plantation owners built their homes at the water's edge, which accommodated large merchant vessels that could tie up at their wharves. Building on the water's edge was all about economic necessity. Those who resided even one or two miles from the water's edge often found it difficult to get their goods to public landings. If a colonist lived on a small creek, he, too, used shallops and canoes to move his cargo to larger ships for shipment to Norfolk. There were many hazards to getting cargo from North Carolina's rivers and sounds, from groundings on one of the islands in Currituck Sound, to squalls over the water and piracy. Ships' captains could heave a sigh of relief on reaching the calm waters of the Elizabeth River. Approaching buildings and storehouses, captains either headed for the wharf of the merchant set to buy their goods or anchored in the river and rowed ashore to negotiate the sale of their cargo. It was rare for a schooner to leave the harbor without having executed a sale for all the goods aboard the vessel. Cargoes varied from Indian corn, tar, pitch or turpentine, to salted beef and pork, and sometimes farm produce, butter and cheese, beeswax, animal hides and myrtle wax, according to the third volume of *Colonial Records of North Carolina*. A number of these early North Carolina captains also bypassed customs collectors before leaving their homeports, taking aboard a few hundred pounds of tobacco without paying the one-penny-per-pound duty required of intercolonial trade, a practice revealed later by records from this important period of goods exchange between the colonies. On the return trip to North Carolina schooners loaded up on Jamaica rum, two or three hogshead of sugar or molasses and a variety of European household goods. There were occasionally slaves sent on these North Carolina–bound schooners, brought from Guinea for sale to farmers in the Albemarle region.

No story of North Carolina–Virginia trade would be complete without pirates. Early eighteenth-century piracy was a constant threat to intercolonial trade between North Carolina and Virginia. Captain Edward Teach ("Blackbeard") ran a band of pirates equipped with armed sloops from his headquarters near Ocracoke Inlet. From this vantage point Teach's pirates targeted incoming and outgoing merchant vessels, occasionally striking at West Indian oceangoing vessels in the Atlantic Ocean. Merchants in Norfolk were economically affected by the decrease of North Carolina captains traveling north to deliver their goods; pirates had begun a reign of terror that left schooner crews deathly afraid their vessels would be boarded, cargo seized and the ship wrecked or burned in some remote inlet. Colonists in Norfolk were also frightened by rumors that Teach planned to take up headquarters along the Elizabeth to target the harbor's steady stream of merchant vessels. North Carolina's traders and ships' captains requested protection from Virginia Governor Alexander Spotswood, as their own colony was not strong enough to combat Teach and his pirates. The British already had two warships, the HMS *Pearle* and HMS *Lyme*, on convoy duty in Virginia waters, but because they drafted too much water to follow Teach's pirates into the shallows of Albemarle and Pamlico Sounds, Governor Spotswood dispatched fifty-five sailors on two sloops, *Ranger* and *Jane*, led by First Lieutenant Robert Maynard. Pilots were hired, and off they went after the elusive Blackbeard and his band. Teach's hideout at Ocracoke Island was discovered on November 21, 1718, and soon thereafter British sailors spotted his sloop, *Adventure*,

Brambleton, Norfolk's first suburb, began as a subdivision of a farm owned by George Bramble in 1872. It was added to the city of Norfolk in 1887. Brambleton was joined to the old area of the city by a causeway at the east end of what was then Queen Street and a bridge at the foot of Holt Street, both crossing Plume's Creek, formerly Newton's and earlier Dun-in-the-Mire. The old creek bed was filled in over a short period of time, though part of it remained as Mahone's Lake at what was later known as Jackson Park and northward. Much of the area that was subsequently drained by a culvert was known as Mahone's Canal for many years.

flying the pirate's distinctive flag. The following day an engagement occurred between the British sloops and Blackbeard's *Adventure*; *Ranger* took a lethal broadside from the nine-gun *Adventure* and was effectively taken out of the fight. Teach was soon outwitted by Maynard, aboard *Jane*. Maynard ordered his crew below deck to make Teach believe the crew was dead. Soon Teach's pirates came alongside with a boarding party, only to be surprised by Maynard's men. Hand-to-hand fighting broke out and the infamous Blackbeard was killed. First Lieutenant Maynard later stated that Teach had at least five gunshots and multiple—upward of twenty—sword wounds; the pirate went down after many blows and having wounded several of *Jane*'s crew, including Maynard. Teach's severed head was tied to the bowsprit of the *Jane*, proof for the governor of Virginia and the colonists in North Carolina and Virginia that he was truly dead. North Carolina sloops soon reappeared on the Elizabeth River, their goods once again filling up Norfolk merchants' warehouses. With improved roads, too, much overland trade began to flourish between North Carolina and Virginia. There were then two main highways from Northeastern North Carolina to Norfolk, one running on each side of the Dismal Swamp. The first, beginning at Edenton, North Carolina, extended north from the Chowan area, rounded the swamp to the west and connected at the Nansemond River near Suffolk. But from that point to Norfolk the road wound to the head of the Elizabeth River's Western Branch, brushing the northern edge of the Dismal Swamp before passing over the upper reaches of the river's Southern Branch at Great Bridge, then turning northeast to Kempe's Landing, then around the Eastern Branch and Broad Creek by way of Newton's Creek, to then enter Norfolk north of Church Street. For those on foot or horseback, the route was somewhat shorter. Upon leaving the reaches of the Nansemond these travelers would head off to the left and follow the road to Sayer's Point, at the mouth of the Elizabeth's Western Branch, and then take the ferry to Norfolk. Another route, still, ran from the headwaters of the Western Branch to Crawford's Point, where Portsmouth soon developed, and then by ferry to the Norfolk County wharf near the market. Major Samuel Boush was running both ferries by 1715, according to the record preserved within *Norfolk County Deed Book*, number nine.

The second route from North Carolina also began at Edenton, running northeast where it crossed the Perquimans River at Vewby's ferry, then through the Pasquotank area, and over the Pasquotank River at Sawyer's ferry, and from there the road ran north of Currituck and then proceeded north to Great Bridge, where the road merged with the one from the west side of the Dismal Swamp. William Byrd wrote on March 15, 1728, that he had traveled along the east side of the Dismal Swamp, and "passed the long bridge that lies over the south branch of Elizabeth River. At the end of eighteen miles we reached Timothy Ivy's plantation, where we pitched our tent for the first time." His expedition had already traversed the Northwest River and the swamp surrounding it, which was then an obstacle to early travelers, but according to *Norfolk County Deed Book*, number ten, residents of Currituck paid out of their own pockets to erect a bridge over the Northwest River in 1719 at what was called Samuel Ballance's old landing. Norfolk County authorities, the British king's appointees and often prominent landowners watched after the upkeep of roads and bridges at all times, as these were the routes of important overland trade and travel. On March 4, 1728, William Byrd rowed about eighteen miles down the Northwest River, as far as the mouth of it, where it empties into the Albemarle Sound. He remarked that it was a delightful sight, all the way, to see the banks of the river adorned with myrtle, laurel and bay trees, which preserved their verdure year round. Byrd observed,

The Boush-Tazewell-Waller residence, originally located on the west side of Granby Street between what is now College Place and Tazewell Street with a view to the Elizabeth River, was the oldest house in downtown Norfolk for over a century. This late Georgian mansion was the first important private residence completed in Norfolk after the British burned Norfolk on January 1, 1776. Constructed for John Boush, shipyard owner and great-grandson of Norfolk's first mayor, Colonel Samuel Boush, and John's wife, Anne Waller, daughter of Judge Benjamin Waller of Williamsburg, the house was begun in 1779 and finished in 1783. Perfectly balanced and proportioned, each section of the home was created as ship's compartments, supported by tremendous hand-hewn timbers, and shiplap wooden siding was used for the exterior in the absence of brick at the time. The second floor repeats the plan. In 1810 the house was acquired by the nephew of Anne Waller Boush, Littleton Waller Tazewell, who added a two-story wing on each side. Tazewell served Virginia as a United States senator and as governor. Among the notables he entertained in the house were Marie Jean Paul Joseph Roche Yves Gilbert du Motier, Marquis de Lafayette, Henry Clay, John Tyler, Andrew Jackson and John Randolph. The house remained in the Tazewell family until 1894, when it was bought by Arthur Clarico and Emma Blow Freeman; Emma Freeman was a descendant of Judge Waller. This picture was taken in 1893. *Courtesy of the author.*

too, that these plants, which owned the banks of the river, grow commonly in very dirty soil. He found it remarkable that the river was never known to ebb and flow until the year 1713, when a violent storm opened an inlet, about five miles south of the old one. "The old inlet is almost choked up by the shifting of the sand, and grows both narrower and shoaler every day," he noted.

Great Bridge, where the two roads from North Carolina to Virginia converged, was bustling with activity by the mid-eighteenth century. Two long causeways extended across marshland on either side of the Southern Branch of the Elizabeth River, connected by a wooden bridge over the waterway. Warehouses and wharves were built on the southern causeway and it was here that two-wheeled carts bearing goods from the Dismal Swamp and Currituck unloaded barrels of tar, pitch or turpentine, or bundles of shingles and hogsheads of tobacco. Small vessels brought cargo to the wharves on the southern causeway, and some stopped to replenish and prepare cargo for delivery up the Southern Branch to Norfolk. Herdsmen from North Carolina drove herds of cattle, sheep and hogs over the wooden bridge on their way to Norfolk slaughterhouses. The sights and smells of large numbers of animals being herded to market, tar burners brining their tar, pitch and turpentine to market and the activity at the causeway wharves were memorable, and captured by an erstwhile Byrd, who surveyed the Dismal Swamp and its winding reaches.

In 1894 Arthur and Emma Freeman dismantled the Boush-Tazewell-Waller house and had it moved to its present location at 6225 Powhatan Avenue in Edgewater, three miles north on a waterfront site near the mouth of Tanner's Creek (now the Lafayette River). The house has undergone two major restorations since 1969. It was named to the Virginia Historic Landmarks Register on February 19, 1974, and the National Register of Historic Places on July 18, 1974. This picture was taken in the mid-twentieth century, at a time when the house had fallen into disrepair. *Courtesy of the author.*

By 1728 business in Norfolk was brisk. Trade with the West Indies, whither large quantities of flour, lumber, beef and pork, among other items, were exported, was abundant, in return for which were imported substantive quantities of sugar, molasses, rum and fruits. Twenty or thirty brigs and smaller vessels constantly rode at the wharves; merchants and mechanics were actively engaged and prospering. A number of stores and dwellings were built, real estate advanced in price and there was no reason to believe that Norfolk would not—or could not—flourish; after all, its lifeblood was the Elizabeth. Much of what is known of Norfolk at this time has been documented in William Byrd's *History of the Dividing Line*. In it, on March 1 of that year, he described Norfolk's trade thusly:

> *Norfolk has most the air of a town of any in Virginia. There were then near 20 brigantines and sloops riding at the wharves, and oftentimes they have more. It has all the advantages of situation requisite for trade and navigation. There is a secure harbour for a good number of ships of any burthen. Their river divides itself into three several branches, which are all navigable. The town is so near the sea that its vessels may sail in and out in a few hours. Their trade is chiefly to the West Indies, whither they export abundance of beef, pork, flour and lumber. The worst of it is, they contribute much towards debauching the country by importing abundance of rum, which, like gin in Great Britain, breaks the constitutions, vitiates the morals, and ruins the industry of most of the poor people of this country. This place is the mart for most of the commodities produced in the adjacent parts of North Carolina. They have a pretty deal of lumber from the borderers on the Dismal, who make bold with the king's land thereabouts, without the least ceremony. They not only maintain their stocks upon it, but get boards, shingles and other lumber out of it in great abundance.*

Four years later, in 1733, North Carolina records indicate that Virginia "imports" from the Tar Heel State amounted to fifty thousand pounds. Norfolk merchants marketed North Carolina goods abroad, sending some of the consumables and textiles, in particular, aboard Norfolk schooners to Barbados, Nevis and Antigua. A decade later, interestingly, four ships, six or seven brigantines, two or three snows (a two-masted merchant vessel popular from the sixteenth to the nineteenth centuries), seven or eight schooners and a half-dozen sloops composed the entire Virginia merchant marine. This was a surprisingly small number given the intense trade going on in the Norfolk harbor.

*William Byrd II
wrote on March
3, 1728, in his
History of the
Dividing Line of
the method used to
lay down wharves
in the communities
along the Elizabeth
River. "They lay
down long pine logs
that reach from the
shore to the edge of
the channel. These are
bound fast together,"
he observed, "by
cross-pieces notched
into them according
to the architecture of
log houses in North
Carolina. A wharf
built thus will stand
several years in spite
of the worm, which
bites here very much,
but may soon be
repaired in a place
where so many
pines grow in the
neighborhood."*

Within the two decades that followed, expansion of trade gave way to far more shipbuilding, and by 1764 Virginians owned 102 seagoing vessels, manned by some 827 sailors. When Norfolk was laid out in 1680, some of the first property owners were ship carpenters. The firm of John Glasford and Company, of Glasgow, Scotland, contracted with Smith Sparrows for a ship built in Norfolk in 1761; this vessel was some sixty feet long, twenty-two feet wide, ten feet in the lower hold and four feet between decks. The ship cost fifty shillings per ton to construct. Shipbuilding was most assuredly active in or near Norfolk, particularly up on Tanner's Creek and Broad Creek on the river's Eastern Branch.

Norfolk ship carpenters were constantly busy refitting and repairing seagoing vessels and coastal cargo runners in the colonial era. When ships in need of repair came up the Elizabeth, captains ordered their cargo dropped quickly, sails and rigging stored nearby in a loft and crews put up in lodging, usually at the most available ordinary. With a minimal number of ship handlers aboard, most of these damaged vessels were drawn to the shallows and careened with aid of fall and blocks. A lighter with steaming kettles of tar or pitch would then run up beside one ship bottom after another, caulking up leaking seams in the hull. Glaziers replaced broken glass, ironworkers fit new bolts, coopers repaired damaged hogsheads, sail makers patched torn canvas and carpenters made new hatches and replaced masts and spars that had perhaps been lost at sea. William Byrd wrote that the inhabitants of Norfolk were largely merchants, ship carpenters and "other useful artisans." Some vessels remained in Norfolk for repairs for a month or more, which could be costly to ships' owners and masters.

English tobacco ships gradually became large in size; commensurately, Virginia and Maryland agriculture diversified to the point that Norfolk had become the primary trading center for the entire Chesapeake Bay region. Thomas Wertenbaker concluded from his research that it was of no great difficulty for a vessel of 60 to 70 tons to move from plantation to plantation up the rivers and creeks, but for those of 250 tons it was tedious and dangerous. British owners did not want their cargo divvied out piecemeal; one location from which to load tobacco and other precious commodities was preferred over many small trips. Norfolk's expansive harbor was ideally suited to trade, and while resistant at first to send their tobacco and other goods south to the Elizabeth, plantation owners on the James, York, Rappahannock and even the Potomac Rivers eventually came to the conclusion that the town on mother water was the most amenable to their English brethren across the Atlantic. During this period of agricultural diversification, farmers had begun to plant wheat and corn bound for the West Indies. Merchant ships bound for the Caribbean stopped regularly in Norfolk, and it was there, on the waters of the Elizabeth, that it became commonplace to see shallops and sloops loaded with barrels of flour, wheat and corn, coming down the rivers to the bay and across Hampton Roads to the Norfolk waterfront. Gazing out on the Elizabeth in the mid-eighteenth century, one saw a river choked with merchant vessels of varying size and purpose; the harbor was soon to fulfill its destiny as the primary port of Virginia.

The most prominent of Norfolk merchants who traded widely with Virginia and Maryland farmers was Neil Jamieson, a Scotsman tied to the Glasgow firm John Glasford and Company. From Cabin Point, up in Surry County, Jamieson was able to secure substantive quantities of corn, wheat, peas, pork and tobacco, observed Wertenbaker, most of it gained through his factor, Adam Fleming; from Maryland he obtained wheat, iron and tobacco; from Petersburg, flour and corn; from Falmouth, on the Rappahannock, tobacco, butter and beeswax; from Alexandria, flour and herring; from Richmond, wheat; and from Fredericksburg, corn and pig iron. Jamieson sent tar, pitch and turpentine to Suffolk, which in turn traded with North Carolina's Chowan area. This very busy Scotsman had large warehouses in Norfolk and Gosport. Jamieson dealt

The John Boswell Whitehead residence (left) was constructed in 1791 by Patrick Parker. The home came into the possession of John McPhail in 1808; McPhail's mother married Hugh McPherson, her second husband. After the marriage, the McPhersons took ownership of the home from Mrs. McPherson's son, John McPhail. Her daughter, Elizabeth, married the Reverend Benjamin Grigsby, and the Grigsbys' son, Hugh Blair Grigsby, born in 1806, spent his boyhood in the house. Hugh Blair Grigsby would become a renowned Virginia historian; he died in 1861. After Reverend Grigsby's death, Elizabeth married Dr. Nathan Colgate Whitehead, in whose family the house remained for three generations. The Whitehead house was razed in the 1930s. The house, located on the southeast corner of Bank and Freemason Streets, was situated across Bank Street from the Moses Myers residence (right), built in 1792. Myers was the town's first Jewish resident and a wealthy merchant who made his living from the flourishing trade along the Elizabeth River. The Whitehead and Myers homes were among the first brick residences constructed after the Revolutionary War. *Courtesy of the author.*

The doorway of Norfolk's Moses Myers house, built in 1792, is shown here ca. 1907. The photograph is by Harry C. Mann. *Courtesy of the author.*

in many goods, from the aforementioned tobacco and farmers' crops to wine from Lisbon, Cadiz and Madeira; salt from Turks Island; barrels of coffee, pimento, chocolate, spices, cocoa nuts, all from different parts of the globe; a multitude of European goods, from Irish linens to large pieces of furniture—Jamieson saw all of it come and go regularly from his wharves. Though Jamieson later adhered to the British Crown during the Revolutionary War, George Washington was one of his most regular clients before the first Patriot fired a shot. In a letter from Mount Vernon dated June 4, 1771, Washington ordered the sails and rigging for his schooner from Jamieson. "If the sails and rigging, which I bespoke for Mr. John West, are not already come of, be so good," wrote Washington, "as to dispatch them by the first vessel bound to Alexandria. Captain Olife says he shall be up again immediately." Jamieson was not the only merchant who claimed great success in this time period. Other early merchants who made their fortunes on the Elizabeth included Samuel Smith, George Mason, Robert Tucker, Lewis Conner, Peter Malbone, Lawrence Smith, Thomas Nelson, Samuel Boush, John Phripp, Nathaniel Tatem, John Hutchings, Anthony Walke, Mason Calvert and John Taylor. The Elizabeth, with its superior harbor, had shifted the trade paradigm, so much so that Virginia Governor Francis Fauquier wrote on January 30, 1764, to the Board of Trade of England, "The seat of trade is altered, the northern part of the colony employing fewer vessels than heretofore, the southern many more." But William Byrd described the underpinning of Norfolk's enterprising merchants' success when he wrote, again from March 1, 1728, "The two cardinal virtues that make a place thrive, industry and frugality, are seen here in perfection; and so long as they can banish luxury and idleness, the town will remain in a happy and flourishing condition." What is not usually quoted is William Byrd's comment preceding this one. In it, he wrote of Norfolk, "With all these conveniences, it lies under the two great disadvantages that most of the towns in Holland do, by having neither good air nor good water"—a reference to waters already contaminated by tar, pitch, turpentine, bilge water and cast-off garbage from daily life.

Norfolk County, Norfolk Borough at its heart, originally included Princess Anne and Nansemond Counties, formerly called Nandzimum and Nansimum; Captain John Smith wrote it as Nandsamund. Shortly after being explored and named by Colonel Adam Thorowgood, the land was designated as Upper and Lower Norfolk. The part known later as Nansemond was called Upper Norfolk, and the rest was included in the two counties of Norfolk and Princess Anne, also called Lower Norfolk. In 1691, the inhabitants in the eastern and northeastern portions of Lower Norfolk, including Lynnhaven Parish, were subject to another subdivision, which created the parishes of Saint Bride's, Lynnhaven, Portsmouth and Elizabeth River. This was opposed by people in the parishes of Saint Bride's and the others, largely because of the consequent increase in the poll tax.

The name Princess Anne was adopted in honor of Anne, the princess of Denmark and daughter of James II, who ascended the throne in 1702, at thirty-eight years of age, and whose loyal subjects gave her the title "the good Queen Anne." The first courthouse in Princess Anne County was built on a branch of the "River of Chesapeake," today known as the Lynnhaven River, at the ferry landing located on the farm owned in the early nineteenth century by Lieutenant Charles McIntosh, of the United States Navy. The old courthouse building was razed about 1840; it had been used as one of the outhouses of the farm. The seat of justice was removed from the McIntosh property to Newtown, on the Eastern Branch of the Elizabeth, and situated on the land of James Kempe at the head of that stream, later the village of Kempsville. In the early 1800s yet another change was made when the courthouse was moved ten miles below Kempsville, and twenty from Norfolk. By 1752, with another Act of Assembly, the building of a courthouse was authorized for Norfolk Borough; this building was later consumed by the burning of Norfolk during the Revolutionary War.

Prior to 1761 Elizabeth River Parish comprised a large portion of the land on both sides of the Elizabeth River, resulting in considerable inconvenience to its residents, who petitioned the Virginia General Assembly to have it divided into three distinct parishes. An Act of Assembly dated April 6, 1761, realigned these parishes. The bounds of three new parishes were established: Elizabeth River Parish, comprising all that part of Norfolk County north of the Elizabeth River and its Eastern Branch; Saint Bride's Parish, taking in all the county south of the Eastern Branch and east of the Southern Branch, extending to a mill on Mill Creek, then southwardly into the Dismal Swamp, as far as the North Carolina line; and Portsmouth Parish, which took in all the county south of the Elizabeth River and west of the Southern Branch. It was enacted "that from and after the first day of May 1761 the parish should be divided into three, to be called Elizabeth River, Saint Bride's, and Portsmouth Parishes," which was accordingly done. The fate of the chapels placed in these parishes after the division in 1761 is worth noting here. Since the division was made along the lines of the areas served by the chapels, it would seem logical that these buildings would have stood the test of time and become chapels in the new parishes. The Western Branch Chapel became a chapel of ease for Portsmouth Parish, and disappeared after the American Revolution. A new parish church was subsequently completed in the new town of Portsmouth in 1762, and though many times altered, remains today as Trinity Episcopal Church at the southwest corner of High and Court Streets. Another chapel of ease for Portsmouth Parish was built in Deep Creek in 1762, but it, too, disappeared after the Revolution. This chapel of ease stood near the northwest corner of State Route 166 and United States Route 17. The Borough Church in Norfolk continued to be used as the parish church of a smaller Elizabeth River Parish, and Tanner's Creek Chapel was its chapel of ease. The latter chapel was abandoned after the Revolution, but later repaired and used by a Baptist congregation, which is discussed later in this volume. Saint Bride's Parish also got a new church in 1762; it stood at the southwest corner of State Routes 170 and 614. It is known that the Great Bridge Chapel served as a parish church until this new church was finished, and then continued in use as a chapel of ease for Saint Bride's Parish. While it is considered unlikely that either the 1762 parish church or Great Bridge Chapel were used as houses of worship after the Revolution, they were not dismantled until 1853 and 1845, respectively.

The mantel in the drawing room of the Moses Myers house was photographed by Harry C. Mann, ca. 1907. The décor in this and an accompanying photograph reflect the culmination of generations of Myers family members' belongings, which include some exquisite, though out-of-period, pieces of this important late-Georgian-era home. The fine neoclassical architectural ornaments of the drawing room went through restoration in 2004 and 2005, revealing detailed gilding on the mantel. *Courtesy of the author.*

While Portsmouth as a town did not begin until 1752, its history started with Bacon's Rebellion in 1676, when Captain William Carver, the owner of the plantation on which the city was built, followed the leaders of the rebellion and gave his life for the cause of liberty. The records of Norfolk County indicate that Carver was a man of prominence in the community. In addition to serving as justice, burgess and high-sheriff for the county, Carver also held the position of surveyor for the Southern and Eastern Branches of the Elizabeth River. In his early deeds Carver called himself a mariner, but in later ones he changed his occupation to merchant, thus conveying land at Church Point—Scot's or Scott's Creek—to his "well beloved cozens, Edward Davis and Rachel, his wife." Documentation by 1666 lists Carver only as "merchant."

Carver married twice, but of his two wives history leaves little record beyond their names. The first wife was called Elizabeth; the second Rose. Richard Carver, William's son, owned the tract of land later

The dining room of the Moses Myers residence, also photographed by Harry C. Mann about 1907, includes family portraits by Gilbert Stuart and Thomas Scully. Stuart's portrait of Moses Myers, ca. 1808, an oil-on-poplar, is visible in the alcove (right), over the buffet. There is a companion portrait of Myers's wife, Eliza Judah Myers, also by Stuart, ca. 1808. *Courtesy of the author.*

known as Lambert's Point. Though little is known of William Carver's private life, his official career was recorded. As justice he was active, and while on the bench, he, in person, presented Jone Jenkins as being too familiar with evil spirits and using witchcraft. When the Quakers were tried, he was one of the justices who sentenced them. But Carver also had a very dark side to his personality. In 1672, while attending a dinner party, Carver turned suddenly on Thomas Gilbert, who was seated next to him, and stabbed him to death. The trial's record indicates that Carver was perfectly unconscious of the crime he had committed; he claimed, in effect, a mental aberration at the time he killed Gilbert. The most important episode in Carver's checkered life was told by his contemporary, Edward Good, secretary to Nathaniel Bacon. Good recorded that he had been busy with Bacon nearly all night, helping him fill in the blank commissions that the governor had finally been compelled to give him. Bacon had scarcely left, according to Good, "when in came Captain Carver, who told me that he had been to wait upon the general for a commission, saying that he had decided to risk his old bones against the Indian rogues. The next news that I heard after going home," Good continued, "was that the general had marched against the Indians with a thousand men. Then came the governor's call to the militia of Middlesex and Gloucester to suppress Bacon. When Bacon had burned Jamestown he pressed the best boat on the James River into his service, and placed his lieutenant-general, Giles Bland,

onboard with Captain Carver, formerly in charge of the merchant vessel, to curb the small ships sent out by the governor."

The ship in Good's narrative was a large one belonging to Captain Thomas Larramore. The vessel, a merchant ship converted to man-of-war, was armed with a number of cannon and manned by two hundred men. Bacon gave secret orders to Carver, but being a little uncertain of Bland, failed to inform him of his plans; Carver, observed Bacon, he could trust completely. They were to go to the Accomack for the purpose of capturing Royal Governor William Berkeley, who was to be carried to England as a prisoner and tried before the king for reprehensible treatment of his subjects in Virginia. After peace was declared between Berkeley and Bacon, Good noted that the former sent for Carver, "who would not agree to go to Berkeley until his written pledge had been given him. This done, Carver went to the governor, who feasted and petted him, offering large promises if he would quit Bacon and serve with him. Carver told him if he had served the devil he would be true to him; but he thought he would go home and live quietly."

From Good's record of events, it is known that while Berkeley and Carver were together, Berkeley had a secret message from Larramore, telling him that he would seize Carver's ship, if he would send him men and seamen. The governor was delighted with this news, and complied at once with the request. While doing so, however, he had to stretch out the interview with Carver, who, when finally dismissed, started out to join his ship. Carver was amazed to find it under attack by the enemy and decided to run away. "He changed his mind," wrote Good, "and went tamely on board." Carver was angry enough when he reached Bland, whom he

The home of Robert Barraud Taylor was built in 1816. It stood at the corner of Granby and Market Streets in Norfolk. The picture was taken ca. 1895. The house was torn down in the early 1900s and the six-story Taylor Building constructed in its place. *Courtesy of the author.*

cursed as a traitor to Bacon's cause, that he ignored the immediate danger posed by Larramore. Bland and Carver were put in irons and three days later, on March 15, 1677, hanged at Bacon's Trench near Jamestown. Thus the first owner of Portsmouth died and his 890-acre property on the west side of the Elizabeth River was forfeited. Carver's Portsmouth tract, plus an additional 239 acres, was re-granted to Colonel William Crawford in 1715. It is probable that the Crawford family took up the lands soon after the forfeiture, the legal title not being conveyed until later.

The bounds of Crawford's patent were approximately Crab Creek, a small stream that once separated Portsmouth and New Town (South Portsmouth); Paradise Creek, also on the south; and Church Point (Scot's or Scott's Creek) on the west. The northern boundary was the land of Joshua Curle, later included as part of the Portsmouth Naval Hospital property, and also a small body of water called Island Creek. This creek was subsequently reclaimed and filled in by the United States government and the owners of the land known as Crawford Place. Island Creek once ran well into what is today the Park View neighborhood and took its name from an island at its juncture with the Elizabeth River. This island was gradually submerged, but could be seen plainly until the early twentieth

The James Wilson Hunter residence, right, was photographed ca. 1900. The Hunter home, located at 240 West Freemason Street in Norfolk's Freemason section, was designed by well-known Boston architect W.P. Wentworth and completed in 1894.

The Richardsonian-inspired Romanesque-revival townhouse was Hunter's dream home. James Hunter was highly successful in the mercantile business. About two years after this picture was taken he founded, organized and became president of the Virginia Bank and Trust Company; he also participated in the organization of the Jamestown Exposition. Hunter had married Lizzie Ayer Barnes in 1877. The couple had three children, James Wilson Hunter Jr., Harriet Cornelia Hunter and Eloise Dexter Hunter. Dr. James W. Hunter Jr. graduated from the University of Virginia School of Medicine and returned to Norfolk in 1901 to practice cardiology and radiology; he had the distinction of being one of Norfolk's first radiologists.

Courtesy of the author.

century. The eastern boundary of Crawford's patent was, of course, the river. Another point of land, on the Western Branch of the Elizabeth River, was also known as Crawford Point, where ferry service was available between his land and the town of Norfolk.

Like Carver, there is much about Colonel William Crawford's life that remains unknown. One tradition has it that Colonel Crawford was born in Portsmouth, England, and named his town for his native city. Another legend indicates he was born in Hull, England, and laid off the town after that city. While it is not known where, with certainty, Crawford was born, it is more than likely that Norfolk County was his birthplace, since his grandparents and perhaps his parents lived there. The will of William Crawford, Gent, was on record in the City Clerk's Office in Portsmouth, dated 1699 for many years. Though slightly damaged, its contents are plainly set forth. He left no children; his heirs being his grandson, William, and his granddaughter, Abigail Crawford, both minors. There is one English city mentioned in this will—Plymouth. It requests that his manservant be sent back there as it was his home. The deceased William Crawford also appointed a Plymouth man as his attorney in England. Of Colonel Crawford's father and mother there is no mention. His sister, Abigail, married a gentleman named Kader Conner and lived in Portsmouth. Colonel Crawford never married; his will, dated 1761, would bequeath the bulk of his property to Abigail Crawford Conner. A portion of his estate was left to the children of Mary Veale (deceased), but not as a whole—that is, each child was called by name and had a separate legacy. It

The earliest known photograph of downtown Portsmouth, looking west down High Street from Crawford Street, was taken after a snowfall ca. 1872. Howlett's Photography Studio is seen in the right foreground. The third building on the left was the home of the Reverend Richard Cleveland, who was pastor of Portsmouth's First Presbyterian Church and father of President Grover Cleveland. *Courtesy of the author.*

101

is further known that Crawford was a successful, prosperous merchant and ship owner who became a planter, served as justice, burgess and sheriff just as his predecessor had done, and became a respected member of the local militia, whence came his title.

Colonel Crawford was on the bench of Norfolk County for years and served in the House of Burgesses a number of terms. That he was a man of broad vision and great ability was well known in his day. Crawford kept ferries, successors to the enterprise begun by Colonel Adam Thorowgood in 1636, plying the Elizabeth River. He also established the county court. Much of what is known today about Colonel Crawford was initially compiled by Portsmouth-born Crawford chronicler Louisa Emmerson, born December 21, 1819, and who died there on May 24, 1907. Emmerson's information was gleaned largely from documents and interviews conducted with older members of the Portsmouth community. She remembered well the Crawford homestead and recorded that "it stood at the southeastern corner of High and Crawford Streets; a comfortable brick dwelling, built in the colonial style. High Street was then the private plantation road leading to the county road. About three hundred feet to the east," she recalled, "and directly in front of the house, was the Elizabeth River with its healthy breezes and pleasant odors." To return to Colonel Crawford's residences, the pleasure grounds are said to have been well shaded, and certainly he did not have to go far for his shade trees; it is said of the variety that he planted, the oak, sycamore and beech long survived him. New settlers, as they died out, planted the streets of Portsmouth with Lombardy poplars, Pride of China, elms and paper mulberries. The northern border of the plantation was planted with swamp laurel, jasmine, fringe trees, myrtle and woodbine, forming a beautiful view, as well as being conducive to health, warding off malaria, according to Emmerson's recollections. Here, too, were partridges, robins and wild ducks, and song birds, martins and hummingbirds. On Crawford's land grew crops of Indian corn and tobacco alongside seasonal vegetables, ready for his table.

Emmerson's account of Crawford includes graphic descriptions of Crawford's pleasures, reminding subsequent generations "that in colonial days as planters were separated from one another by watercourses, the sailboat and bateau were their only conveyances; and that when Mr. Crawford went to Jamestown, Hampton or Smithfield he would be conveyed in one of these boats." When Colonel Crawford and his contemporaries from adjacent waters of the Nansemond and the Lower James and branches of the Elizabeth River proposed a fishing trip, Craney Island was their rendezvous point. "The little fleet," wrote Emmerson, "made a gay appearance, rowed by black oarsmen, with flags flying. When the fatigue of drawing in the lines and hauling in the seines was over," the planters turned over the tasks to their slaves. The planters, with nothing left to do, talked politics, told jokes and discussed important topics of the day: the Spanish War, France and Sir Robert Walpole.

In the autumn Colonel Crawford and his fellow planters would hunt in the extensive land bordering on the Dismal Swamp. Suffolk was the meeting place and there would gather hunters from Southampton and Surry to hunt with their friends from the reaches of the Elizabeth. Dinner would follow the hunt. Crawford and the others would sit late into the night, discussing their duties in the county court, Indian problems and news from England, conveyed by Surry planters who received their news through Williamsburg.

It is not difficult to picture Colonel William Crawford, as the years caught up to him, setting aside his pleasures in return for tranquil evenings on his porch, perhaps planning the city that would eventually arise from sixty-five acres of his estate in 1752, and in the distant future would become part of one of the great ports of the world. From documentation left by Louisa Emmerson, it is not difficult to "see" what Crawford did—gazing west he saw a more convenient location for the county courthouse than the one at Washington Point, today's Berkley; already he had provided a landing place on his farm for the ferry to Norfolk—for both of these purposes Crawford gave up some of his best land. Crawford lived to see

The residence shown here was believed to have been an early home of Colonel William Crawford, built for the manager of his plantations, and from which was derived the name Crawford Bay, the body of water between Hospital Point and Portsmouth's north shore. The home is located at Swimming Point. The photograph was taken about 1950. Courtesy of the author.

the town outgrow the bounds that he had given it. Provisions were made to add additional lots at the time of Crawford's death in 1762. Crawford was likely buried in a private cemetery on his own plantation, the custom of the day, but it is unknown today where, in fact, this burial plot is located, although local construction workers digging the foundation for an annex on the old Merchants and Farmers Bank disinterred human bones, among them three skulls. At the time of this early twentieth-century discovery, it was suggested that this location was once the Crawford burial plot; it was definitely part of his garden.

The town of Portsmouth came into existence in February 1752. The town's act of incorporation stated, "Whereas it has been represented to the General Assembly that William Crawford, of the County of Norfolk, Gentleman, hath lately laid out a parcel of land on the south side of the Elizabeth River, opposite to the town of Norfolk, into one hundred and twenty-two lots, commodious streets, places, courthouse market and landing, for a town by the name of Portsmouth, and made sale of the said lots to divers persons who are desirous to settle and build thereon; and also that the said town lies very convenient for trade and navigation; be it enacted that said piece or parcel of land be hereby constituted, appointed, erected and established as a town to be called the name of Portsmouth." This act forbade the construction of any wooden chimneys within the town limits, and further granted it the same privilege accorded to other towns in Virginia. Portsmouth was surveyed by Gershom Nimmo, of Norfolk. The eastern boundary of the town was the Elizabeth River, which also marked its northern limit. The north side of South Street and Crab Creek bounded it on the south, while what was later the eastern side of Dinwiddie Street was the western border. Crawford Street, at first called Main, was the last street on that side of the town, the lots on its eastern side extending to the river. Next to it and running parallel to it was Middle Street, so called from its position, Court Street being the only one west of it. North Street was originally called Ferry Street, the Norfolk ferry then running from the end of it, where the Seaboard warehouses were eventually constructed. Columbia Street was called Crabbe until about 1906, when its name was changed at the request of property owners. This street was originally spelled "Crab," so called for the creek of the same name that flowed through a part of it, cutting off Crawford and Middle Streets and running far up into Court. At that time there was only sufficient land above the high water mark to make one large lot at the southeastern intersection of South and Court Streets. What later became the rest of the block was then under water at high tide and was called Widow's Point, likely for its first purchaser, Mary Avery, a widow. Avery was an ancestor of many families in old Portsmouth and two of her sons fought in the Revolutionary War.

The establishment of towns was not so much the concentration of administrative activities, both church and lay, in one place for each county or parish, as it was the establishment of ports and market areas where trade, both export and import, could be controlled.

This photograph, looking west along Portsmouth's North Street from Dinwiddie about 1890, shows a creek in the foreground that crossed North, running parallel to and adjoining Dinwiddie on the west. The boats mark the west end of Dinwiddie Street. The Colonel Dempsey Watts residence (right) was constructed in 1799, about midway between Washington and Dinwiddie Streets. The Watts residence was subsequently moved, in 1908, to the northwest corner of Dinwiddie and North, after Hampton Place was laid out. *Courtesy of the author.*

Portsmouth was laid off in squares, each of them bearing old English names such as Buckingham, Red Lyon and Golden. The squares bounded on one side by the river were called rows, and took their names from the square next to them. The lot frontage on the streets running east and west was 360 feet, while on those extending north and south the frontage was only 326 feet. Only four lots were allowed to a square and tradition that has come down through the years indicates that narrow streets, such as Glasgow, King and Bart, were intended as alleyways or back entrances. In 1763 the town was extended, incorporating lands devised to Thomas Veale by Colonel Crawford. This addition included the west side of Dinwiddie Street, Washington from Bart to North, a part of Green Street and South Street was extended across the new streets. Bart Street, too, was added at this time. The new squares were also given names. That same year, by an act of the Virginia General Assembly, the town was empowered to appoint nine trustees: Andrew Sprowle, Thomas Veale, Charles Stewart, Humphrey Roberts, Dr. David Purcell, Francis Miller, James Rae and Amos Etheridge. The first official act of the new body was the laying off of lots in the town's newly annexed territory. Sprowle, one of the town's most prominent citizens and also one of the richest merchants in Virginia, had purchased land across Crab Creek from Thomas Bustin, and there began the village of Gosport, establishing a marine yard, later the navy yard, and many other industries in his settlement. He also constructed for himself an impressive residence behind the marine yard.

Sprowle's Gosport community before the Revolutionary War was once described by a French traveler who visited the Virginia colony in 1764. The diary of this Frenchman was found in a Paris archive in the early 1930s. The writer's name was unknown and the manuscript incomplete, but it is believed that the author of the diary was a secret agent dispatched by the French government to obtain information about the British colonies. The traveler arrived in Norfolk and remained only a few days, but on visiting

Portsmouth he liked the smaller town so much better that he immediately engaged lodging at Roberts' Ordinary, taking up his quarters there on April 17, 1764, and dining at six o'clock each evening. "Portsmouth," he wrote, "has the advantage of Norfolk, having deeper water on its side. Ships of any size can come to their wharves, of which there are several very convenient. This harbour is safe for ships of any burden. It is the only part of Virginia where they build anything of ships. They have all the conveniences possible for that purpose." The Frenchman noted that there was a fine ropery there, but also plenty of masts of all proportions to be had and great quantities, he remarked, "were shipped to all parts, especially to Havana, where they have a contract for that article. I look upon this place," he continued, "as one of the properest on the continent for a King's port. As to the harbor, none can be better, and the country is well stocked with timber; they make their own cordage; have plenty of iron and all kinds of naval stores. The drinking water in Norfolk is bad, but very good in Portsmouth." The traveler did find that both towns were chiefly inhabited by the Scots, all Presbyterians. He observed of the Scots that they were "the most bigoted" people in the world and, to his surprise, had no house of worship of their own at that time. There was a church in both towns of what the traveler called "the English Establishment."

Whoever the French agent was, he dined with Andrew Sprowle, whom he called "the headman of Portsmouth." He described Sprowle's Gosport homestead as a pleasant place separated from the town by a creek, his house "goes by the name of Gosporte, and he has a very fine wharf before his door where the King's ships generally heave down. This merchant," he wrote, "is a gentleman of great reputation." The traveler went on to describe the launching of a ship at Western Branch, and there he met with an accident, his horse having run away. The unknown Frenchman ended up tending his cuts and bruises, with the aid of Dr. Purcell, who bled his bruises frequently. The ferry at that time, he recollected, used three boats, and covered a distance of three-quarters of a mile.

By the end of the colonial era, Norfolk and Portsmouth were prosperous and progressive. While at first Norfolk was a port for Southeastern Virginia and Northeastern North Carolina, the town became, in time, the point of shipment for the entire Lower Tidewater and, eventually, the commonwealth of Virginia. The Elizabeth River's commodious harbor was crowded with ships. Norfolk's, Portsmouth's and Gosport's streets teemed with merchants and shoppers, wharves and warehouses traded every manner of goods and in the shipyards that dotted the Elizabeth and her expansive tributaries were sloops, schooners, snows and other ships.

CHAPTER FOUR
EARLY COMMERCE AND UNFORTUNATE EVENTS DEFINE THE PRINCESS

An astute nineteenth-century observer once noted that Portsmouth, as Colonel William Crawford foresaw it, had been fortunate in her attenuation; that the town's hinterland was covered by vast forests of oak and pine, ready to build the ships that would bring great trade to the magnificent harbor at her shores. An unknown early twentieth-century Portsmouth resident once said that "nature has done much for us, and it only requires energy and enterprise to utilize these advantages and turn them to good account. With…a location unsurpassed by any on the Atlantic Coast—why should we not attain a position of great commercial importance and prosperity?" Few perhaps ever realized the great advantages of this port more than the numerous Scot and English settlers who flocked to Colonel Crawford's Portsmouth as soon as it was established. To later observers it was astonishing how rapidly Portsmouth developed up to the Revolutionary War, and for many years after it. Going back as far as 1770 the merchants of Portsmouth in conjunction with those of Norfolk established a board of trade for the "better conduct of business." The meeting for the board of trade took place in the house of Anthony Hay in Norfolk, but Portsmouth resident Andrew Sprowle was appointed chairman of the board. The other merchants from Portsmouth present at the meeting were James Marsden, German Baker, Humphrey Roberts, David Ross, Robert Seddon and Thomas Hepburn. When Great Britain levied oppressive taxes, Portsmouth merchants turned indignant and the majority of them signed the "Association," which was an agreement refusing to purchase from English merchants.

When war loomed with England, Portsmouth merchants were forced to take action, but some of them played both sides of the confrontation, looking for the best bargain. A few threw in their lots with the Virginia colony; some returned to their homes in Great Britain, fully intending to return when hostilities ended and they might resume their roles in business

Moses Myers, a prosperous Jewish merchant, came to Norfolk from New York after the Revolutionary War. Here, as a respected member of the community and a customs agent for the Norfolk port, he built an impressive Federal-style home in 1792 that was lived in successively by members of his family into the 1930s.

On March 3, 1828, Moses Myers sent this correspondence from the District and Port of Norfolk and Portsmouth to the collector of customs in Bath, Maine, certifying that the list of men of the brig *Mary and Nancy*, F.R. Theobald, master, granted in the District of Bath, Maine, on January 10, 1828, had been returned to his office, with a certificate of the boarding officer that all men were returned. Moses Myers was the collector for the District and Port of Norfolk and Portsmouth. *Courtesy of the author.*

District and Port of Norfolk and Portsmouth,

March 3. 1828

SIR,

The Certified Copy of the List of Men of the *Brig Mary & Nancy* *F.R. Theobald* — Master, granted in the District of *Bath* on the *10th January* 1828 has been returned to this Office, with a Certificate of the Boarding Officer thereon, stating that the Persons produced to him correspond with said List, except where they are otherwise noted—to wit :

All returned.

and the community. After the Revolutionary War ended many of these merchants made application to return to Portsmouth and later some of them did do so. These men were largely not interested in politics; they were focused on business. It was at this time that Portsmouth is said to have made perhaps its greatest error. If the Revolution caused a setback to Portsmouth's commercial growth, it certainly offered an opportunity when hostilities ended to take advantage of the burning of Norfolk, which was leveled to the ground in January 1776. William Forrest, in his *History of Norfolk*, stated that Portsmouth should have grown more rapidly under these conditions, but for the judicious behavior of Portsmouth's leadership. When the Scot families came to the town to settle after the war, they were ordered to leave Portsmouth at once. They came in such numbers that houses could not be found for them all. Many Scot families encamped on the open square in front of the ferry, at the foot of North Street. These settlers were much annoyed by the town's rougher element, who visited the Scots to harangue them daily, asking after King George III, making inquiries about Lord Cornwallis, while some of them even stooped to personal violence, occasionally throwing stones. The citizens of Portsmouth at-large sought to rid the town of these Tories in a more dignified way, but the result was the same—Portsmouth drove out the Tory settlers.

From a document found about eighty years ago in the Virginia State Archives in Richmond, much has been learned of measures taken by Portsmouth's leadership to prevent the Tory "invasion" of the town. The record was addressed to John Kerr, a former resident of Portsmouth, and it said, "We, the subscribers, the inhabitants of the town of Portsmouth, having yet very recent in our memory the treasonable and most traitorous act perpetrated by these execrable miscreants called Tories, and to our great astonishment now see a number of them and have reason to believe that many more will have the audacity to attempt to settle in our town, and it is a measure as insolent and as audacious as their late past actions have been treasonable and diabolical, we find it indispensably necessary for measures to be immediately adopted to stop the same." During this period, 1783–84, only twelve houses had been rebuilt in Norfolk, and Norfolkians realized that an opportunity had come with the expulsion of the Scots from Portsmouth. The people of Norfolk enjoined together and offered Portsmouth's exiled Tories opportunities on particularly advantageous terms, extending them every facility to aid the Scots' business careers. "In consequence," wrote Forrest later, "Norfolk soon rose from her ruins and acquired an ascendancy over Portsmouth, both in commerce and population." These Scot merchants became the leading factor in the success of Norfolk; some of Norfolk's most prominent citizens, even today, are descendants of these Scot Tories.

Portsmouth's tax list of 1784 documented only 584 white males; this, of course, referred only to property owners, but from that snapshot of the town's population some idea of the number of inhabitants can be ascertained. It was not a town flush with residents to rebuild after the Revolution. Tax rolls do not reflect, however, the influx of men, some with families, who came to Portsmouth to work in the shipyards and other industries clustered along Portsmouth's waterfront. In a town with officially few property owners, the town's taverns sheltered homeless mariners who came to the Elizabeth's western shore, while other establishments became temporary hostelries to travelers moving north to south. Eventually boarding houses and hotels would dot Portsmouth.

Within a few years of the end of the Revolutionary War, it had become dangerous to cross the Elizabeth River by ferry—there were so many vessels in the harbor, many of them from foreign ports of call. Ships from those foreign ports brought in luxuries and commodities, carrying away from the port in return lumber, cattle, pork and ship stores. The river's wharves employed hundreds, as did the ships, shipyards and ship trades. The front pages of Norfolk and Portsmouth newspapers dating to the 1800s were given up to shipping news and items pertaining to it. Sailing dates were published; boats advertised for charter; lists of cargoes carried out and brought in; and crew assignments were not uncommon to read in the papers. In 1804 there were ships in port at one time from Isle de Re, Lisbon, Cardiz, Suriname, Bordeaux, Liverpool, London, Glasgow, Madeira, Bermuda, Bahamas, Rotterdam, Antwerp and many other prominent cities. The waterfront of Gosport was lined with warehouses belonging to merchants trading with the West Indies. The Dickson family owned several of these warehouses at Gosport and kept a fleet of ships going and coming. Captain John Cox, noteworthy for his role in the Revolutionary War, had warehouses on the waterfront, too. In 1784 the

A number of wharves had been built off the south end of Norfolk's Water Street, their names indicative of a cross-section of mercantile activity in 1802. Beginning at Fayette Street, over which is today's World Trade Center fronting West Main Street, moving west to east, were wharves called Pennock's; Moore and McLeare's; Warren's; Holt and Woodside's; Commerce, at the foot of Commerce Street; Rothery's; Marsden's; Maxwell's; Campbell's; County Wharf, the county ferry terminal; Newton's; Moore and McLeare's, a second location; Loyall's; John Calvert's, at the foot of Church Street; Cornelius Calvert's; Lee's, at the foot of Read's Lane; and after a protracted gap from Read's, Hutchings' and Frost's, the latter located at the east end of Water Street.

The Norfolk branch of the American Colonization Society was organized in 1821, four years after its parent organization, for the purpose of sending an increasingly large number of free blacks to Africa, their freedom the result of considerable post–Revolutionary War debate to end slavery. Many of the emigrants from Virginia and North Carolina embarked from this port. Norfolk native Joseph Jenkins Roberts was the first president of Liberia when it became a republic in 1848. Portsmouth, too, formed its own chapter of the society; it was chosen as a principal port for the embarkation of free blacks. The American Colonization Society was a tight-knit group of politicians, financial backers and Quaker clergymen who all had their particular reasons for backing the resettlement.

government ordered tobacco warehouses built in Portsmouth and the lots selected for this purpose were numbers 183 and 184. The tobacco warehouses were positioned at the extreme southern end of Court Street just below Bart, fronting on Crab Creek, which was navigable at that time far to the west. All tobacco had to be inspected and shipped from a warehouse owned by the Virginia government, which also appointed its own inspectors. John Cowper was made inspector in Portsmouth.

The year 1784 was also when Laban Goffigan, who had served as a lieutenant in the Continental navy during the Revolution, was appointed harbormaster for Portsmouth. Goffigan was much interested in the harbor and seemed to those who knew him to have studied its advantages carefully. During Goffigan's tenure it was urged that Portsmouth be made a "capital port" by building a canal. Goffigan encouraged plans to develop such a canal, and among other advantages declared that between Devil's Reach and the Gosport Navy Yard there was ample room for five large shipyards. Goffigan placed Devil's Reach five miles above Portsmouth on the Southern Branch of the Elizabeth River.

Norfolk's port trade experienced a revival at the end of the eighteenth century. The town's Indian corn, lumber, tobacco and naval stores were cheaper than those that could be purchased in the North, and were superior in quality to those found in South Carolina and Georgia, noted one observer of the remarkable trade taking place on the Elizabeth River. Norfolk and Portsmouth traders could supply all the demands of the West Indian islands save rice and yellow pine. The *Norfolk Herald* of October 26, 1835, provides historical records of this valuable trade, noting that clearances for foreign ports from Norfolk and Portsmouth rose to 307 in 1798, 405 in 1799 and 448 in 1801. The *Herald* of January 13, 1803, remarked that on one day alone that month there were in the Elizabeth River 42 ships, 31 brigs, 56 schooners and 40 sloops. The *Norfolk Directory* of 1806 documented that the number of vessels from foreign ports to enter at Norfolk rose from 356 in 1800, to 368 in 1801, to 453 in 1802 and to 484 in 1803. Though in 1804 and 1805 the number of vessels from foreign ports entering the harbor declined, the total tonnage from foreign countries continued to grow. Exports rose from a little over a million dollars in 1792, to two million in 1795, to over four million dollars in 1804, according to François-Alexandre-Frédéric duc de La Rochefoucauld-Liancourt's *Voyage dans les États-Unis d'Amérique, fait en 1795, 1796 et 1797*, published in 1799. La Rochefoucauld-Liancourt (1747–1827) was a French social reformer. The French Revolution forced him to flee to England in 1792 and from there he traveled to the United States and wrote of his travels, a good part of which were spent in the American South. From newspaper accounts in 1834 and the *Norfolk Directory*, it is known that in the years from 1804 to 1807, on the cusp of renewed hostilities with Great Britain, exports had

Norfolk native Joseph Jenkins Roberts was a free black sent back to Africa by the Norfolk Colonization Society. Roberts arrived in Liberia in 1829 from Virginia waters. In 1839 he was appointed vice-colonial governor of the commonwealth of Liberia and took over as governor of the commonwealth in 1841, when Thomas Buchanan died. He served as the first and seventh president of Liberia. This sixth-plate daguerrotype of Roberts was the work of photographer Rufus Anson and is ca. 1851. *Courtesy of the Library of Congress Prints and Photographs Division.*

spiked from five to seven million dollars annually. The *American Beacon* dated December 13, 1834, noted that tonnage owned by Norfolk citizens, negligible in 1785, was 15,567 in 1796 and 31,292 in 1805. The *Norfolk Herald* of October 26, 1835, stated that in 1806 Norfolk merchants owned 120 vessels, aggregating 23,207 tons, used exclusively in the foreign trade, some of them stately ships of from 350 to 450 tons. La Rochefoucauld-Liancourt wrote, "Six years ago there were not ten large vessels belonging to Norfolk; today there are fifty, to say nothing of fifty more smaller ones, engaged chiefly in the West India trade."

Shipbuilding, which had fallen into a lull after the Revolution, sprung to life as the sun set on the eighteenth century. Old shipyards experienced unexampled expansion. La Rochefoucauld-Liancourt observed that Gosport was crowded with partly completed hulls, while every slip along the banks of the Elizabeth River and its tributaries was engaged in building ships. The waterfront cadence was kept to the beat of hammer and saw. The Frenchman also wrote that from eighty to ninety vessels of all sizes were built at Norfolk annually, most of them for the Philadelphia market. The *Norfolk Gazette and Public Ledger* dated October 30, 1804, remarked that the capacity of some of the shipyards was indicated by the launching from the establishment of John Foster, at Portsmouth, of a 380-ton ship, the *Dumfries*, intended for the London trade. Interestingly, the cost of construction for the hull of a vessel of 120 tons or more was twenty-four dollars a ton, and for completed ships, ready to be put to sea, from forty-seven to fifty dollars. The pay for ship carpenters, published in the newspaper, was two to three dollars per day, which was considered high for anyone in those days. Men who had built something as small as a shallop or rowboat represented themselves as skilled ship carpenters. In William S. Forrest's *Sketches of Norfolk*, he wrote that a visitor to the town observed, "Your harbor, capacious as it is, was filled with ships from foreign parts. The coasting trade, which distributed your imports, employed hundreds of vessels, whose streamers, mingling on a gala day with the flags of the foreign ships, presented a cheering spectacle." The visitor

In 1784 the government ordered the construction of tobacco warehouses on the Portsmouth side of the Elizabeth. The warehouses were positioned at the extreme southern end of Court Street just below Bart, fronting on Crab Creek, which was navigable at that time far to the west. All tobacco had to

Virginia Tobacco Field.— Tobacco was one of the earliest products raised in the State, the colonial clergy receiving their salary in so many pounds of "sweet Virginia." In fact, in those days it was the monetary standard. One Norfolk tobacco stemmery employs 700 operatives.

be inspected at and shipped from a warehouse owned by the Virginia government, which also appointed its own inspectors. John Cowper was made inspector in Portsmouth. Tobacco was one of the earliest and most important products raised in Virginia and shipped from wharves in Norfolk and Portsmouth.

Colonial-era clergy received their salaries in "sweet Virginia," and, in fact, in those days tobacco had become the monetary standard. One late nineteenth-century Norfolk stemmery, a facility that processes tobacco to produce redried tobacco per customer specifications employed seven hundred men. This ca. 1895 photograph depicts a typical Virginia tobacco field. *Courtesy of the author.*

went on to note that it was difficult "to cross in a ferry boat from Norfolk to Portsmouth, on account of the great number of vessels in the harbor. Your warehouses were full of foreign and domestic products. Besides your stated population, there was always a body of transient people" who demanded houseroom and board. Norfolk was a cosmopolitan place as the curtain closed on the eighteenth century. On its bustling wharves and crowded streets, wrote Thomas Wertenbaker in his *Norfolk: Historic Southern Port*, one could brush elbows with merchants from Glasgow, Liverpool, Kingston or Philadelphia; with North Carolina shippers, just in from the Albemarle Sound with a cargo of lumber, tar and turpentine; with traders from Richmond and Petersburg; perhaps with sailors from some French brigantine lying in the river awaiting a consignment of tobacco. The town then had among its most prominent merchants not only native Virginians and recent Scot immigrants, but also Englishmen, Irish and French West Indians. There were even a few Dutch, Spanish and Portuguese. Norfolk-born people, though, were the base population.

In July 1793 there came into Hampton Roads a fleet of 137 square-rigged vessels under the escort of 2 ships of the line, 3 frigates and 3 smaller warships, all carrying the flag of France. The decks of these ships were crowded with men, women and children, many of them quite sick. They were French refugees driven from their homes in San Domingo by a slave uprising, according to an account of their plight in the July 13, 1793 edition of the *Virginia Chronicle and Norfolk and Portsmouth General Advertiser*. Many of the French ships came up the Elizabeth River and deposited hundreds of weary, sick passengers in Norfolk. Most of these formerly wealthy planters and merchants had escaped San Domingo with only the clothes on their backs; they had no money. Donations to help these refugees poured in from across Virginia, an outpouring driven by the strong bond between France and the United States, but also the fact, noted La Rochefoucauld-Liancourt, that the slaves who accompanied their masters from the West Indies could be put to work in Virginia. The French who came, however briefly, to live in Norfolk numbered between two and three thousand. Those who stayed here opened shops to make a living.

Gosport was not all navy yard in the early 1800s. There were distilleries in Gosport making hundreds of gallons of rum a day. There were ropewalks on Portsmouth's South Street and also on Bart. Brick kilns were scattered through the town, one of the best known being on the northwest corner of Middle and High Streets. There were also several windmills there and in the 1820s Commodore James Barron built one of the most approved types of mill structures for his son-in-law, Wilton Hope, the father of James Barron Hope, the poet and noted editor. This mill was at what was later the intersection of South and Chestnut Streets, but it was not a great success financially and was

Swimming Point, shown here ca. 1895, had extraordinary views of the Elizabeth River. The turreted mansion in this picture was the home of R.T.K. Bain, and later owned by Goodrich Hatton, a noted Portsmouth attorney and Portsmouth delegate to the Virginia Constitutional Convention held between 1901 and 1902. *Courtesy of the author.*

Swimming Point, shown here ca. 1895, had extraordinary views of the Elizabeth River. The turreted mansion in this picture was the home of R.T.K. Bain, and later owned by Goodrich Hatton, a noted Portsmouth attorney and Portsmouth delegate to the Virginia Constitutional Convention held between 1901 and 1902. *Courtesy of the author.*

subsequently abandoned. As early as 1827 steamboats began to be built at Portsmouth shipyards; Joseph Porter's shipyard at the foot of High Street launched one of the first steamboats to be built on the west side of the Elizabeth. The vessel was named *Fredericksburg* and intended for travel on the Rappahannock River.

The Dismal Swamp Canal, discussed in more detail later in this volume, was begun in 1793 and opened for business in 1805, after a dozen years spent in construction, but it was too shallow and it was not until June 1814 that it was put into full operation. A twenty-ton vessel arrived in the Elizabeth with goods from Scotland Neck, thus inaugurating steady commerce via larger ships down the canal. Apart from its commercial value to the community, it is significant as the work of George Washington, who planned and superintended its construction. Washington's work on the canal brought him frequently to Portsmouth. There was an ancient and spreading oak tree on the canal bank called Washington's Oak, for under its shade it was said Washington often rested. When the road to Elizabeth City, North Carolina, was constructed, the tree stood in its path. The road was curved to spare it. Washington had a personal interest in land on the west side of the Elizabeth; he owned a vast tract of swamped acreage between Portsmouth and Driver. As for the Dismal Swamp Canal, it passed through a densely wooded section and ships heavily laden with lumber regularly plied its waters. Its trade was practically ruined, however, when the federal government took over the nearby Albemarle and Chesapeake Canal and made it free passage. By 1931 the Dismal Swamp Canal, too, proffered the same.

About two years after the Dismal Swamp Canal was opened, a second round of hostilities with the British clearly loomed on the horizon. The

Chesapeake-Leopard affair, described further in chapter five, lit a firestorm of indignation across the country, but did little to persuade President Thomas Jefferson that the nation needed to go to war to prevent further transgressions by the English. Jefferson's way of dealing with the problem was a proclamation that required armed British vessels to depart American waters and to prohibit Americans from intercourse with them. He then sought reparations through diplomatic channels. This was far too tame an approach for the citizens of Norfolk, who had witnessed, firsthand, the USS *Chesapeake*'s humiliating return down the Elizabeth River, and who tended wounded sailors. The *Chesapeake-Leopard* affair served as fair warning of what was to come. Jefferson's diplomatic solution failed and impressments and seizures continued unabated. American merchant vessels were being robbed at sea. While Norfolk's experience in the Revolutionary War made the townspeople attuned to river defenses, the War Department did not keep fortifications along the Elizabeth River in good repair. In fact, when Secretary of War Henry Dearborn toured Norfolk in 1802, he ordered the dismounting of Fort Norfolk and the creation of a new fort at Ferry Point in what is today Berkley. According to Wertenbaker, the *Norfolk Herald* would comment rather sarcastically on Dearborn's decision, stating that a fort situated at Ferry Point, above both towns, "is an invincible protection to the little place called Kempe's, ten miles up the Eastern Branch, and to Great Bridge, twelve miles up the Southern Branch, to both of which places a lighter for wood can go with tolerable safety on the flood tide." The citizens of Norfolk and Portsmouth relied on their own efforts to keep Fort Norfolk and Fort Nelson, respectively, in reasonable condition, though the rush to war that was to come placed the heavy burden of major repairs to both forts' walls on the shoulders of those left poorer by President Jefferson's subsequent embargo on foreign trade in the port. Jefferson's decision to put American naval frigates in dry dock and protect the rivers and harbors with a fleet of gunboats made him fair fodder for newspaper editors. On September 20, 1804, the *Norfolk Gazette and Public Ledger* editors chided Jefferson's decision, writing, "We understand Gunboat No. 1 was by the late storm safely moored in the middle of a cornfield." The newspaper's editors later recommended that it was far more prudent to construct seven ships-of-the-line, eight frigates, three sloops-of-war and four bomb ketches to carry in all 908 guns. Jefferson would not hear of it. Realizing, noted Wertenbaker, that Great Britain was trying to weaken France with her Orders of Council while Napoleon was retaliating with his arbitrary decrees, and Americans were finding it difficult to engage in foreign commerce of any kind without seizure and confiscation, President Jefferson recommended an embargo on foreign trade. He believed that this coercive measure would compel the British to reason; after all, the American market would thus be closed to British

Extensive shipbuilding operations were carried out by private concerns. Among their noteworthy accomplishments were the construction of the 420-ton ship General Washington *by Porter and Dyson, launched in 1815; the packet* Newburn, *by John P. Colley, and the steamship* North Carolina, *by Ryan and Gayle, both launched in 1829; the 470-ton* Madison *and 530-ton* Washington, *launched from the yards of Isaac Talbot, the former in 1828 and the latter in 1833. In 1853 Page and Allen, of Portsmouth, had under construction a 1,515-ton clipper ship, at that time the largest vessel ever laid down south of New York—Neptune's Car.*

Trinity Episcopal, on the southwest corner of High and Court Streets, is Portsmouth's oldest church. It was first built in 1762 as the parish church of Portsmouth Parish, established in 1761. Later named Trinity, the church was rebuilt in 1829 and remodeled in 1893. This picture of Trinity Episcopal dates to about 1895. *Courtesy of the author.*

manufacturers and the West Indies would be cut off from provisions. Norfolk merchants and their counterparts in America's shipping centers protested this measure, but it passed through Congress quickly and there was little anyone in the country's premier port towns could do to stop it. On December 22, 1807, Jefferson signed the embargo act that prevented the departure of any ships for foreign ports, and forced coasting ships to give bond to put in only at ports in the United States. Thousands of sailors were thus unemployed and the shipping trades, without their imports and exports, had no source of income.

The embargo was devastating to Norfolk. Warehouses were boarded up, wharves empty and ships in port moved away to fresh water to prevent damage from teredo worms. Property values plummeted, many of Norfolk's and Portsmouth's merchants met with financial ruin, formerly busy shipyards were shuttered and hundreds of sailors and ship tradesmen left the towns along the Elizabeth River for foreign ports to find work. The embargo, in part a protest of British impressment of American sailors, was driving unemployed American and ex-British seamen back to the British fleet in droves. The West Indies were supplied by Canada and, to some degree, by Europe. People living within the reaches of the Elizabeth River, particularly those whose livelihoods had depended solely on the sea trade for their income, were literally starving. In March 1809 the embargo act was repealed and Norfolk again became an active hub of foreign trade, and while non-intercourse with Great Britain and France was still in effect, traders found ways to go around the restrictions. The Elizabeth River was once again full of ships bearing cargo bound for foreign ports and those bringing goods to wharves in Norfolk and Portsmouth. Norfolk merchants would continue to be disappointed by lower prices for their goods in the Caribbean and South America, and continued seizures of American vessels by the British and French. The *Norfolk Gazette and Public Ledger* reported regularly on British and French boardings at sea. The newspaper's February 25, 1811 edition noted, "If our vessels go to any port of Europe except Great Britain, they are seized by Napoleon. If they go to Great Britain, they are seized by the United States when they come home. Between the emperor and Mr. Madison, our merchants, shipwrights, and all concerned in commerce may soon cease their avocations." An act of violence against the French privateer *Ravanche de Cerf*, at anchor in the Elizabeth River, was a good indication of the citizens of Norfolk's animosity toward Napoleon. The *Norfolk Gazette and Public Ledger* reported two days after the incident that on the evening of April 15, 1811, while the *Ravanche de Cerf*'s crew was ashore, two boats filled with armed men came alongside, overpowered two young men left to guard the ship and placed a tub of combustibles in the hold, setting the privateer ablaze. The ship burned to the waterline. The War of 1812, covered in the following chapter, would turn the tide of commerce and secure protection of rivers and harbors for decades to come.

A picture of the Elizabeth River after the war was painted for posterity by observers who penned eloquent descriptions, among them George Tucker (1775–1861), in his *Letters from Virginia*, published by Fielding Lucas of Baltimore in 1816. While authorship of this work is debated, some believing the narrative written by William Maxwell and others by James Kirke Paulding, the words bear repeating:

> *Passing one or two neat country boxes on your left, you come to Fort Norfolk, a strong fortification with a brick wall, in the shape of a half-moon. Fort Nelson is a little above on the other shore, and makes quite a pleasing show with its green banks and white houses in the rear. You are now up, and the town sits to you in all her charms, to paint her if you choose. It is on our left in the landscape, and appears to be almost divided into two parts, by the water running and shining between. Bridges are thrown over to unite these divisions, and the lower one, or the Point, as they call it, shows a number of neat, white houses, almost lost*

in trees. On your right the harbor opens before you in a beautiful basin, nearly a mile wide.

An account in the Norfolk Herald described the September 2–3, 1821 hurricane as a "tremendous storm," causing great damage to ships in the harbor. The new stone bridge on Granby Street was damaged by the incessant banging of heavy timbers against it. The tides inundated the ground floors of all the warehouses on the wharf lining the Elizabeth River. The waters surged as far inland as Widewater Street, several hundred yards from the river. The surging waters of the Elizabeth River swept away the bridge on Catherine Street. The drawbridge across the Elizabeth River was swept away. The frigates USSs Congress *and* Guerriere *were grounded while numerous other brigs, schooners and smaller ships suffered an untimely demise.*

Tucker observed that the Marine Hospital, on Washington Point, at the head of it, "comes out to meet you in the front. Portsmouth, a neat rural village, sits in smiling silence on the other side; and still further up, Gosport with her navy yard, ships and bridge, finishes the prospect." Anne Royall, who came to Norfolk in 1828, wrote the following year in *The Black Book: A Continuation of Travels in the United States* that the town contained three banks, a courthouse, a jail, an academy, three insurance offices, an orphans' asylum, an athenaeum containing six thousand volumes of well-chosen books and seven churches. In an account that appeared in the *American Beacon and North Carolina Gazette* dated January 7, 1834, another visitor observed that approaching Norfolk, "you sail up the bold Elizabeth River, passing Craney Island on your right, where you see the remains of military works, and two or three country boxes on your left. You reach Fort Norfolk, now dismantled, on the same side. The new naval hospital is on the opposite shore, and forms a splendid vision with its Doric colonnade in front. Before you is the town, divided, as you see, in two parts, but united again by yonder stone bridge." The bridge described by this traveler was the stone bridge linking the southern and northern ends of Granby Street. "And there, a little to the left of it, is the house of our ex-senator, Mr. Tazewell, with its white portico and green lawn in front, making a very agreeable point in the picture. The right, or business part of the town, is well built up with brick houses, and appears to be a thriving mart," continued the visitor's narrative. As he entered the harbor, he, too, remarked that it was a beautiful basin, "and full of ships and brigs and innumerable smaller vessels, all along the wharves."

In the years following the War of 1812, Norfolk and Portsmouth pioneered many forms of trade. Portsmouth was the first among Elizabeth River towns in handling Maine ice. In 1830 Captain Samuel Watts and his brother established their ice business, bringing in ice cut from ponds in Maine to Portsmouth via schooners. Two years later, in 1832, Watts's firm built an icehouse on Queen Street on a site long used for that purpose, between Middle and Crawford Streets. The capacity of the building was only about twenty to thirty tons, but three years later it was enlarged and held about three hundred tons. Maine ice proved so successful in Portsmouth that businessmen in Norfolk decided to provide it on the east side of the river. The Wattses eventually sold their icehouse to William E. Maupin, who renamed the business George W. Maupin Ice and Coal Company, but Maupin eventually had competition from Portsmouth Ice and Coal Company and Isaac Fass.

Over in Norfolk, there were innumerable items being imported and distributed, many necessities but others wonderful luxuries. The September 6, 1839 morning edition of the *American Beacon* ran Norfolk advertisements for Spanish cigars, William S. Forrest, agent, and choice wines, imported to the United States by the houses of Cruse and Hirschfield, of Bordeaux, and C. Sauteren and Son, Chalons su Marne, placed by Robert Soutter Jr. The wines included selections of Chateau Marge Claret, Chateau Lafitte Claret, Palm Margeaux Claret, Sauterne, baskets of Eagle Champagne, Rudesheimer Hock, Sparkling Hock Yellow Label and many others, all advertised of superior quality. The other curious item advertised was isinglass, specifically Russian isinglass, a substance obtained from the swim bladders of fish, particularly Beluga sturgeon, used largely for the clarification of wine and beer. But it was also used as a collagen. Prior to inexpensive production of gelatin and other products of similar nature, isinglass was used in confections and desserts. Isinglass was originally made exclusively from sturgeon until the 1795 invention of a cheap

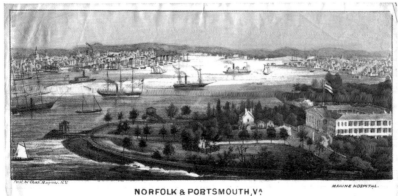

NORFOLK & PORTSMOUTH, VA

According to the New York Historical Society, pictorial lettersheets were an early precursor to picture postcards. Lettersheets were created to comply with, yet cleverly circumvent, postal regulations. Before 1855, postage was calculated based on the number of sheets enclosed in each envelope. Lettersheets became very popular because of their folio format, usually an 8½- by 21-inch piece of paper folded in half, which provided four pages on which to write but were considered as one sheet by the post office. Some publishers, particularly Charles Magnus of New York and many California stationers, included printed illustrations on the lettersheets to increase their commercial appeal. These illustrations, often bird's-eye views or detailed street scenes of cities, usually appeared in a rectangular space at the top of the first page of the folio, as shown here of the Elizabeth River, ca. 1850, with Hospital Point in the foreground, by Charles Magnus. The historical society also indicates that in the United States this form of stationery was popular mainly in New York and San Francisco, perhaps because of those cities' coastal locations and importance as ports of entry. Most lettersheets were printed lithographically in black and white, but occasionally colors were added by hand, or colored stock was used. Magnus, a German immigrant, often used a photograph as a base to achieve an accurate perspective and architectural detail, adding hand-drawn figures, ships and landscape detail. *Courtesy of the author.*

substitute using cod. This was extensively used in British and Russian isinglass. The *Beacon*'s advertisement for Russian isinglass promoted its use in table jellies. "It improves by age if kept dry," noted the advertisement, "and can be made into soup in a few minutes, and is of great service in clarifying cider, beer and wine."

Another industry that was important to the port in its earliest days was oyster pickling. Pickled oysters were shipped in large quantities to the West Indies, New York and New Orleans. One of the largest shippers in Portsmouth was John Benson, whose plant was on the Western Branch of the Elizabeth River. He advertised his pickled oysters in any quantity up to three thousand gallons. Shops in Portsmouth and Norfolk furnished Benson's pickled oysters in smaller quantities. The Virginia General Assembly enacted very strict laws forbidding the sale of oysters between May and October. If the bivalves were found on any ship during that season, the masters of the vessels were subject to a heavy fine. This clause of the act caused some excitement among the picklers, who demanded that it be changed and amended, declaring that pickled oysters did not come within the law.

At the Page and Allen shipyard in 1853 the largest clipper ship ever built south of New York was launched, and a few years earlier the engines and boilers for the USS *Powhatan* were constructed at Mahaffy's Iron Works in Gosport. That clipper ship, *Neptune's Car*, was launched April 16, 1853, on the banks of the Elizabeth River by workers at Page and Allen for Foster and Nickerson of New York. This was, in all likelihood, the only extreme clipper ever built in Virginia at 1.515 tons, 216 feet long, 40 feet broad and 23.5 feet deep. The clipper would reach its peak of notoriety, however, when it was captained from the fall of 1854 to late 1856 by Captain Joshua Patten. While not unusual for the master of a merchant vessel to be accompanied by his wife on a voyage, Mary Ann Brown Patten, a native of Boston, Massachusetts, proved exceptional, familiarizing herself, as one chronicler later wrote, "with every foot of *Neptune's Car* from bow to stern." Spending long days at sea, Mary Patten watched and learned as her husband pored over charts and navigated *Neptune's Car* on long journeys from New York to San Francisco, Foo Chow to London and on a particularly fateful trip, from New York to San Francisco again, traversing the dangerous passage around Cape Horn. This trip, begun on June 30, 1856, started out unremarkably until Mary Patten's husband came down with fatigue and "brain fever" after taking on first mate as well as his captain's duties. With a new first mate, inexperienced with navigation, unable to take the helm of *Neptune's Car* in the Straights of Le Maire, Mary Patten became the first woman clipper captain in history, but not without challenges. The deposed first mate tried to spark a mutiny; Captain Patten became blind and deaf from his illness; and Mary Patten, nurse and

The United States Custom House, shown in this Harry C. Mann picture, ca. 1917, came about as the result of the federal government's need for a larger building to accommodate its operations in the port. In 1852 a site was chosen on the south side of the western end of Norfolk's Main Street at the head of Granby Street. Plans were drawn by government architect Ami B. Young. The contract was let in 1853 and the new building opened in December 1857, with a post office on the ground level and the custom house operation on the floors above. *Courtesy of the author.*

captain, was pregnant. The February 18, 1857 *New York Times* reported that *Neptune's Car* entered San Francisco Harbor as a smart ship: "Those who saw her enter the harbor say that no vessel ever came into that port looking better in every respect." The beautiful Mary Patten gave birth to a son on March 10, 1857, and four months later, on July 25, Captain Patten died in a lunatic hospital in Somerville, Massachusetts. Sadly, though, Patten herself died of consumption at the tender age of twenty-four on March 17, 1861, in her native Boston, and nearly two years later, in February 1863, the seagoing life of *Neptune's Car* ended thousands of miles from her birth on the banks of the Elizabeth River. This magnificent clipper, the progeny of a Southern shipyard, was sold at auction to Barclay and Company of Liverpool for £8,000 sterling.

Before the Civil War, coal played little part in Portsmouth's trade; it was still being sold for twenty-five cents a bushel in antebellum newspaper advertisements. All firewood was brought to town in lighters or vessels and had to be landed at the wood wharf, located on the Portsmouth waterfront just south of King Street, which later became part of the Seaboard Railroad property. Firewood was weighed by the wharf master, who received, according to early historical accounts, six-and-a-quarter cents for each cord he weighed. The wood brought in by the cars was weighed on them. The first wood yard was not begun in Portsmouth until 1854. The *American Beacon*, a newspaper with the subtitle "the

The Norfolk Light Artillery Blues, shown here standing in front of the New York, Philadelphia and Norfolk Railroad warehouse at the foot of Brooke Avenue ca. 1890, dated to 1829. Second Lieutenant John T. Kevill, standing directly under the light, had been a powder boy on the CSS *Virginia* during the Civil War. *Courtesy of the author.*

Norfolk and Portsmouth Advertiser," stated in 1825 that Portsmouth was growing very rapidly, and from that time until the yellow fever epidemic in 1855, that growth remained steady; commerce flourished. The first railroad opened there in 1834, Richard Dale's house on Swimming Point was purchased for an almshouse and new streets and lots were added to the town, all spurned on by the trade coming to Portsmouth from the Elizabeth, which was choked with vessels of every description moving in and out of wharves on both sides of the harbor, and up and down the river's lengthy tributaries.

Norfolk's trade had shifted dramatically from a reliance on European trade to more coasting trade in the years prior to the Civil War. Of the ships in Norfolk's harbor on a given day in 1839, there would be ships from New York, other Northern ports of call, familiar parts of Virginia, Maryland and other Southern states, a few from the West Indies and none from Europe. Of the forty-one vessels entering the Elizabeth River from Northern ports in the early weeks of 1839, fourteen came in ballast, ten brought merchandise, five potatoes, three hay, two ice, one produce, one plaster, one oil and candles, one lime and potatoes, one hay and two fish and potatoes. Coastal trade more than made up for the loss of the port's European markets. The earlier introduction of steam-powered vessels, particularly New York packets running under steam power, made it possible for steamers to go up Virginia's winding rivers directly to wharves that had been largely inaccessible to ocean-going sailing ships with deeper drafts. Later, the *Norfolk Post* of September 27, 1865, would report that the introduction of steam made seacoast towns no longer necessary to commerce and, for the time being, the old town was left gradually to fall in ruin and decay on the small business and traffic of the immediate neighborhood. "Steamers that can take good direct to the point of destination on the rivers and bays, and receive their return cargoes at the same points," reported the *Post*, "possess a great advantage over the old sailing vessels, which were compelled to discharge their cargoes at the large harbors on the seacoast. This is the true cause of the gradual decadence of cities on the seacoast like Norfolk, which unlike New York, New Orleans, Boston, and other great centers of trade, had not became fully established as commercial marts before the era of railroads and steamboats." Clearly,

The Portsmouth Naval Hospital, sans dome, is shown ca. 1895. The hospital was begun in 1827 and completed in 1830. It remains the oldest naval hospital in the United States. Situated on the Elizabeth River and devoted to the treatment of sick and wounded sailors and marines, the hospital was built on the site of Fort Nelson of 1812 fame. Located in the corner of the grounds is a cemetery where Confederate and Union soldiers and sailors of other countries sleep side by side. Upon some of the tombstones are found names of the earliest ships of the United States Navy and battles in which these ships were engaged. *Courtesy of the author.*

The June 3–5, 1825 hurricane that struck Norfolk stayed over the town for twenty-seven hours as the storm passed to the east. Trees were uprooted. At noon on the second day, stores on the wharves were flooded up to five feet in depth. In an account of the storm, Ann Waller Tazewell, wife of then-Governor Littleton Waller Tazewell, noted that some vessels she saw pass rapidly by "were driven ashore at the Hospital Point." She compared the storm to the September 1821 hurricane, although all noted that the tides were higher during the June 1825 storm. "The whole Town Point to within a few feet of Main Street was overflown, as also was that part of town extending eastward from Market Place to the drawbridge," according to an account published in the newspapers.

This oblique view of the east portion of the Portsmouth Naval Hospital complex shows in the middle ground, from left to right, Medical Wards A, B and C, Portsmouth Naval Hospital Building and Hospital Point, and in the foreground, from left to right, the gardener's tool shed, service building, garage and Medical Officers' Quarters C and B. The photograph was taken with a view north from the roof of the 1960 high-rise hospital building. *Courtesy of the Library of Congress Historic American Buildings Survey/Historic American Engineering Record.*

given the prosperity being experienced by Richmond and other Fall Line cities before the Civil War, Norfolk needed to regain its footing in foreign trade. To those who recalled the Elizabeth River crowded with ships from foreign ports, it was a reminder that Norfolk had the best harbor in the United States. Enterprising merchants declared that the city's trade would be best served shipping products from the back country around the world, in packet lines controlled by her Norfolk merchants. But to do so would require avenues of commerce that extended to the west, enterprising merchants akin to Moses Myers and William Pennock and the money to back such enterprise.

The *American Beacon*'s editors could not have foreseen the devastating setback of the yellow fever epidemic of 1855. There had been mild yellow fever epidemics in Portsmouth and Norfolk in preceding years, most notably in 1795, 1802, 1821 and 1826, but they did not reach alarming proportions. Yellow fever had also not been the only disease to enter the Elizabeth River's harbor aboard ships. On December 6, 1746, a smallpox-infested ship from the West Indies arrived; it was ordered that an infirmary be established on the glebe land for the care of the afflicted sailors and for the protection of the rest of the population. This glebe, on the Western Branch of the river, was not the old glebe, which was sold in 1734; the glebe land was part of the seizure of the Reverend Charles Smith. Reverend Smith ministered to the Borough Church in Norfolk and to the entire Elizabeth River Parish from 1742 to 1761. In the latter year, when the parish was divided, Smith took over Portsmouth Parish, where he remained until his death in 1773. The borough council order of March 25, 1750, indicated that the limits and bounds of the borough went from the place called Town Bridge west northwest until merging with the head

of Boush's Creek to a marked pine between the property of Samuel Boush and Josiah Smith, thence down the west side of Boush's Creek to Town Back Creek.

The official chronicler of the 1855 yellow fever epidemic recorded that on July 8, 1855, "a perfect tremor of fear swept over the town when it was learned that a young workman had died of yellow fever in Gosport. It was Sunday, but the town council met in extraordinary session to hear the reports of various physicians who had attended the man." The victim, a Richmond machinist named Carter, had been working on the steamer *Ben Franklin*, a vessel that had come to Page and Allen's shipyard for repairs. The *Franklin* had been in the tropical waters of Saint Thomas, Virgin Islands, where a yellow fever outbreak was already raging, and was en route to New York before reaching the Elizabeth's expansive harbor on June 7 in distress. It was in the Elizabeth that the *Franklin* discharged its bilge water and opened its hold, releasing *Aedes eagypti* mosquitoes, which carried deadly "yellow jack"—the yellow fever. Evidence convinced the council that the ship was the source of infection and orders were issued to the town sergeant to have the vessel removed to quarantine. The *Franklin*'s captain, after much controversy and legal consultation, moved his ship out of the harbor. In the meantime new cases of yellow fever developed on Irish or Leigh's Row, just opposite the shipyard, on First Street. Irish Row consisted of eight tenements with two stories and basements, two rooms on each floor. At the time of the fever every room was said to have been the home of a large family, and pigs and calves, it is known, were kept in the basement rooms with the families. By July 27

This view of the Portsmouth Naval Hospital grounds to the east from the roof of the central powerhouse also shows the adjacent medical storage building and World War I tent camp. The photograph, originally provided by the Portsmouth Naval Shipyard Museum, is dated September 26, 1918. *Courtesy of the Library of Congress Historic American Buildings Survey/Historic American Engineering Record.*

the fever was rapidly spreading in Gosport, which was found to be in a filthy and crowded condition that certainly facilitated the disease's spread. Filth also abounded in the grog shops, kept in the basement of some of the tenements. The families occupying the row had not long been over from Ireland and were desperately poor. A newly organized sanitary committee decided that patients there were to be moved to healthier, cleaner quarters. Thus, a makeshift hospital was built in the town proper, where no case had yet to appear. Procuring the site for this hospital proved difficult, but one was eventually found near Portlock's, also known as Oak Grove, Cemetery. The hospital was not opened until the last day of July to receive patients, with Drs. George W.O. Maupin and John Trugien in charge, both physicians serving without pay. Dr. Maupin survived a bout of yellow fever, but Dr. Trugien did not, dying of the disease before the epidemic ended.

Every attempt was made to move patients from Gosport to the new hospital, but many would not budge. Reverend James Chisholm, rector of Saint John's Church, witnessed the resistance of Gosport residents to being taken to other quarters, recording an appalling picture in his diary of events that would later be included in historical accounts of the period.

Looking southwest toward Parkview Avenue and showing a portion of the cemetery, this picture shows construction of World War I emergency buildings; it is dated December 20, 1918. The original photograph was provided by the Portsmouth Naval Shipyard Museum. *Courtesy of the Library of Congress Historic American Buildings Survey/Historic American Engineering Record.*

"The wretched and squalid patients in Irish Row positively refused to leave their pestilential abodes," penned Chisholm. "These in number between two and three hundred reeking in nameless abomination of filth and stench, and exhibiting in their conduct to one another a hard heartedness of which we would not have dared believe human nature capable of under such circumstances: reveling, fighting and quarreling amongst the dying and over the dead; they refused to stir." Reverend Chisholm went on to write that Father Frances Devlin, pastor of Saint Paul's Catholic Church, had to be sent to Irish Row to use his official authority; he later succumbed to the fever that took many of his parishioners. In addition to the eventual movement of Gosport's Irish Row residents to the newly built hospital, Norfolk gave shelter to some of the families that had been evicted from Irish Row and quartered them in an equally rundown tenement on South Church Street called Barry's Row. It was there that the fever broke out in Norfolk on July 30, after which it spread rapidly throughout the city.

By August 1855 Portsmouth and Norfolk residents realized that the yellow fever had reached epidemic proportions. A delegation had been sent to Washington, D.C., to petition the secretary of the navy to temporarily turn over the naval hospital to Portsmouth for the use of yellow fever patients. The committee returned with news that the naval hospital was being made available for the use of the sanitary committee, but the navy's surgeon and staff would remain in charge of the premises. The committee's move had come too late for many, as hundreds of residents in Norfolk and Portsmouth left the epidemic-stricken towns

Located at Hospital Point, the Saunders Monument was erected as a memorial to Major John Saunders, commander of Fort Nelson in 1805. The view is looking northeast. The monument was designed by John Haviland, an architect from Philadelphia. Haviland also designed Portsmouth Naval Hospital. The cornerstone of Building Number One at the naval hospital was laid on April 2, 1827. It began treating patients three years later in April of 1830, or just as soon as the north wing was finished. Haviland directly oversaw construction, which was not finished until 1833. Half a million bricks from the Revolutionary-era Fort Nelson, positioned at that location since the Revolutionary War, were incorporated into the hospital. *Courtesy of the Library of Congress Historic American Buildings Survey/Historic American Engineering Record.*

by train and boat, and by mid-August it could be said that all who were able-bodied enough to do so had left the pest-ridden communities on the banks of the Elizabeth. Suffolk and Smithfield had quarantined against Portsmouth and Norfolk, it should be noted, and the stagecoach to Elizabeth City had been turned back when within ten miles of the town, with only the mailbags sent on. Worse yet, the boats to Old Point Comfort on Virginia's peninsula were the only means of going back and forth to leave the Southside in a hurry, and it took very little time for Old Point to be shut down to residents coming from Norfolk and Portsmouth. Residents desperate to escape the fever panicked and tried to make Old Point despite word that they would be turned back. Their worst fears proved true. Going to Old Point proved fruitless. The United States Army deployed a detachment of soldiers to its wharves, bayonets fixed, to order them back. A fortunate few took the Bay Line steamer from Old Point to Baltimore, where they were well received.

The cities of Baltimore and Philadelphia did come to the aid of yellow fever victims in Norfolk and Portsmouth, sending supplies of food and medicine, but also doctors, nurses and druggists, several of whom gave their lives aiding yellow fever patients. Reverend Chisholm reported, again in his diary, that at the lowest ebb of the epidemic came a sight he did not expect to see. "At this moment," he wrote, "an astonishing spectacle is presented to our gaze. A schooner under full sail is entering our harbor, probably bringing ice, for the supply in both cities has given out. There has been nothing seen like this for the last six weeks." On September 4 he wrote again that the Baltimore boat came into port, "among other things to land a load of coffins, and so great was the need for them that there was actually quarreling and fighting over them." But in the wake of the fever also came famine, a reality that Norfolk's and Portsmouth's survivors had already begun to experience as the veil of pestilence lingered. During this time provisions sent from Baltimore and Philadelphia saved many lives. There was a point at the peak of the epidemic when the city of Baltimore proffered Norfolk and Portsmouth residents a helping hand, should they come north to their city, promising clothing, bedding and provisions.

Portsmouth was generally cut off, however, from the outside world, even as residents recovered from the yellow fever epidemic and needed to go away from their city to recuperate further. Those who left for recuperative periods elsewhere had to travel a considerable distance on the old road to Suffolk, and at some point along the Nansemond River, take a rowboat to meet a small steamer that plied between Suffolk and Newport News, at which point they boarded the Bay Line steamer for points north in the Chesapeake Bay. The 1850 census indicated that Portsmouth had 8,000 residents, but it was estimated that the number of people in the city and its key areas such as Gosport had reached 10,000 by 1855. About 4,000 people remained in the town during the epidemic, the population divided evenly between white and black residents. Of this number 1,080 are known to have died of the fever. Across the river in Norfolk, about 2,000 died.

The yellow fever epidemic of 1855 was defined by the heroic acts and tragic sacrifices of many men and women, who were not forgotten as cold weather set in and the disease that had killed thousands took its leave from the shores of the Elizabeth. Within a year of the outbreak, the city of Portsmouth honored those who had come to its aid. Medals of gold were struck and presented to surgeons of the naval hospital who had rendered their assistance, including Drs. Lewis Minor, Randolph Harrison, James F. Harrison, Frank Anthony Walke, Thomas H. Steele and John C. Coleman. Drs. James Harrison and Minor had been presented medals by the French government in 1854 in appreciation of their care of yellow fever patients on the French man-of-war *Chimere*, which was anchored in the Norfolk harbor. On January 12, 1856, a party from Philadelphia arrived to escort the bodies of doctors and nurses of that city who had died aiding Portsmouth's fever victims. The Philadelphians who died in Portsmouth were Drs. Cortlandt Cole and Edwin Barrett; the nurses and druggists were R.W. Graham, Henry Spriggman, Singleton Mercer, E. Perry Miller, Fred Mushfeldt, Charles Shrieve, William Husen, Mrs. Clive Whittier and Lucy Johnson.

To the people of Portsmouth, who registered the first victims of the 1855 yellow fever epidemic, it was clear that the *Ben Franklin* had been the vector for the disease. Portsmouth physicians, knowing little then about the root cause of the fever, the *Aedes eagypti* mosquito, attributed "the germ" to the *Franklin*'s bilge water, which spilled into the Elizabeth River. Another point had been noted during the epidemic as well as in other epidemics of yellow fever that is worth noting here. Observers wrote of "a fly"—of an unusual kind—that seemed plentiful. The people along the river called them "yellow fever flies" and it was not uncommon for decades to follow for residents, particularly older people, to say, "That looks like a yellow fever fly."

CHAPTER FIVE
WAR ON THE RIVER

Unpopular British levies, particularly those involving taxation without representation, prompted strong response from communities along the Elizabeth River—just as strong as those well known in Northern colonies. The Boston Tea Party of December 1773 was the most prominent demonstration against English taxation on tea, but of lesser fame but no less significance was the Norfolk Tea Party, which occurred later than events in Massachusetts. In August 1774, the *Mary and John*, a merchant vessel, arrived in the Norfolk harbor bearing in its cargo nine chests of tea. Norfolk citizens held a large public meeting to protest against the importation of tea and made known their intention not to pay tax on it; the shipment was returned to England without ever being offloaded from the ship. Thus was the beginning of patriotic protests in the towns along the edges of the Elizabeth River.

At the outbreak of the Revolution, a fortification was built near Portsmouth for the protection of the harbor, and thereafter one near Norfolk, an earthwork, located directly across the river from the other. The land selected for the fort near Portsmouth was known as Windmill Point, owned by Robert Tucker, of Norfolk. Windmill Point was part of the patent of Joshua Curle, from whom Tucker bought it. When the purchase was made this tract was known as Mosquito Point, but the Tucker family, who owned the land for three generations, built windmills on it and thus the new name. The third Robert Tucker indicated in his will that he wanted the land sold to settle a gambling debt he had incurred while visiting Williamsburg. His wishes were not carried out. Windmill Point was not sold to settle the debt; in fact, it was not sold until 1749. The land was eventually occupied by Fort Nelson, built on part of the Tucker estate, later owned by his son-in-law, Thomas Newton, until 1799, when it was sold to the United States government. At the time John Murray, Lord Dunmore, bombarded the towns of Norfolk and Portsmouth, there

The Portsmouth Rifle Company was commissioned on October 29, 1801. This company was organized by Captain Jesse Nicholson, who was its first commanding officer. He was followed, in turn, by Francis Benson, Richard Kelsick, John Kay, James Jarvis, William D. Young, John P. Young, Nat Gayle and William P. Sanger, and in 1846 again by John P. Young. The company banner displayed their motto, "Don't Tread on Me," placed over a rattlesnake twined around a tree. Also on the banner was a staff with a liberty cap on it. This company was called to service during the War of 1812.

were two large bakehouses and several windmills on the point and all of them were damaged by Dunmore's cannon. The bakehouses were used to bake hard bread or hardtacks that were supplied to ships of the period, particularly those making long voyages. The fort itself had a parapet fourteen feet high and fifteen feet thick. It was surrounded by strong dovetailed timbers, the middle part filled with earth that had been hard rammed. There were forty-two embrasures in the fort, and there were a number of heavy cannon and much ammunition as well as large stores of food on hand. British Admiral Sir George Collier would later observe that when the order came for the English to evacuate Portsmouth in May 1779 all attempts by his troops and battery failed to demolish Fort Nelson, and it had to be set on fire to accomplish any damage whatsoever to the structure of the fort. After the British had gone and the Americans returned to Portsmouth the fort was hurriedly rebuilt, but there were no further details of it until 1794, when the United States government sent an engineer, John Jacob Ulrich Rivardi, to lay off plans for the fortification of the harbor and the United States Congress appropriated $3,000 to rebuild Fort Nelson and construct Fort Norfolk. From the *Simmons Directory of Norfolk*, dated 1809, it is learned that Fort Nelson was a star-shaped fort on the water's edge, occupying about six acres of ground and holding a commanding position guarding the harbor. At the time the directory was published, the fort was undergoing extensive repairs; a bomb-proof magazine and forty-two cannon were added.

Over the years several locations were designated as the site of Fort Nelson, but a survey made by a Revolutionary War soldier, Jesse Nicholson, provided the actual position of the fort. It stood on the point, but farther down than the present-day naval hospital buildings. A small creek separated the land on which the medical director's house and officers' houses stood from the point on which the original naval hospital building is situated. The land on which these quarters stood was not then the property of Fort Nelson or the federal government, but was owned by Richard Nestor, whose claim to it remains an obscure fact of history. Nestor had bought the land from Thomas Edwards across Island Creek or Swimming Point in 1787, but Island Creek separated the two tracts. The land, when first purchased by the government, was used to house a powder magazine. Island Creek was named for an island of small size that stretched out east of the hospital bridge and for a smaller one in the middle of the creek. There was no connection between Fort Nelson and Portsmouth. No bridges had been built and to reach it from the town, it was necessary to go by way of Fort Lane. When the government took over the site for the naval hospital, Fort Lane was claimed as private property and the United States had to buy the lane. While there are no physical vestiges of the fort that remain on the hospital site today, nearly six

The post at Great Bridge, located on the Southern Branch of the Elizabeth River, was established on February 5, 1781. The post plan was wrought by Royal Engineer James Straton. *Courtesy of the Library of Congress Geography and Map Division.*

hundred thousand bricks from the fort were used in building the original naval hospital building, as was much of the fort's stone. The walls of Trinity Episcopal Church, rebuilt in 1829, were made from the rubble of Fort Nelson.

The first and most important battle of the Revolutionary War in Virginia took place at Great Bridge, then in Norfolk County. According to later accounts in the *Virginia Gazette*, John Murray, the fourth earl of Dunmore ("Lord Dunmore"), after defeating the Virginians at Kempe's

Landing, now Kempsville, moved ten miles south to Great Bridge on the Southern Branch of the Elizabeth River. Great Bridge was the shipping point to nearby Norfolk of shingles, tar potash and turpentine from the Carolinas. The battle of Great Bridge had a significant influence on events that followed. Lord Dunmore, Virginia's last royal governor, had fled Williamsburg, taking refuge with the British fleet then in the York River. By July 1775 this fleet was in the Elizabeth River off Norfolk, where Dunmore planned to make his headquarters for the retaking of the Virginia colony. The Virginia Convention determined that Dunmore would not be permitted to take Norfolk, and Virginia troops were ordered there to rid the communities on both sides of the Elizabeth River of Dunmore's presence. Among the forces dispatched to face off with Dunmore were the Culpeper Minutemen and militia from Fauquier and Orange Counties, composing the Second Virginia Regiment under Colonel William Woodford. Among those from Fauquier were Major (later Colonel) Thomas Marshall and his son, John, not yet a captain and who was later the first chief justice of the United States Supreme Court. As the

Virginia troops moved toward Norfolk, they were joined by others from points closer at hand, including companies from Isle of Wight, Elizabeth City, Princess Anne and Norfolk Counties and also North Carolina. The Norfolk County militia was under Colonel John Wilson. Dunmore's forces included the Fourteenth Regiment of Infantry and some local Tory units, the Queen's Rangers under Colonel Jacob Ellegood of Princess Anne, the Norfolk Militia of Loyalists under Colonel Alexander Gordon, who was a physician, and the Ethiopian Corps, composed of fugitive slaves.

Dunmore and his commanders made a strategic blunder that cost the British a stronghold in Southeastern Virginia: they overlooked their lines of communication with the outside world until it was far too late to stop the course of events that would unfold at Great Bridge. The route by which the Virginia troops approached Norfolk extended northeasterly from Suffolk, brushing the northern edge of the Great Dismal Swamp at Shoulder's Hill, then turned southeasterly, crossing Western Branch near what is today Bower's Hill. The Virginians then passed by Batchelor's Mill on Deep Creek, Tucker's Mill on Willis Creek, Corbury's Mill and Bell's Mill, then passed Great Bridge Chapel to arrive at the village of Great Bridge. The road then crossed the Southern Branch of the Elizabeth River, circled the head of the Eastern Branch at Kempsville, crossed the forked head of Broad Creek at Moore's Bridges and entered Norfolk on Princess Anne Road and Church Street. Had the detachment of the Fourteenth Regiment, quartered at Andrew Sprowle's shipyard at Gosport since early November, been positioned six miles away at Batchelor's Mill, where the road crossed Deep Creek, the line of approach to Norfolk could have been cut off. But Dunmore had turned his efforts to fortifying the northern edge of Norfolk, and by the time he realized that Great Bridge was of key importance, Woodford's men were already on their way.

The Southern Branch of the Elizabeth River at Great Bridge flowed between swamps with a bridge across it, hence the name of the village, which had to be approached on either side by a causeway. The bridge connected two solid riverbanks that, due to the swampy nature of the streams draining them, were more akin to islands. At the south end of the bridge were the yards and warehouses from which were loaded lumber, cooperage, shingles and numerous other products bound for Norfolk and Portsmouth. Facilities at the south end of the bridge were connected to the village of Great Bridge, which had previously been known as Bridgetown. The British tried to fortify the north causeway, building a stockade fort and bringing in two twelve-pound cannon. The Virginians camped on the grounds of the Great Bridge Chapel on their arrival and from there put up breastworks athwart the south causeway head and on the solid riverbank on their left flank. Woodford's men numbered about one thousand; the British had fewer. A snapshot of the situation as it stood in early December

In the early nineteenth century the professional separation between architecture and engineering was much less marked. Architects such as Benjamin Henry Latrobe and Robert Mills were involved in the designs of canals, shipyards and railroads as well as buildings.

1775: a stalemate in which neither side was willing to cross the bridge or causeway to engage in an all-out fight.

The stalemate lasted until Thomas Marshall's black servant feigned desertion to the British and told them the Virginians numbered only in the hundreds. On the morning of the ninth, the British began their attack with a grenadier company of the Fourteenth Regiment, followed by infantry, Tories and the Ethiopian Corps. The British carried planks to lay over the partially dismantled bridge, over which they drug two field artillery pieces, advancing over the south causeway toward the Virginians' breastwork. The Virginians skillfully laid down fire as the British came within fifty yards of their positions; additional assistance came from Colonel Woodford's reinforcements, who flanked the enemy. The battle lasted a little over half an hour, but in their victory, Woodford's men had made it impossible for Dunmore to hold Southeastern Virginia from a headquarters in Norfolk, although Dunmore, as retribution, would be certain the town of Norfolk was destroyed before his departure. Colonel Woodford's Virginians, reinforced by Colonel Robert Howe's North Carolinians, quickly turned from Great Bridge and took the undefended road through Kempe's Landing to Norfolk. Dunmore and most of the Tories took refuge onboard the ships of his fleet and accompanying vessels. After Major General Charles Lee was put in command of the Southern Department, posts were established where it was believed attacks were most likely to occur.

The Revolutionary War caused much damage to the communities that dotted the Elizabeth River's main stem and branches. Before Christmas 1775 Lord Dunmore brought seven of his best ships within range of Norfolk and covered the town with heavy fire from what is now the area of the Berkley Bridge to the western end of Main Street. The HMS *Liverpool* remained off Church Street, flanked by the HMSs *Otter, Kingfisher, Eilbeck, Dunmore, Mercury* and *William.* The few Norfolk residents left in the town at that point had been finishing preparations for Christmas when Dunmore's ships sent up a barrage of bar shot, chain shot and grape that tore through the trees and buildings located nearest the waterfront; he burned thirty-two houses, for what reason was never clear. British troops were considered likely to attempt an amphibious landing after such an attack, a preemptive blow before a more devastating attack to come. Colonel Edward Stephens and two hundred Culpeper Minutemen charged Dunmore's landing parties, forcing them back to their ships. The minutemen's success was short-lived. On January 1, 1776, Dunmore bombarded the city and a number of buildings caught fire; women and children fled to the Borough Church, protecting themselves under the eaves from the hail of shells raining down on the town. Early accounts of the bombardment state that eighty houses were burned in Norfolk and the American troops burned

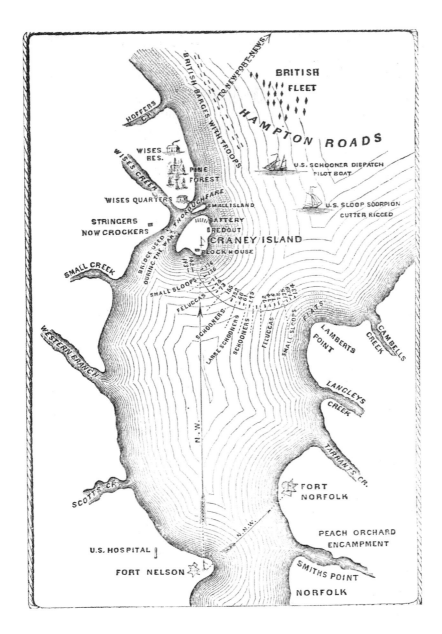

This is the plan of operations at Craney Island in 1813. *Courtesy of the* Pictorial Field-Book of the War of 1812, *by Benson J. Lossing, published 1868, from chapter XXX, "Predatory warfare of the British on the coast."*

the rest. Eyewitness accounts of the burning of Norfolk and the earlier battle of Great Bridge—certainly not unprejudiced—found their way into London newspapers during the months of March and April 1776. A letter penned on Christmas Day 1775, from the HMS *William* "off Norfolk," told readers that the British had been obliged to abandon their fort at Great Bridge and Norfolk and take shelter on their ships. It was then estimated that there were two thousand Patriots under arms in the borough and "they having stopt [*sic*] all supplies to the ships, it is imagined the ships of war will destroy the town in a few days. The *Liverpool*,

Kingfisher, and *Otter*, are now laying before the town for that purpose. Lord Dunmore has done everything for the cause of his King and country which man could do," wrote the English soldier. This account went on to relate that "the Provincials set fire to every house, the owner of which was supposed to be well affected to government. Upwards of three hundred houses were burnt down in the fine town of Norfolk." On January 9, 1776, a midshipman onboard HMS *Otter* wrote a letter that appeared in the March 5 *London Chronicle*:

> *The detested town of Norfolk is no more! Its destruction happened on New Year's Day! About four o'clock in the afternoon the signal was given from the* Liverpool, *when a dreadful cannonading began from the three ships, which lasted till it was too hot for the rebels to stand on their wharfs. Our boats now landed and set fire to the town in several places. It burnt fiercely all night, and the next day; nor are the flames yet extinguished; but no more of Norfolk remains than about twelve houses, which have escaped the flames.*

An issue of the *Virginia Gazette*, published on January 18, 1776, printed onboard Lord Dunmore's ship, HMS *Dunmore*, read like an official report. It was stated that Captain Henry Bellew of the HMS *Liverpool*, soon after his arrival on scene, demanded under flag of truce whether his ships would be supplied; they would not be. Thus, it reportedly became necessary for Bellew to destroy that part of the town next to the water from which the ships were being fired on. Bellew gave notice to Norfolk's inhabitants that Lord Dunmore's ships would bombard the town, a warning largely for the benefit of women and children. Shortly thereafter, at about four o'clock in the afternoon, men were landed from boats to set fire to the houses next to the water. Since there was a moderate offshore breeze, it was believed that only the waterfront area would be destroyed. Such was not the case. "The Rebels cruelly and unnecessarily completed the Destruction of the whole Town, by setting Fire to the Houses in the Streets back, which were before safe from the flames," reported the *Virginia Gazette*. Among the critical facilities destroyed, according to this report, was a distillery, "a Work of great Value and publick [*sic*] Utility with a large stock of Rum and Molasses."

A Commission of Investigation was sent to Norfolk by the Virginia government in 1777 to determine who had actually burned the town. The report revealed that 51 houses had been burned by January 2, 1776, and that 32 of those had been destroyed by Dunmore the previous November. Another version of the report on October 10, 1777, on record in the *Journal of the House of Delegates* for 1835, stated that 54 houses had been

THE U.S. FRIGATE UNITED STATES CAPTURING H.B.M. FRIGATE MACEDONIAN.
Fought Oct 25 1812.

The USS *United States*, a 1,576-ton sailing frigate, was built at Philadelphia as one of the first warships of the new United States Navy. Commissioned in July 1797, she cruised heavily during the 1798–1800 quasi-war with France, taking several prizes. The *United States* was active again between 1812 and 1813 against the British, and captured the Royal Navy frigate HMS *Macedonian* on October 25, 1812. That capture is depicted in this hand-colored N. Currier lithograph dated between 1835 and 1856. *Courtesy of the Library of Congress Prints and Photographs Division.*

burned by the second of January, without attempting to specify when. Both versions concur that 863 houses were burned by Virginia troops between the bombardment and January 15, and 416 more were burned by order of the Virginia Convention in February 1776 "to deprive Dunmore of shelter." The truth as to who burned Norfolk lies in the aforementioned Commission of Investigation reports.

In Portsmouth there was little damage from Lord Dunmore's ships, but the people were nonetheless infuriated. Major General Charles Lee came later, sent by the Committee for Safety, and made every effort to drive out the Tory element from the town. Lee was first commander of the Continental army's Southern Department. Though history assigns complete blame for the firing of Norfolk on Lord Dunmore, it is actually not known for certain whether he alone is responsible, or if American Patriots under the command of Colonel Robert Howe set fire to the city to prevent it from quartering British troops in the town or serving as a provisioning hub for the British fleet. Of the burning of Norfolk by the British, General George Washington wrote from his headquarters to Jeremiah Wadsworth on May 25, 1779. The letter's draft in Alexander Hamilton's handwriting provided the following direction:

> *It is probable the enemy may have it in view to hover along the Southern coast and endeavor by sudden incursions to destroy our stores dispersed about in that quarter. I am therefore to request, as they may otherwise have it in their power to do us a great deal of mischief, that your attention may be fully turned to this matter and that all the stores in your department at places accessible to the enemy may be immediately removed to other places of greater*

The mast house in this undated photograph was located on the west side of Warrington Avenue between Shubrick and Breeze Streets on the Norfolk Naval Shipyard before being razed in 1992 for new construction. Also known as Building 28, the mast house was built between 1828 and 1836 and served as the shipyard's mast construction facility between 1836 and 1904. The building was historically associated with the shipyard's early role in the construction of wooden sailing vessels for the United States Navy. Historic documents suggest that this load-bearing masonry building was supported by piles driven into the riverbed to a depth ranging between forty and twelve feet. *Courtesy of the Library of Congress Historic American Buildings Survey/Historic American Engineering Record.*

security. The Head of Elk [Elkton, Maryland] appears to be an unsafe deposit for considerable quantity and should be attended to without delay. The injury we have just sustained [Norfolk's burning] should be a caution to us carefully to avoid accumulating stores on the sea coast and on the borders of navigable rivers, where the enemy's shipping and troops can easily penetrate. There are strong reasons to believe the plan of this campaign will be to distress the Country and destroy our supplies by desultory operations along our coast.

After the burning of Norfolk, posts were thrown up at points considered most likely to be attacked. In Norfolk County, where many inhabitants of destroyed Norfolk had fled, protected locations included Great Bridge, the overland key to the northern part of the county and Princess Anne; and at Ferry Point, formerly known as Powder Point and, later, Berkley, at the junction of the Eastern and Southern Branches of the Elizabeth River. Dunmore took the *Liverpool* and *Otter* up the Southern Branch above Deep Creek, and established a camp at Tucker's Mill. The *Dunmore* was anchored on the other side of the river near the ruins of a distillery that the Virginians had destroyed. In August 1776 Dunmore left the river's shores never to come back.

In the years immediately preceding the Revolutionary War, tradition that has come down through the years indicates that the Gosport shipyard had been used by the ships of the British king as a careening ground long before Portsmouth was in existence; thus Dunmore's residency there during the war was not unexpected. Portsmouth had barely been established when Andrew Sprowle, an enterprising Scot merchant, purchased from Thomas Bustin a tract of land across Crab Creek in Portsmouth and built on it not only his home, but also warehouses and tenements, thus giving

Portsmouth its first "suburb" of Gosport. This pivotal place on Elizabeth River, Sprowle's marine yard, was his crowning achievement. Into the early twentieth century Sprowle's original yard was known as the oldest part of the modern navy yard. Under Sprowle, Gosport took little time to become a flourishing village and the marine yard was so much in favor with British ships that the government took it over in nearly all aspects and appointed Sprowle as navy agent here in 1762, an office that he held until the outbreak of the Revolutionary War. The British officially established the yard as a government facility on November 1, 1767, under the Union Jack. Thus, Sprowle's yard predated the creation of the United States Department of the Navy by thirty-one years. It has since experienced the impact of ten wars in which it was three times burned; from its staff have flown flags of four sovereign powers.

The Gosport Navy Yard was greatly affected by the beginning of the Revolution. At that time Great Britain was preparing to enlarge and equip the yard, and it appeared for a time that the British could hold the port, which was a Tory stronghold in the beginning of the war. It had become the last seat of royal government in Virginia in May 1775, when Lord Dunmore came quietly up the river on the *Hoebuck* and moored at Sprowle's wharf. The great warehouses were filled with Dunmore's soldiers, who used them as barracks. Sprowle was one of Dunmore's most intimate friends, giving him a fitting welcome. Dunmore and his men remained at the Gosport Navy Yard for six months and then, on January 1, 1776, bombarded Norfolk and Portsmouth. The bombardment greatly angered the populace of both towns; Sprowle fled to Dunmore's ships for safety and his home and the home of other prominent Tories were burned on the order of Major General Lee. The colony of Virginia immediately took possession of all property owned by Sprowle, confiscating, in particular, his marine yard, which was stocked with materials needed for warfare. Although Virginia held title to the land after the Revolution, the Gosport shipyard continued to operate as a private enterprise. The property was not converted to military use because the public would not support maintenance of a standing armed force. This policy resulted in the eventual disbanding of the Continental and Virginia navies after the war with Great Britain.

By June 1776 Virginia had been declared an independent state and that October the Virginia Convention directed the commissioners of the Virginia Colonial Navy to provide materials for building two thirty-gun frigates and four galleys and authorized the enlistment of crews for these ships to serve three years from March 1, 1777. The commissioners of the navy at this time were Paul Loyall and David Stoddard. It was estimated that it would require 200 oak and 150 pine trees to build these two ships. The contract for furnishing this timber was awarded to Thomas Talbot

Fort Norfolk is located at the point on the Elizabeth River that was once commonly known as The Narrows, where the river extends out to the east to form Norfolk's inner harbor. The fort is opposite the Portsmouth Naval Hospital, also once the site of Fort Nelson, a Revolutionary War fortification.

and the price was \$3,333.33. Virginia would build the largest navy of the American colonies and also operated several shipyards for this purpose, all in an effort to protect its shores and vast network of inland waters from being taken by the British. Of these yards, Gosport was the largest and would play a key role between 1776 and 1782. But in May 1779, a British fleet under Vice Admiral Sir George Collier made its way up the Elizabeth River carrying troops commanded by Major General Edward Matthews. Debarking his men from their transports anchored in the Elizabeth River, Matthews attacked and occupied Portsmouth's lightly defended Fort Nelson and burned the Gosport Navy Yard; this action was protested strongly by Vice Admiral Sir George Collier, who wanted to take possession of the yard for its facilities. Collier considered the yard the largest and most important in America—and extremely convenient. Writing of the incident later, he noted the five thousand loads of fine seasoned oak knees for shipbuilding, an infinite quantity of plank, masts, cordage and numbers of beautiful ships of war on the stocks, which were set ablaze. Existing records of the Virginia navy tell an interesting story of the Revolutionary War. Of the ships built at Gosport, it is known that the *Sally Norton* was fitted out there for one of the most daring exploits of the war: under Captain John Cox, of Portsmouth, the *Sally Norton* went to Bermuda to aid in the capture of powder that was brought up to Williamsburg.

The British expedition that sailed from New York on October 16, 1780, was commanded by Major General Alexander Leslie, with orders to carry out Major General Lord Charles Cornwallis's recommendation that a division be posted in Chesapeake Bay to facilitate his operations. "Untill [*sic*] I am certain that Earl Cornwallis sees the propriety of establishing a post on Elizabeth River, which I heartily wish his Lordship may find expedient to do, I do not of course think of adding to the Corps already under his Orders," wrote Sir Henry Clinton to Lord George Germain on November 10, 1780. Leslie arrived at Portsmouth from New York with orders to proceed immediately up the James River and seize or destroy any magazine the enemy might have at Petersburg or Richmond. Major General Leslie was provided a formidable assemblage of ships and men to achieve his military objective. His naval escort, under the command of Commodore Clark Gayton, included his flagship, the forty-four gun HMS *Romulus*; two frigates, the HMS *Blonde* and the HMS *Iris*, both thirty-two guns each; three sloops of war, the HMS *Delight*, HMS *Halifax* and HMS *Otter*, all sixteen guns; the ten-gun schooner HMS *Apollo*; two row galleys and several smaller vessels. Also accompanying Leslie's naval contingent was the twenty-gun privateer *Arbuthnot* under the command of John Goodrich, whose participation had been prompted by Sir Henry Clinton's agreement to appoint a vessel for the removal of Goodrich's wife and son's family, who had been in Virginia since the beginning of the war. Aboard the transports were the Eighty-Second, Eighty-Fourth and part of the Seventeenth Regiments of British troops; the Hessian Regiment von Bose; the Royal Provincials, a Loyalist regiment commanded by Colonel Edmund Fanning; about one hundred horses of the Queen's Rangers; a detachment of Highlanders; and a company of German Jagers.

Leslie's force of twenty-five hundred troops arrived in the Chesapeake Bay on the twentieth of October, landing parties at Lynnhaven to gather intelligence. By the reaction of the Virginians questioned by his troops, Leslie concluded that his attack was no surprise. He thus concluded that it would be unwise to advance to Petersburg and Richmond. The British troops aboard Gayton's ships never made it farther than Smithfield, where they met Virginia militia in the area. Rather than risk direct confrontation with the Virginians, Leslie went for his secondary objective and landed without opposition in Portsmouth on November 15, 1780, in order to assist Cornwallis in the Carolinas. While quartered in Portsmouth, Leslie would

UNITED STATES STEAM-FRIGATE "MERRIMAC." B a Navy Yard.

On April 20, 1861, as Virginia's Confederate forces took over the Gosport Navy Yard after its evacuation by Federal authorities, they found, among other valuable items, the hulk of the steam frigate USS *Merrimack*. Though burned to the waterline and sunk, the large ship's lower hull and machinery were intact and salvageable. During the balance of 1861 and the first two months of 1862, the Confederate States Navy raised, dry docked and converted her into a casemate ironclad ram, a new warship type that promised to overcome the Union's great superiority in conventional warships. The *Merrimack* was placed in commission as the CSS *Virginia* in mid-February 1862, her armor virtually impenetrable to contemporary gunfire. She carried ten guns of her own, a seven-inch pivot-mounted rifle at each end and a broadside battery of two six-inch rifles and six nine-inch smoothbores. Affixed to her bow would be an iron ram, allowing the *Virginia* to be employed as a deadly weapon. This wood engraving of the United States steam frigate *Merrimack* appeared in *Frank Leslie's Illustrated Newspaper* on November 29, 1856. *Courtesy of the Library of Congress Prints and Photographs Division.*

maintain a strong post, though short-lived. To the astonishment of Leslie and the American commander, Brigadier General Peter Muhlenberg, Cornwallis ordered Leslie to evacuate Portsmouth; the British were gone shortly after their arrival. The day after Leslie's Portsmouth landing, November 16, Lieutenant General Friedrich Wilhelm Rudolf Gerhard August von Steuben, one of the fathers of the United States Army, arrived in Richmond to take command of all military forces in Virginia. Leslie's presence had precipitated a change in leadership of the Virginia militia.

The British fleet sailing at-will into the Chesapeake Bay and up the Elizabeth River had not stopped, but with Leslie's departure, the Virginia General Assembly, which had convened in October 1780, turned its attention to prosecution of the war. Among the assembly's priorities was protection for American ships traversing the Chesapeake Bay and for inhabitants living along the shores of Virginia's navigable rivers and bays. The Elizabeth River was high on the list. Twenty-seven British ships arrived in the Chesapeake Bay carrying an expeditionary force commanded by traitor and newly appointed brigadier general in the British army, Benedict Arnold, on December 30, 1780. Arnold had initially been instructed to complete a strong garrison and fortifications at Portsmouth. He was to concentrate on destroying any supplies or equipment that would be useful to the Continental Southern army, which had been very active in the Carolinas by this point in the war. After occupying Portsmouth and building a defensive fortified line with several redoubts around the town, Arnold's force went up the James River and burned parts of Richmond after weak defense from the Virginia militia in the area. The same fate was in store for Petersburg, as warehouses and public buildings were burned to the ground. From Portsmouth Arnold established a base for British vessels blocking the mouth of the Chesapeake Bay, effectively bringing commerce on the bay to a halt. Among the ships affected by the British blockade was the privateer *Marquis Lafayette*, which was being fitted out for her maiden voyage. The *Marquis Lafayette* was owned by Willis Cowper and Company, merchants from Suffolk. In October 1780, on the eve of the *Marquis*'s launching, Leslie's invasion force had landed near Portsmouth and overrun the surrounding countryside. To keep the ship out of British hands, her owners hurriedly launched the privateer and scuttled her in eighteen feet of water, but the British discovered the *Marquis Lafayette*'s location, pumped her out and towed her back to Portsmouth. Leslie's men never finished fitting out the ship; they evacuated and the *Marquis Lafayette* was scuttled again and sunk, this time in proximity of Gosport on the Elizabeth River. Once Leslie was completely gone, the Cowpers refloated the *Marquis Lafayette* and towed her back to Nansemond to step her masts, complete her rigging and fully equip the privateer for sea. Captain Joseph Meredith of Hampton, Virginia, was put in command of

TERRIFIC ENGAGEMENT BETWEEN THE "MONITOR" AND "MERRIMAC"

This depiction of the first battle of the ironclads was published by the McCormick Harvesting Machine Company on March 2, 1891. *Courtesy of the Library of Congress Prints and Photographs Division.*

the fated ship. In the final days of December 1780, just before the *Marquis Lafayette*'s departure, Arnold's invasion fleet unexpectedly sailed through the Virginia Capes, eventually settling into Portsmouth and blockading the bay. Despite British fleet presence in the bay, Meredith and his crew slipped through the blockade and moved past the capes to begin a rich career as privateers.

Writing from New Windsor on February 19, 1781, to Jean B. Donatien de Vimeur, Comte de Rochambeau, General George Washington remarked that the subsequent destruction of a detachment under the command of General Benedict Arnold was of "immense importance to the welfare of the Southern states" to the point he had resolved to attempt it with a detachment sent in conjunction with the militia. Washington addressed the need for French Admiral Charles Rene Dominique Gochet Destouches to detach part of his naval squadron from Newport, Rhode Island, to provide support for American and French forces in the Chesapeake Bay. "If Mr. Destouches should send any ships into the bay on the principle of cooperation it will be necessary," wrote Washington, "that a light frigate should come up to the Head of Elk to protect the passage of the troops across the bay." But part of Destouches's fleet was already in the Chesapeake. Commodore Arnaud de Tilly's squadron had slipped by the British blockade at Newport, Rhode Island, on the thirteenth of February 1781 and headed for Virginia to pursue General Arnold's forces, which had gone south in December 1780. De Tilly entered the Chesapeake Bay and anchored in Lynnhaven Bay. Though Arnold sent his ships up the Elizabeth River where the water was too shallow to permit the heaviest French ship to

This Jamestown
Exposition souvenir
postcard depicted
the CSS *Virginia*
passing Fort Norfolk
on March 8, 1862.
The image is from
an original painting
by B.A. Richardson;
the postcard was
published by the
Merrimack and
Monitor Postcard
Company of
Norfolk, Virginia.
Courtesy of the author.

get within range, Commodore de Tilly captured the forty-four-gun frigate
HMS *Romulus*, and two privateers. One of the French frigates actually ran
aground giving chase, but de Tilly had done what he had been asked to
do—remain in the Chesapeake Bay no longer than necessary; the frigate
that had run aground was a casualty of unfortunate circumstance. General
Charles Rene D. Gochet Destouches, Comte de Rochambeau, reported to
General Washington that "our vessels were unable to enter the Elizabeth
River because there was not water enough for ships of sixty-four [guns];
that their cruise resulted only in the capture of *Romulus*, of forty-four, of two
privateers of eighteen and fourteen, of a few other transports, one of which
is of considerable value, and of about five hundred prisoners."

George Washington wrote Comte de Rochambeau on February 22,
1781, concerning Washington's intention to keep Arnold bottled up in
the Chesapeake Bay using the French fleet. On Comte de Tilly's return
from the Chesapeake in mid-February, a further expedition from Newport
to Virginia was pondered. "The letters, found on board the vessels taken
by Mr. de Tilly, have decided Mr. Destouches to follow at full the plan
given by your Excellency, and to risk everything to hinder Arnold from
establishing himself at Portsmouth in Virginia…Mr. Destouches is arming
with the greatest diligence the forty-four-gun ship that was taken, and he
hopes that with the frigates, will be able to go up the Elizabeth River, Mr.
Destouches will protect this expedition with his whole fleet," Rochambeau
wrote Washington on the twenty-fifth of February, three days later. "Your
Excellency has given me orders to join thereto 1,000 men. I will send
1,120, all my grenadiers and chasseurs will be there, which corps shall
be commanded by the Baron Antoine de Viomenil. I will join to them,
four four-pounders, four twelve-pounders, and four Obusiers. The navy
will furnish the twenty-four-pounders, if necessary, but it is presumed that
against earthen entrenchments, the twelve-pounders will be sufficient."

The ruins of the
United States Navy
Yard, Norfolk,
Virginia, were
photographed by
Alexander Gardner
in December 1864.
Courtesy of the Library
of Congress Prints and
Photographs Division.

Washington's concern that Arnold would take Portsmouth was founded, as evidenced by Rochambeau dispatching Destouches yet again to the waters of the Chesapeake Bay to confront the British fleet. This would become the first battle of the Virginia Capes. The second would not occur until September 5–9, 1781, when the most well-known naval engagement of the American Revolution, on which the success of the defeat of Cornwallis at Yorktown hinged, was fought. The battle pitted Admiral Comte François Joseph Paul de Grasse, Marquis de Grasse Tilly's twenty-four French ships of the line against nineteen British ships under Admiral Thomas Graves. The consequence of Graves's defeat was the isolation of Cornwallis's forces at Yorktown.

When the war ended in 1781, the Virginia and Continental navies disbanded, ships were disposed of and personnel sent home. Gosport Navy Yard was used largely to service merchant vessels carrying the American flag to ports of the world. The appearance on the scene, however, of Barbary pirates, who seized unprotected American ships, cargoes and men at will, aroused considerable public opinion against these acts of piracy. The subject of raising an American naval force was brought to the attention of the United States Congress as early as 1791, but it was not until March 27, 1794, that Congress passed "An Act to Provide a Naval Armament." This act authorized the construction of six frigates, the first American naval vessels built since the Revolution. The act

founded the United States Navy, although, there being no Department of the Navy at that time, the new navy was administered by the secretary of war. The federal government owned no shipyard, thus it was decided to lease the necessary facilities and build the ships under the supervision of their captains and government-employed naval contractors. Navy agents in charge of the shipyards and yard clerks were also appointed. The names eventually given to the frigates were USSs *United States*, *Constitution*, *President*, *Congress*, *Constellation* and *Chesapeake*. Of the six, the *Chesapeake* was to be built at Gosport. Each frigate was originally designed with forty-four guns, but it was finally decided that the last three—*Congress*, *Constellation* and *Chesapeake*—would be constructed with only thirty-six guns.

By an act of the Virginia General Assembly, passed in May 1784, Joseph Jones, Paul Loyall, William Lee, Mann Page, Benjamin Harrison, Thomas Nelson, Miles King, Henry Tazewell and John Kearnes were appointed commissioners for the sale of certain public lands belonging to the commonwealth, among which were the lands commonly called Gosport, adjoining the town of Portsmouth, except such part thereof as in their opinion might be necessary for the use of the public, taking care to lay off the said lands into lots, so as to make them uniform with the town of Portsmouth. It would seem, however, that the commissioners never procured a meeting of a sufficient number to act, in consequence of which the law was amended in October of the same year to place the appointing of the commissioners in the hands of the governor, by and with the advice of the council. The commissioners were also empowered to sell such portions of the Gosport lands as the governor and council should direct, after having laid them off into lots and convenient streets. The persons appointed and who acted as commissioners for the carrying out of the law were William Ronald, Edward Carrington and Benjamin Temple. The marine yard was retained for the benefit of the commonwealth, though no use is known to have been made of it until the year 1794. The lands adjoining the yard were sold in 1785. A large portion of them, in addition to the yard, was afterward purchased by the United States. In a report submitted to the House of Representatives by Secretary Henry Knox, dated December 27, 1794, after stating the character (armament, as such) that was required of the vessels ordered, the materials to be used and how they should be obtained and prepared, he goes on to say that in order to distribute the advantages arising from the operation, and as to ascertain where the work could be executed to the greatest advantage, the building of the ships had been ordered in six different ports of the Union; one of the ports selected was Portsmouth, Virginia, where a frigate of thirty-six guns, the USS *Chesapeake*, would be laid down. In 1794 the shipyard at Gosport was, indeed, leased from the Commonwealth of Virginia by the federal government. Captain Richard Dale, already famous as John Paul Jones's lieutenant aboard the *Bonhomme Richard*, having himself taken a prominent role in the fight with HMS *Serapis*, a British frigate captured by the Americans during the war, was placed in charge of the construction department at Gosport, and William Pennock was made the navy agent. Pennock, by virtue of his office, became custodian and administrator of the entire yard. While John Morgan had been provisionally appointed constructor, he was succeeded by Josiah Fox. This method of managing the yard was actually retained until about 1810.

The *Chesapeake*'s construction would drag on for years. An agent was immediately dispatched to Georgia for the best pine, and by December 1795 two-thirds of the white oak frames were cut and shaped for the *Chesapeake* and most of her material, including cedar and the pine from Georgia, was in store, but its keel, due to many delays, had not been laid when peace was declared in 1796 between Algiers, home to the Barbary pirates, and the United States. Further work on the *Chesapeake* was thus suspended. But work commenced again when threat of war with France was believed imminent. Congress created the Department of the Navy on April 30, 1798, and the laying of the keel for the *Chesapeake* occurred on the tenth of December that year. The new Navy Department ordered the purchase of some vessels and the construction of others. Richard Dale was put in command of one of them, the *Ganges*, the first of these vessels that sailed from Gosport in 1798. The *Chesapeake*, the first United States Navy ship built at Gosport, was launched the following year on December 2, 1799, commissioned in May 1800 and placed under the command of Captain Samuel Barron during

As another war with Great Britain seemed certain, in 1807 preparations were made to fortify and repair Fort Norfolk. At this time a heavy chain was stretched across the river from the fort to Fort Nelson to prevent British men-of-war from entering Norfolk's inner harbor. Chains of this nature were used in port communities up and down the East Coast as a protective measure. A chain was actually stretched across the Hudson River, in fact, forged of iron links, each two feet long and weighing between 140 and 180 pounds. Anchored to shore by huge blocks of wood and stone, the chain was attached to logs and floated out into the river, where it ran, in the case of the Hudson, between West Point and Constitution Island.

The steamer USS
Fort Donelson, the
former Confederate
blockade runner
Robert E. Lee, is
shown anchored in
the Elizabeth River
in December 1864.
*Courtesy of the Library
of Congress Prints and
Photographs Division.*

the quasi-war with France. Given her early fits and starts, observers called the *Chesapeake* an unlucky ship from the moment of her inception. When launched in 1799 the *Chesapeake* had cost $220,678.80. Her first cruise was under Samuel Barron to the West Indies in 1800, where she captured the *Young Creole* and remained off Bermuda until recalled in 1801.

The first secretary of the navy, Benjamin Stoddart, recognized that it would be more cost effective for the navy to purchase its own shipyards rather than rent space at privately owned facilities. He convinced the United States Congress to fund the purchase of six established shipyards, including Gosport. The federal government purchased the 15.25-acre shipyard at Gosport from the Commonwealth of Virginia for $12,000; the deed was executed on June 15, 1801, by James Monroe, then governor of Virginia. This tract was situated in the northeast corner of the present shipyard; the first buildings at Gosport constructed to accommodate naval ship construction were a spar shed, a timber shed and riverfront wharves. Prior to 1827 other buildings were enjoined to the original structures, including an office; a commandant's house; marine barracks; a brick storehouse, which stood near the First Street gate; a powder magazine; a smithery; and two large covered building-ways known as ship houses. In the center of the yard stood a large two-story frame building used as a marine hospital, and also as a rigging loft and gunners' storeroom. The original boundaries of the Gosport Navy Yard were the Southern Branch of the Elizabeth River to the east, Lincoln Street to the north, Second Street to the west and a creek, now Slip Number One, to the south.

In 1803 the United States Congress appropriated $10,000 for improvements to the Gosport Navy Yard, specifically for the construction of a warehouse and timber shed. The superintendent of the yard, Daniel Bedinger, subsequently authorized construction of a brick perimeter wall, which marked the northern and western boundaries, while wooden docks, requiring frequent repairs, stood along the waterfront. Bedinger also authorized a brick dwelling for himself, another timber shed and a warehouse. The wall was finished in 1805, thus enclosing the entire plant with the exception of the east side that was bounded by the river. A United States Marine guard, ordered to the yard in October 1801, was detached in August 1804, but was reestablished in November 1807. The commandant's house can be attributed to William Pennock, who had it completed in 1804. By order of Pennock, the first commandant to occupy the house completed in 1804 was Samuel Barron. Squadrons and ships under the command of Richard Dale, Thomas Truxtun and Stephen Decatur were frequently repaired or fitted out at Gosport in the years leading up to the War of 1812, and other vessels, renowned in their day, were built or reconstructed at Gosport during this early period. Prior to 1810, the yard's administrative officers, who had sometimes been civilians, had been called superintendents and navy agents, but on July 7, 1810, Commodore Samuel Barron was appointed the Gosport Navy Yard's first commandant.

In early June 1807 the *Chesapeake* came to Portsmouth to be fitted out and while there yet another stroke of bad fortune happened. Just before June 1807, two French frigates made their way into Norfolk to repair damages incurred during a storm. The French and British were at war, but since the United States did not take sides, both countries' vessels were permitted in and out of American ports for legitimate repairs, but not to fight or hide from an enemy force on the high seas. When the British navy discovered the French ships were in Gosport Navy Yard, the admiralty dispatched the fifty-gun HMS *Leopard* to lay in wait off the Virginia coast to destroy the French frigates as they made their way out to sea. It happened that the USS *Chesapeake*, a thirty-six-gun frigate under the command of Commodore James Barron, was deploying to the Mediterranean Sea to become the flagship of her squadron—and she had onboard seven men who had sworn that they were Americans and so were taken on as part of the crew. As the *Chesapeake* passed from the Elizabeth River into Hampton Roads and out to the bay, the captain of the *Leopard* demanded to search the American vessel for deserted British seamen. When Commodore Barron refused, the British fired on the *Chesapeake*, boarded her and took off four seamen—three Americans and one Brit— as deserters. In the course of this incident eighteen sailors were wounded and three killed onboard the *Chesapeake*. What came to be known as the

After the Confederacy evacuated Norfolk in May 1862, the Hampton Roads anchorage filled with Union naval forces waiting to enter Norfolk waters. The ammunition schooners shown here in December 1864 moved their cargo up and down the Elizabeth River. These schooners were photographed off historic Fort Norfolk by one of Mathew Brady's field photographers. Fort Norfolk was an ammunition store for the Union army, thus the vessels were a frequent sight in close proximity to the fort's wharf. *Courtesy of the Library of Congress Prints and Photographs Division.*

Chesapeake-Leopard affair only exacerbated tensions with Great Britain, which still held out hopes that the new United States would fail and come back to the motherland. The indignity of taking American sailors from one of their vessels, particularly in coastal waters, inflamed the American public. Newspaper editorials and public debates urged Thomas Jefferson, president of the United States, to take retaliatory action. Nowhere was this outcry louder than Norfolk, where the town's citizens were up in arms to go after the British for their attack on the *Chesapeake*, which had limped back into the protected waters of the Elizabeth River.

The *Chesapeake-Leopard* affair was not Barron's finest hour. At the time of the incident Stephen Decatur was commander of the United States Navy's force in Norfolk. Four days after the event, on the twenty-sixth of June, Decatur was also given command of the *Chesapeake*; Commodore Barron was relieved of command and a court martial followed in 1808. Secretary of the Navy Robert Smith wrote Decatur on July 3, 1807, that by the letter of June 26, "I gave you command of the frigate *Chesapeake*. You are still to command her, and in addition you are to command all gun boats now at Norfolk, including those lately built there, and all the gun boats lately built at Hampton, and in Mathews County, Virginia." The postscript to this event, however, became as famous as the *Chesapeake-Leopard* incident: the duel between Barron and Decatur. One of Decatur's naval duties as commander of the force in Norfolk was to sit on the board of Barron's court martial. Although Decatur and Barron had been friends, Decatur agreed to a verdict that expelled Barron from the navy for five years. This event began the thirteen-year dispute that was fueled by comments Decatur made regarding Barron's crushing defeat at the hands of the *Leopard*, and which would not end until Barron killed Decatur on the dueling grounds in Maryland in 1820.

As for the *Chesapeake*, once repaired, this unlucky ship was hard pressed to find a crew. Officers, too, were prejudiced against her. Even the newly promoted Captain James Lawrence, who commanded the *Chesapeake* during the War of 1812, and on her met his death, was originally opposed to commanding the fated frigate. When the *Chesapeake* met HMS *Shannon*, captained by Philip B. Vere Broke, off Boston on June 1, 1813, she was no match for the more experienced British crew. Captain Lawrence was mortally wounded by small-arms fire and taken below deck, but not before declaring the famous phrase that has carried through the United States Navy's history: "Don't give up the ship!" HMS *Shannon* came alongside, a skirmish on the *Chesapeake*'s deck ensued and she was captured and taken into Halifax, Nova Scotia, as a prize of war. The *Chesapeake*, however, had not yet reached the worst of her humiliation; her end would be ignoble. The *Chesapeake* was sold to a miller in Wickham, in Hampshire, England, who used her timbers to build his flour mill. They could be seen with the battle scars for many years to come.

Tensions quickly turned into more menacing blockades and seizures. The British navy was more than willing to escalate hostilities, blockading American goods bound for Europe and the Caribbean along the traditional trade routes and conscripting sailors off American ships. The British embargo, coupled with crop blight in Princess Anne County, led to the opening up of areas west of the county, making farming so unprofitable that John Randolph, the great Virginia statesman, observed, "Instead of a slave running away from his master, the master felt like running away from the slave." The *Chesapeake-Leopard* affair, often called the Douglas War for Commodore John E. Douglas, commander of the British fleet in Hampton Roads in the summer of 1807, turned out to be the opening salvo of England's renewed aggression toward her former colonies. As time would tell, British sailors and marines would embark on a direct attack of Craney Island in the Norfolk harbor in an attempt to break American defenders and take the town, an important port of commercial trade.

Tolerance for British bad behavior waned quickly; American trade from the Elizabeth River had been severely curtailed by English warships. A war message was dispatched to the United States Congress from President James Madison on June 18, 1812. Norfolk and Princess Anne Counties, harangued regularly by the British fleet from coastal and inland waters, were already on Admiral Sir John Bolase Warren's list to be taken. Early in January 1813 it was known that the British squadron, carrying a

Naval Medical Center Portsmouth is the oldest continuously running hospital in the U.S. Navy. The cornerstone for the country's first naval hospital was laid on April 2, 1827. John Haviland, a Philadelphia architect, designed and oversaw the construction of the hospital. The hospital admitted its first patients in 1830, although only one wing was ready for occupation. The first hospital building, which stands at the opposite end of Hospital Point, was finally completed in 1833.

The USS *Texas*, photographed in 1907, was a participant only years earlier in what ranks as one of the greatest sea fights in American history as part of the flying squadrons that engaged Spanish Admiral Pascual Cervera y Topete in the Battle of Santiago on July 3, 1898. During the heat of battle, it was Captain J.W. Philip of the *Texas* who is quoted as saying, "Don't cheer, the poor devils are dying." The keel of the *Texas* was laid for this twin-screw battleship on June 1, 1889, at the Norfolk Navy Yard. On June 28, 1892, the ship was launched with much fanfare as she became the United States Navy's first battleship. *Courtesy of the author.*

significant number of troops, had landed at Bermuda with ships stocked with bombs, rockets and ammunition. On hearing these reports in the newspapers, Americans were certain that this well-provisioned squadron was making preparations to attack key Southern cities. Warren's fleet anchored in Lynnhaven Roads on February 4, 1813, to enforce Great Britain's declaration that all American ports and harbors in and around the Chesapeake Bay would be blockaded. The British squadron, among them two line-of-battle ships, three frigates and a tender, took possession of Hampton Roads and it was clear that an attack on Virginia was imminent. Norfolk had been opposed to a war with England, but its citizens were willing to uphold the honor of the nation if needed. Most residents along the Elizabeth knew all too well that the United States Navy was incapable of matching British naval power; there were no frigates or ships-of-the-line to defend the harbor.

During this time, Gosport Navy Yard had little protective force with the exception of that provided by a flotilla of small gunboats that were inadequately manned. The frigate USS *Constellation*, sailing from Washington, D.C., had been prevented from putting to sea through the Virginia Capes by a large British blockading squadron. With great difficulty the *Constellation* was kedged to a position in the Elizabeth River opposite Fort Norfolk, where it furnished detachments of seamen and marines to reinforce the harbor's weak defenses. Capture of the yard, which would almost certainly have led to the fall of Portsmouth, would be prevented with the aid of local militia and regular forces.

Before the attack, Warren took his squadron back to Bermuda and returned in early June with more reinforcements. With him was the 102nd Regiment of Infantry, the Royal Marine Brigade, two companies of Canadian Chasseurs and about eight hundred foreign renegades and prisoners, called Chasseurs Britannique, under the command of Sir Sidney Beckwith. The entire force numbered about five thousand men, commanded by Admiral Warren and Rear Admiral George Cockburn. Hampton Roads had been blockaded since early February, a situation that strangled off Norfolk's vibrant maritime trade. To counter Warren's forces, militia were mustered along with some Regulars and the officers and crew of the USS *Constellation* and numerous gunboats. The Regulars and militia were posted in the immediate vicinity of Norfolk and Portsmouth, largely at Forts Nelson, Norfolk and Barbour. The *Constellation* rode at anchor between the two cities. The gunboats were moored east of Craney Island in a crescent shape extending from Lambert's Point across the channel. Craney Island, where the battle would be fought, lay just north of Portsmouth near the mouth of the Elizabeth River, commanding the approach from Hampton Roads. Craney Island was then very small; at that time about 900 yards long and 233 yards wide. There was no house on it then and but one tree, a lone cedar. It was separated from the mainland by a narrow inlet, which could be forded at low tide—or even half tide. "This," observed one witness to the battle, "was the most exposed of our military line—the nearest in contact with the enemy—a position of great importance as a key to the harbor and it was [so] indispensable that the enemy should possess it before they could reach the ultimate objective of attack—the cities of Portsmouth and Norfolk." A small breastwork had been thrown up on the east end of the island, but it had not been completed. There, on Craney Island's incomplete breastworks, were three cannon: two twenty-four-pounders and one eighteen-pounder.

On June 21, 1813, the whole force on the island consisted of two companies of artillery, Captain Arthur Emmerson's Portsmouth Light Artillery and Captain Richardson's light artillery, under the command of Major James Faulkner of the Virginia State Artillery; Captain Roberts's company of riflemen; and 416 infantry, commanded by Lieutenant Colonel Henry Beatty and Major Andrew Waggoner. The British had anchored their ships east of the mouth of the Nansemond River, roughly five miles from Craney Island. American defenders took immediate action to reinforce the troops on the island with forces that could be spared from anywhere they could be found. General Robert Barraud Taylor came with great speed from Fort Norfolk and ordered Captain Richard Pollard of the United States Army, who was stationed there, to send 30 men of his company; Taylor would add another 30 men and 2 officers. This detachment with Lieutenant Johnson of Culpeper and Ensign Archibald

Atkinson of Isle of Wight were promptly at Fort Norfolk, from which they embarked in boats wildly cheered by the garrison at Craney Island upon their twilight arrival. In the meantime, General Taylor had applied to Captain John Tarbell of the USS *Constellation*, urging that he add such forces to those on the island as he could spare from the frigate, including officers, sailors and marines. As a result of this request, Captain Tarbell dispatched First Lieutenant B.J. Neale with 100 officers, midshipmen and sailors, and Lieutenant Henry B. Breckinridge reported with 50 marines. This contingent arrived under the cover of darkness. The whole force on the island from that fateful day forward numbered 50 riflemen, 416 militia infantry of the line, 30 Regulars of the United States Army, 91 state artillery, 100 sailors and 50 marines. About midnight on the twenty-first, the fire from a sentinel, thinking that he saw a boat pass between the island and the mainland, gave the alarm. Troops were called to arms and remained on duty until dawn the next day, when they were dismissed. The sentinel had made a mistake; no ship had passed and troops had been unnecessarily scrambled to meet an enemy who was not yet ready to pounce.

Just as Craney Island's troops stood down on the morning of June 22, a horseman dashed across the inlet at low tide to report that the enemy was landing in great number at Major William Hoffler's, about two miles west of the island. Quickly every man reached his post. As sunrise came the enemy's boats could be plainly seen passing from ship to shore, landing great numbers of troops. The three heavy cannon that had been placed in Craney Island's unfinished battlement on the east end of the island were promptly brought to the west by order of Major Faulkner, who had already had four six-pounders moved to meet the enemy. At this time there had been a low breastwork temporarily erected and the cannon were mounted immediately to the rear of it. These seven cannon were all that composed the American battery. Behind the low breastwork were arranged the six four-pounders to the north, next to them the eighteen-pounder and on the left of the battery were placed the two twenty-four-pounders.

There was no flagstaff on the island, but a long pole was soon erected and the American flag nailed to it. The pole was mounted in the breastwork. Major Faulkner assigned the guns: one twenty-four-pounder to Captain Arthur Emmerson and the other to Second Lieutenant Thomas Godwin, who was assisted by Captain Thomas Rourke of the merchant ship *Manhattan* that was blockaded in the Elizabeth River. Rourke was also a former member of the Portsmouth Light Artillery. The four six-pounders were put under Lieutenant Parke G. Howle, Corporal William Moffat, First Sergeant William P. Young and Sergeant Samuel Livingston. The whole battery was thus arranged under orders and direction of Major Faulkner of the state artillery.

Battleships are moored alongside the United States Navy Yard Norfolk's coal piers in 1907. The destroyer USS *Stewart* (DD-13) is foreground and the receiving ship USS *Richmond* can be seen across the Elizabeth River (right). Commissioned on December 1, 1902, the *Bainbridge*-class *Stewart* had been placed in reserve at Norfolk, but was recommissioned in 1907 in the Atlantic Fleet. The *Richmond* had been launched at the navy yard as a wooden steam sloop in 1860, but in 1887 was completely overhauled, and by October 7, 1890, began its service as a training ship. When the picture was taken, she was serving as an auxiliary to the receiving ship *Franklin* until the end of World War I. *Courtesy of the author.*

As the Americans were making their order of battle, the British had landed about twenty-five hundred infantry and marines. They could be distinctly seen marching and counter-marching on the beach; the weather was calm and clear, and the sun shone directly upon them. After forming a column they took up the line of march, but due to thick underbrush near the beach, they were soon lost to view. Two hours later the British reappeared from the woods on the point of land made by the junction of Wise's Creek and a narrow inlet that separated the island from shore called the Thorofare; they were intent on reaching the island on the south. This land assault was led by Colonel Sir Sidney Beckwith. To divert the attention of the Americans from their movement, the British fired Congreve rockets on Craney Island. Faulkner's battery directed fire at the British column, by then in sight, sending off canisters and grape shot in the direction of the enemy, who took cover in the woods and a house belonging to Captain George Wise. The shot directed at the house through the trees tore off the roof and collapsed the chimney. There was no safe retreat for the British, who fell back with many killed and wounded, two officers among them. Moving beyond the range of the Americans' cannon and rifle, the British waited for the movement of their barges south of the island, the attack now coming from the water. By this time two American guns had been disabled. Fifty of the largest British barges filled with men from their ships, containing roughly fifteen hundred

The six-thousand-pound anchor of the USS *Merrimack* was dredged from the mud of the Southern Branch of the Elizabeth River during operations to deepen the channel near the United States Navy Yard Norfolk in April 1911. Fifty years before, when Federal troops evacuated Norfolk, the gunboat USS *Pawnee* was sent to destroy the *Merrimack* and other ships still in their berths, the dry dock and the navy yard's stores. The *Merrimack* was set afire and went adrift in the water. Blazing and sending up columns of smoke, she drifted across the Southern Branch into shallow water on the opposite shore. There she burned to her berth deck, filled with water and sank. She was raised by the Confederates, who converted the *Merrimack* to the CSS *Virginia. Courtesy of the author.*

sailors and marines, began to approach within range of American artillery. They were advancing toward Craney Island in column order in two distinct divisions, following the channel, between the island and mainland, led on by Admiral Warren's barge, the fifty-two-foot-long HMS *Centipede*, rowing twenty-four oars. There was a brass three-pounder—a "grasshopper"—in the bow under command of Captain John Martin Hanchett, of HMS *Diadem*, and a natural son of George III, born some time after his marriage to the queen. This line of barges was under the overall command of Captain Samuel J. Pechell, commander of Admiral Warren's flagship HMS *San Domingo*. In both arms of the British attack, about twenty-five hundred men were committed. Captain Hanchett is said to have been sitting in the stern of the green-hulled *Centipede*, holding an umbrella over his head as a mark of disdain for the Americans. The barge was otherwise crammed with seventy-five men.

While the British were approaching, Captain Emmerson asked Major Faulkner if the enemy had drawn close enough to American cannon. Faulkner replied that they were not, "let them draw a little nearer." When the time had come, Emmerson called to his men to fire. The British, with nowhere to go, beat a hasty retreat. The barges, however, continued to advance in the face of destructive fire until they could no longer maintain formation under fire. The *Centipede* took particularly heavy fire and was sunk by shot from one of the Americans' guns that passed through the boat as the barge tried to maneuver to the north of Craney Island; Hanchett was severely wounded in the thigh, but removed by his men before he could be taken prisoner. The *Centipede* and many other barges in the British landing party were so damaged that it was with great difficulty that they were kept afloat. The Americans kept up the round shot until the British got beyond the reach of their guns. As the British made their retreat, Lieutenant Neale sent a detachment of his sailors to haul up the boats that had sunk and to secure the British sailors and marines who were making to the shore for safety. A detachment of sailors under the command of Midshipman Bladen Dulaney and Acting Master George F. de la Roche rounded up prisoners and the *Centipede* was drawn up. After the *Centipede* was made watertight, Acting Master de la Roche was given the honor of taking it to the navy yard at Gosport, where workers found the brass three-pounder, a number of small arms and a quantity of pistols and cutlasses, placed there for use had the British succeeded in making their landing. Twenty-four of her men had initially been brought to Craney Island with the vessel and surrendered themselves as prisoners of war. Among them was a Frenchman, with both legs shot off. He died a few hours later. After the battle thirty deserters came to the island, too.

In this important engagement—one of the most significant of the War of 1812—in which fewer Americans than British were actually engaged, British soldiers, sailors and marines had been led into combat by brave, yet inexperienced, officers. Opposed by 544 Virginia militia and volunteers, 30 soldiers of the Regular army and 150 sailors and marines, the enemy had 200 killed, wounded and drowned, exclusive of prisoners and deserters. Captain Samuel Travis, commander of the revenue cutter *Surveyor* who, prior to the action, had been taken prisoner himself by the British, conversed freely with British officers after the engagement at Craney Island. He arrived in Norfolk on his parole on August 6, 1813, with valuable observations of the battle from the British perspective. He noted that the British found fire from the battery at Craney Island far more destructive than they had anticipated. A single shot, as he learned from the British, cut off the legs and feet of nearly a whole boat's crew. Another shot struck among a crowd of soldiers and killed 7. Nothing, he added, could exceed the confidence of the enemy

In 1827, in response to An Act for the Gradual Improvement of the Navy of the United States passed by Congress, work was begun on Dry Dock Number One at Gosport Navy Yard, today the Norfolk Naval Shipyard, one of the first two built in the United States. The dry dock was constructed of Massachusetts granite and completed in 1834. Before completion, the dry dock was opened on June 17, 1833, and the USS Delaware became the first ship to be dry docked in the United States. Since that time Dry Dock Number One has had a long and illustrious history.

in taking Norfolk on June 22 except their astonishment and mortification at being beaten, noted the *Norfolk Herald* of August 10, 1813.

Admiral Warren's official report of the British repulse at Craney Island, dated onboard the ship *San Domingo* on June 24, 1813, set forth the necessity of his obtaining Craney Island to enable warships to proceed up the narrow channel toward Norfolk. The report acknowledged the failure of the attempt and his repulse by the militia of Virginia and the seamen assisting them. He complimented his men and officers for their bravery and expressed his regret that Captain Hanchett, who had volunteered, was so severely wounded. The Virginia militia sent some of the prisoners and deserters to a penitentiary at Richmond until arrangements could be made to send them on to Annapolis; in the interim, they were important sources of information for the Americans. Prisoners and deserters told their captors that the British had been so confident of victory that they brought their dogs and shaving kits as well as extra clothing to the fight. The French prisoners stated that Cockburn assured them that they would have no difficulty getting the island and when that was won they could march right to Norfolk and have three days of pillaging and a reward of twenty-five pounds sterling if they exerted themselves. He also informed the Americans that Cockburn had told his troops of the beauty of the women in Norfolk and promised to place them at their disposal. When the British finally left the Elizabeth, beaten by the Virginia militia, they were fond of a song that went something like this:

> *Ross, Cockburn, Beckwith, Warren*
> *With twenty thousand men,*
> *Came sailing into the Chesapeake*
> *And just one half went back again.*

Other stories would emerge after the battle of Craney Island. A strange incident was the discovery after the actual fighting of a leg with a silk stocking still on it. For many years no one knew to whom it belonged. By chance a British officer who had served with the 102nd Regiment of Infantry knew the story behind the leg. He noted that a British officer, who wanted to see what was going on among the American troops on Craney Island, took his spyglass and climbed a pine tree. As the column passed him, an officer observed to him that he had better look out for the enemy, who might knock him off his perch. The officer in the tree purportedly told them, "Oh, I'm too high for them." Just at that moment a ball struck the tree, bringing it down. In the fall the officer's leg was so badly injured that it had to be amputated on the spot. Almost immediately, however, the officer was shot and another ball struck four men nearby, killing two of them. By this time the captain called to his men to push on.

One of the saddest events of this period was the assassination of Lieutenant William Ball Jr. of the Fourth Virginia Regiment. He was stationed with his company at Fort Nelson in 1813. That May he started from the fort to carry orders to Norfolk, and was accosted by a sentinel. He answered but the sentinel was not satisfied with Ball's response, called again and started toward him. The sentinel fired and Ball was fatally wounded; this was an intentional murder in daylight. Ball was well liked and highly respected. He was an artist who specialized in etching and line engraving. He was buried in Portsmouth at the old Methodist church on Glasgow Street, and, in addition to the men of many companies encamped in the vicinity who were ordered out for his funeral, there was an enormous gathering of civilians. The murderer was sentenced to eighteen years in prison. A marble slab was placed over Ball's remains by his fellow soldiers. It bore the following inscription:

In memory of William Ball Jr., of the Winchester Rifle Company, (late adjutant in the 4th Regt. Va. Mil., in the service of the United States) who was inhumanly shot by a sentinel at Fort Nelson, on the 24th day of May 1813. He was born in Winchester, Frederick County, the fourteenth day of October 1792.

As a son dutiful and affectionate, as a friend faithful and sincere, as a man scrupulously honorable. He was endowed with talents of a superior order, in an evil hour cut off in the morning of a military career.

His companions in arms of the 4th Regt. as a lasting testimony of their high respect for his virtues have erected this monument.

In 1815 the newspapers of the day reported the death of Captain William Miller of Gosport, in Halifax, Nova Scotia. Captain Miller had been captured by the British and remained in Halifax as a prisoner of war; the report came over two years after his capture. In 1854 friends and admirers of Captain Edward Carter met at his home located just outside Portsmouth on land opposite Fort Norfolk, bordering on the river. The meeting had been convened to present a cane to Captain Carter in appreciation of his services at the battle of Craney Island. The cane, carved from a piece of the USS *Constellation*, was inscribed with the following: "Young America to one of its old defenders." It was capped with a gold top. Captain James Jarvis, a veteran of the Craney Island battle, was chairman of the presentation committee; Claudius Murdaugh, a prominent Portsmouth lawyer, delivered the address, telling all in attendance of Carter's heroism during the battle to stave off defeat at the hands of the British in 1813.

Much was also owed to the hero of Craney Island, Captain Arthur Emmerson, and the Portsmouth Light Artillery, whose roster also included First Lieutenant Parke G. Howle; Second Lieutenant Thomas Godwin, Nansemond; First Sergeant William P. Young; Second Sergeant William Drury; Third Sergeant James B. Butt; Fourth Sergeant Samuel Livingston; First Corporal William Moffat; Second Corporal Daniel Cameron; Third Corporal John M. Kidd; and Privates Richard Atkinson, William Barber, Edward Carter, Benjamin Cox, James Deale, George Evans, T.L. Emmerson, James Foster, John Purdie, James Hughes, Philip Hockaday, William Hoffler (the younger), Richard Keeling, Watson Kelly, John Lawton, Aaron McAdow, Abner Nash, Lane Owens, George Pell, John Pully, John Roper, Francis Lousedo, James H. Simmons, Nicholas Scott, George Sweeney, Nathaniel Walker, John Newell and Joseph Whiterock. When the Civil War began, the name of this company was changed to the Grimes Battery.

Among the most important figures who plied the Elizabeth River in the early nineteenth century, and whose services were much in demand during the War of 1812, was Captain William Tee, a resident of Portsmouth. Tee was hired by the United States government as sailing master in the navy and made chief pilot of the fleet, which consisted of the frigate USS *Constellation*, some gunboats and smaller vessels and barges. One of Tee's duties during the war was to superintend the blockading of the Norfolk harbor, sinking wrecks in the channel to prevent the approaching enemy's vessels from successfully navigating their way to attack the cities of Norfolk and Portsmouth. When the war was over Captain Tee was again employed by the government to lift the wreckage out of the harbor, clearing the channel for navigation. When the first light boat was placed at Craney Island, Tee was put in charge of it, and held the position for over thirty years. Tee's home in Portsmouth stood on the northwest corner of Washington and London Streets, on the site later occupied by Saint John's Church. He died in 1849 at the age of ninety-one and was buried in Cedar Grove Cemetery.

After the War of 1812, expansion and improvement took place at the Gosport Navy Yard. This was a period marked by a number of significant events. The keel of the ship-of-the-line USS *Delaware*, the first of its kind ever built at Gosport, was laid in the summer of 1817; it was launched on October 21, 1820. The HMS *Alert*, the first British man-of-war captured in the War of 1812, was assigned to the yard in June 1818 as its first receiving ship. Three years later, in August 1821, a school for midshipmen was established at Gosport onboard the forty-four-gun USS *Guerriere*, with Chaplain David P. Adams in charge. The school was the product of

The United States
Coast Guard
Headquarters,
United States Navy
Yard Norfolk Annex,
is shown here, ca.
1920. *Courtesy of the
author.*

yard commandant Commodore Lewis Warrington's vision. Warrington
was stationed in Portsmouth frequently, and made his home in the town,
building a brick house on First Street near the old timber dock. It was
occupied by his descendants for many years. A member of Saint John's
Church, Warrington presented the congregation with a font, the pedestal
made from one of the live oak stanchions of the old USS *Constitution.* The
bowl, too, was live oak. When the original Saint John's was razed, the font
and bowl passed to Dr. Gray Holladay. During this time the Gosport Navy
Yard supplied other naval establishments with timber, cordage and other
naval stores readily available in the communities along the Elizabeth River
and its tributaries. A second house for the commandant of the Gosport
Navy Yard was built on Lincoln Street in 1824, and two others on the
same street were added two to three years later. Few of the buildings now
standing antedate the burning of the yard in 1861.

Importantly, in 1825 Secretary of the Navy Samuel Southard authorized
a study of the navy's shore facilities to identify potential sites for the
department's first two dry docks. The cost of land acquisition required
for dry dock construction persuaded Southard initially to abandon the
project. Plans for navy dry dock construction were revived by arguments
presented by the commandant of the Gosport Navy Yard, Commodore
James Barron. Barron argued that construction delays at the yard were
due to the lack of a dry dock. Water, and the toredo worms that inhabited
it, led to the rapid decomposition of wooden wharves, which in turn
left submerged remains that impaired navigation. The following year, in
1826, following a survey of Portsmouth, New Hampshire; Boston; New
York; and Gosport, Congress selected the Boston and Gosport shipyards
as the locations of the United States Navy's first dry docks. The necessary
improvements to the yards were inaugurated on March 3, 1827, when
Congress passed "An Act for the Gradual Improvement of the Navy of
the United States," which provided the navy with a half-million dollars per
year for a period of six years to upgrade facilities.

The Gosport site was expanded. The navy's agent, a Mr. King, reported
on March 25, 1827, that "the lands from Jefferson Street, along the line

of Third Street to the county road, and thence down to the water, could be purchased for $7,825." King was authorized to purchase the parcel and to procure as much land to the south of the yard as he deemed necessary. The Board of Naval Commissioners developed a plan for the expansion of the Gosport yard during the winter of 1827, predicated on a facility survey conducted by Loammi Baldwin Jr., considered the father of American civil engineering, and son of noted engineer Colonel Loammi Baldwin. It was the younger Baldwin who accepted the appointment of the United States government in 1827 to construct the two great works of his career—the naval dry docks at Charlestown, Massachusetts, and at Gosport. Forty-three town lots were subsequently bought by the Gosport navy agent between 1826 and 1829. The total purchase price was $23,622.

In November 1828 development plans for the Gosport Navy Yard were approved and work began. The plans included reclaiming parts of the Elizabeth River and the timber dock, lining the fill with stone walls and constructing new buildings on the reclaimed land. Building 28 was constructed as the mast house, and built almost entirely on land reclaimed from the river. The construction contract records for Building 28 were not found; however, the construction contract records for masonry work on Building 29 name local masons Jefferies Wilkman and John A. Metz in June 1829; the craftsmen may have worked on Building 28 as well. Construction estimates for Building 28 were not prepared, "as it was out of our power to come to anything like the precise cost of such an edifice in such a place; the site being, with the exception of a few feet on the west side, covered by the river, and the bottom of unequal tenacity; the piles, in some places, driving forty feet and in others twelve or fifteen…additional expense has also been incurred, by laying the second story floor on trusses instead of beams, by which stations or pillars, are dispensed with; throughout its whole length, their whole space saved, and an uninterrupted passage over the whole lower floor secured," according to a federal government report on expenditures and estimates for the years 1836 and 1837. The mast house was completed at the cost of $101,004.74. Building 29, a boathouse located west of Building 28, also was completed at that time. The timber dock was under construction. Two ship houses, office buildings located in the vicinity of the north wall, the commandant's house and sections of the marine barracks were the only pre-1827 buildings retained in the shipyard expansion project. After 1836 the antebellum development of the shipyard progressed slowly.

Begun in 1827 and finally completed in 1834, Gosport's dry dock, Loammi Baldwin Jr.'s masterpiece, was built of huge blocks of Massachusetts granite and cost $974,365.65, a large sum in that time period. This dry dock is still in daily use, only the caisson having been

The battleship USS *New York* (BB-34) was in the United States Navy Yard Norfolk's Dry Dock Number Four, then one of the world's largest dry docks, undergoing remodeling and modernization post World War I, ca. 1920. During her World War I service, *New York* was frequently visited by royal and other high-ranking representatives of the Allies, and she was present for one of the most dramatic moments of the war—the surrender of the German High Seas Fleet in the Firth of Forth on November 21, 1918. As a last European mission, *New York* joined the ships escorting President Woodrow Wilson from an ocean rendezvous to Brest en route to the Versailles Conference. *Courtesy of the author.*

replaced as required. Before the dry dock was formally completed, it was christened on June 17, 1833, by the reception of the ship USS *Delaware*, the first vessel to be dry-docked in the United States. The ceremonies, in keeping with the importance of the occasion, were attended by many national and local dignitaries and attracted widespread attention. A snapshot of the yard at this time would reveal four hundred men working there building the *Delaware* and the *New York*. The *New York* was never finished and still rested in the stocks in 1861; it was set on fire in April of that year. On completion the *Delaware* bore a figurehead that represented Tecumseh, Indian chief of the Delaware tribe, which had been carved by a Portsmouth carver, William Luke, who did much carving of this kind for the United States Navy. It was considered a masterpiece; the *Delaware*'s figurehead was eventually sent to the United States Naval Academy for display. The opening of the dry dock was a particularly significant event. President Andrew Jackson came into town with his cabinet for the ceremony.

The USS *North Carolina* was the next ship, after the *Delaware*, to use the dry dock. There is a story that the *North Carolina* was preparing for a three-year cruise and, just as it was about to start, the bakehouse in Norfolk burned with three thousand barrels of ship bread, otherwise known as hardtack, which was to have been the ship's supply for the deployment. The cruise was delayed for three months, until another stock of hardtack could be made. The *North Carolina* was the first seventy-gun ship to be repaired at the Gosport Navy Yard. By 1837 the yard employed twelve

The tar house, Building Number 3, is one of the oldest surviving structures at Norfolk Naval Shipyard, dating to 1834. This small, octagonal-shaped building, possibly designed by Architect Benjamin Henry Latrobe, designer of the south wing of the U.S. Capitol, was built with leftover granite blocks from the construction of Dry Dock Number One and is predated only by the dry dock and by Quarters B, C and D. Originally used as a tar pitch cooking house, it has since been used as a storage facility. Former British Royal Navy officer and commissioner of the Virginia State Navy Captain James Maxwell claimed that he provided the money for the construction of this structure.

hundred men. At the various docks was an array of ships fitting out for exploring expeditions. Among them were the USS *Delaware, Relief, Consort, Pioneer* and the schooner *Pilot.* Also at the pier was the thirty-six-gun frigate USS *Macedonian,* which was a magnificent ship that had been rebuilt from the keel at Gosport in 1836. The *Macedonian's* cannon bore the insignia of George III, which made them very interesting, as they were part of Stephen Decatur's prize of war. As the story goes, in January 1812, the then-British-flagged *Macedonian* was ordered to secretly deliver some bills of exchange to Norfolk, Virginia, and to bring back an equivalent quantity of gold and silver specie as part of a scheme to keep the Bank of England solvent. During the visit, Captain John Carden socialized with the notables of Norfolk, including Commodore Stephen Decatur, whom he would soon meet under less hospitable circumstances. But Carden bungled the mission by inadvertently revealing what was planned, and had to return to Lisbon empty-handed. Months later, on October 25, 1812, the war with Great Britain and the United States well underway, *Macedonian* was steering northwest about one thousand miles west of the Canary Islands when, at daybreak, a sail was seen on the lee beam. Captain Carden soon made out a large American frigate. After exchanging shots at long range for an hour a close action commenced. The enemy's force was so superior that there could only be one end to the battle; after two hours and ten minutes with all her masts badly damaged, all the guns on the quarter-deck and forecastle disabled except for two and a great proportion of the crew killed or wounded, Carden was forced to surrender his ship. His opponent was the USS *United States,* commanded by Stephen Decatur and built with the scantlings of a seventy-four-gun ship, armed with thirty long twenty-four-pounders on her main deck and twenty-two forty-two-pounder carronades and two long twenty-four-pounders on her quarter-deck and forecastle. Decatur took the *Macedonian* into American service, but by 1828, the USS *Macedonian* was decommissioned. Rather than broken up, the *Macedonian* was rebuilt. In fact, the old ship's figurehead, the likeness of Alexander the Great, was transferred over to the newly constructed ship. In the dry dock would eventually be the *Columbian* and nearby were the frigates *Brandywine* and *Potomac,* among others. It was from Gosport that Commodore Matthew Calbraith Perry went out on the side-wheel steamer *Susquehanna,* the first ship in the navy named for a river, on June 8, 1851, to join his fleet for the opening up of Japan. The *Susquehanna* became the flagship of Perry's Black Fleet on July 8, 1853, entering Tokyo Bay with his squadron.

Decatur was quartered at the Gosport Navy Yard in 1804 to superintend construction of four gunboats, and again in 1812 when his fleet was fitted out to enforce the embargo. He was in the port so often and became so interested in the harbor that he published an article about it in the

American Beacon. Though Decatur did not die in Portsmouth, he met his end at the hands of a man who had spent his boyhood, as well as much of his adulthood, in and around Portsmouth. Commodore James Barron's second wife was Mary Ann Wilson, a Portsmouth native, and Barron's grandson, James Barron Hope, for many years was editor of the *Norfolk Landmark* and a distinguished poet, also born in Portsmouth.

The tract of land on the eastern side of the Southern Branch of the Elizabeth River, known as Saint Helena, was originally purchased for the storage and repair of ordnance and was added to the navy yard on August 26, 1846. The price paid for this land was considered particularly reasonable, due largely to the foresight and planning of Commodore Jesse Wilkerson, who anticipated the need for this land. Wilkerson, born in Nansemond County, Virginia, was familiar with the land and people who owned it. He quietly purchased the tract and held it until the government wanted it. He sold it to the federal government for $2,403.50. This was the amount he had paid for it plus the interest to date. Cedar Grove, which was later purchased as part of Saint Helena, was sold to the government for $135,000 in 1900. Other tracts were added to the yard until it eventually grew to 819 acres.

In 1850 the side-wheel steam frigate USS *Powhatan*, one of the last and largest of American paddle frigates, was built at Gosport Navy Yard; its engines were constructed by Mahaffy's Iron Works on First Street, also in Gosport. The *Powhatan* was an all-Portsmouth product. She was built by constructor Samuel Hartt, who had made Portsmouth his home and had married a city daughter, Celestia Pendleton. Hartt's grandsons, William and Beverley Hartt, of Portsmouth, became officers in the United States Navy. The *Powhatan* was designed by Francis Grice, another constructor at the yard who had adopted Portsmouth as his home of record. During the *Powhatan*'s launching celebration, the homes of Commodore John Drake Sloat, the first to ever be promoted to the rank of commodore in the United States Navy, and Captain David Glasgow Farragut, among others, were thrown open to the public, and elegant hors d'oeuvres were served at each house. Commodore Silas Stringham, who succeeded Sloat, made many improvements to the yard.

After the yellow fever epidemic of 1855 the yard did recover. The frigates *Roanoke* and *Colorado* were launched. The *Dakota* was built soon after, followed by the *Richmond* in 1860. The *Richmond* would serve in three wars, first the Civil War and then as a receiving ship in the Spanish-American War and as quarters for the commandant of the naval training station at Saint Helena during World War I. The *Richmond* was also at one time Rear Admiral Farragut's flagship and the vessel selected to take General Ulysses S. Grant on his tour around the world. *Richmond* returned to Portsmouth in 1903 to serve as an auxiliary to the receiving ship USS *Franklin*, and it was from that time on that the ship stayed in the waters in which she was built.

Newspapers of 1859 and 1860 sounded repeated notes of warning that war was looming on the horizon, not a war against a foreign enemy, but one between America's North and South. Portsmouth remained loyal to the Union until the bitter end, electing by large majority a Union candidate, James G. Holladay, as its representative at the secession convention. Norfolk County also chose a nominee with the same bent: Dr. William H. White, of Deep Creek. Both Holladay and White voted against secession until President Abraham Lincoln called for troops to maintain the Union. Then, on April 18, 1861, Virginia seceded by the unanimous vote of all representatives at the convention. On the morning of April 20, Holladay returned to Portsmouth, bringing with him word that Virginia had seceded. The town was immediately thrown into turmoil. Many of the town's most well-respected citizens and numerous skilled workers were from the North. Exulting cheers mingled with the groans of those who realized almost immediately that lifelong friends would become enemies, and families might be divided brother against brother.

A plan was formulated for blocking the harbor and six young men were detailed for this duty: Henry C. Hudgins and Joe Sam Browne, of the Old Dominion Guards; as well as John C. Tee, William Hanrahan and Henry Allen. The name of the sixth participant is unknown. The work was to be done by two vessels, which were to be towed down to Seawell's Point by the tug *Jane Smith*. One boat was quickly put in position, but the other proved harder to manage and while working on her side the *Pawnee*, a light-draft steam sloop of war, appeared at dawn and gave chase. John Tee observed later that the *Pawnee* pursued them a fair distance before his crew escaped. The young men engaged in this undertaking were all from Portsmouth and lived to tell their stories long after the Civil War was over.

While the towns of Norfolk and Portsmouth marshaled their forces, confusion reigned at the Gosport Navy Yard, which the Commonwealth of Virginia claimed as its rightful possession. When workmen left at noon the gates to the yard were closed to the public. The yard's commandant, Commodore Charles S. McCauley, was too old and anxious to cope with the turn of events that had now put him in the untenable position of protecting the navy's finest shipbuilding facility from the local population. United States Secretary of War Gideon Welles, fearing that Gosport would fall into the hands of Virginia troops, dispatched a contingent of one hundred marines from Washington, D.C., on April 19, 1861, under orders to destroy the facilities at Gosport and retrieve the ships stationed there. The marines arrived as the commander of the navy yard, Commodore McCauley, was boarding the USS *Cumberland* in Hampton Roads,

A machine shop at the United States Navy Yard Norfolk was photographed ca. 1920. *Courtesy of the author.*

following the evacuation of the yard. McCauley was severely criticized for surrendering the yard without a struggle, but his hasty departure owed much to the president of the Atlantic, Mississippi and Ohio Railroad, precursor of the Norfolk and Western, William Mahone, who became a celebrated general of the Confederacy and whose fame would be forever linked to the battle of the Crater. A lookout in the crow's nest of the USS *Delaware* saw trainload after trainload of Confederate soldiers brought to the outskirts of Norfolk on the Portsmouth side. Thousands of them, as far as the lookout could tell, had disembarked. In fact, Mahone had brought his soldiers into town on rail cars, standing up, then sent them out lying down in the cars, repeating the procedure, so that anyone watching would think the soldiers had only been brought *in*—no one could see them to get an accurate count of their number. The general had brought the same troops back and forth from Petersburg through the night, in some cases with band playing and colors flying—all for show.

While Mahone pulled off his ruse, the populace of Norfolk and Portsmouth became frantic as rumors spread that Federal troops intended to bombard them. A number of citizens worked together to block the harbor, but this failed. This was the final straw for McCauley, who, after some correspondence with Major General William Booth Taliaferro of the Virginia militia, who had taken command of Norfolk and Portsmouth on April 18, 1861, agreed that there would be no bombardment, provided the harbor was not blocked. This agreement had been strictly kept. A mass meeting of citizens was subsequently held, and Captain Samuel Watts, James Murdaugh and William H. Peters were appointed to a committee to confer with the commander of the navy yard. As they approached the gate, they met a number of officers who had just resigned and left their ships. These men told the committee that McCauley would not see them, and this proved true—McCauley had already left. Morning became evening. At dusk the USS *Pawnee* sailed into port, colors flying, her band playing the national anthem, and loaded with cannon pointed at the shore from her ports. That evening the *Pawnee* opened up on the shipyard. It was the *Pawnee*'s commanding officer, Captain Hiram Paulding, who gave the order to burn the yard and its contents; his crew left the ship and joined the wrecking force in the yard, where the marines had set charges and helped burn scuttled ships in the Elizabeth River. Many United States Navy vessels were burned that day; some of them, like the *United States*, which under Stephen Decatur had captured the *Macedonian* in one of the most thrilling exploits in navy history, escaped the firing of the yard, as did the USS *Cumberland*, which was towed into the harbor to escape the fire. The *Dolphin*, *Plymouth*, *Raritan*, *Germantown*, *Merrimack* and *Pennsylvania* were burned to the waterline. Why Paulding's sailors did not set fire to the *United States* before they left was never known. Several of the charges set by sailors and marines also did not detonate and some contemporary reports credit Confederate sympathizers among McCauley's junior officers as responsible for the incomplete demolition of the yard. Captured by the Confederates, the *United States* was placed in Southern service as CSS *United States*; she was used as a receiving ship but was sunk when the Confederates abandoned Norfolk in May 1862. Though subsequently salvaged by the United States Navy, it was determined the *United States* was not worth repairing and she met her end following the war.

During the firing of the Gosport Navy Yard, hundreds of oxen and horses were burned alive, and what could not be burned was destroyed by other means. Stores were thrown overboard and heavy cannon spiked. When the liquor supplies were poured out many of the sailors and workmen became so drunk that they were unable to do their work properly, and some of the larger guns were not spiked well enough to preclude Confederate troops from returning them to service. Just before dawn the navy yard was a seething mass of flames, as ships of the line fell prey to the conflagration. Adding to the horror of the scene was the booming of the *Pennsylvania*'s guns, which had been left loaded, firing as they reached high heat in the flames. The fire quickly spread from the yard to Lincoln Street—but for the shifting of the wind the city of Portsmouth might also have caught fire. As daylight broke the navy yard was blackened ruins, but from those ruins the Confederate flag was raised and Captain French Forrest was placed in command of the yard, with Captain Sidney Smith Lee, a brother of General Robert E. Lee, as executive officer. To the surprise of Portsmouth members of the Virginia militia who walked down to the stone dry dock the morning after the fire, it was intact. The soldiers, David A. Williams and Joseph Weaver, examined it carefully and found a trail of powder had been laid, leading to a culvert at the northwest corner. Weaver ran down to the dock and severed the connection to the explosives. They then looked for the fuse, but could not find one. Later, when water was let into the dry dock, roughly thirty barrels of powder floated out of the dock. Williams and Weaver concluded that the order to destroy the dry dock had been either countermanded or the word never came in time to execute it. The following spring the answer to this question came when Weaver, who had been commissioned a carpenter in the Confederate States Navy, was captured by the Federals and placed aboard a Union gunboat. Weaver spoke often with the gunboat's master's mate, who ate at the same mess with him. When the mate heard that Weaver was from Portsmouth, he asked him about the dry dock at the yard and then told him why it was not destroyed. Just as sailors at the yard were ready to fire the dry dock, they were called back to their quarters. As soon as they left the mate lit the fuse, but instead he threw it overboard, feeling certain that no one would ever find out he had disobeyed the order. His reason for not destroying the dry dock had to do with the many people who lived in proximity of the yard. Had he blown the dry dock, the great stones that line it might well have been thrown beyond the walls of the yard, striking homes and likely killing many people. Near the yard lived families who had been particularly kind to the master's mate. The mate's description of the powder train matched what Weaver had found, and thus he believed his story.

Portsmouth defenders placed cannon along the entire waterfront, from the navy yard to the hospital at a distance of a hundred feet apart. Camps surrounded the town, placed a half-mile from each other. Breastworks were thrown up near the navy yard at Third Street and later the wall was lowered in places to afford a lookout. Confederate troops poured into Portsmouth in the days that followed the navy yard's burning. The first company from outside the city was the Columbus Life Guards of Georgia under Colonel Peyton H. Colquitt. They encamped at the naval hospital, where bales of cotton had been hastily piled to form temporary breastworks. The commandant of the hospital had not resigned, but he was approached by a local committee bent on finding out where he stood in the hostilities. Called upon to declare his loyalties, Dr. Samuel Barrinton resigned. The Confederates replaced him with Dr. George Blacknell, who had earlier been commanding officer of the hospital from 1839 to 1842; this time Blacknell took over as an officer of the Confederacy.

By the afternoon of the twenty-first of April, crowds poured down to the Portsmouth waterfront, to the batteries that had been hastily begun. Men and women, shovels in hand, threw up the earth to complete construction of the batteries, which were soon ready for the guns

The mast house at the Gosport Navy Yard was built in 1836, when the American navy was composed of wooden sailing vessels. This building housed the construction of ships' masts, a process similar to that of hewing timbers. Oak and pine were the two species preferred for the masts of naval vessels. Smaller masts were constructed from single trees. Logs were elevated above the floor level on a series of wooden blocks. The timber was squared with, and reworked into, an octagon shape with an adze. Masts were finished by adze again to level sixteen faces. Corners were planed smooth, and plane marks were removed by sanding.

salvaged from wrecks at the navy yard. By the end of that fateful week in April, twelve cannon were in place and Hospital Point was ready for an attack. The frigate *United States*, rechristened by the Confederacy, was placed at the mouth of the Elizabeth River to guard the approaches to Norfolk and Portsmouth. Pinner's Point and Pig Point had been fortified and garrisoned, and it was at the latter place that Confederate soldiers had their first engagement. This was a skirmish with the steamer *Harriet Lane* and Captain Robert Baker Pegram's battery at Pig Point. In his official report of the battle, Pegram stated that the Confederates had no casualties. The *Harriet Lane*, however, was disabled and retreated to the Washington Navy Yard for repairs. About the same time Colquitt's Georgia troops had a brush with enemy troops off Seawell's Point. During this skirmish it was observed that the Georgia troops did not have a unit flag. The ladies of Portsmouth set out to make them one, which was presented to the Columbus Life Guards by Belle Bilisoly. Belle later married Griffen F. Edwards, a Portsmouth lawyer. Despite the number of Confederate troops in and around Norfolk and Portsmouth, Union troops were getting information of value through spies who could not be pinpointed, largely because their work was being done at the river's edge. Men disguised as fishermen gathered information that they wrote on scraps of paper and enclosed in bottles to which they attached a small flag or signal, then set them adrift at the proper tide. Harbor police organized under Captain John Young of Norfolk soon put a stop to this practice, but the information continued to flow. Women moved about the shipyard and in and around the communities of the Elizabeth River, taking with them Confederate secrets onboard outbound watercraft.

The Virginia troops who occupied the Gosport Navy Yard on April 21, 1861, found the yard badly damaged, but serviceable. The new Confederate paymaster, William H. Peters, was detailed to compile a list of serviceable buildings. This list was not found after the war, but an adjunct report by Peters noted that several substantial workshops were undamaged and the dry dock was operational. The Confederates wasted no time otherwise repairing the navy yard and from their watery graves, the *Plymouth*, *Dolphin*, *Germantown* and *Merrimack* were raised by the Baker Salvage Company, under the Confederate authorities. Work on the first three started at once, but the *Merrimack* was rejected as worthless—at first. A skilled workman at the yard, Thomas Carr of Portsmouth, after seeing the Parrott guns used by the Georgia troops assigned to the Third Street Battery, had an idea. He rifled the Dahlgren guns that had been left at the navy yard half spiked, just as the Confederates had done with the Parrott guns. When the Dahlgrens had been rifled, Carr went back to Lieutenant Reginald Fairfax, who took the tug *Harmony*, owned by Captain James Brown and used to carry freight between Norfolk and Portsmouth, mounted one of the guns onboard and went down the Elizabeth River to Hampton Roads to meet the Federal fleet anchored there. It was a bold attack. Fairfax first attacked the frigate *Savannah* lying at the mouth of the James River. The rifled gun did its work, throwing shot well into the frigate while the return shot fell far short of the *Harmony*. Fairfax continued to shoot until his ammunition was exhausted, and then returned quietly to Portsmouth, satisfied with his experiment. Under Fairfax was a Portsmouth mechanic, George Maxwell, who manipulated the gun. Carr himself never received credit for his skill and ingenuity at rifling the Dahlgren guns.

On July 12, 1861, work began on the *Merrimack*—a unique experiment in naval warfare. The iron used to cover the *Merrimack* for her transformation to the world's first ironclad was initially hard to acquire. The iron plates with which the vessel was eventually covered came from rails of the railroad. As the *Merrimack* was being transformed, so, too, were the *Richmond*, another ironclad vessel, as well as the gunboats *Hampton*, *Nansemond*, *Elizabeth* and

The USS *Mendota* was in dry dock at the United States Navy Yard Norfolk about 1925 for refurbishing when this picture was taken. The *Mendota* had a brief but interesting service life. Built in 1898 by Charles Hillman at Philadelphia, the tug was commandeered by the U.S. Navy on September 22, 1917, from the Staples Transportation Company of New York City, and subsequently commissioned the USS *Concord* (SP-773) on the twentieth of November. In late 1917, the *Concord* helped tow French submarine chasers from Bermuda to the Azores, then went on to Brest, France, where she served through the end of World War I and for nearly another year afterward. The tug was placed in service at the Washington Navy Yard in December 1919, but less than a year later, on November 20, 1920, was reclassified the *Mendota* (YT-33). In January 1932, *Mendota* was renamed *Muscotah*; she was placed out of service on November 4, 1934, and sold less than three years later. The fate of this tug is unknown. *Courtesy of the author.*

Escambia. Many of the Dahlgrens and other guns were rifled and put into service. Early in March 1862 the *Merrimack* emerged from the Gosport Navy Yard as the CSS *Virginia*. Built in Portsmouth by a native son, John L. Porter, a constructor in the Confederate States Navy, this amazing vessel sailed quietly down the Elizabeth River on the eighth of March to fight a battle that would revolutionize naval warfare.

There have been many accounts of the CSS *Virginia*'s place in naval history, but the one most poignantly and vividly told was by Henry Ashton Ramsay, the *Virginia*'s chief engineer, in the February 10, 1912 issue of *Harper's Weekly*. "The *Merrimack* was built in 1856 as a full-rigged frigate," Ramsay recounted, "of thirty-one tons burden, with auxiliary steam power to be used in case of headwinds. She was a hybrid from her birth, marking the transition from sail to steam, as well as from wooden ships to ironclads. I became her second assistant engineer in 1859, cruising around the Horn and back to Norfolk. Her chief engineer was Allan Stimers." Ramsay remarked, too, that little did the *Merrimack*'s crew dream that Stimers would become the right-hand man of Swedish engineer John Ericsson, constructor of the USS *Monitor*, "while I was to hold a similar post in the conversion of our own ship into an ironclad, or that in less than a year we would be seeking to destroy each other, he as the chief engineer of the *Monitor*, and I in the corresponding position on the *Merrimack*." Captain Ramsay went on to observe that the *Merrimack*, after being set on fire as the Federals evacuated the yard, was scuttled by workmen, thus putting out the flames. When raised by the Confederates, she was only a blackened and burned hulk. "Naval officers were skeptical," he noted, "as to results. The plates were rolled at the Tredegar Mills, Richmond, and arrived so slowly that we were nearly a year finishing her. We could have rolled them at the yard here and built four *Merrimacks* in that time had the South understood the importance of a navy at the outbreak of the war." Rifled guns were just coming into use, he continued, and Lieutenant John Mercer Brooke, the former United States Navy officer who designed the *Merrimack*, later *Virginia*, considered the question of having some of the vessel's guns rifled. Interestingly, Brooke was the Confederate naval officer who had submitted a plan for raising and reconstructing the sunken *Merrimack* as an ironclad warship at the request of Confederate Secretary of the Navy Stephen Russell Mallory. Naval constructor John L. Porter also worked on the project and made the first formal drawings for the project, as well as supervising the construction, though with frequent input from Lieutenant Brooke. Soon after the battle with the *Monitor*, the parties and their friends began arguing in the newspapers about who was the true inventor of the ironclad. Brooke decided that the place to have the controversy settled was in the Confederate Patent Office, and thus he filed an application for a patent on his invention on May 2, 1862. His drawings were tracings of the drawings that Porter had made of the original plans; however, constructor Porter did not contest the patent application, and a patent on the invention was granted to John M. Brooke on July 29, 1862, as Confederate patent Number 100.

The use of rifled guns aboard the ironclad *Virginia* would present problems. There were no foundries in the South at that time capable of turning out such guns. There were many cast-iron cannon that had fallen into Confederate possession at Norfolk, and Lieutenant Brooke thus conceived of the idea of turning some of this ordnance into rifles. In order to enable these guns to withstand additional bursting strain, the Confederates forged wrought-iron bands and shrank them over the chambers; they also devised a special tool for rifling the bore of the guns. Many details of this process remained incomplete when the *Virginia* floated out of the dry dock, but the Confederates were desperate to halt General George Brinton McClellan's advance down the Virginia Peninsula. "The ship was full of workmen hurrying her to completion," remembered Ramsay, when Commodore Franklin Buchanan arrived from Richmond one March morning and ordered everything out of the ship, except her crew of 350 men, who had been hastily drilled on shore in the management of guns, and directed executive officer Lieutenant Catesby ap Roger Jones to prepare to sail at once. After some discussion of details with his commander, Ramsay decided that a trial run would be needed, as they would have to go several miles down the Elizabeth River, and all of the ironclad's systems would have to be monitored at all times. "Across the river at Newport News gleamed the batteries and white tents of Federal camps and vessels of the fleet blockading the mouth of the James," Ramsay noted, and chief among them were the USS *Congress* and the USS *Cumberland*, tall and stately, with every line and spar clearly defined against the blue March sky, their decks and ports bristling with guns, while the rigging of the *Cumberland* was gay with the red, white and blue of the sailors' garments hung out to dry. "The ship had been sighted from Old Point and help was sent to the Federal vessels," Ramsay noted. The *Congress* shook out her topsails and the clothesline on the *Cumberland* was hauled down.

"Our crew was summoned to the gun deck, and Buchanan addressed us," Ramsay recalled later, telling his men, "'Sailors, in a few minutes you will have the long looked for opportunity of showing your devotion to our cause. Remember that you are about to strike for your country and your homes. The Confederacy expects every man to do his duty. Beat it to quarters.'" As the CSS *Virginia*, née *Merrimack*, approached the Federal fleet, it was met by a barrage of fire that Ramsay noted would have sunk a conventional wooden vessel, "except the *Merrimack*. They struck our sloping sides, were deflected upward to burst harmlessly in the air, or rolled down and fell hissing into the water, dashing the spray up into our very ports. As we drew nearer the *Cumberland*, above the roar of the battle, rang the voice of Buchanan: 'Do you surrender?' 'Never, I'll sink alongside,'" came the reply from *Cumberland*'s executive officer, Lieutenant George Upham Morris. "The crux of what followed was down in the engine room," noted Ramsay. "Two gongs the signal to stop, were quickly followed by three, and the signal to reverse. There was an ominous pause, then a crash, shaking us all off our feet. The engine labored. The vessel was shaken in every fiber. Our bow was visibly depressed. We seemed to be bearing down with a weight on our prow," he continued. "We had rushed on the doomed ship, relentless as fate, crashing through her heavy barricade of spars and torpedo fenders, striking her below her starboard forechains and crushing into her." For a moment, he would observe, the whole weight of the *Cumberland* hung on the *Virginia*'s prow, threatening to carry it down with the stricken Federal sloop, the return wave of the collision hurling up the *Virginia*'s port bow. The *Cumberland*, with heavy casualties onboard, began to sink slowly bow first and continued to fight desperately for some forty minutes after its fate was sealed. "We had left our cast iron beak in the side of the *Cumberland*," Ramsay recounted. "Like the wasp we could sting but once, leaving the sting in the wound.

"Our smokestack was riddled and our flag shot down several times," Ramsay continued. The flag was finally secured to a rent in the stock. On the gun deck the *Virginia*'s crew fought ferociously, giving little thought to the wounded and dying, he would say later, as they tugged away at their guns, training and sighting their pieces, while the orders rang out, "Sponge, load, fire." At times, there would be the cry, "The muzzle of my gun has been blown away," to the reply by Catesby Jones, "No matter, keep on loading and firing; do the best you can with her." The gunners onboard *Virginia* were covered with powder grime, so much so that Ramsay described them as "looking like negroes. Human hearts were beating and bleeding there, human lives were being sacrificed. Pain, death, wounds, glory—that was the sum of it." On the doomed ship *Cumberland* the battle raged with equal fury. The sanded deck was red and slippery with blood. Delirium seized the crew, who cheered and fought, by all accounts, as their ship sunk beneath Hampton Roads. As the ship listed, a pivot gun broke loose, leaving a mass of mangled flesh in its wake. The *Congress* was then attacked. Though the Federal frigate tried to escape, it ran aground and after desperate firing came the order to surrender.

"The whole scene," recalled Ramsay, "was changed: a pall of black hung about the ships and obscured the clean outline of the three frigates, *Saint Lawrence*, *Roanoke*, and *Minnesota*, also enveloped in the clouds of battle that now and then reflected the crimson lightning of the god of war." The masts of the *Cumberland* protruded above the water. The *Congress* presented a terrible scene of carnage. The gunboats CSS *Beaufort* and CSS *Raleigh* were summoned to take off the wounded and to fire the ship. They were driven away by sharpshooters on shore, who suddenly turned their fire on the *Virginia*, notwithstanding the white flag of the *Congress*. Buchanan fell severely wounded in the groin. While being carried below deck, Buchanan instructed Jones, "Plug hot shot into her [the *Congress*] and don't leave her until she is on fire. They must look after their own wounded since they won't let us." Buchanan's brother was paymaster on the *Congress*.

After the *Congress* was fired, the *Virginia* next went after the three frigates, but all made off except for the *Minnesota*, which could not be reached by the *Virginia* enough to do serious damage. The ironclad then pulled up to Seawell's Point for the night, planning to make short work of the *Minnesota* in the morning. What happened in the morning can best be told in the words of Ramsay, who said, "We left our anchorage shortly before eight o'clock in the morning, and steamed across and upstream toward the *Minnesota*, thinking to make short work of her. We approached slowly, feeling our way along the edge of the channel, when suddenly a black object that looked like the historic description, 'a barrel head with a cheese box on it,' moved slowly out from under the *Minnesota* and boldly confronted us." The great fight was on, a fight the likes of which the world had never seen before, when "the battle of yesterday" passed away, and with it the experience of "a thousand years of 'battle and of breeze'" was brought to an end. The books of all navies were burned with the *Congress*, Ramsay would rightly observe, by a conflagration as ruthless as the torch of Omar. "We hovered about each other in spirals," he remembered, "gradually contacting the circuits until we were in point-blank range, but our shells glanced from the *Monitor*'s turret, just as hers did from our sloping sides. For two hours the cannonade continued without perceptible damage to either combatant." Then an accident occurred—the *Virginia* was aground.

The use of coal over a period of two days had made the *Virginia* much lighter, thus exposing the part of it that was not covered by iron. The *Virginia* had been hurried out of the dry dock before the plates of metal could be put below the waterline. Had the crew of the *Monitor* known this, the Federal ironclad could have sunk the *Virginia* without any problem whatsoever. "Fearing that she might discover our vulnerable heel of Achilles," noted Ramsay, "while she had us in chancery, we had to take all our chances. We lashed down the safety valves, heaped quick burning combustibles into the already raging fires and brought down the boilers to a pressure that would have been unsafe under ordinary circumstances." The *Virginia*'s propeller churned the mud and water furiously, but the ship did not move. "We piled on oil cotton waste, splints of wood, anything that would burn faster than coal," Ramsay continued. "It seemed impossible that the boilers could long stand the pressure that was crowding upon them. Just as we were beginning to despair there was a perceptible movement and the *Merrimack* [*Virginia*] slowly dragged herself off the shoal by main strength. We were saved." The crew of the *Monitor* had not noticed the *Virginia*'s troubles. Gliding by the *Monitor*, the *Virginia* fired on the *Minnesota*. As the Federal ironclad came to the frigate's rescue, the ironclads fired upon one another. The shot carried away the *Monitor*'s steering gear, damaged the pilothouse and blinded Captain John Lorimer Worden, who was replaced by Lieutenant Samuel Dana Green as the engagement with the *Virginia* continued. The *Minnesota* was about to give up ship, but *Minnesota*'s crew saw the *Virginia* turn toward Norfolk. It was decided during a consultation of officers onboard *Virginia* that they would not attack the *Monitor* until the needed plates could be put on; at that time the *Virginia* was not completely "ironclad."

As the *Virginia* passed up the Elizabeth River, it trailed the ensign of the USS *Congress* under the Stars and Bars of the Confederacy; there was a tremendous ovation from the crowd that lined the shores, while hundreds of small boats, flying colorful flags and bunting, converted the *Virginia*'s course back to the shipyard into a victorious procession. About three weeks after the *Virginia*'s two-day engagement in Hampton Roads, the ironclad was ready to return to battle, but the *Monitor*, though reinforced by two additional ironclads, the *Galena* and the *Naugatuck*, and every available vessel of the United States Navy, was under orders from Washington, D.C., to refuse the *Virginia*'s challenge; the Federal navy blockaded the *Virginia* in the Elizabeth River. The North's strategy proved highly effective. From Lieutenant Catesby Jones's October 1874 article for the Southern Historical Society, it is known that after the fated engagement with the *Monitor*, the *Virginia* returned to her berth at the shipyard where a prow of steel and wrought iron was put on, and a course of two-inch iron on the hull below the roof extending in length 180 feet was applied. "Want of time and material prevented its completion," wrote Jones. "The damage to the armor was repaired; wrought-iron port shutters were fitted…The rifle guns were supplied with bolts of wrought and chilled iron. The ship was brought a foot deeper into the water, making her draft twenty-three feet." Commodore Josiah Tatnall (also spelled Tattnall) relieved Buchanan in command, but he soon grew impatient with the Federal blockade, which effectively hemmed in the *Virginia*'s movement. On April 11, 1862, Tatnall took the *Virginia* down to Hampton Roads, expecting to have a desperate encounter with the *Monitor*. "Greatly to our surprise," recalled Jones, "the *Monitor* refused to fight us. She closely hugged the shore under the guns of the fort, with her steam up. Hoping to provoke her to come out, the CSS *Jamestown* was sent in, and captured several prizes, but the *Monitor* would not budge. It was proposed to take the vessel to the York River, but it was decided in Richmond that she should stay near Norfolk for its protection." Commodore Tatnall commanded the *Virginia* for forty-five days, of which time there were only thirteen days she was not in dock or in the hands of the navy yard. It was determined imprudent for the *Virginia* to risk capture lest Confederate Major General Benjamin Huger's army at Norfolk and Portsmouth be left unprotected. "We were to receive a signal when Huger evacuated, but this we never got," observed Ramsay of the situation. "Learning that part of the waters that we had to cross in following Huger up the James River drew only fourteen feet of water, we were prepared to risk this, but the wind changed and blew the water off the bar. It was decided to abandon the vessel and set her on fire." The *Virginia* was taken to the bight of Craney Island and about midnight that night Norfolk was evacuated by the Confederacy; the intention was to fire the *Virginia*, which had a draft too deep to take her up the James River to avoid capture. According to Tatnall, the *Virginia*'s "shield was out of water; we were not in fighting condition." Running her ashore at Craney Island, the crew alighted and the vessel was set on fire. "We had but two boats and it was sunrise before our three hundred and fifty were ashore," stated Ramsay, in his description of events. "Cotton waste and trains of powder were strewn about the deck and Executive Officer Jones, who was the last to leave the ship, applied the slow match." The *Virginia*'s

The USS *Missouri* (BB-63)—the "Big Mo"—was photographed by H.D. Vollmer at Norfolk Naval Station on May 9, 1946. Commissioned in June 1944, the *Iowa*-class battleship was the Third Fleet flagship at the end of World War II.

The Big Mo was the site of the September 2, 1945 Japanese surrender ceremony that ended the war. With the exception of March 1946, when she was sent to the Mediterranean on a diplomatic mission, through the rest of the 1940s and into 1950, the battleship operated extensively in the Atlantic area. She was the centerpiece of a major grounding incident off Hampton Roads, Virginia, in January 1950 but was quickly repaired and returned to service. Stricken from the Naval Vessel Register in 1995, *Missouri* was transferred to Pearl Harbor, Hawaii, in June 1998 to become a memorial. *Courtesy of the author.*

crew marched silently through the woods to join Huger, who was on his way to Suffolk. The ironclad's magazine exploded about half past four on the morning of May 11, 1862, its low deep mournful boom heard by her crew. The *Virginia*'s crew arrived at Drury's Bluff the next day, and assisted in defeating the *Monitor*, *Galena* and other vessels the fifteenth of May. Years after the *Virginia*'s destruction, many parts of the ironclad became personal trophies to people in Norfolk and Portsmouth. Crosses made of its live oak beams and tipped in gold were in the possession of many of the people of Portsmouth. One of the *Virginia*'s bells was brought up in dredging and was displayed for many years in Norfolk.

The story of how Norfolk and Portsmouth fell so quickly had much to do with Northern operatives at work in both communities along the Elizabeth River; they did, in fact, use the river to their advantage in betraying the South. William H. Peters, who had been commissioned a paymaster in the Confederate States Navy, had charge of all the stores at the Gosport Navy Yard. In late April 1861, rumors of Confederate evacuation of both cities were rife. Peters soon received orders to remove the stores to Charlotte, North Carolina. He was quietly going about with this work, and nearly finished, when it was learned that the Gosport community had harbored a traitor. Captain James Byers and his little steamer *J.P. White* had been held in the Elizabeth River by the Confederacy, but in the spring of 1862 the Confederates required his services. But when Byers learned of their plans to fire the shipyard and the naval hospital, he determined to spare these properties by running the forts and batteries along the river to inform Federal authorities camped at Newport News under Major General Joseph K.F. Mansfield. With his friends, George W. Griggs and John Nolen, Byers made his move. On May 6, 1862, four days before Norfolk fell, the three men took the *J.P. White*, flying the Confederate flag, and steamed down the Elizabeth River past Rebel forts and batteries. They landed at Newport News, where Byers surrendered the steamer to Mansfield. President Abraham Lincoln, Secretary Edwin M. Stanton and General John E. Wool were at Old Point Comfort, a few miles away, and Byers was quickly dispatched there to deliver his news of Confederate plans for Norfolk and Portsmouth to the president's party. Lincoln later wrote, "On the morning of May 7, 1862, I was at Fortress Monroe, Va., when two or three men came there and said that they had just come from Norfolk, and that Norfolk was being evacuated by the enemy. This information proved true, and to a great extent led to the movements which resulted in our occupation of that city and the destruction of the Merrimac [*sic*]. It was said, and I believe truly, that they came on a tug, which they surrendered to the United States authorities."

Engaging in a strategic withdrawal, Confederate General Joseph Johnston ordered the Gosport Navy Yard abandoned and destroyed. On the tenth of May 1862 Confederate forces burned the facility. General Wool wrote to Secretary Stanton on May 12, summarizing the capture of Norfolk two days before, describing the events as he knew them. Wool informed the secretary that on the ninth of May, a Friday afternoon, he had organized a force to march against Norfolk. The following morning, Federal troops were landed at Ocean View and commenced the march toward Major General Mansfield and Brigadier General Max Weber who proceeded on the direct route by way of Tanner's Creek Bridge. Finding the bridge on fire, Mansfield and Weber returned to Newton's Crossroads where Wool joined them and took the direction of the column. Wool arrived by the old road, entering the entrenchments in front of the city at twenty minutes to five that evening. He reported later that he immediately proceeded toward Norfolk accompanied by Secretary Salmon P. Chase and met the mayor and a select committee of the common council of Norfolk at the limits of the city, where they surrendered Norfolk according to the terms set forth in the resolutions of the common council presented by Mayor William W. Lamb, which were accepted by Wool, as the terms pertained to the civil rights of the city's citizens. Wool appointed Brigadier General Egbert Ludovicus Vièle to the post of military governor of Norfolk with directions to see that the citizens were protected in all their civil rights. Shortly thereafter Wool crossed the Elizabeth River and took possession of Gosport and Portsmouth. On the eleventh of May Wool visited the navy yard and found all the workshops, storehouses and other buildings in ruins, having been set on fire by the Confederates, who at the same time partially blew up the dry dock. The general also visited Craney Island, where he discovered thirty-nine guns of large caliber, most of which had been spiked. There was also a large number of shot and shells with about five thousand pounds of powder, all of which, with the buildings, were in good order. As far as Wool was able to ascertain, the Federals captured two hundred cannon, including those at Seawell's Point batteries, also with a large quantity of shot and shells as well as many other articles of value stationed at the navy yard, Craney Island, Seawell's Point and other places. As a footnote to the Confederate abandonment of their Gosport and Portsmouth positions, Major General Huger had ordered all saloons closed and liquor destroyed. Gutters ran, literally, with brandy and other liquors, washing into the Elizabeth River.

The Union contingent that occupied the yard following the Confederate withdrawal found all of the buildings, with the exception of the officers' quarters, substantially damaged by fire. John H. Livingston was appointed commander of the yard; he officially rechristened it the United States Navy Yard, Norfolk, Virginia (referred to herein as United States Navy Yard Norfolk), on May 20, 1862. In early June, he reported to Joseph Smith, chief of the United States Navy's Yards and Docks Bureau, that the marines assigned to protect the base were housed in tents because "there are no buildings in this yard suitable to house them, but the two buildings composing the first lieutenant's and master's houses." The first priority of the new commander was to return the base to operational status, and comprehensive repair of the fire-damaged buildings was not part of this priority. An albumen print of the shipyard, executed by Alexander Gardner in December 1864 and shown herein, depicts damage to the yard in the vicinity of the mast house. The building shell of the mast house is intact in the picture.

In January 1866 the first postwar commandant of the United States Navy Yard Norfolk, Vice Commodore R.B. Hitchcock, reported that the quality of wartime repairs to the yard was very poor and recommended building replacement. An 1866 map of the navy yard indicated that the mast house, along with other structures, was damaged during the war. The mast house was repaired by the time the map was printed. Adjoining Buildings 29, 30 and 31 sustained greater damage. Major repair work was undertaken at a cost in excess of $100,000. Vice Commodore Hitchcock directed that former one-story buildings be expanded to two-story structures during this rebuilding process. Building 29, located west of the mast house, was one of the structures expanded to two stories in February 1866.

During the postwar period, the United States Navy experienced an increased demand for shore facilities. The expansion of the fleet during the Civil War occurred without a commensurate increase in the construction of shore facilities to service the larger number of vessels. The shore establishment was less capable of serving the fleet than during the prewar years due to the extensive damage incurred at Norfolk and Pensacola Navy Yards, coupled with the closing of the shipyard at Memphis, Tennessee. The 1865 annual report to the secretary of war identified the lack of space at navy shore facilities as hampering the ability of the fleet to operate effectively. Exacerbating the problem was the rise of ironclad technology. All of the existing navy yards were designed for the construction and maintenance of a wooden fleet. The national debt created by the prosecution of the Civil War restrained Congress from appropriating funds to improve navy facilities. In 1874 the United States Senate Committee on Naval Affairs was asked by Congress to study the feasibility of naval yard closures. The committee recommended the expansion of the Norfolk yard, citing its strategic location. Nine years later, in 1883, a similar committee was convened by Congress. The committee noted that the United States Navy Yard Norfolk had the capability to build and repair wooden ships of all sizes, but was unable to construct, or even dry dock, the new iron-hulled *Chicago*-class vessels.

The Norfolk Navy Yard's strategic location made it, even then, the most important naval shipyard on the Atlantic Coast. The nine-o'clock-gun, a time-honored tradition in the local community, had been fired again in 1866 on the order of Rear Admiral Stephen C. Rowan, then commandant of the yard, and the following year a large bell was installed in the cupola that surmounted the First Street gate. Navy Commander Edward P. Lull, in his *History of the United States Navy Yard at Gosport, Virginia*, published in 1874, wrote:

> *No navy yard belonging to the United States is from its geographical position more important than that of Gosport, Virginia. Located near enough to the entrance of Chesapeake Bay to be easily accessible, it is, at the same time, in a position readily defended from attacks either by land or by water, and one, as has been repeatedly shown, which can be held by a small force against a very largely superior one. There is in the vicinity an abundant supply of timber and other material, while the close proximity of a populous city secures to it the command of all the skilled labor that can be required. Such is the mildness of the climate that work of all sorts can be carried on at all seasons of the year without interruption. Hampton Roads, the outer harbor, is an excellent point of rendezvous for a fleet or squadron.*

Lull went on to remark that a glance at the map would demonstrate the great importance of a naval station in vicinity of the yard. "The Chesapeake, with its navigable tributaries, penetrates into the heart of several of the richest states in the Union, reaching to the national capitol," noted Lull. "A foothold in its waters would, therefore, be of the utmost strategic importance to an invading enemy, and would probably be one of the earliest objects sought by them, as past history has fully shown. The width of the entrance of the bay is so great that it would be impossible to defend it except by a naval force, which should have a repairing, coaling and victualing station as near at hand as possible consistent with entire defensibility for itself, with a reasonably secure outer harbor, large enough for the necessary maneuvers of a squadron in getting under way and forming. All of these conditions are admirably filled by the location of the Gosport yard."

The United States moved to modernize its fleet and naval shore facilities in the 1880s. An electrical fire-alarm system was fitted at the navy yard in 1886, and in 1887, the celebrated Naval Post Band, which for many years played in the community's festive and social occasions, gave its first concert. The telephone system was installed in 1888, followed the next year by the first use of a railroad car in the yard, which also completed a second dry dock. As war with Spain approached, wood and canvas gave way to steel and steam. The navy yard at Norfolk built two of the first ships of the modern navy: the steel-sheathed USS *Raleigh* (C-8), a protected cruiser, and the steel-hulled USS *Texas*, a second-class battleship, both launched in 1892. The *Raleigh* was the first ship of the new navy to be completely built by the United States government and the *Texas* was the navy's first battleship, but she was also powered exclusively by steam. The launching of the *Raleigh* corresponded with the International Columbian Naval Rendezvous in Hampton Roads celebrating the four-hundredth anniversary of European awareness of the Americas.

The mission of the United States Navy Yard Norfolk prior to the Spanish-American War was to build, supply and maintain the United States fleet. Both the *Texas* and *Raleigh*, the progeny of the Norfolk yard, became famous for participation in the Spanish-American War, the *Texas* at Santiago, where with the assistance of USS *Massachusetts*, designated BB-2, sank the *Reina Mercedes*. The *Raleigh* brought home its reputation from its participation in the thickest of the fight at the battle of Manila Bay. The captured *Reina Mercedes* was brought to the United States Navy Yard Norfolk on May 27, 1899. On that day the riverbanks were lined with crowds anxious to see the captured Spanish warship. Portsmouth and Norfolk both sent ships to Old Point Comfort to escort the *Reina Mercedes* to the yard; there were twenty-two tugs, all with flags flying and whistles tied down as thousands watched. As the *Reina Mercedes* rounded Hospital Point, too, the cannon of the Grimes Battery commenced firing and continued to do so until the Spanish prize of war was moored at the dock.

The Portsmouth Naval Hospital, particularly Hospital Point, mentioned throughout this chapter, has long played a prominent role in the river's history. Tied to the Spanish-American War period, it should be noted that the hospital was connected to a project to widen the Elizabeth River at Hospital Point. This was accomplished by removing about four hundred feet at the point. The old lighthouse that stood there had already been toppled during an August storm in 1879. A new bridge was built about the time the river was widened; the land where the bridge was erected had been extended by filling in and the little islands that had given the name to Island Creek were submerged in that process of filling in.

After the Spanish-American War, the traditional role of naval yards was expanded and altered by the demands of the steel navy. At Norfolk, land-based schools for sailors were established. Down the waterfront from the hospital, the Norfolk yard's third dry dock was begun in 1903 and completed in 1911. Constructed of granite and concrete, this dock was only one of many new shipbuilding facilities, necessitating expansion to the south and west. Rear Admiral Purnell Harrington, commander of the yard, complained to the Board of Navy Yard Plans in October 1904 that the functions housed in the yard were ill-organized and scattered throughout the base. Harrington recommended reorganization. To

The aircraft carrier USS *Midway* (CVB-41) is pictured on December 27, 1954, as she returns from deployment to Norfolk Naval Station. The base's ship and submarine piers face the Elizabeth River as it spills into Hampton Roads. The photograph was taken by Charles S. Borjes. *Courtesy of the Sargeant Memorial Room, Norfolk Public Library.*

support his recommendation, he provided a building-by-building list of the operations housed at the shipyard accompanied by a description of the operational responsibility. On the date of the assessment, October 14, 1904, Building 28, for example, was not identified as housing the mast construction division of a sail-powered navy. During the eight years between the preparation of the 1896 map and the 1904 yard assessment, the mast house was converted to the mast and spar shed, the patternmakers' shop, a storehouse for finished boats, the office of shipkeepers and the storeroom for the Construction and Repair Division's cellulose material. As a result of the 1904 assessment, a reorganization of the base was initiated. A large area containing just a little over 272 acres, known as the Schmoele tract, was purchased in 1904; this was the most extensive growth the yard had experienced to that point. The land, juxtaposed on both sides of Paradise Creek, and which flowed into the river, belonged to an old Portsmouth resident, Dr. William Schmoele Jr.

Two events in 1907 proved particularly memorable, attracting widespread attention to the United States Navy Yard Norfolk and the Elizabeth River: the Jamestown Exposition and the sailing of the Great White Fleet—the Atlantic Squadron—on its around-the-world cruise from Hampton Roads. Both events told the world the United States had become a world power. In November 1910, the yard hosted yet another momentous event—the first flight of an airplane off of a United States Navy vessel by Eugene Barton Ely. Ely's aircraft, the *Hudson Flyer*, was transported to the navy yard at Norfolk from Pine Beach aboard the naval tug *Nice*. The evening of the thirteenth of November the *Hudson*

Flyer's engine was due to arrive by boat from Baltimore. By the time it was delivered, Ely was already on the ferry to Portsmouth to find his mechanics. The *Hudson Flyer* was craned aboard the ship and secured aft on the platform. Securing the plane required nothing fancy. The tail was tied just over the USS *Birmingham*'s (CL-2) ship's wheel, leaving only fifty-seven feet of platform for takeoff.

The *Birmingham* left its berth at the navy yard about half past eleven the following morning, the fourteenth, and steamed down the river in full view of the Norfolk waterfront. The scout cruiser was accompanied downriver by one destroyer while another stopped on the Norfolk side to fetch Ely's wife, Mabel, and a growing number of anxious Norfolk newspaper reporters. Ely, the consummate perfectionist, helped his mechanics install the plane's engine, a task that was completed by the time the *Birmingham* passed Pine Beach and headed into the harbor. The *Birmingham* was accompanied by four torpedo craft, the USSs *Bailey*, *Rowe*, *Stringham* and *Terry*. The *Rowe*, the fastest craft on station, was to be positioned closest to the *Birmingham* in the event Ely was unsuccessful on takeoff or mid-flight, which would require plucking from the Chesapeake Bay. The *Rowe* also served as the press boat. Ely's original destination on takeoff from the *Birmingham* was the marine barracks parade ground at the navy yard. As it was, when Ely landed, it would be at Willoughby Beach adjacent to Ocean View, but had the weather cooperated, he intended to begin his route beyond the Rip Raps (Fort Wool), rounding Seawell's Point, Lambert's Point and following the center of the Elizabeth River over the inner harbor, turning to the south then above the county ferry wharf and going directly to the navy yard. The flight was to take forty minutes.

While far less riveting than Ely's flight, a discovery in the mud of the Southern Branch of the Elizabeth River held the attention of Norfolk and Portsmouth residents for several days in April 1911. For fifty years and a few days an anchor that had once hung from the side of the United States first-class, full-rigged frigate *Merrimack*, later converted to the Confederate ironclad CSS *Virginia*, was found. The anchor, a six-thousand-pound piece of wrought iron with a huge stock of black walnut, was taken from its resting place by a dredge that was deepening the channel to the navy yard. The anchor was removed to a wharf near Norfolk's Roanoke Dock, having been purchased by R.W. Hudgins and Son, who intended to scrape off accumulated rust, repaint and put an iron stock on it before selling the piece to the master of a windjammer. The most noticeable aspect of the anchor was its particularly large black walnut stock, which was still covered in part by the copper sheeting put on it to protect the wood from the ravages of worms inhabiting Southern waters. While the copper had come away in places, all of the iron bands, except one, which had been forged around the wood, had dropped away. The wooden stock measured seventeen feet in length and was twenty-four inches thick and sixteen inches wide. The shank of the anchor was thirteen feet long; from tip to tip of the flukes the anchor was nine feet, seven inches. About two feet of one of the flukes stuck up above the mud, and it was this fluke that had the most rust damage. Interestingly, when the Confederates decided to rebuild the *Merrimack* as an ironclad, not a single anchor was found onboard; new ones had to be secured from the navy yard's supply. The only chain link left at the end of the *Merrimack*'s anchor, when found in the spring of 1911, was snapped in two from the strain of an attempt a half-century before to raise it from the mud. An anchor carried by the CSS *Virginia* (ex-*Merrimack*) was dredged from the bight of Craney Island in 1907, and it was this anchor, not to be confused with the discovery four years later of the original *Merrimack* anchor, that was displayed at the Jamestown Exposition.

Europe was drawn into World War I in 1914, and before the United States followed less than three years later, the navy yard played host to two interned German sea raiders, the *Kronprinz Wilhelm* and the *Prinz Eitel Frederick*. The year was 1915 and the crews of these vessels, numbering approximately one thousand officers and men, built a makeshift German village from scraps found at the yard. They dubbed it Eitel Wilhelm; it attracted many visitors and soon German sailors became fixtures on the streets of Portsmouth. Eitel Wilhelm was complete in every detail, from streets and avenues carefully laid off and named, to cottages by the scores, covering a large area, each surrounded by a garden with an attractive fence. Almost every house had its pet: dovecotes, chicken coops and rabbit hutches. Everything was carefully painted, just as it would have been at home in Germany. There was a chapel, a station house, a windmill—all the appurtenances of a real village. When work on the new dry dock began the ships were sent to the navy yard at Philadelphia. The village was taken down and packed, to be rebuilt elsewhere.

During the First World War, after the United States entered the fight in 1917, the yard was expanded; dry docks number four, six and seven, begun in the first year of America's involvement in the war in Europe, were finished in 1919. A number of ships interned in the United States before it entered the war were seized from Germany and sent to the yard to be converted, among them the *Pennsylvania*, *Neckar* and the *Rhein*. The first was rechristened *Nansemond*, the second became the *Antigone* and the third was known as the *Susquehanna*. These steamers supplemented the United States troop transport fleet. Many new shop facilities were added at the shipyard as well, with employment reaching its peak in February, nearly four months after the war ended. The yard had 11,234 workers, a considerable increase from the 2,718 who were there in 1914; an immense amount of work took place at the yard during this period. Due to the large influx of employees, many from outside Lower Tidewater, two wartime housing projects were developed, Cradock and Truxtun, which were built on the outskirts of Portsmouth. During the war years, vessels were repaired, converted and fitted out and four destroyers were built: the 1,020-ton *Caldwell*-class destroyer *Craven* (destroyer number seventy, later DD-70), launched in 1918; and the USSs *Hulbert* (DD-342), *Noa* (DD-343) and *William B. Preston* (DD-344), launched in 1919. The 43,200-ton battleship USS *North Carolina* (BB-52) was constructed at the yard, and though more than a third completed, this ship, more powerful than any then in the fleet, was scrapped in 1923 as the result of the Washington Naval Limitation Treaty.

While World War I increased shipyard production, it also limited the mission of the United States Navy Yard Norfolk. Fleet support and shore training functions were transferred to a new installation at Seawell's Point named the Norfolk Naval Operating Base, now the Norfolk Naval Station. Commander C.F. Stansworth noted in his book, *Naval Bases of the World*, "The dredged channel of the Elizabeth River from Hampton Roads to Norfolk, eleven and three-fourths miles, is crooked, congested with commerce, and it has been necessary to establish a supply depot at Hampton Roads, entitled 'Operating Base.'" From this point forward, the function of the shipyard was confined to ship construction and repair. While many of the facility's operations were transferred to Seawell's Point, war demand created a need for more industrial space and a new round of shipyard construction began. Structures built at the yard during the World War I period included a new power plant, a machine shop, a foundry, a paint shop, oil storage tanks, a pattern shop, a forge shop, a galvanizing plant, a shipfitters' building, several storage sheds and other structures. Building 28, the mast house, had a sail loft on the second floor at this time. During the era of wind propulsion, the duties performed in the sail lofts of navy yards were sail making and repair. When the navy ceased placing masts on steam-driven vessels as auxiliary power in the event of engine failure, the duties performed in the sail loft changed. Rope product construction, such as assembling hammocks and rigging loops; the fabrication of bumpers for ships; and the sewing of various canvas items, such as hatch and lifeboat covers, were the most common activities carried out by the sail loft crew.

During the years 1919 to 1922 the yard converted the collier USS *Jupiter* (collier number three) into the United States Navy's first aircraft carrier, the USS *Langley* (CV-1). The yard had its fair share of famous visitors, too. When the king and queen of Belgium visited the United States in 1919, the 23,788-ton steamer SS *George Washington*, put at their disposal, was docked at the navy yard while the Belgians went into Portsmouth and were present at the flooding of dry docks six and seven. Speaking at the ceremony, Navy Lieutenant J.J. Carey observed that the equipment, facilities and accessibility of the yard were unsurpassed by any other shipyard in the United States as a naval repair yard. "Approached by Hampton Roads," he said, "with a channel forty feet deep, and a width at minimum of four hundred and fifty feet, ending at the south of this yard in a turning basin, large enough to accommodate the largest ships afloat, this yard is equipped to build, dock and repair such vessels as the *Majestic* and the *Leviathan* on down to the lesser tonnage liners." The lieutenant also noted something else: "The yard also manufactures turbine blades, paint, buoys, gas engines, metal furniture, gas for industrial purposes, coal and oil burning ranges and small boats."

After the Washington Naval Limitation Treaty took effect, the yard's employment figures once again plummeted to 2,538, less than it had been in 1914. In 1929 the name of the navy yard was changed to Norfolk Navy Yard, Portsmouth, Virginia. During the twenties and into the early thirties, no new ships were constructed and little improvement occurred to the yard itself. But the freeze on shipbuilding was eventually alleviated by a battleship modernization initiative that started in 1925. Six of the fleet's oldest battleships were modernized at the United States Navy Yard Norfolk (the name having changed again), including the USS *Texas* (BB-35), 1925–26; the USS *New York* (BB-34), 1926–27; the USS *Nevada* (BB-36), 1927–29; the USS *Arizona* (BB-39), 1929–31; the USS *Mississippi* (BB-41), 1931–33; and the USS *Idaho* (BB-42), 1931–34. In the spring of 1933 navy yard employees, along with other government workers, had their pay cut during the Great Depression. With the passage of the National Industrial Recovery Act in July 1933, which included a naval construction program, the economic crisis of the national depression was broken. The yard was allotted a total of nine destroyers, built and launched during the period between 1934 and 1939. With its battleship modernization program, yard employment had risen by the end of 1932 to 3,819 but, with a workload of nine destroyers, there began a steady climb in yard employment that reached a total of 7,625 by September 1, 1939, the day the Germans invaded Poland, the opening salvo of World War II in Europe.

During World War II the navy yard expanded in size and development of its facilities surpassed its growth many times over from World War I. Yard statistics are telling. From January 1, 1940, four months after the outbreak of war in Europe, to the end of the war with Japan, on September 2, 1945, a period of five years, eight months, the Norfolk Navy Yard repaired, altered, converted or otherwise worked on 6,850 naval vessels, aggregating more than 27 million tons. But the yard also built 101 new ships and landing craft for the fleet, and millions of dollars worth of manufactured products were turned out for forces afloat and other naval establishments. The yard's work during World War II reached the staggering total, at that time, of over one billion dollars. To achieve these

A salvaging operation to recover what was left of the CSS Virginia *was conducted over a ten-year period from September 2, 1867, to June 2, 1876. According to the logbook of Navy Yard Dry Dock Number One, dated May 30, 1876, the* Virginia *(ex-*Merrimack*) entered the dock on that date to be cut up.*

numbers, the yard more than doubled in size, its reservation expanding from 352.76 acres to 746.88 acres with nearly four and a quarter miles of waterfront on the Elizabeth River. A dry dock 1,100 feet in length, capable of taking the largest ship afloat, was constructed, and 685 buildings, both permanent and temporary, were built. By February 1943 there were 42,893 workers at the yard, nearly four times the maximum employment during the prior world war. The influx of workers became a stressor on the Elizabeth River ecosystem. Housing facilities in the community, exceptionally inadequate, were supplemented on the Portsmouth side of the river by the construction of no fewer than 45 public and private war housing projects, totaling 16,487 units. In addition to the 9 destroyers built between 1934 and 1939, the yard also constructed and launched 30 major vessels during the World War II period. This number does not include 20 tank landing ships (LSTs), and many other smaller watercraft that came out of the yard during this time. With the end of World War II the shipyard resumed a familiar peace-time posture, and on December 1, 1945, the Norfolk Navy Yard was renamed the Norfolk Naval Shipyard, Portsmouth, Virginia.

With the outbreak of hostilities on the Korean peninsula in June 1950, the shipyard was assigned a heavy workload and operated again during wartime conditions largely as a repair station. During the three-year conflict, the yard completed repairs and other work on more than 1,250 naval vessels and in addition built two new ships, USS *Bold* (MSO 424) and USS *Bulwark* (MSO 425), non-magnetic minesweepers of laminated wood construction. There were 16,100 employees on the yard by July 1952, but when the fighting ended, employment began to drop off, falling to a low of 9,100 in early 1965, the year that the shipyard attained nuclear technology capability when the USS *Skate* (SSN 578) became the first modern submarine to undergo a major overhaul in the Norfolk Naval Shipyard. Within the span of history of this storied shipyard, it has hosted presidents, promulgated the United States Navy's first hospital, recruited workers from many states, repaired and overhauled thousands of American and allied ships and earned a host of awards. Just as it had been charged with building a ship capable of protecting American merchant ships from the Barbary pirates, the shipyard is still serving the nation with its work on ships that ply the waters of the Elizabeth on their way to and from the sea.

Chapter Six
Living on
Mother Water

As pleasant a country as ever the sun shined on: temperate and full of all sorts of excellent viands; wild boar is as common as the tamest bacon; and venison as mutton.

And you shall live freely there, without sergeants, or courtiers, or lawyers—You may be an alderman there and never be a scavenger; you may be any other officer and never be a slave. You may come to preferment enough—to riches and fortune enough, and have never the more villainy nor the less wit. Besides, there we shall have no more law than conscience, and not too much of either; serve God enough, eat and drink enough and enough is as good as a feast.

So wrote an English playwright in *Eastward Ho*, an English comedy of 1605 and such was his countryman's opinion of life in Southeastern Virginia. With four centuries of development, and perhaps some rewording of the description above, the same would be the opinion today of the area that begins on the shores of Seawell's Point (now Sewell's Point) and centers on the cities of Norfolk and Portsmouth as the Elizabeth River begins, eventually making its way east, west and south. For it is here that people *live*.

By 1618 two important Virginia institutions came into being that are still at work today, though modified from their original form—the county-parish system of local government, and the bicameral representative legislative assembly. The orders establishing these two institutions both originated with the Virginia Company's London council on November 18, 1618, the same day that Sir George Yeardley (also Yardley) was chosen as governor by the council. On this date, it was also ordered by the council in London that the Virginia Colony be divided into four great corporations for the purpose of local administration. The term "borough" was also frequently applied to these corporations but was almost entirely suspended by the latter term. Representatives took the

Town Back Creek, shown here, once extended nearly to Church Street, today Saint Paul's Boulevard, and to the stone bridge, to the left in this ca. 1845 lithograph. The stone bridge was built in 1818 to connect the northern and southern ends of Granby Street before the creek was later filled in—to Granby Street by 1884 and to Boush Street by 1905. *Courtesy of the author.*

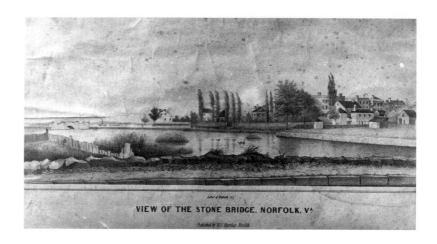

VIEW OF THE STONE BRIDGE, NORFOLK, Vᵃ

name burgesses, meaning borough inhabitants, and the lower house of the Virginia General Assembly became known as the House of Burgesses, a custom that prevailed throughout the colonial period. In the early days of the seventeenth century a borough was not, as the term implies, a corporation or incorporated town; there were no charters or other articles of incorporation. A borough was merely a territorial division entitled to be represented in the assembly. Yeardley arrived and assumed governorship of the colony on April 19, 1619, and with him also came the duty of carrying out the London council's instruction to create the corporations, which he completed by April 28, when the Virginia Company records start.

The first assembly convened on July 30, 1619, and was composed of the governor, then Sir George Yeardley, the council and two burgesses from each corporation and from each of seven particular plantations—twenty-two burgesses in all. There seems to have been some degree of inconsistency in this method of representation, since not only were the corporations represented, but also the other settlements within their boundaries. The burgesses from the corporations represented the company plantations, whereas the others represented particular plantations that were territorially within a corporation's bounds. The corporations were organized like the Hundreds in England. These territorial divisions in England originated at the time of Alfred the Great, but went back much further, in truth, to beginnings of Teutonic law and custom. Alfred is reported to have divided his kingdom in the late ninth century into shires, hundreds and tithings, a tithing being a community of ten freeholders and their families. Ten tithings composed a hundred—hence the name—which was subordinate in size to the shire. The designation "hundred" in Virginia referred to an area inferior in size to a shire or county, largely because it was traditionally referenced as such in England. There was no regularity in size here either in number of families or in acreage, for some Virginia hundreds included as many as eight thousand acres.

Another kind of early settlement in the colony was called a particular plantation. Little separated the hundred from a particular plantation. Some settlements bearing the name "hundred" had been established by the Virginia Company itself and some by individuals or associations of individuals, but those with the name "plantation," without exception, were "particular" or privately owned. Private plantation ownership was the outgrowth of the Virginia Company having run out of money, thus particular company shareholders joined together in societies to establish plantations on their own. The hundreds, the particular plantations and their parishes were begun about 1618. Of the four corporations and fourteen other settlements that came into existence before the first assembly in 1619, only two were in Lower Tidewater Virginia—the company settlement of Kecoughtan, which became the seat of the corporation of Elizabeth City, and Captain Christopher Lawne's plantation, located on the present boundary between Isle of Wight and Surry Counties. When Lawne died in 1620, the patent was renewed by his heirs and associates under the name Isle of Wight Plantation. There was nothing down the Elizabeth River at that time, but this would soon change.

Land grant records in patent books begin about 1623 with scattered grants of a few years prior recorded at that time. Records are more complete beginning in 1624, when the Virginia Company was dissolved. Grants were not made in the name of the British Crown until three years later, in 1627, but it is important to remember that the date of the grant does not always coincide with when it was seated. Though the records are not comprehensive, there are numerous grantees who are known from other sources for which land grants have not been otherwise preserved in the official books. A list produced in 1626 is a source of landowners in geographical sequence, which provides an approximate location of many very early land grants. In each of the list sequences, the names and properties start upstream and move downward on the riverbank and shoreline of the Elizabeth River, unless otherwise noted. The first tracts taken up on the south side of Hampton Roads started at Willoughby's Point, today called Willoughby Spit, then on to Seawell's Point (now Sewell's Point), then south to Tanner's Creek (now the Lafayette River). In 1624 Thomas Willoughby and Thomas Chapman were each granted 100 acres; Thomas Breewood, 200 acres, all on the north side of Mason's Creek; and John Downman, 100 acres on the other side of the creek. Four years earlier, in 1620, Captain William Tucker had been granted 650 acres on Seawell's Point and between this and John Sipsey's (also Sibsey) land was a creek, also a reference to Mason's Creek. John Sipsey, yeoman, was also granted 250 acres in 1624 adjoining Tucker's, and 200 acres were

The militia in each county relevant to the Elizabeth River, its tributaries and the Great Dismal Swamp was headed by a county lieutenant, counterpart of the Lord Lieutenant of Shire in England. Men in the militia had to be between the ages of sixteen and sixty, for whom service was compulsory. The governor remained the titular head of the colonial militia with the rank of lieutenant general (more often called captain general), and he appointed county lieutenants (rank of colonel), their deputies (rank of lieutenant colonel) and, in the case of counties with distant, inaccessible areas, sub-deputies were appointed with the rank of major.

Thelaball's Creek was named for James Thelaball, a Huguenot refugee from France who arrived in Lower Norfolk in 1648. The Southern Branch of Mason's Creek, at the head of which was Tanner's Creek Chapel, was still traditionally called Thelaball's Creek, a name that remained on maps until the early twentieth century. The creek disappeared when it was filled in as the principal landing field for the U.S. naval air station. Thelaball lived on the creek with his family, three sons and three daughters. He died in 1693, two years after the division of the county.

granted Lieutenant John Cheesman (also Chisman). Importantly, however, John Wood, shipbuilder, applied for land on the Elizabeth River "because thereon is timber fitting for his trade, and water sufficient to launch such ships as shall be there built for the use and service of the Company," a reference to the Virginia Company. Wood's entry in July 1620 was in the patent books but not the 1626 list, and there is no acreage listed to indicate how large the yard might have been. These are all of the earliest grants in the corporation of Elizabeth City that pertain to holdings along the Elizabeth River. Notably, two grants at Seawell's Point were preserved in records—properties belonging to Sipsey and Cheesman. Information regarding Tucker's 650-acre grant from a deed of a much later date—1661—on record for Lower Norfolk County, was described thusly: that Captain Tucker, in 1620, patented the six hundred and fifty acres "knowne and commonly called by the name of the plantations scituate, lyeing and being on the south side of the James River"; that this patent had been granted earlier confirmed by general court order in December 1633, but Tucker subsequently assigned the whole tract to Sipsey. Henry Seawell did also "cleare, seate, build and plant" on 150 acres on the tract known as Seawell's Point adjoining land occupied by Sipsey. Sipsey and Seawell had been burgesses for the upper part of Elizabeth City in 1632, which Thomas Willoughby had represented since 1629 by virtue of his residence on Salford's Creek east of Newport News in 1628. Willoughby did not live on the land he owned "on the south side" of Hampton Roads in the early years of his ownership, and Tucker did not maintain his principal residence there either, but it is very likely that Sipsey was the first to have his principal residence at Seawell's Point and running a close second was Henry Seawell, possibly after 1633. Of note, too, Virginia also had its cadre of men called "ancient" planters, those who came to Virginia before May 1616. Of these men, Francis Mason, his wife Anne and his daughter, also Anne, arrived in the colony in 1613 aboard the ship *John and Francis*. The Masons were on Mason's Creek before November 1635. Another would be Thomas Willoughby, who had come to the colony at the age of nine in 1610, and whose uncle, Sir Percival Willoughby of Nottingham, was a shareholder in the Virginia Company and member of a distinguished English family.

A land grant by the colony's governor, John Harvey, in the name of the British Crown, under the date of January 22, 1637/38, provided instructions essentially setting up New Norfolk County from land formerly part of Elizabeth City County, dividing it into its upper and lower components. On April 13, 1637, a patent was drawn up by the Virginia assembly for land in Upper New Norfolk County, which had not been transcribed correctly, for the land was on the Western Branch of the Elizabeth River; this was the first occurrence of the name Norfolk in early

This picture may be the oldest existing photograph of Norfolk, dating to 1865; it was taken from the top of a building near the corner of Bank and Main Streets. The street running up the center of the photograph is the part of Bank Street running between Main Street and what later became City Hall Avenue, but what was then Town Back Creek, which was gradually filled in after the Civil War. The Merchants' and Mechanics' Bank, chartered in 1849, is in the foreground. A squad of Federal troops can also be seen at the bottom of the picture, marching up Bank Street toward the creek. *Courtesy of the author.*

records. Almost exactly a month later, on May 15, 1637, the court for the Lower County of New Norfolk met for the first time. This was eight months prior to the Virginia governor's grant to Henry Frederick, Lord Maltravers, whose desire to take part in the colonization of Virginia had led, on July 5, 1636, to Charles I writing a letter of instruction to Harvey on behalf of Maltravers ordering "to assign and sett out to the said Lord Maltravers and his heirs a competent tract of land in the southern part of that country as may beare the name of a county and be called the county of Norfolk." The governor's grant to Maltravers not only encroached a whole degree of latitude, sixty nautical miles, on the Carolina grant of 1629, but also covered a part of Elizabeth River reaches in which only a few individual grants had been made in the 1620 to 1624 period, and which in 1635 and 1636 thus became the center of much granting of land and settlements.

By 1635 patent books dramatically changed; landowners increased exponentially on the Elizabeth River and its tributaries and creeks. On April 21, 1635, Francis Towers was granted 200 acres one mile up the Western Branch of the Elizabeth River, and John Hill, 350 acres four miles up the same branch between Clark's Creek and Brown's Bay. John Hill came to the colony in 1621 and was well connected to Adam Thorowgood. It was, in fact, from the Thorowgood patent that it is known of Hill that he "doth affirme himself formerly to have lived in the university of Oxford of the trade of booke binder, and that he is the Sonne of Stephen Hill of Oxford aforesaid ffletcher," an arrow maker, per Sadie Scott and V. Hope Kellam's *Old Houses in Princess Anne, Virginia.*

Other grants on the Western Branch included a May 30, 1635 grant of 200 acres to John Slaughter adjacent to Brown's Bay, a patent that was renewed in John Radford's name shortly thereafter; a June 1, 1635 grant to John Sipsey for 1,500 acres in the present area of West Norfolk; a June 2, 1635 grant of 800 acres to Cornelius Lloyd east on Merchant's Creek, west on Muddy Creek; a June 14, 1635 200-acre-grant to Captain William Tucker on the north side of the Western Branch; and a July 14, 1635 150-acre grant to Thomas Wright near Captain Tucker. On the main stem of the Elizabeth River three grants were made between June 1 and July 2, 1635, one to Thomas Lambert of 100 acres on the east side of the river that is still called Lambert's Point; a 200-acre tract to William Ramshaw on the south side of the river; and an 800-acre tract to Cornelius Lloyd. On November 19, 1635, Thomas Willoughby was granted 300 acres on the Southern Branch of the Elizabeth. From the grants named herein and those that had also occurred on the Lynnhaven River, settlement of the area in 1635 spread first from the Western Branch before the end of June that year, then on the river main stem, the Lynnhaven River during the latter half of the year and, lastly, the Southern Branch and the Elizabeth's confluence with the waters of Hampton Roads and the Chesapeake Bay.

The following year, 1636, there were many new grants made, some to established settlers, but a considerable number went to new arrivals. On the Western Branch were Edward Lloyd, brother of Cornelius, and Robert Page; on the main stem, John Yates, William Ramshaw, Thomas Burbage, John Gater, Cornelius Lloyd and Thomas Willoughby; on the Southern Branch, John Yates, again, and John Roberts; and on the Eastern Branch, the first there, William Julian, another yeoman and ancient planter, and John Gater, again. Willoughby's "dwelling house" is first noted on patent in 1635 on his land on the south shore of the Chesapeake Bay. This house, long gone, was likely near the conjoining of Willoughby Spit to the mainland, then called Willoughby's Point. His fellow ancient planter, Francis Mason, first lived in Charles City above Westover. When Mason ultimately came to Norfolk is not known for certain, but he was here by 1635, as indicated by Willoughby's patent, on the west side of the creek that soon took his name. Interestingly, most of the land between the Lynnhaven River and Seawell's Point was in the hands of three men in 1636: Thomas Willoughby, Adam Thorowgood and Francis Mason. A later name that would be added to the list is Henry Seawell. Willoughby added further patents to his already expansive land holdings when he acquired additional acreage at Willoughby Point and the Elizabeth River where Norfolk Town was later to be sited. He added further to his estate with patents in 1643 for fifteen hundred acres and 1654 for fourteen hundred acres, the latter extending from Willoughby's Point Manor inland to the head of Mason's Creek, which almost met Old Seawell's Point

The stone bridge over Town Back Creek is shown in this photograph, taken about 1870. The brick home to the left of the bridge was the residence of Cincinnatus W. Newton; it was built in the early 1800s, but torn down in 1905, when the Law Building was constructed on its site. To the right of the Newton home, the sails of a merchant vessel are visible in the background, and the piers and warehouses of the Merchants' and Miners' Transportation Company can be seen. After the creek was filled in, the Haddington Building was built in 1890 roughly on the site of the wooden building to the immediate left of the bridge. To the right of the bridge the Royster Building was erected in 1912, and to the extreme right, the Monticello Hotel in 1898. *Courtesy of the author.*

(now Little Creek) Road at one point, and Old Ocean View Road where Fisherman's Road branched into it. This 1654 patent was interesting, too, because of the names of twenty-eight headrights listed on it, some of whom were Alice, Thomas and Elizabeth Willoughby, James Wishard and Matthew Hancock.

When the division of communities was made between Upper and Lower New Norfolk, the Nansemond River area became the heart of Upper New Norfolk. The boundary between Upper and Lower Norfolk Counties became what is known today as Hoffler's Creek, the first creek west of Craney Island, demarcated on a 1636 land grant belonging to Richard Bennett. By April 1637 it was clear, by virtue of land grants, that these two counties were operating independently, but there is not a Virginia statute separating an area of Elizabeth City County to create the Lower County of New Norfolk. One month later, in May 1637, the area south and east of Hampton Roads first appeared in legal records as two counties and parishes, named distinctly the Upper County of New Norfolk and the Lower County of New Norfolk; both locales would soon drop the "New" from their titles. It was not until an Act of Assembly in 1639–40, establishing the bounds of Isle of Wight, Upper Norfolk and Lower Norfolk, that there is an official separation recorded. In March 1642–43 the boundary between the parishes was official, and at the same time the 1639–40 act was reiterated and the boundary between Upper and Lower Counties of New Norfolk was defined. The latter is particularly important, as it was stated that the common boundary was that "first creek west of Crayne Point in no way trenching upon the Western Branch of Elizabeth River nor the creeks thereof which belong to the County of Lower Norfolk." The only good source of information of this time has come from

This Levytype of Granby Street, looking north from Main Street, ca. 1880, includes a horse-drawn trolley and a number of trees, still part of the landscape at that time. Horse-drawn trolleys were capable of carrying about twenty passengers. *Courtesy of the author.*

county record books, which are predominantly court records that provide orders and minutes of proceedings, deeds for land that it permitted to be recorded, wills that it admitted to probate, estate inventories and audits that it ordered. From this information it is possible to ascertain details of landowners' daily lives, purchases of land and considerable demographics, real and personal property left at death and to whom. The records of Lower Norfolk County, one of the first ten counties in existence in 1637, largely survived. Lower Norfolk County Records, Book A (1636–46) noted that a court was held in the Lower County of New Norfolk on May 15, 1637, with Captain Adam Thorowgood, Captain John Sipsey, Francis Mason, Edward Windham, Robert Came (also Camm) and William Julian present; this is the first entry in Book A. Thorowgood was commander and presiding justice. While it would be some years before this county was divided into two parishes, two natural divisions were represented on the court. Thorowgood, Windham and Came lived in the eastern section of the county at Lynnhaven, while Sipsey, Julian and Mason lived in the western section near Seawell's Point and the Elizabeth River. Henry Seawell replaced Camm on the Court of Lower Norfolk on February 6,

1639. By July 6, 1640, Captain Thomas Willoughby was commander and presiding justice; Thorowgood had died early in the year. There would be a steady stream of prominent citizens who served on this court for the half-century that it existed.

Men with military rank or title preceding their names are not to be taken lightly nor are they used indiscriminately as titles would come to be interpreted later. These men held titles from appointments and commissions in His Majesty's Colonial Militia for Virginia. The militia in each county relevant to the Elizabeth River, its tributaries and the Great Dismal Swamp was headed by a county lieutenant, counterpart of the Lord Lieutenant of Shire in England. Men in the militia had to be between the ages of sixteen and sixty, for whom service was compulsory. The governor remained the titular head of the colonial militia with the rank of lieutenant general (more often called captain general), and he appointed county lieutenants (with the rank of colonel), their deputies (with the rank of lieutenant colonel) and, in the case of counties with distant, inaccessible areas, sub-deputies were appointed with the rank of major. In one or more companies of foot, lighthorse and dragoons there were the usual officers, such as captains, lieutenants and ensigns, commissioned by the governor on the recommendation of the county lieutenant. A clerk of the militia kept the records. In Lower Norfolk County that person was known to be John Ferebee, the county surveyor in 1680. This rank structure was not always strictly adhered to; Adam Thorowgood had qualified as captain of militia at its first meeting on May 15, 1637, but it is possible he was also county lieutenant. John Sipsey qualified as captain.

There were other officers of the Court of Lower Norfolk, including sheriffs, constables and clerks. The earliest records did not consistently list the clerk, but a document dated February 1, 1657–58, was signed Thomas Bridge. Another, dated August 15, 1665, was signed William Jermy (also Jeremie), clerk of the court, who was also listed as a headright in a land grant of 1664. If this is true, Jermy had been in the county for some time, as John Sipsey bequeathed to Jermy his "black-hilted Rapier" in his will, which was proved in August 1652. Jermy died before January 15, 1666/67, and from his will it is known that he was living in Lynnhaven Parish then, and that William Langley II was his godson. The best known of the seventeenth-century clerks of court was William Porten, who came to his post on February 18, 1668/69, and continued to serve until his death twenty-five years later. While the court may have held its first meeting at Captain Adam Thorowgood's house on the Lynnhaven River, subsequent meetings were successively convened at William Shipp's, Thomas Lambert's and Thomas Mears', all on the Elizabeth River, and then at Savill Gaskin's at Lynnhaven, which may have meant

Port Norfolk, built west of downtown Portsmouth along the banks of the Elizabeth, was developed in the late nineteenth century to accommodate a growing demand for more suburban-style neighborhoods with more convenient access to downtown Portsmouth. This planned suburb was designed with freestanding Queen Anne–style wooden houses and bungalows. Port Norfolk served as the glebe of Portsmouth Parish and Trinity Episcopal Church, a strategic landing point during the Revolutionary War and as a farm.

Atlantic City was a suburb of Norfolk that referred to a small area of Norfolk riverfront on both sides of Colley Avenue, southwest of Olney Road. When annexed in 1890, Atlantic City reached from the Norfolk and Western terminal at Lambert's Point and touched the railway tracks at Twenty-third Street as far as Elmwood Cemetery.

Thorowgood's or the glebe land. William Shipp's quickly became the favorite location for court meetings; Shipp lived on the Elizabeth, where he kept a tavern or ordinary, thus it made reasonable accommodation for the justices to do business and socialize accordingly. In May 1646 it was ordered that the meetings be held at Shipp's exclusively. The Assembly of March 1654–55 passed a law entitled "An Act for Regulating Trade and Establishing Ports and Places for Markets." This law was the first step toward establishing towns in the colony, but it is interesting that at this point the act carried provisions concerning the county court. It stipulated that ports and marketplaces should be established in *each parish on a river* and that within these sites should be located the county court, the clerk's office, the sheriff's office and the prison; the justices were further enjoined to "endeavor to have meeting places or churches and ordinaries for entertainment and lodging within the same." Lower Norfolk County Court complied with the provisions of the act by a court order of July 16, 1655, that read:

> *Uppon the land of Mr. William Shipp on Elizabeth River to be the place for both Church and Market for Elizabeth River Parish, two myles in length Northward and Southward and noe further…Uppon the land or plantation of William Johnson, being Mistress Yeardley's land scituate on Linhaven River* [sic] *to be the place for both Church and Market for Linhaven Parish, two myles in length Northward and Southward and no further.*

Had this act not been repealed in 1656, the courthouses would have been built in each parish as specified above. William Shipp's was "on the Elizabeth River," not on its branches. This would indicate that his property was between its wide mouth, Craney Island to Tanner's Creek, perhaps Lambert's Point, and where the river divides into its Eastern and Southern Branches. This would put Shipp's most likely between Lambert's Point and what later became Town Point, the west end of Main Street in downtown Norfolk. The court continued to rotate between Mistress Yeardley's (she was the widow of both Adam Thorowgood and John Gookin) and the Elizabeth River for years to come. On January 16, 1660/61, the courthouse was ordered, the first in Lower Norfolk County, built at Thomas Harding's plantation on Broad Creek. Harding's plantation was on the dividing line of the two parishes (and, eventually, two counties). This two-hundred-acre site was deeded to the county by Harding on November 15, 1661, but its bounds were so vague that its location is uncertain. The Norfolk courthouse was not built as a permanent structure for some time to come; there was no evidence that it was begun while Lower Norfolk County was still in existence. The county levy of November 18, 1690, indicates that

James Joseling was paid for clearing the courthouse field, on land that had been set aside for this purpose. But there is no record of the building being erected there until after the county was divided in 1691, the beginning of Norfolk and Princess Anne Counties.

Interestingly, the parishes' churches followed many of the same organizational conventions as the courts. Parish churches or chapels of ease maintained governing bodies who appointed a succession of reverends. Depending on where landowners lived along the Elizabeth, larger property owners took responsibility for a portion of their reverend's salary, dividing it into thirds among three geographical areas of the Elizabeth. In 1640 those living from Captain Willoughby's plantation to Daniel Tanner's creek would have a portion of the reverend's one-hundred-pound salary paid by Captain John Sipsey, Lieutenant Francis Mason and Henry Seawell. Inhabitants of the stretch of river from the Western Branch and Craney Point placed Cornelius Lloyd, Henry Gatlin and John Hill in charge of paying their part of the salary, and William Julian, John Gater, Ensign Thomas Lambert, Thomas Sawyer, Thomas Mears and John Watkins paid for those inhabitants on the Eastern and Southern Branches. Most of these men's names have been attached to prominent waterways and points of land and are well known, but others are not. Saint Julian's Creek, flowing into the Southern Branch from the west, is now misspelled Saint Julien's Creek. There are also Sawyer's Point, which is better known as Lovett's Point, on the west side of the mouth of the Western Branch; Watkins' Land was, in 1644, the name of the tract that later became part of the town of Norfolk in 1680. In the same court order of May 25, 1640, covering reverends' salaries, there was also the first direct reference to a parish church at "Mr. Seawell's Point." It is further noted that there was a disagreement among inhabitants of the parish: those living from Tanner's Creek up the three branches of the

The Elizabeth River

Elizabeth River did not think it was right that they should pay two-thirds of the reverend's salary, unless he intended to teach and instruct them as often as he preached at the parish church at Seawell's Point, which was not easy to get to for any of them. About this time discussion of additional chapels began. The Elizabeth River Chapel was likely in close proximity to the court, somewhere between Lambert's Point and Town Point on William Shipp's land or that of Robert Glascocke, purchased from him by Shipp, but there are some who continue to believe the site now occupied by Saint Paul's Episcopal Church was the site of this chapel, though the land under it had nothing to do with Shipp. The Act of Assembly of March 1642/43 provides for the division of Lower Norfolk County into parishes: Elizabeth, Lynnhaven and Southern Shore. Southern Shore Parish was on the south bank of the Eastern Branch of the Elizabeth River, and had been there since mid-1639. A grant in 1649 to Richard Whitehurst mentions a Church Creek, the first stream flowing into the Eastern Branch, east of Indian River, and on this site is early evidence that a church building was constructed to accommodate its earliest inhabitants. Later, in the early 1650s, spreading settlement in the Elizabeth River Parish necessitated additional chapels of ease. The first such chapel of this kind was included in a 1653 grant to Richard Pinner for land on the Western Branch "between two branches of Church Creek." This Western Branch Chapel was on the north side of the branch near an early ferry, and where the later Atlantic Coast Line Railroad bridge crossed it, bricks of its foundation were dug up during bridge construction.

The second chapel of ease to reach inhabitants in growing settlements away from designated towns was known as Tanner's Creek Chapel. This chapel was built between 1659 and 1661, at the head of a branch of Mason's Creek, later called Thelaball's Creek, and was at the angle of the former Virginian Railway line to Seawell's Point and its branch line to the old United States Army Sub-Port of Embarkation. At the turn of the twentieth century the brick foundation of this church was still visible, but is now gone. This site was only three miles from the original parish church at Seawell's Point. The chapel was needed because by the time the

Tanner's Creek Chapel was finished in 1661 the first parish church was dilapidated and had been abandoned.

The third Elizabeth River Parish chapel serving the area's population sprawl was called the Southern Branch Chapel. It was built in 1662 and was referred to indirectly in a grant in 1664 to William Carver for land on the Southern Branch near another Church Creek. This was on the east side of the branch and likely between two tidal streams now called Jones Creek and Scuffletown Creek; it is unknown which of these two might have been called Church Creek. Information contained in the *Journal of the House of Burgesses* under the date August 30, 1701, titled "A Grievance from Norfolk County Complaining that a Chapel of Ease Formerly Built by the Inhabitants of the Southerne Branch Precinct of the Said County Is Pulled Down and Rebuilt in An Inconvenient Place," made clear the residents' displeasure with available religious facilities. The original site was on the east side of the Southern Branch, almost directly opposite the entrance to Paradise Creek, and the site to which it was moved in 1701 was Great Bridge. This was the place that William Byrd II referred to during his journey into Carolina in 1728 as "the long bridge built over the Southern Branch." The chapel was still called Southern Branch Chapel in April 1728, but by October 1749, it was referred to as the Great Bridge Chapel. During the Revolutionary War battle of Great Bridge, this chapel was damaged, but was not abandoned and dismantled until 1845.

There would be additional parish divisions in the early eighteenth century. By mid-century, Elizabeth River Parish comprised Norfolk County north of the Elizabeth River and its Eastern Branch; Saint Bride's Parish took in the entire county south of the Eastern Branch and east of the Southern Branch; and Portsmouth Parish took up the entire county south of the Elizabeth River and west of the Southern Branch. The southern part of the county was presumably divided by a line running north and south, an extension of the north-to-south boundary of the Southern Branch. The Act of Assembly of April 6, 1761, that had created these new boundaries was accepted without much argument.

One additional mention should be made here: the Tanner's Creek Chapel of Elizabeth River Parish was abandoned by 1785, and in 1828 repaired and put back into service as a Baptist meetinghouse. The following year, 1829, this congregation was formally constituted as the Tanner's Creek Baptist Church, though this structure was apparently dismantled and later rebuilt, in 1836, at the corner of Old Ocean View Road and Seawell's Point Road, and thus rechristened Salem Baptist Church. A new building was built in 1870. There would be several additional antebellum churches constructed in Norfolk County, but those would best be discussed in another work.

Park View's development was facilitated by electric trolleys running from Portsmouth Naval Medical Center. The neighborhood, named after the hospital's public park, cropped up along the Elizabeth between 1888 and 1892, and was one of the first residential areas outside Portsmouth's original eighteenth-century core, Olde Towne. There are more than three hundred homes of varying styles in Park View, although Queen Anne homes with towers and gables are the most popular.

Below and Opposite: The Edgewater section of Norfolk County, shown here ca. 1900, was annexed by the City of Norfolk in 1923. Edgewater, with picturesque views of the main stem of the Elizabeth River, is located off Hampton Boulevard, which was formerly known as Atlantic Boulevard—until it was renamed in the 1920s. *Courtesy of the author*.

About five miles up the Southern Branch of the Elizabeth River, on the west, near Julian's Creek, now Saint Julian's Creek, was also the residence of Thomas Nash, first of another family, long seated and widely spread over the area. From an agreement dated November 4, 1664, Thomas Nash and Richard Taylor owned 500 acres in partnership, and a patent was issued to them just one year later, on November 6, 1665, for 446 acres "neere the head of Julian's Creek in the southward branch of the Elizabeth River beginning at a point on the south side of the creek." When Thomas Nash died in 1672–73, there was a deed of apprenticeship for his son dated February 10 that year noting that Thomas Nash II was to work under John Nichols to learn "the art of a shoemaker or cordwinder," but the most interesting aspect was that Thomas II was only going to be six years old the following March 18; thus it is known that he was born exactly on March 18, 1666/67. The apprenticeship was to last until Thomas II turned twenty-one, thus he probably did not marry until 1688. His wife, Ann, was the daughter of William Etheridge, and they had three sons and four daughters. The Etheridge family also lived on the Southern Branch. Thomas Etheridge died in December 1671, and his wife, Christian, died the month before; they had five children, three sons and two daughters.

It was not until the Virginia General Assembly convened at Jamestown in June 1680 and passed "An Act for Cohabitation and the Encouragement of Trade and Manufacture" that towns came to pass in counties, which in the case of Lower Norfolk, were named according to the convention dictated in the act, which specified that it be called the town of Lower Norfolk County. In the clause regarding this county, it was referred to as the town "in Lower Norfolk County on Nicholas Wise his land on the Eastern Branch of the Elizabeth River at the entrance of the Branch." This strip of land, on which the heart of today's downtown Norfolk has

risen up, was considered a well-protected site, having at its western end a fort—the Half-Moone Fort—that was provided by the Act of 1673 and was completed a few years later. The town site was surveyed by the county surveyor, John Ferebee, in 1680 and 1681, and early settlement began shortly thereafter, but most certainly before the end of 1683. Economic upheaval, prompted by turmoil on the river, was caused by large losses sustained in 1667 and 1673 as the result of acts of war committed in the waters of the Elizabeth by Dutch naval forces. But far more serious were the effects of Mother Nature on the Elizabeth River and her well-protected towns, including residents in what later became Portsmouth on the south bank of the Elizabeth. The trouble began with a spring hailstorm in April 1667, described by Thomas J. Wertenbaker in his 1931 writings on Norfolk. Hailstones fell as big as turkey eggs, which destroyed newly planted crops and killed livestock in large number. Inhabitants had not recovered from this storm when it began to rain—for forty days—and grain planted after the hailstorm rotted in the ground. Two months passed and a third disaster struck. On August 27, 1667, a storm swept over the coast and bay with gale-force winds accompanied by torrential rain that lasted twenty-four hours. From the time of year and its duration and intensity, this was a hurricane—one of the earliest recorded. The day after this storm came through, August 28, an observer wrote that it was a scene of utter desolation; houses and barns were ruined, chimneys wrecked, fences flattened and tobacco in the fields had been cut to pieces. The waters of the Chesapeake Bay had been driven into the rivers and creeks, forcing rowboats and sailboats onto land, and during the height of the storm, the rising tide overflowed banks and forced people "who lived not in sight of the water" to take refuge on rooftops. A fourth catastrophe struck in the winter of 1672–73 that was particularly disastrous, when

a disease of epidemic proportions struck down thousands of head of livestock. The winter that year was particularly cold; the mortality rate for cattle in the colony was estimated to have been half the population.

As indicated earlier in this chapter, Lower Norfolk County was, by an act of the Virginia General Assembly in April 1691, divided into two separate units to be named Norfolk County and Princess Anne County. The common boundary between the two counties was identical with that established between Elizabeth River and Lynnhaven Parishes in March 1642/43, almost four years after the separate establishment of these two parishes, which is believed to have taken place in late 1639. The act of March 1642/43 gave the boundary line of the two parishes as "the first creek shooting out of the Chesopeiack bay called the Little Creek," and continued, "all the branches of the said creek," then on to the Lynnhaven River, including all branches of the river, and thus to the head of the Eastern Branch of the Elizabeth River, actually to the head of the Eastern Branch and to Broad Creek on its north side and to Indian Creek, now Indian River, on its south side. This particular boundary put the plantations on Broad Creek in the bounds of the Lynnhaven Parish and, eventually, Princess Anne County. The boundary did not specify further due largely to the existence of the Southern Shore Parish, which disappeared later but existed at that time on the sparsely populated south bank of the Eastern Branch. The "Act for Dividing Lower Norfolk County" provided more specific information on the boundary, but it, too, had its vagaries. The description in the act of 1691 began with a new inlet at Little Creek and up that creek to the dams between the lands of Jacob Johnson and Richard Drout; most likely this was the land up to the point of today's Norfolk International Airport, and "up a branch at the head of which is the dwelling house of William Moseley, Senior, and the new dwelling house of Edward Webb." From that point the boundary ran to the head of the said branch in a direct line to the dams at the head of the Eastern Branch of the Elizabeth River between James Kempe and Thomas Ivy; this was most certainly the present village of Kempsville. From there the line followed modern maps very closely, going down the Eastern Branch, not to Indian River, but to a small gut east of it where James Porter lived, thence overland to the "great swamp (later the Norfolk County reservoir and Gum Swamp) east of John Showlands"; this was a point on the Kempsville-Great Bridge road a mile southwest of Bethel Church to the North River (later the North Landing Reservoir) of Currituck and down the North River to the mouth of Simpson's Creek, the first creek south of the Albemarle and Chesapeake Canal, "up the said creek to the head thereof, from thence by a south line to the bounds of Carolina." There were problems with this boundary that were rectified in April 1695 by the assembly, which passed "An Act to Extend the Bounds of Princess Anne

Charles Bliven was one of Berkley's best-known and highly respected citizens. He was instrumental in the development of Berkley Electric Light and Water Company and made significant improvements to the wharf adjoining the Chestnut Street Ferry Bridge. In 1882, after engaging in planing mill enterprises, he started wharf building and ended up constructing some of the most important wharves and piers, iron bridges, railroad bridges and other key structures ever built on the river. Among his important works was the connection of the stone dry dock with the pumps of the Simpson Dry Dock at Norfolk Navy Yard.

A balmy, calm-water day on the Elizabeth River was the perfect setting for this Harry C. Mann photograph of a few sailing craft in 1910. The two single-masted, gray-hulled vessels on the left were commercial freight sloops. *Courtesy of the author.*

County." The act made note of complaints received from residents of Princess Anne County and that part of Norfolk County that belonged to Lynnhaven Parish, thus the boundary was changed so that the limits of Princess Anne County were enlarged and extended to coincide with the bounds of Lynnhaven Parish. This was essentially called the "triangle" bounded by Broad Creek, the Eastern Branch of the Elizabeth River and a line from what later became the Norfolk City Waterworks at Moore's Bridges to Kempsville, an area that was put in Princess Anne, where it belonged at that time.

Norfolk and the settlements of Portsmouth and Gosport, as well as others dotting the Elizabeth River and her tributaries, were included in Norfolk County under the new division. By the turn of the eighteenth century, Norfolk County began to profit from improved communications in the colony. An additional ferry was established on the Elizabeth River in 1702 from the town of Norfolk to Lovett's Point in West Norfolk, and the earlier ferry, first established in 1636 by Adam Thorowgood, was still in operation. Three years later, in 1705, a ferry was established between Seawell's Point to Hampton, and a law was passed for building roads to connect Williamsburg, the new capital of the Virginia colony, with each parish church, county courthouse and public mill and ferry. This was a tall order that took years to achieve. A third attempt was further made in 1705, albeit unsuccessful, to establish towns by law; towns or boroughs, ports and markets were given proper names at this time instead of simply being called, for example, the town of Norfolk in Norfolk County. Norfolk's county seat was officially named Norfolk Town. It would not be until September 15, 1736, that the corporation of the borough of Norfolk was chartered by an Act of Assembly, and its mayor and aldermen permitted to set up as a Hustings Court for the borough. Jumping ahead

This photograph of the extreme end of Botetourt Street below Freemason Street was a tranquil waterfront retreat with an unobstructed view of the river. The houses shown here were built in the 1870s. Lending perspective to this ca. 1910 picture, part of the Monticello Hotel, completed in 1898, is visible to the right. *Courtesy of the author.*

in the story, after the borough came close to being completely destroyed by fire on January 1, 1776, the borough courthouse was repaired but the county courthouse was not. From 1777 to 1785 the county court was seated but met in the town hall, and also rented private rooms or buildings for lesser tribunals and as a repository for its records. Among the private residences used for this purpose were those of Eunice Smith in August 1776; Edmund Allmand from 1777 to 1779; before 1785, rooms at Pat McCauley's, William Smith's and Abram Wormington's; and at Westwood, Samuel Boush III's home near Great Bridge.

In 1785 there was a petition to remove the county court outside Norfolk, and four years later, in November 1789, an "Act to Remove the Court of the County of Norfolk Without the Borough of Norfolk." County commissioners sold the courthouse lot in Norfolk and commenced building a new courthouse at Washington Point, formerly known as Powder Point, later Ferry Point, and today Berkley, where the jail had been since November 1790. The new county courthouse was finished in June 1792, and was situated at the southwest corner of Walnut (this used to be Washington) and Pine Streets. But the courthouse did not remain at Washington Point for very long. An act of 1801 authorized its removal "from the town of Washington to the town of Portsmouth," which is covered in additional detail elsewhere in this volume. When the town of Portsmouth (established by law in 1752, though it had existed for decades without official designation) received its city charter in 1858, the county court found itself operating from the city's downtown and in a territory in which it thus had no jurisdiction. The latter point had been true, however, for some time, as the county had already lost the territory north of the Elizabeth River through annexation to the city of Norfolk and large portions ended up removed from its bounds on the south side of the river not only to Norfolk but also to Portsmouth and South Norfolk (today part of the city of Chesapeake).

After the Revolutionary War a new form of government, one that involved town mayors and councils, was implemented. Divisions or districts of Norfolk County were also sculpted; under this system emerged Tanner's Creek, Western Branch, Deep Creek, Pleasant Grove, Washington, Cradock and Butt's Road. Judicial responsibilities were folded under circuit courts presided over by judges who meted out justice in a "circuit" that might include courts in up to three counties. Charted as a city in 1845, Norfolk had not grown significantly from its borough limits of 1736. Beginning in 1887, however, it began to absorb large portions of Tanner's Creek District until 1955, when the latter district completely disappeared. Portions of the Kempsville District adjoining Princess Anne to the east were subsequently annexed by Norfolk; Washington District was similarly reduced in size by the annexation of Berkley by the City of Norfolk in 1906; and Campostella became part of Norfolk in 1923. Portsmouth expanded into Western Branch and the Norfolk Naval Shipyard grew larger in another annexation.

While many prominent families with homes along the Elizabeth River and its tributaries have already been mentioned, there are others of equal importance, as well as particular communities, worth mentioning to provide a better picture of those people and places that remain in name and significance, some centuries after their passing. At the end of the seventeenth century the name Talbot was first recorded in association with life on the river. Isaac and Jacob Talbot appeared as witnesses to the will of John Fulcher, who had died in 1712. Jacob Talbot's will was proved in 1732, when he died, and from this document it is known that he had one son, William; but the will also gave the names of Jacob's brother John's children, eight sons and one daughter. Two of John Talbot's sons, Kader and Thomas, are worth mention. Kader Talbot died unmarried in 1752, and his will mentions "a schooner now in the docks," indicating that he was involved in shipbuilding activities. Thomas Talbot, who died in 1777, was captain of the militia in 1760 and headed a family that reached prominence in Norfolk Borough; all that is known of these Talbots was gleaned from *Norfolk County Records*, Books 1 and 11, and accompanying will book. Their county holdings are of primary importance. An 1863 map contains a legend for H. Talbot in two places, indicating the Talbots owned large tracts on the west side of Granby Street north of the bridge; they also owned much of what was on the east side as well. The southernmost of the two Talbot houses is Talbot Hall, which remains. Solomon Butt Talbot, son of Thomas, had provided in his will, about 1800, for the building of this summer home for his son Thomas Talbot.

In 1906 the town of Berkley, approximately a square mile at the confluence of the Eastern and Southern Branches of the Elizabeth River, was annexed by the City of Norfolk. Five years later, in 1911, came Lambert's Point and Huntersville. Lambert's Point was north of the Norfolk and Western tracks, west of Park Place, with its northern boundary at Forty-ninth Street. Huntersville, at the time of annexation, was sandwiched in between the old city of Norfolk and Brambleton on the south and Park Place on the north, and extended nearly to Lafayette Park, to include Villa Heights.

In the River and Harbor Act of March 3, 1909, Congress authorized the first complete surveys for an intracoastal waterway along the Atlantic Coast. Three years later, the U.S. Army Corps of Engineers recommended the purchase of the Chesapeake and Delaware Canal and its conversion into a ship canal. On February 17, 1912, Congress authorized the purchase of the Albemarle and Chesapeake Canal for $500,000, and the construction of a waterway twelve feet deep and at least ninety feet wide from Norfolk to Beaufort Inlet. Construction was completed in 1932.

There is a seal of the United States over the mantel of Talbot Hall with seventeen stars, dating the building's completion between 1802 and 1803. The seal saved the house when Union troops entered the area in 1862, as Federal troops gave the home special consideration and did not deface the property. On the latter Thomas Talbot's death in 1838, the property passed to his son, William Henry Talbot, the actual Talbot indicated on the map as "H. Talbot," who left the property in 1884 to his son, another Thomas Talbot, who died in 1932 and passed it to his brother, Minton Wright Talbot, the last of the Talbot male heirs. After Minton's death, the property was donated by his daughter to the Protestant Episcopal Diocese of Southern Virginia.

On the south side of Tanner's Creek, just across from the Minton Wright Talbot house, was a country house called Lebanon. The house, no longer standing, was constructed by Captain John Johnston in 1793 and was home for Johnston and his wife, the former Mary Bayard Wooten. The Johnstons had two daughters, both of whom successively married Captain Ethan Allen of Fort Ticonderoga renown. The private lane leading to the house from the country road was planted by Captain Allen with two rows of magnolia trees, which he imported from Mississippi. Many of these old trees are still standing on Magnolia Avenue in Norfolk's Larchmont neighborhood. Captain Allen had a daughter, Mary, who married Andrew Weir and their son, Allen Weir, who died in 1933, was the last family member to own Lebanon. The Johnston family burial plot was moved to Elmwood Cemetery in 1925.

Captain Samuel Watts, another large landowner in the northern part of Norfolk County, was actually one of Portsmouth's most respected citizens and son of Colonel Dempsey Watts. But Captain Watts owned land on both sides of today's Granby Street from Ward's Corner to Mason's Creek including most of Forest Lawn Cemetery. The location of Watts's land and the house on it are shown on the 1863 map of the county as S. Watts. When Samuel Watts died in 1878, his property passed to his daughter, Margaret Leigh Watts; she later told early Norfolk chroniclers that the name of her father's country seat on Mason's Creek was Pilgrim's Rest. This property, as well as land owned by the Talbots and Johnstons, is now all within the bounds of the city of Norfolk.

On the west bank of the Elizabeth River, Gosport had been partially burned in 1776. Shipyard founder Andrew Sprowle's house was set on fire by an infuriated mob in retaliation for John Murray, the fourth earl of Dunmore's bombardment of Portsmouth. Sprowle, as one of the Lord Dunmore's intimate friends, left Portsmouth with him and Sprowle's property was forfeited. In 1784 the General Assembly of Virginia appointed three commissioners to sell Sprowle's land. Gosport was to be laid out in conformity with the town of Portsmouth, the lots

The Norfolk Boat
Club, now over
a century old, is
shown here ca.
1910. The club is
located at the foot
of West Freemason
Street. *Courtesy of the
author.*

corresponding in size. Portsmouth would rise from the ashes of revolution
to build a community along the Elizabeth that quartered everyone from
wealthy men to the poorest immigrant. Before the year was out the lots
from 1 to 212 were sold with the exception of those reserved for the navy
yard, from 19 to 56. Many of the purchasers of these lots did not live in
the vicinity of Portsmouth, and deeds were recorded in various clerks'
offices. Bonds were given with payments at the end of 1784, but many
of them did not comply with their contracts, these parcels were sold
again with the remainder of available public land in 1795. This sale was
made by lottery, bringing the sum of $490,000. The amount was applied
immediately to the building of a road to Deep Creek and a causeway
between Portsmouth and Gosport. This bridge had draws near each end,
for Crab Creek at that time was a busy thoroughfare. It was an outlet for
the farms in the nearby section. It ran far into the west, and schooners and
sloops plied its waters, carrying necessities to the farms and bringing from
them the crops and timber. Portsmouth, too, was growing rapidly, and as
time went by the residents of the town felt the need for a street closer to
the water. The riverfront on the east was lined with shipyards, sail lofts and
machine shops. A street was opened up by those who owned lots on the
east side of Crawford Street, but the right of way was subject to the will of
property owners, who could close it whenever they chose to do so. In 1791
an appeal was made to the General Assembly for the right to lay off the
street. This act forbade injury to private property if the owners objected.
With such a provision, the street was not legally laid off at that time. Forty
years later there was yet another appeal to the General Assembly, with far
better results. The act this time authorized the town's trustees to lay off a
street 40 feet wide, beginning 216 feet from Crawford Street, and running
from one end of the town to the other. Should any property owner be

unwilling to cede the required land, twelve impartial freeholders were to be selected and empowered to condemn the land needed. Many of the Water Street lots were sold off in 1839.

From the time that Gosport was rebuilt the east side of First Street was lined with docks and warehouses used for the East India trade. These wharves were owned largely by the Dickson, Young and Cox families. These, with several other families, built impressive brick residences on First Street. The Young house, later called the Neville residence, for General Wendell Cushing Neville, had an interesting history. It was the birthplace of General Neville, the hero of Chateau-Thierry during World War I, who also won high praise during the Spanish-American War. General Neville's father fought in the Confederate service during the American Civil War. The builder of the house was James Young, a captain in the Continental army. The house stood on part of the land later used by the government as a buoy yard. The Dickson home, also long gone, was marred by personal tragedy. One of the Dickson brothers died under unfortunate circumstances. He had married a young Scot lady, whom he had met on one of his trips. She was much troubled whenever he started out to sea, so much so that he finally gave in to her wishes that he settle down to tend his land. Obligated to one more sea voyage, he could not know it would truly be his last. The ship was lost at sea and he was drowned. The Cox home stood on the western side of First Street and was torn down in 1928.

In the early 1800s two bridges besides the Gosport causeway spanned Crab Creek: Lafayette Bridge, which extended from a point on South Street to Third, and Union Bridge, which started at the foot of Court and joined it to Fourth Street. Both bridges had draws. Lafayette Bridge was not used within the memory of anyone living a century later, but Union Bridge remained until the part of the creek that it crossed was filled in to make a roadway for the street cars.

Not much changed until the mid-1930s, when the last block on Dinwiddie Street at its northern end, which had been water, was extended well into the yards of Court Street lots. The west side of Court Street ended just a few feet beyond the home of Mrs. Ellis Butt, at number thirty. At the foot of Court Street was the Swimming Point Bridge, which began from the middle of the street and ran diagonally to where it terminated at the boathouse of the Portsmouth Boat Club. The lots beyond Mrs. Butt's were all land, filled in by deposits of mud. The Dinwiddie Street end was filled in at the same time, in the late 1870s. For many years the land was not used and locals called it "the Desert." The bridge route was changed in this area because "the Desert" was prone to being under water during heavy storms for days at a time. High Street and streets running parallel to it ended at Chestnut Street. Cooke Street, its name changed to Elm

The Norfolk County Ferry Building at the foot of Commercial Place in Norfolk was photographed on April 3, 1915, after a hurricane; it was still raining when the picture was taken. *Courtesy of the author.*

Avenue, was cut through the Cooke family plantation, the country home of Colonel Mordecai Cooke, called Misery Thicket, due to the dense woods that surrounded it. During the Civil War, Misery Thicket was seized by the Federals and used as a hospital. Misery Thicket was inherited by Patrick Henry Cooke, who married Olivia Bilisoly, and their daughter, Virginia Cooke, continued to live there for many years.

Another Portsmouth point of interest is Scottsville, named for the Scott family who owned the land in that area from the early part of the eighteenth century, and had a shipyard there. There was an old house on the Scott farm engraved with the name, or rather the initials, of the builder and the date of construction—T.S. 1734. The original name of the place was Church Point and the creek was called Church Creek (later also Scot's or Scott's Creek on nautical charts). The old house stood on the portion of the land that was used as a farm well into the twentieth century. Park View was, until the 1880s, the farm of the Hatton family called Alabama. It was laid off at that time by the owners, Alexander Hatton, William Hatton and Dr. James L. Hatton. John G. Hatton, when he took ownership of Alabama, claimed that Fort Lane, then the only way to access the naval hospital, belonged to him. The matter was settled when the federal government bought the strip of land called Fort Lane from him. West Park View was the Matthews family farm. There was an interesting old house on this property that legend says was built in one week, as its family was reportedly anxious to have it ready for a celebration, which could not be postponed. This house was destroyed by fire in the early 1920s. Alfred Wilson, a grandson of the original Matthews who owned the property, assumed its ownership for many years, until it passed to the Guthrie family, who developed it.

Norfolk's largest annexation came in 1923, when the city's boundary was extended to include Campostella, Newton Park, Chesterfield Heights, Ballentine Place, Lafayette Residence Park and Annex, Winona, Lakewood, North Granby Street, Larchmont, Edgewater, Algonquin Park, Meadowbrook, Lochhaven, all the area north of Willoughby Bay, with the exception of federally owned property, Willoughby Beach, Ocean View and the Cottage Line to Princess Anne County. This left only the Tanner's Creek District, Norfolk County, bounded by Ocean View, Princess Anne County, the Eastern Branch of the Elizabeth River and the Virginian Railway; this was taken into the city in 1955.

Pinner's Point, named in the mid-1650s for Richard Pinner, was later the home of John Kearnes, one of the most prominent citizens of Portsmouth, in 1796. Kearnes's widow married Edwin Gray, of Southampton County, the first representative of his district to the United States Congress. Gray was elected as a Republican at large from 1799 to 1807, and to the Nineteenth District from 1807 to 1813. It was Gray who introduced the bill into Congress to make it unlawful to fight a duel. Virginia Cooke, a descendant of John Kearnes, once had in her possession a picture of Pinner's Point done in needlework by Kearnes's daughter, Margaret, who later married Mordecai Cooke. Pinner's Point was fortified and occupied by troops in the Civil War.

Port Norfolk was the glebe of Portsmouth Parish until after the Revolutionary War, when it was confiscated with other glebes by the Commonwealth of Virginia. It was at this point—Port Norfolk—that the British landed when they captured Portsmouth in 1779. The troops, upon landing there, marched to Scott's Creek, which they crossed, and entered Fort Nelson from the rear while Commodore Sir George Collier bombarded the fort from the Elizabeth River. The old glebe house stood facing the river on what was later the southeastern corner of Mount Vernon Avenue and the boulevard. On its lawn were particularly large shade trees, some of them pomegranate trees.

Waterview and Glensheallah were suburbs of Portsmouth originally developed outside the city limits. Waterview was Dale's Point, the birthplace of Commodore Richard Dale. It was then his grandfather's farm, and had been the home of the Dale family for several generations. Dale had a large family of sisters and brothers who lived in Portsmouth, and left descendants, among them the Luke and Porter families. The old Dale home in which the commodore was born has long since been razed, but the house in which he spent his childhood was on Swimming Point. This house was constructed for Dale's father by Colonel William Crawford and devised to him in his father's will. Dale was a deeply religious man who constantly worried about the welfare of his men. He organized a mariner's church in Philadelphia, making every effort to get sailors to attend. A simple but beautiful monument was erected in Portsmouth to the memory of Dale; it was unveiled on May 9, 1917. The stonework of the monument was done by Archibald Ogg; the bronze tablet was originally designed for Colonel William Lamb, of Norfolk, by an artist named Couper. The tablet did not suit Lamb's heirs, but fulfilled the monument committee's effort to honor Dale. The heads of the rivets that hold the small tablet to the stone were buttons from the uniform of Captain Kenneth McAlpine, United States Army, a distinguished officer who rendered valiant service as chief of the engineers on the USS *Texas* in the Spanish-American War. The United States Navy subsequently named its first ship for Dale, a sloop

With a wide-open view up the Elizabeth River, these Portsmouth ferry boats carried passengers to Portsmouth when this picture was taken about 1900. The ferry in the middle of the channel was the *City of Portsmouth. Courtesy of the author.*

of war, in 1839; there were at least five United States Navy ships that have carried the USS *Dale* name. Glensheallah was part of the Herbert property, until the Herbert family sold it to Beverly Bayton. It was later that Bayton's grandson, Beverly Armistead, had a farm, later developing the property. Seven to eight miles away from Portsmouth sat Deep Creek, the older of the two communities.

The appearance of substantive pomegranate trees on Portsmouth's glebe land, which at first might appear a minor point of the river's natural history, was actually indicative of events that would take place on the western shore of the Elizabeth, significantly boom periods, the first one dating to 1790, when refugees fleeing the Reign of Terror in France arrived on the scene. Within a brief span of time, the French who arrived in Portsmouth planned agricultural schemes, aided by an onslaught of immigrants from Italy and the West Indies. Sugar cane and tropical fruits were planted; English planters followed suit, learning from these immigrants how to cultivate such oddities to Hampton Roads as oranges and olives—and the pomegranate, which flourished. While tropical fruits could not survive in the climate here, subsequent waves of immigrants, more French and Italians during the Napoleonic Wars, tried their fortunes at almond trees, which also did not survive. Despite these failures, another generation of foreign settlers to Portsmouth imported merino sheep from the mountains of Spain, only to realize their mistake too late. The next venture of this kind was the mulberry boom of 1838.

Newspapers of the day devoted columns to accounts of a special variety of the white mulberry tree, on whose leaves silkworms fed, discussing it from every angle. There was a large cocoonery built just outside of town and another in Norfolk, not surprising given the mulberry craze of the 1830s that had swept the East Coast from New York to the Carolinas. One of Portsmouth's most respected citizens, George M. Bain, sold fifty

The Norfolk County Ferry Building at the foot of Portsmouth's High Street is shown in this ca. 1940 postcard. *Courtesy of the author.*

thousand mulberry trees in one day. They were one foot high and brought 30¢ each. Within the week the purchaser sold the entire lot for 50¢ apiece. At the same time another citizen sold trees for the amount of $18,000 in one lot. The mania for mulberry trees spread. This boom accounted years later for the large number of gnarled and spent mulberry trees dotting the gardens of older Portsmouth and Norfolk residents, for even flowers and vegetables had been uprooted to make room for these trees with nearly everyone in both towns interested in the silkworm business to greater or lesser degree. The *American Beacon* of September 6, 1839, ran a notice from the local silk agency expressing deep interest in the culture of silk and the introduction of *morus multicaulis* trees among local farmers, believing that in years to come one of the staples of the South would be the growing of silkworms. The advertisement included an offer for sale of 400,000 silkworm eggs, of three crop mammoth white species in quantities to suit the buyer. In the advertisement that followed the Robinson and Martin offer of silkworm eggs was another by R.C. Barclay for *Jonathan Dennis' Silk Manual*, containing complete directions for cultivating the different kinds of mulberry trees, feeding silkworms and manufacturing silk for profit. Dennis, of Portsmouth, Rhode Island, promoted himself as an experienced silk grower and inventor of the patent premium silk spinner and twister, and the patent central silk reel. But the climate was not as conducive to silkworm production as its promoters had hoped. When the mulberry trees failed to attract silkworms, the trees remained, promulgating in large number along the shores of the Elizabeth as a non-native species.

There is an interesting account of the mulberry craze from an unidentified woman living in Portsmouth in the 1830s that further illuminates this story. The woman, interviewed by Mildred M. Holladay, recounted later that "Mr. Jones, a chaplain in the navy, owned a farm just where the southeast end of the town joins the Deep Creek Road. He was a pioneer in planting the mulberry, or as he called it 'the *morus multicaulis*.'" The *morus multicaulis* cultivated by Mr. Jones was actually the *morus multicaulis* Loud, which comes from China. This particular white mulberry has been successfully cultivated in southern reaches of Russia's Asian region, Europe, the Far East and India, but was not the red mulberry, *morus rubra* L., that is also found today in the Elizabeth River watershed; there are differences in the trees that are clear to the trained eye. The woman went on to observe that from Mr. Jones's enthusiasm for mulberry cultivation came an excitement for mulberry speculation that reached a fever pitch on both sides of the Elizabeth. "Every vacant lot in town was in demand," she wrote, "and much of the farming land in the county was turned into mulberry plantations. The fever ran into an epidemic, those who had laughed at it as a wild fancy now caught the contagion." Men, women and children laid down cuttings, counted the number of joints on each stick, made estimates of trees to be produced and the fortune to be made. "Ladies thought," she continued, "that silk dresses would be as common in this country as cotton prints. The servants believed that the time had come when they would wear silk bandanas on their heads. Then the bubble burst and what subject was as disgusting as the silk worm?"

Many place names along the Elizabeth ring familiar, others simply intrigue. Paradise Creek, today an urban waterway two miles long with industries on one side and working-class homes on the other, hardly seems to fit its name—or does it? The name of the creek originated, according to local tradition, with the once-bucolic Paradise Plantation. Historical records indicate that large plantations once lined the shores of Paradise Creek throughout the nineteenth century. An 1817 advertisement in the *American Beacon* promoted the sale of "a plantation handsomely situated on the north shore of Paradise Creek." The plantation was 150 acres with an excellent landing place, so the advertisement read, for boats or lighters within a few yards of the house, along with another 112-acre plantation for sale on the south side of the creek. Dr. Charles O. Barclay and Robert Barclay, cousins and Portsmouth residents, have reported that their family owned the 310-acre Barclay Farm on the southern shore of the creek, starting in 1801. The family cemetery is still located there, next to Cradock Middle School.

With World War I came the rapid expansion of the United States Navy Yard Norfolk, roughly two miles north of Paradise Creek. The Barclay Farm was sold to house shipyard workers in 1918, becoming one of the nation's first government-planned housing communities. Thus was born historic Cradock, an independent town until annexed by the City of

Campostella Heights is situated in the very southeastern part of Norfolk, on the south side of the Elizabeth River. It is bordered by the residential neighborhoods of Campostella to the west, Oakleaf Park to the south and Newton Park to the east. The neighborhood has very distinct physical boundaries that include the main thoroughfares of Campostella Road to the west and Indian River Road to the south, and the shorelines of Steamboat Creek to the east and the Elizabeth River to the north. Houses were built there between 1907 and 1927, but most were constructed in the decade following the First World War.

Portsmouth in 1960. Cradock is laid out in the form of an anchor with Afton Square, the town square, as its focal point. Over 750 cottage-style single-family homes were built, along with schools, recreational land, churches and commercial areas. Cradock still dominates the creek's southern shore. One of America's first planned shopping centers was established in Cradock, and eventually other neighborhoods would be developed, too. Truxtun, on the headwaters of Paradise Creek, was originally a forty-two-acre, 250-home neighborhood and the country's first government housing project for African Americans working at the navy yard during World War I. Developed in 1918 and named for United States Navy Captain Thomas Truxtun, the neighborhood's homes were built close together with varied roof styles. Truxtun's houses offered modern-day conveniences such as indoor plumbing and electric lights. Along with Highland-Biltmore, on the southern shore, and Brighton and Prentis Park on the north shore, about thirty thousand people live today in the immediate watershed of Paradise Creek.

Campostella Heights is situated in the very southeastern part of Norfolk, on the south side of the Eastern Branch of the Elizabeth River. It is bordered by the residential neighborhoods of Campostella to the west, Oakleaf Park to the south and Newton Park to the east. The neighborhood has very distinct physical boundaries that include the main thoroughfares of Campostella Road to the west, Indian River Road to the south and the shorelines of Steamboat Creek to the east and the Elizabeth River to the north. Houses were built there between 1907 and 1927, but most were constructed in the decade following the First World War.

The origin of the name Campostella has its roots in the Civil War. During the war the land from Steamboat Creek to the Southern Branch of the Elizabeth River was owned by Confederate Captain Fred Wilson, who equipped a company of soldiers during the war and built a camp on the site, which he named Camp Stella, after his daughter. The 1889 *Hopkins Atlas* depicts the land west of Campostella Road extending to the railroad tracks as platted but not developed. There was no development on the tract east of Campostella Road and north of Indian River Turnpike, west of Steamboat Creek. This tract of land was owned by Clarence A. Woodard, and had about eight frame buildings along the water. Woodard was president of a wholesale grocery and distribution business with offices in downtown Norfolk, and was a director of the Norfolk Bank for Savings and Trust. According to an undated letter containing personal recollections of E.S. Smith, Woodard's plantation was once the largest in Norfolk County and the first to raise produce for New York markets. A bridge to Norfolk over the Eastern Branch of the Elizabeth River appears on an earlier 1881 map. The 1900 *Bowman Atlas* shows that Campostella Heights had been platted but not developed. While it is noted on the

The Indian Pole Bridge (later the Granby Street Bridge) collapsed in 1916, leaving cars of the Bay Shore Line to Ocean View teetering toward the waters of Tanner's Creek. *Courtesy of the author.*

map as still belonging to Woodard, a 1904 article noted that it had been purchased by the Berkley real estate firm of Tavenner and Keister, whose principals organized the Campostella Heights Company, with Dr. E.F. Truitt as president. The Campostella Heights Company renamed the area, adding the *o* and informing the public that it was named after a place in Italy that meant "bright star" or "starlit field." Much of Steamboat Creek was originally intended to be filled and the neighborhood extended to the east into Newton Park, which was platted by the Ford Motor Company in 1925 for workers at the nearby Ford plant.

Campostella Heights developed from the waterfront south, with the oldest houses along Arlington Avenue, most of which were developed before the First World War. For the most part the rest of the neighborhood was built after the war, primarily in the 1920s. South of Canton Avenue was entirely undeveloped until well after the Second World War.

As was the case with many Norfolk neighborhoods, demolition of downtown slums in the post–World War II era prompted an exodus of white families, characterized as "white flight," to the suburbs. Campostella began to integrate in the early 1960s. The neighborhood today is largely African American, but in the late 1960s was faced with controversy not involving its integration, but a proposed development. William R. Forbes, the private owner of a broad swath of land along the Elizabeth River waterfront, wanted to fill it in to develop a motel and marina. At that time the land was zoned as industrial, and Forbes began to fill it with debris from construction sites across the river. The neighborhood objected and

in 1969 the zoning was changed to single-family residential, thus stopping
the proposed project. The land has since been untouched.

Other prominent homes on the Elizabeth took their names from their
vista of the river. The historic Herbert-Hardy house was built circa 1728.
The house featured Greek Revival architecture, the brickwork of the
main house consisting of Flemish bond fixed with lime mortar made from
crushed oyster shells. The bricks of the kitchen, adjoining the main house,
were only common bond brick, indicating a later period of construction.
The house and outbuildings were constructed by at least three generations
of the Herbert family, who resided on the property they named Riveredge.
The main house had at least twenty rooms. The Herberts had a long
colonial history, much like the Hardys who would later reside in this
magnificent home on the southern bank of the Elizabeth River.

Riveredge was built on land granted by King Charles II in 1664 to John
Herbert. The land grant was 700 acres. Three years later, in 1667, Charles
II granted a second tract to Herbert that consisted of an additional 1,227
acres on the Southern Branch of the Elizabeth River. Henry Herbert,
John's descendant, made his home in what is now Berkley and founded
a shipyard that remained in existence from 1728 to 1828. He died in
1778. Berkley was first known as Herbertsville, then Washington Point
and eventually Ferry Point before coming to its present name. A few miles
east of Berkley was a post office on the colonial plantation of the Herbert
family that bore the name Herbert, Virginia.

Henry Herbert's descendants sold a ship to the United States Navy
during the undeclared war with France in July 1798 that has been credited
as the first ship of the navy to carry the name of the city of Norfolk. W.H.T.
Squires described the vessel as a brig of two hundred tons, which had been
built by the Herberts, and which when nearly ready for launching, was
purchased by the government and fitted out under the name USS *Norfolk*.
Another notable contribution of a Herbert descendant can be reckoned

among the most important to the development of modern-day Norfolk, when a Herbert granted a right-of-way through family property from the Norfolk County line to the Elizabeth River. For many years this was the only route into Norfolk from the Norfolk County line, and subsequently became South Main Street in Berkley and the drawbridge that spanned the river and remained in use until after the Civil War.

The first member of the Hardy family to reside at Riveredge was Thomas Asbury Hardy. Born in 1800 at the family home in Coleraine, Bertie County, North Carolina, Thomas Hardy came to Norfolk in 1826 to start a wholesale cotton business with his brothers. By 1831 he had met his first wife, the former Elizabeth Margaret Pierce, of Norfolk, and they married that year. The first home occupied by the Hardy newlyweds was 300 Granby Street, today the site of the old Smith and Welton Department Store. The Hardy family kept the Granby Street residence until 1907, the year of the Jamestown Exposition and a boon period in Norfolk's business development. Thomas Hardy quickly became a man of significant prominence in the community, and was a well-known

During the Great Depression, funding received by the Public Works Administration (PWA) provided skilled labor for a number of projects in Norfolk, from construction and landscape projects for the Norfolk Museum of Arts and Sciences to the landscape and grading work being performed in this picture at the foot of the Lakewood Bridge. Willow Wood Drive crosses over the bridge into the Lakewood section. Granby Street is the road in the foreground. The PWA made contracts with private companies, including citizens' groups, for public works programs. Created by the National Industrial Recovery Act of 1933, the PWA came under the purview of Secretary of the Interior Harold L. Ickes, who ensured that a fair share of black workers received jobs. Much work was performed under PWA programs until the creation of the Works Progress Administration (WPA) in May 1935, which further expanded employment opportunities during hard times. This picture of black workers in the Lakewood section was taken on January 18, 1934, by *Virginian-Pilot* photographer Charles S. Borjes. The Lakewood Bridge, shown here, was built from the northern end of the new Granby Street to the Lakewood section. Though the bridge was constructed by the city in 1930, residents of the section who benefited most by its being there paid for it through agreeing to higher property assessments. Note the number of houses completed and under construction in Lakewood when this picture was taken. *Courtesy of the Sargeant Memorial Room, Norfolk Public Library.*

member of the old Virginia Club and president of the German Club. On September 28, 1846, Hardy bought Riveredge from Enoch Herbert, and just a few days later, on October 1, he also held title to an adjoining tract of land bought from Lucretia A. Brodie. Mary Pinckney Hardy, one of the Hardys' fourteen children, was born at Riveredge on March 22, 1852.

The future mother of General Douglas A. MacArthur lived almost exclusively in Norfolk until the Civil War, when the family retreated to Burnside, the Hardy family plantation near Henderson, North Carolina. While the family lived at Burnside, Riveredge was occupied by Union army troops who converted it to a hospital and later occupation headquarters. Four of Mary's six brothers fought for the Confederacy. Even in seclusion at Burnside the Hardys were not immune from the ravages of war. Union General William Tecumseh Sherman's army stayed overnight at Burnside on its way north from his March to the Sea Campaign at the end of 1864.

When she was twenty years old, Mary Hardy visited friends in New Orleans; it was 1872. It was in New Orleans that she met a dashing young United States Army officer, Arthur MacArthur, who had frequently visited Norfolk in his youth. MacArthur, of Scottish descent from Massachusetts, had been awarded the Medal of Honor for heroism at the Civil War battle of Missionary Ridge in 1863. Though he had retired in 1865 as a lieutenant, not a year passed before he decided to rejoin the army in February 1866, making it his career. MacArthur was a captain in the Thirty-sixth Infantry when he met Mary and followed her back to Norfolk. The couple was married at Riveredge on May 17, 1875, by the Reverend Father Matthew O'Keefe, rector of Saint Mary's Catholic Church. Though the Hardys were devout Methodists, Mary preferred a Catholic service. She had been educated at the Convent of the Visitation Order in Cantonsville, Maryland. From accounts of her marriage, Mary's brothers refused to attend her service because she was marrying a Yankee. Thomas Hardy passed away in 1876 and Elizabeth in 1881.

The eldest child born to Arthur and Mary MacArthur was Arthur MacArthur III, who was born at Riveredge on August 1, 1876. Arthur graduated from the United States Naval Academy as the youngest man to ever complete the program. He had a distinguished career in the navy until his death in 1923 from appendicitis. The MacArthurs' second son, Malcolm, was born October 17, 1878, also at Riveredge. Malcolm died at age five and was buried at Norfolk's Cedar Grove Cemetery. In his later years, Douglas MacArthur returned to Norfolk regularly to visit Malcolm's grave.

The third son of Arthur and Mary MacArthur was born near Little Rock, Arkansas, on January 26, 1880. Douglas MacArthur recalled in interviews later that he "grew up with the sound of Dixie and the Rebel

yell ringing in my ears. Father was on the other side but he had the good sense to surrender to mother." Douglas MacArthur graduated first in his class from the United States Military Academy at West Point in 1903, his success due largely to his mother's emphasis on the importance of good study habits. Arthur and Douglas MacArthur would become only the second father-son recipients of the Medal of Honor. When Arthur MacArthur died in September 1912, Mary spent the remainder of her life living in Washington, D.C., and New York, with one exception. At eighty-four years of age Mary traveled with Douglas to the Philippines, where he was to become military advisor to President Manuel L. Quezon. On arrival in Manila, Mary was gravely stricken with cerebral thrombosis. She passed away on December 3, 1935. Though initially buried in Manila, MacArthur had his mother's body returned to the United States on his next trip home. She is now laid to rest beside her husband in Arlington National Cemetery.

Riveredge passed out of the Hardy family in the 1890s when it was sold to the Ryland Institute, a girls' school. The home was subsequently occupied by a number of other tenants, including its use as a terminal by the Norfolk and Portsmouth Belt Line Railroad. The home sat vacant for many years, badly damaged by fire and its fair share of trespassers.

Poplar Hall, a graceful, two-story home on Norfolk's Broad Creek, was constructed by the first Thurmer Hoggard on land granted him by the British Crown in 1645. Thurmer and Suzanna Hoggard had married in England before coming to Virginia. The house, like the Herberts' (later Hardys') Riveredge, was built of Flemish-bond brick. Detached from the main house were the original kitchen, ice and smokehouses. The home's interior was constructed of wide panel planks and exquisite paneling of light woods. Originally surrounded by three hundred acres, its name is derived from a row of Lombardy poplars brought from England by the original Hoggards and planted

A new bridge replaced the old Lakewood Bridge in the late 1980s. This picture, taken when construction of the new bridge was nearly complete, is dated 1987. *Courtesy of the author.*

between the house and Broad Creek. The first Hoggards to occupy
the home were shipbuilders. Their shipyard on Broad Creek is
believed to have been the first navy yard in America. The home went
undisturbed by the Continental army and His Majesty's Redcoats
during the Revolutionary War, but just prior to the War of 1812 three
privateers berthed in the Hoggards' shipyard were burned by the
British fleet. During the Civil War a Union garrison of an officer and
ten men occupied one of Poplar Hall's outbuildings, but treated the
family well. This was due largely to the fact that Dr. William Cornick,
a relative of the Hoggards, was a doctor in the Northern Army of
the Potomac. The Union garrison at Poplar had been placed there
to keep down blockade-running activities in which the women and
old people living along the Eastern Branch of the Elizabeth River
took part. It is said that the Union officer and his men played the
blockade-running game "like the gentlemen they must have been."
There were members of the Hoggard family who did not appreciate
the presence of Federal troops on their property. Two Hoggard sons,
Thurmer H. and Horatio E., had joined the Confederacy and served
in the Princess Anne Calvary Company Fifteenth Regiment, Norfolk,
Virginia, from 1862 to 1865 under the command of Captain James
Forbes Simpson.

Poplar Hall, like many of the grandest city homes, summer houses and
plantations along the Elizabeth River and its tributaries, had its share of
great stories, legends and secrets. One of the most interesting stories told
of Poplar Hall is of a very large beech tree that stood near a well in the
yard. Black Hawk, chief of the Sauk and Fox tribes, reportedly spent a
short time at the home in 1833 after being released from prison at Fort
Monroe for instigating what became known only as the Black Hawk
War of 1832. While washing at the well, Black Hawk is reputed to have
thrown his blanket over the beech, then a sapling. Black Hawk's jailer,
and later escort to Poplar Hall, was Jefferson Davis, future president of

the Confederacy. Black Hawk died six years after his visit to the Hoggard home on Broad Creek.

The Poplar Hall way of life was the elegant way of life, reflecting a bygone era on the Elizabeth River that is no more. An 1828 poem, quoted in part, tells of pleasant living on a small Southern plantation:

> *And as we 'próached fir Poplar Hall*
> *Beneath the poplar tree*
> *They were sitting all beneath its shade*
> *And chatting merrille.*
>
> *Now welcoming on ev'ry side.*
> *Right cordially did greet*
> *And full glad in truth were we*
> *Our fair young friends to meet*
>
> *We ate and drank and play'd and sang*
> *And walked about the grove...*

CHAPTER SEVEN
WATERWAYS OF OPPORTUNITY

The Royal Charter of Norfolk Borough, dated September 15, 1736, defined Norfolk's boundaries by water. The northern boundary of the town, when it was incorporated, was defined by a line running from the head of the cove at Town Bridge, in a westerly direction to the river, embracing the whole of the two-hundred-acre tract of Nicholas Wise. In 1761 the limits were enlarged, by Act of Assembly, to encompass all the land south of a line running from the head of Newton's Creek to the head of Smith's Creek. A new survey of the northern boundary conducted in 1807 was ordered by yet another Act of Assembly; the line between the heads of the two creeks was designated by stone landmarks. The jurisdiction of the city then extended over a space of approximately eight hundred acres.

During the period in which the royal charter was obtained, the town had already spread far beyond the limits of the fifty acres purchased from Wise, and extended from the river "out into the country" to a cove that extended from Newton's Creek west to the spot where Church and Charlotte Streets once intersected each other, at which place there was, for a very long time, a bridge that gave the name of Town Bridge to that part of town; that area was still called this long after there was no bridge nor necessity for one. During the Revolutionary War, an entrenchment was thrown up from this place across the town to Smith's Point. By the mid-nineteenth century, chroniclers were documenting stories from persons who could remember boats of considerable size frequently seen at Town Bridge, as late as 1780. Many years later, Fenchurch Street was extended across the spot where the bridge stood, and Charlotte Street was continued through from Church to Fenchurch (and eventually extended to Chapel), covering what was formerly the center of the cove.

The *Virginia Gazette* of November 26, 1736, remarked that the residents of Norfolk Town flourished in trade by sending vessels to sea, loaded

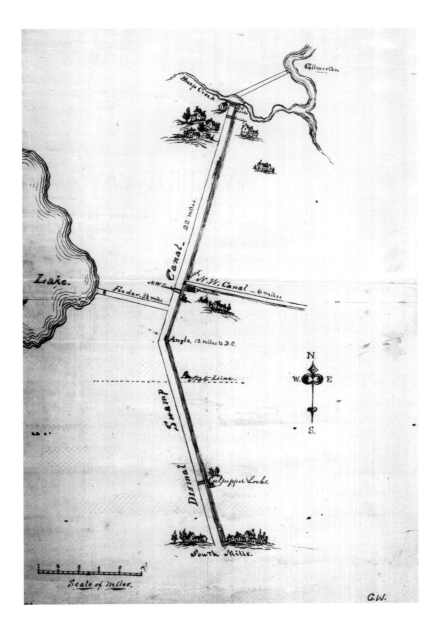

The original plat of the Dismal Swamp Canal, with an inquisition to condemn land along the feeder ditch for the Dismal Swamp Canal Company, was filed on August 4, 1812. The Northwest Canal Locks, indicated just above the feeder ditch and locks to the lake, also pinpoint Wallaceton, where George Thomas Wallace constructed his home and a small town soon developed. The settlement of Wallaceton, situated a short distance from the house, derived its name from Wallace's family, which settled in the southern part of Norfolk County in the early 1700s. *Courtesy of the author.*

with American commodities, which returned to other countries. There were many merchants in Norfolk by that time, and with the population growing steadily, the town's influential merchants had petitioned the governor of Virginia for a charter to incorporate, which was granted. An Act of Assembly passed the last session to confirm and strengthen this charter, by which they incorporated the name of the borough of Norfolk. Before the Revolutionary War the old Norfolk harbor was teeming with vessels, many of them very large. Commerce flourished beyond anyone's expectation.

George Washington is honored in the naming of the Dismal Swamp's Washington Ditch and, later, George Washington Highway, two engineering projects that brought the world to a place that had seen few people.

Norfolk had, indeed, owed its early success to neighboring North Carolina, but the route that promised to make trade between the Elizabeth River communities and the Tar Heel State—a water route between the Elizabeth River and the sounds of North Carolina—took decades to come to fruition. The Great Dismal Swamp extends a distance of fifteen miles in Virginia and twenty-five miles in North Carolina, running north to south; it is about fifteen miles wide and originally contained approximately 400,000 acres, the equivalent of six hundred square miles. Today the Great Dismal Swamp National Wildlife Refuge is about 111,000 acres, less than half the original size of the swamp. In its center is the 3,100-acre Lake Drummond. The lake itself is nearly circular in shape, about three miles in diameter. It was named by a hunter who, with three companions, went to the swamp in the early days of the European settlement. The hunter's companions disappeared and were presumed lost. The hunting party's sole survivor, William Drummond, returned to become the white settlers' first source of information regarding the beautiful lake, tucked away in the depths of the swamp. The year of Drummond's discovery of the lake was 1665. Drummond, a Scotsman, was first colonial governor of the Albemarle Sound settlement in the Province of Carolina from 1664 to 1667, appointed to his post by Sir William Berkeley, one of the North Carolina colony's eight Lords Proprietors and governor of Virginia. Drummond had lived at Jamestown before this appointment. After serving his term as governor, Drummond returned to Jamestown, where he became one of the chief men of Nathaniel Bacon's rebellion, continuing in arms after Bacon's death, until his capture on January 14, 1677. He was hanged the same day. Drummond's daughter married a son of Colonel Thomas Swann, of Swann's Point, where the commissioners resided and held court in 1677. Rather than dispose of Drummond's body in the James River, his supporters spirited it away and buried him at Swann's Point.

Though William Byrd II had platted much of the Dismal Swamp in his surveying trips in 1728 as part of his effort to resolve border disputes between North Carolina and Virginia for the Boundary Commission, no development of the swamp would take place for decades to come. Byrd had proposed a cut—a canal—be made between the Elizabeth River and the sounds at that time. It would be nearly sixty years, following the Revolutionary War, before a canal was begun. The new nation desperately needed good roads connecting the isolated towns and villages with larger cities. If the country was to grow and prosper, an effective means of internal transportation had to be developed. Both George Washington and Patrick Henry felt that canals were the easiest answer and favored a route through the Dismal Swamp. Although Washington was not involved in the canal's construction, he was familiar with the region. Washington Ditch, a

separate cut through the swamp, was built to transport their timber. The earliest known reference to Washington Ditch is an advertisement in the *Virginia Gazette* on November 19, 1772, by the executors of the estate of Josiah Riddick offering seventy-five acres joining the great ditch of the Dismal Swamp. Also for sale was a large gondola, most probably used on the ditch. Riddick's plantation and mill appeared on Gershom Nimmo's map and would also be mentioned in Washington's diary of his travels over Riddick's land.

When Colonel George Washington became interested in the Dismal Swamp in 1763, one of the men who shared in the venture was Robert Tucker. Colonel Robert Tucker was vestryman of the undivided parish in 1750 and of the reduced Elizabeth River Parish in 1761. His son, the third Robert Tucker, was vestryman in 1759 and after 1761 served Saint Bride's. It was Tucker who is most likely to have secured the services of Gershom Nimmo, surveyor of Norfolk County when Washington wanted to survey the land he planned to buy. Tucker's Mill is located at the edge of the Dismal Swamp. Colonel Washington described the mill in his diary as being eight miles from Great Bridge. Washington organized an initiative called "The Adventures of Draining the Great Dismal Swamp" and bought 5,000 acres of swamp land from the Dismal Swamp Land Company, which held upward of 50,000 acres, because he was so confident of its potential for farming. Washington's fellow adventurers included William and Thomas Nelson; Burwell Bassett; Washington's brother-in-law, Fielding Lewis; Robert Tucker Jr., son of the aforementioned Norfolk merchant by the same name; Thomas Walker; William Waters; John Symes; and Samuel Gist. After Nimmo completed his survey for existing patents of swampland, he reported to Washington and Lewis a total of 5,800 acres, of which 3,000 acres already belonged to Tucker.

Jim Pierce, portrayed in David Hunter Strother's *Harper's Weekly* story about the Dismal Swamp, was living and working deep in the swamp. The Dismal Swamp Land Company owned a number of slaves and hired others employed to get the lumber shaped into shingles, among other products taken from the land. "The swamp is said to be inhabited by a number of escaped slaves," he wrote, "who spend their lives, and even raise families, in its impenetrable fastnesses."

Returning from a jaunt in the swamp, Strother found Pierce cooking ham and eggs under a shed that had been recently occupied by fishermen. "Jim was a tall wiry black," wrote Strother, "with his hair plaited into numerous pigtails."
Courtesy of the author.

JIM PIERCE.

George Washington traveled to Suffolk in October 1763 and on the fifteenth began a ride around the swamp on horseback. Washington described this trip in detail in his diary, explaining that he and his party rode south from Suffolk to Pocoson Swamp, roughly six miles, and about four or five miles from Edward Riddick's mill run. This location was northwest of the lake, on lands known as Soldier's Hope, belonging to the estate of Colonel Josiah Riddick, running west to what was called the Reese Farm, on the Edenton road, actually about seven miles from Suffolk. Later, a large quantity of juniper timber was brought through a ditch at this location, which was hauled to the Nansemond River for shipment. Josiah Riddick's estate had passed to his heirs by the time Washington made his famous jaunt around the swamp. Washington wrote that the land within proximity of this distance, especially after passing Willis S. Riddick's, was level and not bad, as was the land of another Riddick brother, Henry, also living nearby. His party then rode to Cypress Swamp, and a short distance to the south, where they went a half-mile straight into the Dismal Swamp toward Lake Drummond. After making the lake, Washington's party rode across Mossey Swamp near John Riddick's land to the North Carolina line. There they went by Marmaduke Norfleet's mill, where Washington and Lewis had bought land, and Luke Sumner's plantation, then circled south and east to the Perquimans River. They crossed the Perquimans and the Pasquotank River by bridges and proceeded to Northwest Landing on the Northwest River in Norfolk County, Great Bridge, Tucker's Mill, Farley's Plantation east of Bower's Hill, Robert's Ordinary east of Shoulder's Hill, Cowper's Mill north of Magnolia, Riddick's Mill near Suffolk's fairgrounds and back to Suffolk. Washington would visit the swamp again in November 1766, April 1767 and October 1768; all total he came to the Great Dismal Swamp six times. On the last visit he wrote in his diary that on the twenty-sixth he breakfasted in Suffolk, dined and lodged in the Dismal Swamp at John Washington's before going the following day to "our Plantation at Norfleet's in Carolina" (this would have been in Gates County) and returned that afternoon. On the twenty-eighth, Washington went to Lake Drummond with Fielding Lewis, Major Riddick and John Washington. The following day he arrived in Smithfield, a stopover on his way to Williamsburg.

The Dismal Swamp Canal was authorized by the Virginia legislature in 1781 and the North Carolina legislature in 1790. Canal construction had long been on the Virginia General Assembly's agenda. The General Assembly approved the Dismal Swamp Canal project in a 1787 compact providing for the cutting of a navigable canal from Deep Creek, an arm of the Elizabeth River, to the Pasquotank River in North Carolina. The compact also provided for the formation of the Dismal Swamp Canal Company. There was an important exchange of correspondence between George Washington and other notables during the critical gap between approval of the Dismal Swamp Canal by the Virginia legislature and the beginning of the canal's construction in 1793. George Washington wrote a letter on March 31, 1784, to Hugh Williamson, who represented North Carolina at the Constitutional Convention and in the first Continental Congress, expressing his lack of familiarity with what had transpired with the management of the swamp company, noting that he had received no correspondence from Williamson until March 24, having heard nothing of his interest in the Dismal Swamp for more than nine years. "I am equally uninformed," wrote Washington, "of the motives which induced the Assembly of Virginia to open a Canal between Kemps [*sic*], and the

The original road later designated U.S. Route 17 was opened in 1804. Drawbridges were constructed at Deep Creek and South Mills in 1934 and the road's width widened twenty to thirty feet.

No. West Landings; but presume territorial jurisdiction must have been the governing principle." He continued, "From an attentive review of the great Dismal Swamp (and it was with a critical eye I examined it) I have long been satisfied of the practicability of opening a communication between the rivers which empty into Albemarle Sound (thro' Drummonds pond) and waters of the Elizabeth or Nansemond Rivers." From Washington's research, at different times, into and around the swamp, he made the following observations:

That the principal rivulets which run into the great dismal, if not all of them, are to the westward of it, from Suffolk southwardly. That Drummonds Pond is the receptacle for all the water which can force its way thro' the reeds, roots, trash and fallen timber (with which the Swamp abounds) into it. That to these obstructions, and the almost perfect level of the Swamp, are to be ascribed the wetness of it. That in wet seasons, when the banks of the pond are overborne by the assemblage of waters from the quarter I have mentioned, it discharges itself with equal difficulty, into the heads of the rivers Albemarle, Elizabeth and Nansemond; for it is a fact, that the late Colo. Tucker of Norfolk, on a branch of the Elizabeth river, and several others on Nansemond river, have Mills which are, or have been worked, by the waters which run out of the Swamp.

The Dismal Swamp Canal is the oldest operating artificial waterway in the United States. It is also rich in history and folklore. It is said that Edgar Allan Poe wrote "The Raven" during one of his stays at the Dismal Swamp Hotel. On the Dismal Swamp Canal James Adams's Floating Theatre is also said to be the place Edna Ferber got the idea to write the novel Showboat, *upon which the famous musical is based.*

Washington went on to make a critical observation, telling Williamson that "with the aid of one Lock," canal waters could be let either into the Elizabeth River or Nansemond River, "neither of which, from the best information I have been able to obtain, would exceed six or seven miles." Interestingly, in a letter dated November 2, of the same year, from Hugh Williamson to Thomas Ruston, Williamson elaborated on the companies that owned portions of the Dismal Swamp. In the letter, he noted that there were two companies to whom the whole of the Great Dismal belonged, including the lake. "The boundary line passes through that great Desart [sic]. General Washington and nine other Gentlemen have taken up the Part that is in Virginia, about 100 Thousd [sic] Acres. Another Company, of which I am one," he wrote, "holds all that part of the Dismal which is within N Carolina, about 50 Thousd As. I consider our Part as by far the most valuable acre for acre on Accot [sic] of the vast Cyprus [sic] forests it includes. This is the Timber generally call'd Cedar of which Shingles are made." He observed that while there was two and a half to three feet of black soil in all parts of the latter company's land, under it was blue clay. After the timber was removed, the land could not be turned to agriculture. From Tucker's Mill dam to Lake Drummond

Pulling up to a horse camp in the Dismal Swamp, David Hunter Strother observed a crudely constructed wharf, piled high with fresh-made shingles. From the landing a road, or causeway of logs, led back into the swamp. The horse camp was the headquarters of the swamp's shingle-makers. Shingle carts, like this one, piled high with loads, were taken from the swamp. *Courtesy of the author.*

Williamson told Ruston it was only about two miles. "The Tide water, in the West Branch of the Elizabeth River, on which Norfolk stands, rises to the very back of Tucker's Mill dam; from this you may calculate the necessary length of a Canal to pass large Boats from our Rivers to those of Virginia to carry off our Lumber and to carry off our redundant waters so as to drain our low ground," he continued. "General Washington, who has view'd [*sic*] the Lake and Virginia Tract carefully, assures me that a Canal four feet deep may convey Boats of sufficient Magnitude from the Lake to any of the contiguous Rivers." Williamson was clearly aware that the Virginia Company had wanted the canal work done immediately, but his own group of investors had requested his assistance in putting "that Business in a Train."

Writing to Marie Joseph Paul Yves Roch Gilbert du Motier, Marquis de Lafayette, from his home at Mount Vernon on February 15, 1785, Washington informed Lafayette that the Virginia General Assembly had authorized the appointment of commissioners to examine the most convenient course for a canal from the waters of the Elizabeth River to those passing through the state of North Carolina. The letter's focus was largely the importance of increasing national prosperity by opening up inland commerce and connectivity through civil works such as the Dismal Swamp Canal. In correspondence to Thomas Jefferson on September 26, Washington also informed Jefferson of the initiative to cut a canal to connect the waters of the Elizabeth to those of the Albemarle. Two months later, on November 30, Washington wrote James Madison Jr. on the same subject. At that time Madison, who had participated in the framing of the Virginia Constitution in 1776 and served in the Continental Congress, was a leader in the Virginia General Assembly. Expressing his pleasure that the assembly had adopted a mode for establishing the cut between the Elizabeth and Pasquotank Rivers, "which was likely to meet the approbation of the State of North Carolina," Washington observed that "no Country in the Universe is better calculated to derive benefits from inland Navigation than this is." Thomas Jefferson would later write Washington on May 10, 1789, after much correspondence between the two men on the subject of the Dismal Swamp Canal and the benefits of opening up navigable inland waterways, that "Canals and locks may be necessary, and they are expensive; but I hardly know what expense would be too great for the object in question…The navigation again between Elizabeth River and the Sound is of vast importance and in my opinion it is much better that these should be done at public than private expense."

Despite George Washington's years of optimism, investment and belief that there was much profit to be made from the Dismal Swamp, the swamp remained largely undeveloped, undrained and, for the most part, unknown for many years after Washington's survey. When Washington did find a use for his land, it was not farming but making juniper shingles, which were in much demand after the Revolutionary War. Washington used his slaves and poor white men to perform the backbreaking work of harvesting the trees, splitting the shingles and preparing staves and wood products for market—and digging ditches to pull timber products from the swamp. In a letter from George Washington to Henry Lee dated February 18, 1793, concerning the possible sale of Washington's Dismal Swamp holdings, he wrote, "Forty thousand Acres of the interior and richest part of the Swamp has been (as the Subscriber is informed) patented in the names of the Members of said Company; and, probably, is all they will ever obtain, altho' [sic] it is far short of what they expected." Washington told Lee that his company had a plantation there, marked on the plat as Dismal Plantation, which was separate and distinct, he iterated, from the forty thousand acres. "On this there are, or were, a number of Negroes, as may be seen by the Agents (Mr. Jameson's) letter to me," he continued. In telling Lee how much he would take for his land, Washington penned, "For the whole of this interest, be it little or much, and it cannot be less than 2/21, parts of forty thousand Acres, I will take Five thousand pounds Virginia Currency; estimating dollars at Six Shillings, and other Silver and gold in that proportion, provided the bargain is now struck; but shall not think myself bound by this offer if it is not." The "Mr. Jameson" to whom Washington referred was John Jameson of Culpeper County, Virginia, who held power of attorney for Washington regarding his interest in the Dismal Swamp Land Company. Disappointed in the management of the Dismal Swamp Canal Company, he disposed of his interests in it in 1795, at just about the time the canal itself was making progress.

Construction had begun on both ends of the Dismal Swamp Canal in 1793. The canal had to be dug completely by hand so progress was slow and expensive. While Jefferson had hoped that public money would be used to build the canal, it was not to be. Private capital was used to complete the project under a charter by the states of North Carolina and Virginia. Most of the labor was done by slaves hired from nearby landowners. It is interesting to note that the slaves became so familiar with the swamp during this period that it eventually became a haven for runaways. Later, in the antislavery era prior to the Civil War, *Harper's Weekly* artist David Hunter Strother visited the area in the winter of 1856 and reported that there were large colonies of runaway slaves in some sections of the swamp. "These people live by woodcraft, external depredation, and more frequently, it is probable, by working for the task shingle-makers at reduced wages," wrote Strother. Harriet Beecher Stowe patterned her main character in the novel *Dred: A Tale of the Great Dismal Swamp* on one of Strother's sketches. Henry Wadsworth Longfellow was inspired to pen his poem, "The Slave in the Dismal Swamp," based on Stowe's character.

The original canal was narrow and only five feet deep, but it was a useful means of transportation between the waters of North Carolina and the Chesapeake Bay via the Elizabeth River. Shortly after the Civil War, a competitive canal, the Albemarle and Chesapeake, connecting the same waters, was built, also with private capital. Since the new canal had larger dimensions, it soon attracted the bulk of maritime traffic and practically put its rival out of business until 1892, when its owners—the Lake Drummond Canal and Water Company—purchased and enlarged the Dismal Swamp Canal and took the competitive advantage over the Albemarle and Chesapeake Canal. This was short-lived prosperity. By 1912, just a few years after this picture was taken, the United States government planned, under the auspices of the U.S. Army Corps of Engineers, to take over the Albemarle and Chesapeake Canal, providing free access to the waterway to commercial traffic. This literally put the owners of the Dismal Swamp Canal, also called the Lake Drummond Canal, a toll-access waterway, out of business. This photograph was taken by Harry C. Mann. *Courtesy of the author.*

By 1796 the costs of building the canal had far exceeded the projected estimates. The company halted work and began a road to connect the two canal sections. The road was completed in 1802. The famous Irish poet, Sir Thomas Moore, visited the area soon after and immortalized "The Lake of the Great Dismal" in a ballad about a legendary love affair. Moore's poetic interpretation was lyrical, conjuring a mysterious, ancient place:

> *Away to the Dismal Swamp he speeds,—*
> *His path was rugged and sore,*
> *Through tangled juniper, beds of reeds,*
> *Through many a fen where the serpent feeds,*
> *And man never trod before.*

Over a hundred years later, in 1910, Walter Prichard Eaton would write a description that conjured that mysterious, dismal place, when he penned that the Dismal Swamp had become his delicious nightmare of the composite wetness and gloom of all those dark corners of a New England woods. To those who came before him, the great, untouched freshwater Dismal Swamp was cloaked not in secret, dark places, but opportunity. But opportunity was costly.

The completed canal would eventually open in 1805, twelve years after it was begun; it was only five feet deep. Because it was so shallow, its use was limited to flat boats and log rafts that were manually poled or towed through. Shipments consisted mainly of logs, shingles and other wood products taken from the swamp's great stands of cedar and juniper. Needless to say, this was a far cry from what farmers, lumbermen and merchants originally envisioned as a regional trade route. Throughout its history, the Dismal Swamp Canal has experienced hard times. The canal's owners would give up trying to maintain it, letting it fall into disrepair. Eventually they tried to sell it. Maintenance problems, the result of flaws in the canal's original concept and design, became particularly problematic. Water levels between the canal's start at Deep Creek and its original end in Joyce's Creek were not correctly measured. This left the canal without an adequate source of water and subject to natural rainfall and drainage conditions. Even with the feeder ditch built to supply water from Lake Drummond, the canal was still dry in periods of low rainfall and drought. The problem remains, even today. To preserve water levels in the federally protected Great Dismal Swamp National Wildlife Refuge, the feeder ditch is periodically shut off during dry spells. This prevents the canal from draining waters of the swamp and damaging its fragile ecosystem.

George Thomas Wallace is pictured about 1887 on this Walter Studios of Norfolk cabinet card. He died two years later. *Courtesy of the author.*

Commerce did not advance until the twenty-two-mile Dismal Swamp Canal was completed. By 1812 the large volume of business required major reconstruction of the canal, including the addition of several locks and a feeder ditch to Lake Drummond to provide a steady and adequate supply of water. The first vessel to make its passage down the Dismal Swamp Canal was a twenty-ton decked boat owned by James Smith that contained a consignment of goods consisting largely of bacon and brandy, from Scotland Neck, North Carolina, bound for Norfolk, which arrived on the Elizabeth River in June 1814. The canal was only navigable for shingle flats and small lighters until the late 1820s, when slaves widened and deepened its channel for the safe passage of vessels with a five-and-a-half-foot draft. The Dismal Swamp Canal Company's African slaves further opened a navigable route to Currituck Sound, digging a six-mile canal to

The Dismal Swamp Canal is on the National Register of Historic Places as a Historic Landmark, and is also noted as a National Historic Civil Engineering Landmark. In February 2004 the Dismal Swamp Canal was included in the National Park Service's Underground Railroad Network to Freedom Program. It is maintained by the U.S. Army Corps of Engineers as a navigational resource along the Atlantic Intracoastal Waterway.

the Northwest River and several smaller canals to float shingles and staves out of the old growth in the swamp's forests in 1829.

By December 1829 First Lieutenant Andrew Talcott of the United States Army Corps of Engineers reported to his chief engineer, Colonel Charles Gratiot, the results of his surveys of Deep Creek, including estimates for improving the Pasquotank, using a dredging machine that was then owned by the Dismal Swamp Canal Company. No action was taken at that time to make Talcott's improvements. More extensive surveys were conducted again in 1838 by J.J. Abert, the corps' chief of the Bureau of Topographical Engineers, from the Dismal Swamp down to Winyah Bay, South Carolina. The unincorporated town of Deep Creek, which in the eighteenth and nineteenth centuries was a small settlement on the edge of the Dismal Swamp, a stagecoach stopover point between Norfolk and Elizabeth City, had remained the principal shipping point for the swamp's vast lumbering enterprises. By 1838 Deep Creek was clamoring for improvements to the canal. After authorization from the Virginia General Assembly, an agreement was reached with the United States government that if the latter would underwrite the cost of erecting a new lock, the company would pay for the needed excavation. Because the silting up of Deep Creek could not be avoided, the decision was made to bypass it as a means of approach by constructing a lift lock at Gilmerton, a new town on the west bank of the Elizabeth River near Portsmouth, and named for Virginia Governor Thomas Walker Gilmer. From Gilmerton a straight cut of two and a quarter miles over land would lead to the existing locks at Deep Creek. Since it was necessary to cross Deep Creek, Gilmerton's elevation was to be maintained by throwing a tumbling dam and spillway across the creek below the debouche of the existing locks. These works, which had been admired by Governor Gilmer in May 1840, were completed in February 1843. The federal government, however, failed to provide funding under the previously reached agreement; the company built the locks with private funding under Abert's advice. The company was eventually reimbursed for its trouble with a Congressional authorization approved on February 26, 1845.

In the years intervening construction of the canals, Lake Drummond maintained its mystic quality. As the most elevated part of the Dismal Swamp, from its margins the swamp tapers off sharply at an incline of roughly 20 percent in all directions, dramatic enough to provide a strong current in ditches three feet deep and four feet wide. The lake's water is amber colored from the gum and juniper trees in nearby woods, and is often, even today, referred to as "juniper water." The water tasted, some would say, like sassafras tea. Ships leaving Norfolk for extended periods at sea would fill barrels with Lake Drummond's juniper water. It is said that Commodore Matthew Calbraith Perry had barrels of it aboard when he

made his trip to Japan in 1853. The water's keeping properties made it ideally suited to such use. The lake's water looked like dark-colored French brandy or strong coffee to David Hunter Strother. "It is fresh, healthful, pleasant to the taste, and, it is said, will keep pure for an unlimited time," Strother observed. Through at least a good part of the twentieth century people were still bringing home the lake's water in barrels, convinced of its good taste and perhaps healing properties. There is a story about a hunter who took a flask of liquor into the swamp and stopped for the night at the Lake Drummond Hotel, built about 1830 across the dividing line between North Carolina and Virginia. In the hunter's room was another bottle containing water from Lake Drummond. Taking a drink from it, he soon realized its sassafras taste and amber color—he panicked, believing he had been accidentally poisoned. He kept drinking, so the story goes, from his liquor flask, which did not help matters. Drowning his impending end in the flask, the hunter reportedly forgot the whole incident and went on his way.

The Lake Drummond Hotel, where the hapless hunter had stayed the night, was popularly known as the Half-Way House. A notice appeared in the *American Beacon* on January 11, 1830, stating:

> *This House of Entertainment is situated on the Dismal Swamp Canal, and half way from Norfolk to Elizabeth City, immediately on the North Carolina-Virginia Line one half the building in each State. The subscriber having erected this establishment at considerable expense during the present year*

President William Howard Taft visited Norfolk to attend the second annual convention of the Atlantic Deeper Waterways Commission at the Monticello Hotel on November 9, 1909. This photograph shows President Taft in a parade as it turned the corner at Granby and Main Streets. *Courtesy of the author.*

The Lake Drummond Locks had become little more than the overgrown entrance to a leafy tunnel on the way to the lake by 1896. The old barn on the right in this Harry C. Mann picture, taken about 1910, had been on the property since the mid-nineteenth century, where it once sat alongside a keeper's house. Lake Drummond was reportedly discovered by North Carolina Governor William Drummond, who held office from 1663 to 1667, while he was on a hunting trip. Drummond did not enjoy any profit from his discovery; he was hanged in 1677 for his role in Bacon's Rebellion. *Courtesy of the author.*

is now prepared to entertain travelers and boarders in a style which he thinks will give satisfaction. His house is large and commodious, being 128 feet long and having eight separate chambers, with fireplaces, so that families traveling, or parties of pleasure, can be accommodated with distinct apartments if they wish. His table will always be supplied with the substantials of Norfolk and neighboring markets. He has an extensive range of stables, well supplied with good provender, and attended by careful hostlers. In addition to improvements already made, he is now building a large carriage house, which will be completed in a few weeks; and he intends providing boats for the convenience of persons wishing to visit the Lake. His prices will be moderate and he hopes with these comforts and his own unremitting attention to please his guests, to merit and receive a share of the public patronage.

Isaiah Rogerson

Later that year, disturbingly to most who read the notice, Rogerson, proprietor of the Lake Drummond Hotel, died after a short illness. The August 6, 1830 edition of the *American Beacon* also stated, "We have no particulars of the death." A month later, on September 6, the newspaper ran a notice from Daniel Rogerson, indicating that he had rented the establishment, which was now open again for public accommodation. Daniel Rogerson was formerly the proprietor of the Tavern in Hertford,

North Carolina, and he was offering a place of hospitable entertainment and accommodation to anyone who might care to see the natural wonders of the swamp. But the Rogersons' hotel was not the only accommodation operating in the Great Dismal. A public notice published in the newspaper on September 8, two days after Rogerson's invitation to visit the Lake Drummond Hotel, gave notice that Farange's House on the Virginia and North Carolina Canal, twenty-four miles from Norfolk, nineteen from Elizabeth City and two and a half south of the boundary line between the states, continued to keep a house of entertainment at "the same old place where he has kept one for twenty-eight years past, and which is said to be the most pleasant and healthy situation on the Canal." Major William Farange, its proprietor, wrote that he was compelled to advertise his establishment, "though so well known," in consequence of "an insidious report" that he had just been informed by his friends was put in circulation by Isaiah Rogerson, before his death, purporting that Farange had discontinued keeping his house of entertainment, so that his customers would stop at another house, "which would have been no house at all if it had not been for the Government money and that of individuals." A Camden County deed was recorded on October 23, 1802, when Charles Chamberlain sold to William Farange fifty acres, which had been inherited from his father, John Chamberlain, and which bound the canal on the west and the Dismal Swamp on the north. This was referred to as Brickhouse Plantation, which later served as Farange's House, an inn for the public. The *American Beacon and Commercial Diary* of June 9, 1818, ran a news item that supports the existence of Farange's House predating the Lake Drummond Hotel.

> *This morning at 5 o'clock, the President with his Secretary and nephew, accompanied by the Secretaries of War and Navy, Generals Swift and Bernard, Colonels McRee and McRae, Com. Cassin, Capt'ns Warrington and Elliott, of the Navy, Col. Bassett, and C.K. Mallory, Esq. with several private gentlemen, will leave here to examine the Canal. They will proceed as far as Elizabeth City, but not cross the Sound. We understand that they will sleep tonight at Major Farange's on the Canal, and proceed on Wednesday to Lake Drummond; thence to Elizabeth City, and return to this place on Thursday evening. On Friday they will partake of a public dinner to be given by the citizens of Norfolk at the Exchange Coffee House.*

The announcement referred to President James Monroe's tour of the area, particularly Camden County, North Carolina, where he spent the night at Farange's House and also went on to Elizabeth City and from there

*Poet Robert Frost
visited the Dismal
Swamp in November
1894. Depressed
at the failure of his
first book of poetry
and initially spurned
by his love Elinor
White, he picked up
the road alongside
the canal and kept
going, intending to
never return. When he
reached a place where
the road seemed to lose
itself in the water, he
thought of wading
in, disappearing
forever. But he
hesitated. Scholars
of Frost's life do not
know what held him
back—perhaps it
was the light of the
lockkeeper's house
that drew him away
from the water, or the
thought of Elinor. He
returned home and the
couple was married in
December 1895.*

crossed the river to be entertained the following night by Enoch Sawyer, collector of the Port of Camden and whose brother was United States Congressman Lemuel Sawyer. As the years went on Farange's House and the Lake Drummond Hotel became poplar spots for marriages, particularly for those who eloped. The *Norfolk and Portsmouth Herald* of November 22, 1830, ran a feature article that stated that the Lake Drummond Hotel was a "convenient resort for matrimonial excursions to those whose impatience is too great for them to journey to our old friend Major Farange's (the original Gretna Green of Lower Virginia; Gretna Green is a locale in Scotland in which runaway marriages were quite famous between those considered too young in England but old enough to the Scots to be wed) about four miles further on." Since the marrying age was lower in North Carolina than Virginia, many of those who eloped to the two hotels were from Virginia. The only duel at the Lake Drummond Hotel that was ever known to have been reported by the Norfolk newspapers appeared in the *American Beacon* of October 2, 1847. Two young men from Greenville, Pitt County, North Carolina, both of them lawyers, fought a duel the day before on the Dismal Swamp Canal just inside the Virginia line. Both were killed. The suggestion has been made that the unexpected death of the hotel's first proprietor, Isaiah Rogerson, was the result of a duel.

Shortly after the *Norfolk and Portsmouth Herald*'s feature on the Dismal Swamp hotels, Daniel Rogerson disappeared and was never heard from again. Less than three months after announcing his proprietorship of the Lake Drummond Hotel, a notice was placed in the *American Beacon* advertising the hotel for sale at public auction on December 15 of that year; the actual sale was postponed until January 11, 1831. The announcement of sale was signed by William Rogerson. In truth, Daniel Rogerson, who had been appointed collector of the Port of Camden in 1827, had been charged with financial improprieties involving his office; the allegations had been made by Farange. It is clear that Rogerson had left town in the face of financial problems, thus making his property subject to United States Treasury Department scrutiny. The *Norfolk and Portsmouth Herald* later published a notice of Rogerson's death in New Orleans in early 1832.

In the midst of scandal and setbacks, major advances were made by enterprising businessmen to take lumber from the swamp. When Robert H. Smith, then president of the Norfolk and Western Railway, delivered an address about the beginnings and growth of his company in 1949, he spoke of the building of sections of track through the Dismal Swamp. He reported that as a swath one hundred feet wide was cut through the forests to establish the narrow-gauge Dismal Swamp Railroad in 1830, the trunks of the cut trees were felled to the center of the cut to make a corduroy mat, on top of which earth was packed. The sunken trees never

Looking south on the Hampton Boulevard Bridge over Tanner's Creek in 1910 a trolley is visible on the track. This was the first bridge built over Tanner's Creek, constructed about 1903 by the Norfolk and Atlantic Railway Company to connect downtown Norfolk to Pine Beach, located at the west end of Taussig Boulevard where the Newport News–Norfolk ferry once docked. The photograph was taken from the draw span at the center of the bridge. The homes visible in the distance were part of the Larchmont suburb, which was just beginning to take shape. *Courtesy of the author.*

rotted, Smith noted, nearly one hundred years after being laid under heavily trafficked rails; seasoned railroaders were astonished that the track required so little maintenance.

The second headwater canal is the Albemarle and Chesapeake. First authorized in 1772, fifteen years prior to the Dismal Swamp Canal, its early history has been characterized as all "acts" and no action. No fewer than ten acts were passed in both Virginia and North Carolina over a period of eighty-three years before construction finally began in 1855. By that time, however, the Dismal Swamp Canal was firmly established. The state of Virginia owned quite a bit of stock in the canal company and a new canal was viewed as a competitive threat. The man who carefully put the pieces together to begin the canal was Marshall Parks Jr. Parks's father had been superintendent and chief engineer of the Dismal Swamp Canal during its first major period of reconstruction in the late 1820s. The younger Parks had also been an official with the Dismal Swamp Company and was thoroughly familiar with the canal's problems. He visualized the Albemarle and Chesapeake Canal as the answer to more efficient commercial trade between the two regions, Northeastern North Carolina and Southeastern Virginia. The new canal would be wider and deeper than most others of its day. Parks planned for it to handle the larger steamers and future growth. It would also have only one lock, instead of the Dismal Swamp Canal's then seven, considerably reducing passage time. Construction of the Albemarle and Chesapeake Canal was accomplished by seven steam dredges on floating platforms. Had an attempt been made to dig the canal prior to steam-powered technology, it would have failed. The dredges had

This is a seldom seen early color view of the Smith and McCoy Shipyard in Norfolk, showing the Old Dominion Line steamer *Berkeley* in dry dock (left) and the steamers *Ocracoke* and *Viking* in the marine railway, ca. 1910. *Courtesy of the author.*

to gouge the canal out of low-lying mucky ground, scooping up huge tree trunks and petrified logs that lay beneath the surface. When the canal was finished in 1859, it was an engineering marvel, consisting of one lock and two relatively short man-made channels, the Virginia Cut and the North Carolina Cut. The single lock, which balanced lunar tides of the Southern Branch of the Elizabeth River with the wind-driven ones of the North Landing River and Currituck Sound, was 40 feet wide and 220 feet long, the longest along the Atlantic Coast and the second largest in the entire United States. The reversible gate heads, allowing ships to lock up or down depending on water levels, were probably the first of their kind. In addition, four times a day when the levels were equal and the winds favorable, the gates were left open to permit clear passage.

The opening of the Albemarle and Chesapeake Canal gave the Dismal Swamp Canal serious competition. The two coexisted for fifty-four years, with the Albemarle and Chesapeake carrying most of the traffic. There was only a short period when the older canal stole away a significant amount of the commercial shipping. This occurred in the years following 1899, when the Dismal reopened after being entirely rebuilt at a cost of over one million dollars. The triumph was short-lived, however. The final blow was delivered when the United States government chose to buy the Albemarle and Chesapeake in 1913. Both canals were considered for purchase, along with building one of the two new routes, as part of the government's plan to establish a continuous inland waterway as provided for in the River and Harbor Act of 1910. The Albemarle and Chesapeake Canal had defaulted on a bank loan and was sold at foreclosure in 1910. Three years later it sold for only half a million dollars. Following the sale, the United States Army Corps of Engineers went to work making improvements, and the Albemarle and Chesapeake was made toll free. For the next sixteen years, in a reversal of roles, the Dismal Swamp Canal wavered on the edge of bankruptcy. Finally, in 1929, the government also purchased the Dismal in an act of fairness. Prosperity had not lasted forever for owners and investors in the Dismal Swamp, but, on the balance, this great natural wonder became known to the world and much happened there that shaped the future of the regions of North Carolina and Virginia that are far more lasting than short-term monetary gain.

Work to make cuts—canals—into the Dismal Swamp to open up inland commercial routes, largely for timbering operations, also had an impact in other quarters of Norfolk and Princess Anne Counties, where efforts were made to connect the Elizabeth River to headwaters of the Lynnhaven River. In the fall of 1807, Colonel William Tatham, the father of topographical and coastal surveys, made a sketch of Norfolk's harbor and surrounding environs and sent it off to Robert Smith, President Thomas Jefferson's secretary of the navy. Smith sent Tatham's sketch and accompanying recommendations to Commodore Stephen Decatur, with a letter, dated October 22, 1807, in which Smith stated, "We are desirous of ascertaining whether a number of gunboats, say from sixty to one hundred, aided by suitable fortifications, stationed near the mouth of the Chesapeake, could not prevent the entrance into the bay of vessels of war, or their retreat out of the bay." Smith noted that it was thought by some that the Chesapeake Bay could thus be effectually protected. To answer these questions, Smith told Decatur he must survey the waters from the Virginia Capes to Seawell's Point, and all the intermediate rivers, creeks and inlets. "We have no chart upon which we can implicitly rely," he wrote. "You will cause one to be made upon which the soundings, the bearings from the land…must particularly be noted, and I shall be happy to receive your opinion and observations at large upon the points herein stated." Decatur did not acknowledge receipt of Tatham's sketch of the Norfolk harbor and environs. From a letter from Decatur to Smith dated November 1, 1807, it is known that Decatur did not employ Tatham to execute the survey requested by Smith, instead employing a Frenchman with prior French service who possessed "merit in the line of his profession."

During the period of the *Chesapeake-Leopard* affair in June 1807, William Tatham was at North Landing. Well acquainted with the coastal area from Cape Henry to Hampton Roads, Tatham was asked by President Jefferson, with whom he frequently corresponded at this time, to observe the activities of British ships entering the Chesapeake Bay from his vantage point at Lynnhaven Inlet and report what he observed directly to the president. Tatham's daily correspondence to the president proffered valuable descriptions of events that turned particularly heated that July, when the people of Norfolk most feared another war with Great Britain. Despite the extent and variety of his activities, Tatham's thoughts inevitably

Gordon's Canal, also called the Ebb Canal, was begun in 1856 to connect the Elizabeth River and Little Creek; it was never completed.

returned to canal building; he became the geographer of Virginia in 1790. The following year, 1791, the Virginia legislature authorized Tatham to raise by lottery a sum of money not to exceed $4,000 to enable him to complete geographic surveys he had contemplated and those already begun. He published *An Address to the Shareholders and Others Interested in Canals in Virginia* in 1794. As relations between the United States with Great Britain and France became more difficult in 1807, Tatham stressed the immediate importance of fortifying Norfolk, economically and militarily, by developing inland navigation routes; he recommended "gunboat cuts" from London Bridge to Dozier's Bridge in Princess Anne County. The construction of a large number of gunboats was the crux of Jefferson's naval policy, punctuated by its defensive and economical tenets. Gunboats of this era were roughly fifty feet long, equipped both with oars and sails and armed with one or two medium-sized cannon. They were manned by forty to sixty men and were designed to be highly maneuverable for coastal defense. The gunboats' shallow draft permitted them, in Jefferson's words, "to assail under advantageous circumstances, and under adverse ones withdraw from the reach of the enemy" into shoal waters. Making his observations for Jefferson, Tatham observed firsthand the danger of a British blockade of the Chesapeake Bay and, consequently, the resulting isolation of Norfolk and Portsmouth. It was during this period, in October 1807, that Tatham also drew a detailed map of the coastal area from the Chesapeake Bay to Cape Fear, North Carolina, which laid out his ideas on junction canals. Among his recommendations was the construction of a canal that would connect the Lynnhaven River to Norfolk, inland, via Kempsville, through the Eastern

Harry C. Mann was standing atop a building in Berkley when he took this panoramic photograph in 1913 of Norfolk's waterfront, but also the expansive Elizabeth River as it transitions from the main stem to the Eastern Branch. Portsmouth's Hospital Point is upper left. The area from Fort Norfolk (center, across from Hospital Point) and Norfolk's Town Point (center, below Fort Norfolk) to the city's Union Station (extreme right) at the end of East Main Street are shown. There are barges, ferries, sailboats and numerous other watercraft going about their business on the river. An Old Bay Line steamer was docked at its pier at Town Point, while just below it a paddle-wheel steamer, the *Luray*, of the Old Dominion Line, made its way down the river. The *Luray* operated between Norfolk and locations up the Nansemond and James Rivers. Norfolk's tallest buildings at that time, the Royster Building (the large white structure) and the National Bank of Commerce building (to the right of the Royster Building), rise above the skyline. Three ferries can be seen in this picture. The ferry (left, foreground) was headed for its berth at the foot of Pear Street in Berkley. The Old Dominion Steamship Company's docks (white buildings, center) had two ships berthed. Old Dominion steamers provided daily service between Norfolk and New York. Union Station opened in 1913. *Courtesy of the author.*

Branch of the Elizabeth River, with an additional cut that would open a waterway from Kempsville to the North River.

Treasury Secretary Albert Gallatin's report on roads and canals, sent to the United States Senate in early April 1808, received national attention; Gallatin had called for internal improvements to America's key transportation routes. Tatham published two pamphlets stating his own views on the subject, *A View of the Proposed Grand Junction Canal, Designed to Bring the Commerce of North Carolina to Norfolk by Inland Navigation, Together with a Proposed Lateral Canal from Kempsville to Lynhaven [sic] River, Calculated for the Defence [sic] of Norfolk, and for Promoting the Gun Boat Service*, dated August 1808, and *A Comparative View of the Four Projected Coastwise Canals, Which Are Supposed by Some to be in Competition for the Trade Between Norfolk and North Carolina*, printed in September. In the first pamphlet Tatham expounded on the commercial and agricultural benefits that might accrue from his proposed canal system, in addition to the increased possibilities of being able to better protect Norfolk and Portsmouth from foreign raiders. He wrote that the North Carolina sounds had "a natural inland tendency towards Norfolk, and an easy, still and deep communication by way of the North River, the head branch of Currituck Sound, and thence the route of the portage over land by the Eastern Branch of the Elizabeth River; requiring a cut or canal of about eight miles in length, through a fine suitable country, to form the junction between the North Landing on the North River, and Whitehurst's Landing on the Eastern Branch of the Elizabeth River, which enters the port of Norfolk at the New Bridge passing out of that town." He believed, too, that southern trade that moved northward by land to Petersburg would be diverted to Norfolk due to a more convenient and less expansive water route. "The port of Norfolk may fairly calculate," he wrote, "on becoming the port of consumption and distribution for an annual locomotion of fifty thousand tons of North Carolina shipping, with its progressive increase," rather than being "the warehouse of the James River." The canal at North Landing on the North River at a point near Kempsville on the Eastern Branch of the Elizabeth River could have supported a town or village at or near North Landing, thus the location of Cypressville.

The Grand Junction Canal had its detractors; objections were loudest from those who perceived Tatham's canal as a direct competitor and duplication of the Dismal Swamp Canal. To those who disparaged his idea, Tatham noted that the Grand Junction Canal would complement the value of the Dismal Swamp Canal by attracting wealth, population and power to Norfolk. Commercial activity, expanded by two canals, would bring greater use of the Dismal Swamp Canal. He promised repeatedly that Norfolk would become the central port of American commerce, and "the grand Mart of the United States." In his mind's eye, Tatham saw the canal system as interdependent, one in which no one canal could be removed from the plan without endangering the entire project. He was particularly concerned that the lateral canal from Kempsville to the Western Branch of the Lynnhaven River might be ignored. To keep the cut in the plan, he emphasized its importance to the maneuverability of Jefferson's gunboats. He wrote of telegraphic signals bringing together North Carolina and James River gunboats at Lynnhaven Inlet, and that the gunboats could be moved quickly from Craney Island by Kempsville to Lynnhaven.

Tatham petitioned the Virginia legislature to proceed with work on his canal, exerting enough pressure on members of the Virginia House of Delegates that on January 5, 1809, the Committee of Propositions and Grievances was presented a bill "incorporating a company to cut a canal from the port of Norfolk through the Eastern Branch of the Elizabeth

Garrett and Company, makers of Virginia Dare wines, popular in the early 1900s, occupied the foot of Chestnut Street in Norfolk's Berkley. The wine company began operations in 1903 and continued until 1916, when Virginia went dry in November 1916. The mansion visible to the right was the residence of Paul Garrett, president of the company. The photograph was taken by Harry C. Mann ca. 1915. *Courtesy of the author.*

River to the channel of Currituck Sound." The bill did not cover all that Tatham had hoped. He complained to Jefferson that the report of the committee appeared to have omitted an essential point, "a lateral branch to Lynhaven [*sic*]." He explained to Jefferson that though he had spent nearly $4,000 of his own money, at great risk of his own ruin he intended to continue to pursue the canal's approval. Tatham was finally successful, when on January 25, 1809, the Virginia House of Delegates read for a third time and passed an engrossed bill authorizing the president of the United States to open an inland navigation route from the Chesapeake Bay or the port of Norfolk to the channel of Currituck Sound, and from Lynhaven Bay to the Eastern Branch of the Elizabeth River. Just as this favorable action was being taken, however, the embargo was taking its toll on national coffers and an increasing number of American citizens had begun to question the advisability of the federal government underwriting such a substantive public works project.

Tatham became more than cartographer and surveyor in the years immediately preceding the outbreak of the War of 1812; he also became landowner. Disregarding the fateful course of events stemming from the embargo and heightened tensions with Great Britain, Tatham turned his attentions to Cypressville. Anthony and Anne Walke deeded Tatham three lots in April 1810, "situated, lying and being in the town of Cypressville, laid out, designed and surveyed by the said William Tatham on the land of the said Anthony Walke." The Walkes paid Tatham for his subdivision of the property with the lots. Tatham laid off the town on the North River, at or in close proximity to North Landing in Princess Anne County. The legend on Tatham's plat of Cypressville read, "Plat of the town of Cypressville, situated at the North Landing, in the county of Princess Anne, being the nearest landing to Norfolk or any inland navigation to North Carolina. The premises being surveyed and delineated by William Tatham in February 1810, there being at this time next to no magnetic variation in this part of the country." Cypressville was laid off in 245 quarter- and half-acre lots, with 110 feet reserved for a right-of-way for a canal. Those invested in Cypressville with Walke and Tatham included James Lewis, Moses Fentress and Caleb Boush, who held titles to various portions of the land; all counted

The knitting mill industry cropped up in the communities along the Elizabeth River in greater number during the late nineteenth and early twentieth centuries, as business became increasingly profitable to mill owners. Mills were built on Tanner's Creek, and several along the Eastern and Southern Branches of the Elizabeth, particularly South Norfolk and Portsmouth. Charlie Culpepper, the boy in the middle, is shown with his family in June 1911. He had been working for two years in the Elizabeth Knitting Mill, located on Bainbridge Boulevard in South Norfolk (later merged to form the city of Chesapeake). His older sisters worked there, too, but when photographer Lewis Wickes Hine (1874–1940) visited the mill to take his pictures, he observed that many of the youngsters were not working that day. Hine took his pictures for the National Child Labor Committee, which was then looking into sweatshop operations illegally employing children. Interestingly, the original Hine captions of these photographs misidentified the location of the Elizabeth and Chesapeake Knitting Mills, putting them incorrectly in Berkley, Virginia (subsequently annexed by the City of Norfolk). *Courtesy of the Library of Congress Prints and Photographs Division.*

on the canal becoming profitable, as it was to be the nearest landing to Norfolk or any inland waterway navigation in North Carolina.

Nothing appears to have come of the town of Cypressville, though there were, at one time, a couple of residences and a dilapidated sawmill still standing in the early twentieth century that dated back to Tatham's survey. Tatham's surveys often held great potential but were difficult to fund. With war looming, his timing could also have not been worse. Among his most promising projects, Kempsville Canal never reached completion. The Kempsville Canal, first promoted by President Thomas Jefferson as a military canal for gunboats prior to the War of 1812, was intended to connect the headwaters of the Elizabeth and Lynnhaven. Tatham's survey recommended it be thirty feet wide, nine feet deep and six to eight miles long. "With a view of this," wrote Jefferson to President James Madison on May 21, 1813, "was a survey made by Colonel Tatham, which was lodged either in the war or navy office, showing the depth and length of the canal which would give them [gunboats] a retreat from Lynhaven [sic] river into the eastern branch of the Elizabeth river. I think the distance is not over six or eight miles, perhaps not so much, through a country entirely flat, and little above sea level." The canal would have to be hand dug, Jefferson estimated, based on what Tatham and his crew estimated, that a cut of ten yards wide and four yards deep would require the removal of forty cubic yards of earth for every yard in length of the canal. "At twenty cents the cubic yard," continued Jefferson, the canal "would cost about $15,000 a mile. But even doubling this to cover all errors of estimate, although in a country offering the cheapest kind of labor, it would be nothing compared to the extent and productions of the country it is to protect."

Concerned that a maritime enemy would again attack Norfolk, Tatham had told Virginia Governor James Barbour that Craney Island was not the place to erect a first line of defense. This should have been done at Lynnhaven, observed Tatham. Just as he had predicted, the British launched an attack on Norfolk in June 1813, but it was stopped at Craney Island in the Elizabeth River, the first and only line of defense to safeguard the valuable port of Norfolk. The heroic efforts of General Robert Barraud Taylor and the Virginia militia and United States Navy and Marine troops did not, however, signal the end of the British blockade. During the summer and fall of 1813 produce from Southeastern Virginia was sent via the James River to Norfolk, and from Norfolk down the Elizabeth River to Kempsville, where it was transported overland roughly ten miles to North Landing. At North Landing the flour, tobacco and other produce was transferred to sloops that made their way down the North River into Currituck, Albemarle and Pamlico Sounds to Beaufort, North Carolina. There, the cargo was loaded aboard ships bound for Charleston, South Carolina, the West Indies trade and Europe. Tatham's canal, had it been built as he had planned, would have benefited planters and merchants immeasurably, and Cypressville would have flourished.

After the War of 1812, his spirit broken, Tatham gave up trying to revive interest in his canal between the Elizabeth and Lynnhaven Rivers, though Jefferson continued for some years to urge its reconsideration. William Tatham was a man ahead of his time, trapped in an era when circumstance and history proved unkind. From accounts of his demise, near the end of Tatham's life he was destitute and drank heavily. "Poor old Colonel Tatham is here," wrote Joseph C. Cabell to Jefferson on December 24, 1818, "half deranged, in great poverty, avoided by everybody, and trying to sell his collections to the assembly, and to get his lottery law revived, in both which attempts I believe he will be disappointed." The depth of Tatham's despair led to his suicide on February 22, 1819, when, on the grounds of the Virginia Capitol in Richmond, he threw himself in front of a cannon being fired in honor of George Washington's birthday.

Drawn up over two decades before, the project to build the Kempsville Canal seemed to show signs of coming to life in 1840, when the first charter was issued for the incorporation of the Princess Anne and Kempsville Canal Company. Colonel Claudius Crozet had surveyed the route originally recommended by Tatham, from the Eastern Branch of the Elizabeth River near Kempsville, to the North River for a new effort to make the cut. The canal company amended its charter on numerous occasions and, as a result, was simply reincorporated in 1851 as the Kempsville Canal Company, a corporate title that seemed to better suit its anticipated progeny. The by-laws of the company, adopted February 3, 1858, also indicated that it was time to start digging—all of it by hand. The canal work was divided into phases, the first of which was a four-mile section divided into four one-mile segments. The two sections closest to Kempsville were nearly finished in 1860, but then came the Civil War and digging stopped completely. Though the canal work picked up after the war, the cut was never finished. The United States Army Corps of Engineers determined in 1890, nearly twenty years after the Kempsville Canal Company's last expenditure was drawn from company accounts for excavation, that it was no longer economically feasible to continue digging the canal.

The two miles of Kempsville Canal completed before all work stopped were finished before the Civil War started. Prior to the digging of the canal, sailing ships, usually two-masted schooners, tugs and all manner of working boats, had to fit through a small drawbridge, and on the other side of the bridge were several warehouses that lined the banks of the river. Merchants shipped large quantities of oak knees and timber of all description from Kempsville to the Norfolk Navy Yard. Kempsville was the shipping center for most of the natural resource and farming

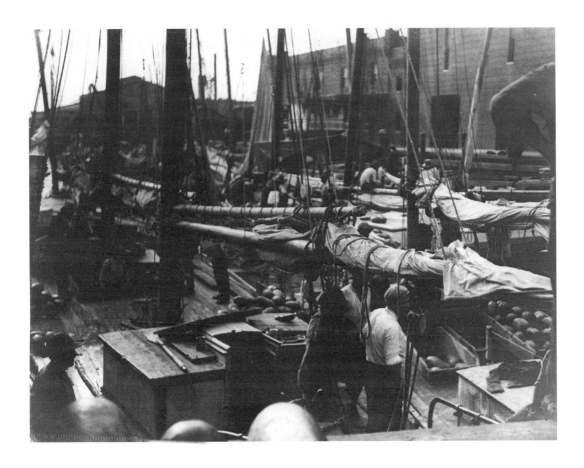

products of Princess Anne County, whose farmers were at that time large producers of corn and wheat crops. But by the 1850s a route connecting the Southern Branch of the Elizabeth River at or near Great Bridge, with the North Landing River, by the construction of a seven-mile canal through Gum Swamp was favored by the Great Bridge Lumber and Canal Company, which published its position in a pamphlet printed in 1855. This latter recommendation eventually developed into the Albemarle and Chesapeake Canal. The Kempsville Canal held greater promise as a faster route to market, had it been finished. Remnants of canal spoil piles, trenching and other tell-tale signs of a massive digging project along the Kempsville Canal route were visible as late as 1988 in the vicinity of Euclid Road in the Kempsville section of Virginia Beach. Continued urban sprawl along the Kempsville Canal route has since obliterated one of the nation's most unique examples of canal-bed construction.

By 1850 the *Norfolk Herald* remarked that the purpose of petitioning the Virginia General Assembly for extension of the city's boundaries to include all the land west of a line from the head of Plume's Creek, for a time the eastern boundary of the city, to Tanner's Creek, however visionary it

Boats laden with watermelons were photographed at the foot of City Hall Avenue at the wharf of the Boush Cold Storage Company (the building to the right in the picture) in 1912. *Courtesy of the author.*

253

The Fosburgh Lumber Company, located on the Berkley waterfront, is shown in this Harry C. Mann photograph dated 1911. *Courtesy of the author.*

might have appeared at first glance, was worth closer consideration. "Our city limits now embrace a space equivalent, we believe, to a square of one mile and a quarter. The contemplated extension would," noted the *Herald*, "make it equal to a square of three miles. It would take in all the farms on the south side of Tanner's Creek, down to the old Quarantine House, and all from that point to Lambert's Point, and thence to Smith's Point, the present western terminus of the city; and it would then be a great deal smaller than one-half of the site of the city of New York." The newspaper went on to remark that a ditch or canal from Plume's to Tanner's Creek—about a mile—would completely insulate the city, while affording a ready means of transportation for wood and marketing for all the farms on the north side of Tanner's Creek to the lower end of the city.

"It is not at all improbable, we think," remarked the *Herald*'s editors, "that if our city were thus extended it would infuse a spirit of energy and enterprise into the people of the new municipality." A few years later, in 1853, city leaders were advised by the *Herald* to be looking for more land to extend the city limits, and while they were at it, to consider extending the boundaries so clearly indicated by nature, commencing at the head of Newton's (or Plume's) Creek and running across the narrow strip of land (three-quarters of a mile in width) between the head of that creek and Tanner's Creek, and following that watercourse to its junction with the Elizabeth River, and thence to the limit of the city's southern waterfront. "It is not generally known," penned the *Herald*'s editors, "that Tanner's Creek, the northern boundary of the city as it would then be, is a bold stream all the way up to the point where it is proposed to be intersected by a canal from the head of Newton's Creek; and that for more than a mile from its mouth it has a sufficient depth of water for ships of large tonnage." There were formerly several shipyards on Tanner's Creek, where vessels of large draft were constructed, the last of which the *Herald*'s editors could recollect being the brig *George Loyall*, built by the late Isaac Talbot, Esquire. In his volume documenting Colonial-era shipbuilding, Joseph A. Goldenberg wrote that from newspaper advertisements of the period, Virginia-built ships began to appear in the 1750s, becoming more common during the decade to follow. How early shipyards appeared along Tanner's Creek is uncertain, but shipyards did exist along Norfolk's Broad Creek most certainly by that time. Norfolk merchants developed a thriving shipbuilding industry, establishing for themselves what Goldenberg observed was thriving commerce with the British West Indian colonies to supplement the transatlantic tobacco trade.

In the years immediately preceding the American Civil War serious consideration was given once again to building the Elizabeth River Canal, a body of water that would connect the head of Tanner's Creek to the head

Harry C. Mann took this picture of Norfolk Coal and Ice Company workers making a coal delivery in 1912. The company was located at 225 Front Street, tucked in Norfolk's Atlantic City section, one of the busiest commercial sectors on the waterfront. There is a horse-drawn dairy cart behind the tipped bed of their Kelly truck. Note also the waterway at the end of the street. *Courtesy of the author.*

of Newton's Creek—a distance that was actually less than a mile when calculated by constructors. In a report of the committee on the improvement of the marsh east of Norfolk's Chapel Street, a recommendation was made to open a canal to the terminus of Marsh Street. "Private enterprise has it in contemplation to connect the upper end of Newton's Creek with Tanner's Creek by a short and cheap canal," reported *Southern Argus* editors on June 10, 1854. Even then, Tanner's Creek was a far more important body of water than most of its inhabitants imagined. "It is, indeed, a deep and beautiful branch of the Elizabeth River, extending through thousands of acres of timbered land; while along its picturesque margin are some handsome and well cultivated farms," continued the *Argus* editors. They also observed that the proposed canal would afford convenient means of conveying wood to market, as there was timber that was cut in large quantities in what was then still Norfolk County.

The Elizabeth River and her tributaries continued to bring opportunity to those making a living on her banks. Attempts to improve water travel,

The old Berkley Bridge extended from the foot of East Main Street to South Main Street in Berkley. Harry C. Mann took this picture from Norfolk looking toward Berkley shortly after the bridge was built in August 1916. The bridge was a privately owned toll bridge that cost travelers two cents to cross. The City of Norfolk acquired the bridge in 1946 and took it down in 1952 after constructing a larger structure. At the far end of the bridge, to the left, is Riveredge, built ca. 1728 by John Herbert and, later, the home of Mary Pinckney Hardy, mother of General Douglas A. MacArthur. *Courtesy of the author.*

This early iteration of the Granby Street Bridge—used by trolleys—extended over Tanner's Creek, now the Lafayette River, and is shown as it appeared in 1908. *Courtesy of the author.*

thus commerce, through the digging of the Kempsville and Elizabeth River Canals fortunately failed. Had they succeeded, the Elizabeth's salinity levels would have been dramatically changed, as would the character of its aquatic life. Much is discussed in other chapters about commerce and the importance of the marriage of water and rail—and even the importance of aquatic life. To conclude here, however, it is worth mentioning that it was the advent of steam-powered vessels that drove a president of the United States to advocate canals for shallow-draft gunboats to protect the Elizabeth's towns and, later, improve the port's trade. Steamers would eventually team with railways to carry freight off to foreign and coasting ports, taking advantage of the Chesapeake Bay, the broad expanse of the Elizabeth River and two canals, the Dismal Swamp Canal and the Albemarle and Chesapeake Canal. A Merchants and Mechanics Exchange report in 1869 described canal boats from 20 to 300 tons burden, many of them making regular trips from Philadelphia and Baltimore to Norfolk, and thence to points on the North Carolina sounds. At that time the New York liners consisted of the *Isaac Bell, Niagara, Saratoga, Albemarle* and the *Hatteras*, all side-wheelers, and the propeller steamship *Virginia.* The Boston line had the *William Lawrence, George Appold* and the *Blackstone*, all propeller steamers, and the side-wheeler *William Kennedy.* While export trade was limited in the 1860s and still carried largely on sailing ships, during the year 1868 83 ships left the Elizabeth River for foreign ports of call, including our steamers. With increasing shipments of cotton, the tonnage of vessels engaged in foreign trade increased quickly, from 12,530 in 1870, to 30,598 in 1873, 65,521 in 1876 and 86,279 in 1878, according to the *Norfolk Landmark* dated August 6, 1879. These numbers would jump

The piers and warehouses of the Old Dominion Steamship Company, located at the foot of old Church Street (today Saint Paul's Boulevard) and Water Street was crowded with small general cargo vessels loaded with baskets of fresh produce from farms located along the waterways of the Elizabeth River and also from Northeastern North Carolina. Before the advent of interstates and the shift to tractor-trailers to ship such goods, boats were the preferred method of moving farmers' produce to the city for local sale and shipment elsewhere, usually to markets in the North. This picture was taken in 1912. *Courtesy of the author.*

to 121,420 in 1882 and 789,396 in 1891. In the five years from 1891 to 1895, over 2,500 vessels left for foreign ports, 2,100 of them steamers. Exports rose from $728,000 in 1871 to $1.25 million in 1873, $7.8 million in 1876, $9.82 million in 1879, $16.2 million in 1881 and $19.84 million in 1882, according to *Fact and Figures about Norfolk*, published in 1890.

Norfolk's foreign trade was restored largely by William W. Lamb, who had been commander of Confederate forces at Fort Fisher, North Carolina, during the Civil War. As part of his duties there, he had assisted British blockade runners, thus establishing many friendships with ship owners. At the war's end these men offered to help Lamb rebuild Norfolk's export business, and in 1866 Lamb dispatched the *Ephesus*, the first steamship ever loaded in Norfolk for Europe. Although the *Ephesus* was wrecked at Sable Island and part of her cargo of cotton lost, Lamb's export business continued to grow. In fact, he became manager of a line of Spanish steamers plying between Norfolk and Liverpool, as well as the Norfolk agent for the Baltimore-Liverpool steamers and the Allen Line. Reynolds Brothers, Ricks and Milhado, Barry Brothers and other companies further restored Norfolk's transatlantic trade in which all made their fortunes.

The coasting trade made great strides from the Civil War well into the twentieth century. The Old Dominion Line operated a fleet of seven steamers to New York; Merchants' and Miners' steamers plied the waters between Norfolk and Baltimore, Boston, Providence and Savannah; the Clyde liners went back and forth to Philadelphia. The number of vessels

The Granby Street Bridge, pictured in 1931, accommodated vehicular traffic; trolleys used the trestle visible just beyond the bridge. The view is looking south over the bridge. The New Year's Day 1931 *Virginian-Pilot* noted that the construction of this new concrete bridge to replace the old Indian Pole Bridge on Granby Street constituted the major public improvement by the city in 1930. *Courtesy of the author.*

engaged in the coasting trade in 1879 was 1,068, totaling 973,459 tons; in 1887 the number was 1,500 vessels, of 1,396,071 tons. A large amount of the coasting trade was in peanuts, fruit and vegetables. After the Civil War Norfolk merchants and farmers discovered the money to be made in peanuts. Before the end of the nineteenth century Norfolk had become the greatest peanut-growing region of the United States. Interestingly, it was in 1842 that two New Jersey farmers came to Eastern Virginia and began intensive truck farming, bringing impressive prices for their barrels of cucumbers and peas. Local farmers were amazed, and immediately began turning their attention to tomatoes, beans, potatoes, cabbage, strawberries, beets, lettuce, onions, corn and other crops. The first truck farms were on the Western Branch of the Elizabeth River, but they spread quickly, first throughout Norfolk County, then on to Princess Anne, Nansemond and Isle of Wight, among others. Farmers brought their crops to market via rivers, sounds and canals in small sailing vessels, at least in the beginning. One observer's account, published in 1893, noted that there were often seen one hundred and fifty of these little vessels entering the harbor a few hours before the sailing time of steamers, racing at full speed, with everything set and loaded high above the decks with a profusion of boxes and barrels packed with melons, cabbages, tomatoes and vegetables of all description and quality. They made an orchestrated mad dash to the wharves, often crowding up so thick that steamers and large vessels could not make their berths. Some were obliged to cast off from the wharves and swarmed like butterflies into the river, waiting to return. The frequent sailings of coasting and bay steamers, together with available freight cars to and from the Eastern Shore via a branch of the Pennsylvania and other railways, gave reasonably prompt and ready access to Eastern markets. By 1893 the annual shipment of truck from Norfolk equaled three million packages. The acreage of truck farms totaled about forty-five thousand,

The Hampton Boulevard Bridge over Tanner's Creek was photographed in 1934. This new concrete bridge was state of the art until replaced in the late 1960s by a wider and more modern bridge intended to increase the flow of traffic. The picture was taken from the roof of a building at the old Public Health Hospital; part of the hospital complex is visible to the right of the bridge. *Courtesy of the author.*

the number of farm workers 22,500 and the value of their product seven million dollars. There was opportunity in the waterways; Norfolk had become a city of the New South, noted an observer of the activity in the port at the end of the nineteenth century.

At the dawn of the twentieth century, and for decades to follow, the course of the Elizabeth River's history was affected most profoundly by war, evidenced in an earlier chapter. War proffered as much opportunity as crisis. Norfolk's exports in 1914, before the United States entered the world war, were $9.5 million and imports $3.12 million; in 1926 exports had spiked to $137.2 million and imports $16.87 million. The population of Hampton Roads was a third of a million, the foreign trade $220 million and the entire waterborne commerce twenty million tons. Norfolk's exports were equal in value to those of San Francisco, and well ahead of Baltimore, Philadelphia and Boston. After America entered World War I, Norfolk and Portsmouth bustled with activity once again. The number and variety of vessels coming up and down the Elizabeth River seemed endless. From the Norfolk side, ships took on cargo and bunker at the coal piers while others waited in the channel to take their turn; around them plied small harbor craft, even an occasional government dredge engaged in the work of making anchorages. In the distance, staying out of the way of naval vessels and large merchant ships, were tramps and sailing craft, barges and schooners. The principal export was coal. Long trains snaked their way from the West Virginia coalfields to dump their load into the holds and bunkers of ships at Seawell's Point and Lambert's Point, and also Newport News. Norfolk and Portsmouth exported a total of 10,903,137 tons in 1917, of which 10,469,060 were coal. According to War Department figures, in 1917 Norfolk's domestic shipments of coal were only 289,710 tons, but in 1918 that number leapt to 5,525,758.

Interestingly, Mother Nature did more to hamper commerce on the Elizabeth River than the Germans during World War I. Reports in the

The opening of the Norfolk-Portsmouth Bridge-Tunnel on May 23, 1952, signaled the arrival of Virginia's first subaqueous tunnel, initially a two-lane 3,300-foot toll facility under the Southern Branch of the Elizabeth River. Virginia Governor John S. Battle addressed a crowd of more than two thousand who came out to see this important link between the two cities. On opening day, automobiles—and people on foot—by the hundreds passed through the tunnel lying 90 feet below the surface of the river, captured by photographer Charles S. Borjes for the *Virginian-Pilot*. The tunnel is better known to daily commuters as the Downtown Tunnel. *Courtesy of the Sargeant Memorial Room, Norfolk Public Library.*

January 6 and February 2, 1918 editions of the *Virginian-Pilot* noted that during the winter of 1917–18 the waters of the Elizabeth (and every major waterway in Hampton Roads) froze solid, leaving shipping paralyzed and freight piled up on the piers and wharves. United States Navy battleships, put to work to break the ice in the harbor, moved slowly, making little progress. When the channel was cleared to the coal piers, steamers waiting for their cargo had to continue waiting because the coal had frozen and could not be dumped until steam pipes had been run through the cars.

In addition to coal, in 1917 Norfolk and Portsmouth sent out to other American ports half a million tons of fruit and vegetables, 76,000 tons of tobacco, 66,000 tons of petroleum products, 36,000 tons of lumber, 76,000 tons of cotton and 23,000 tons of fish, oysters and clams. In return, 546,000 tons of iron- and steel-manufactured articles, 300,000 tons of petroleum products, 136,000 tons of dry goods, 200,000 tons of fertilizer, 337,792 tons of canned goods, 85,000 tons of sugar, and miscellaneous goods amounting to 5,500,00 tons were brought in. The United States used Norwegian, Swedish and Danish vessels to carry on its trade of nitrates for fertilizer with Chile after the supply of kainite was cut off when America joined the war against Germany. The *Virginian-Pilot* reported in December 1918 that no fewer than 363,865 tons of nitrate were brought to Norfolk in 1917, and no fewer than 411,195 tons the following year. The advantages of Norfolk for both ocean and railway traffic induced the federal government to establish the greatest army base in the country, with concrete warehouses, miles of track, a rifle factory and one or more large piers on the Elizabeth River that would later become the basis for the Norfolk Tidewater Terminals, and subsequently the Norfolk International Terminals. Down the waterway, at Seawell's Point, the United States Navy had acquired about 474 acres, of which 367 had been the old Jamestown Exposition grounds and another 100 belonged to the Pine Beach development, to construct its first storehouses and piers. The first objective was to create a naval training camp, which was done by the fall of 1917. This was just the beginning. The federal government designed the naval base at Norfolk not only as an expansive supply station, but also an aviation field, a submarine base and an additional training camp.

During the fall of 1917 and throughout 1918 the U.S. Navy began developing the former Jamestown Exposition grounds at Seawell's Point. As part of the navy's need to provide shore facilities and piers for its ships, two piers, 1,400 feet long and 125 feet wide, were thrown out into the Elizabeth River.

From the end of World War I through the twenties prosperity continued. When the Great Depression came in 1929, Norfolk's marriage to the United States Navy accounted for the lessened impact of the Depression on otherwise hard times. The navy then had a $20 million economic impact on the local economy; sailors patronized businesses and bought homes here; the navy yard employed about four thousand men, the naval base two thousand. The navy continued to grow when other industries curtailed their activities. The people of Norfolk and Portsmouth were heartened by the sight of merchant ships coming and going, unloading at the piers on the Elizabeth River. Freighters headed to London, but were coming in from Bremen and Cuba, loaded with sugar. At one time there were upward of 200,000 tons of Cuban sugar in the warehouses of the army base and various storage facilities along the river. The *Virginian-Pilot*, in its annual review published in January 1931, remarked, "Norfolk is not stopping…to count her blessings nor ponder such misfortunes as have befallen her," a reference to the Depression. "She is engaged in making the most of her opportunities. Her ship lines she prizes. They use the sea as a long green path to the ports of the world that are anxious for her goods. Commerce through this port is a surer thing than it has ever been before."

As the Depression deepened, stores would be shuttered in Norfolk and Portsmouth, yet there were important public works projects that required immediate attention, one of which was a new bridge over the Eastern Branch of the Elizabeth River to replace the wooden structure at Campostella Road. As early as 1931 the city was considering funding for a two-lane bridge by using a system of tolls. Long delays prevented the project from coming to fruition until July 1933, when it was announced that $400,000 from federal funds allotted for roads in Virginia had been designated to the Campostella Bridge project. When ultimately built, the bridge had four lanes and a walk, and a modern draw span over the river channel, reported the *Virginian-Pilot* on July 7 and 8, 1933, and January 24 and November 10 and 18, 1934. Of no less importance was the construction of a new bridge to replace the old one over Tanner's Creek (now the Lafayette River) at Hampton Boulevard. The federal government as well as the City of Norfolk had an interest in Hampton Boulevard Bridge improvements. The bridge was an essential link in the line of communications between the naval base and the marine hospital and the Norfolk Navy Yard. After a period of delay, $119,000 was allocated to the

This Bethlehem Steel advertisement from the time of the tunnel's opening explained that the tunnel connecting Norfolk and Portsmouth, Virginia, was constructed in a shipyard, then towed 180 miles to the construction site and sunk into a trench across the river's bottom. Seven huge double-shelled steel tubes, each as long as a football field, were built on the shipways at Bethlehem's Sparrows Point Shipyard near Baltimore. The tubes were plugged with watertight bulkheads so they would float; they were then launched like ships and towed down the Chesapeake Bay to the Elizabeth River. When each tube arrived at the tunnel site it was lined with concrete while still afloat. Concrete roadways were poured inside of the tube and the completed unit sunk into position. Each tube was then joined to the end of its adjacent tube on the bottom of the river until all seven formed a continuous tunnel section. *Courtesy of the author.*

The Jordan Bridge, originally called the Norfolk-Portsmouth Bridge, was completed at a cost of $1.25 million. The bridge connects to Portsmouth's Elm Avenue, a heavily industrial section of that city near the Norfolk Naval Shipyard. This Waddell and Harrington vertical-lift span, two-lane bridge opened on August 24, 1928, as a toll bridge with a ceremony attended by Virginia Governor Harry Flood Byrd. Designed by Harrington, Howard and Ash, engineers, of Kansas City, Missouri, the bridge was planned by South Norfolk businessman Carl M. Jordan, who also organized the financing. Jordan and his brother Wallace owned Jordan Brothers Lumber Company and they believed that the Norfolk County ferry service was not dependable enough to meet the needs of their business or others in the South Norfolk community.

Contintued on p. 265

project by the Public Works Administration (PWA); the rest of the bridge's funding, some $400,000, was financed locally. Norfolk had always been a city of bridges, built on a peninsula intersected with bays, a river and its tributaries and creeks. Traffic has long been facilitated, in some cases by filling in, in others by ferries, but most often by bridges. With the advent of the automobile, it was obvious that the old wooden structures that dotted the city's landscape, traversing major bodies of water, were in dilapidated condition and outmoded. The replacement of these bridges, such as the Campostella, Hampton Boulevard, Colley Avenue, Granby Street and Lakewood Bridges, began in 1929 with the construction of the bridge over a branch of Tanner's Creek at Colley Avenue. This was soon followed by a new four-lane Granby Street Bridge over the Lafayette River. Construction of the bridge started in early 1935 with the backing of Senator Harry Flood Byrd and Congressman Colgate Whitehead Darden Jr. and approval of President Franklin Delano Roosevelt. Norfolk City Manager Thomas P. Thompson considered the Granby Street Bridge his personal triumph. The following year, more PWA money was needed for other public works projects, among them an improvement project for the Twenty-sixth Street Bridge, completed by 1939. The hard times of the thirties would be forgotten in the glow of prosperity that came as the United States emerged from the Great Depression at the end of the decade.

World War II thrust Norfolk into a flurry of defense-related activity from the outbreak of the war in Europe in September 1939 until Japan's formal surrender in September 1945 in Tokyo Bay. Nearly all of this work was centered on shipbuilding along the Elizabeth River. The largest part of the shipyard work done was performed by the Norfolk Navy Yard, but there were also several small private yards contributing to the war effort. Government shipbuilding in this period often overshadowed substantive gains made by private industry at this time. Commerce, noted one observer, was greatly affected by the war. The sinking of colliers leaving Hampton Roads ports on their way to New England and New York forced coal shipments to all-rail routes, removing the threat of enemy submarines sinking valuable cargo off the coast. Despite the move to ship coal via rail, Norfolk's piers along the Elizabeth were busier than in peacetime. Troop transports were loaded with men, equipment, horses and mules bound largely for North Africa and Europe. Cranes lifted bombs, ammunition and artillery pieces aboard waiting ships. When the threat from German submarines lessened in 1944 and 1945, shipments of coal resumed by collier, both to America's North and transatlantic to Europe. Later, as countries were retaken by the Allies, foodstuffs, livestock and other goods were sent to restore war-torn nations. The Elizabeth River and the communities along her shores emerged from World War II far different from when the war began. Intense shipbuilding and related industries had sprung up along the Elizabeth and all her tributaries to support the war effort. They had left their mark. For all of the ships repaired and built during this period, little concern was paid to the pollutants put in the water or the impact of these pollutants on the water quality and aquatic life in the river. With a war on, there was no time or impetus to think of the river.

World War II was the Elizabeth River's fifth major war, but not its last. The wartime boom continued beyond the war and overcrowded Norfolk looked to expand its land area. The Norfolk City Council called up Dr. Thomas H. and Doris D. Reed, noted annexation and citizenship training authorities, to make recommendations to city leaders. The Reeds' recommendation, in part, included annexation of the Tanner's Creek and Washington Districts of Norfolk County, the former to the north along Tanner's Creek and the latter situated on the south side of the Elizabeth River's Eastern Branch. Tanner's Creek District organized a Council of Civic Leagues to oppose annexation, but this position eventually softened and on May 25, 1954, the courts awarded Norfolk County about eight million dollars in compensation and spent about two million more to make improvements within the district, according to the Norfolk Chamber of Commerce's *The Norfolk Story 1954*. The Tanner's Creek District was largely well on its way to being built out when the City of Norfolk legally completed its annexation on January 1, 1955, thus this area was not intended to offer the city room to grow. But the district had to be acquired before Virginia law would permit the City of Norfolk to annex part of Princess Anne County, which successfully occurred four years later, on January 1, 1959. The physical divisions of land along the Elizabeth River's banks were not nearly as significant—though some would argue they were for other reasons—as the way people saw the river as an opportunity to commit closer ties between communities by bridging over and tunneling under it. While in the seventeenth century waterways were the most expedient form of transportation between towns and villages, by the twentieth century the water that surrounded municipalities embraced by the Elizabeth came to be viewed as an impediment. It was not until the late 1930s that it became possible to reach Norfolk from the west without paying a toll. Most toll-free highways went so far out of the way that automobiles and trucks actually preferred the inconvenience of the ferries plying the waters between Portsmouth and Norfolk.

A tunnel under the Elizabeth River had been discussed for many years. The Virginia General Assembly, in 1942, created the Elizabeth River Tunnel Commission to investigate the possibility of and carry out such a tunnel. When World War II ended, the commission set about its business. By 1947 an engineering report was completed and two years later contracts were let. The first tunnel to open under the Elizabeth

The bridge was renamed for Carl Jordan after his death. Ownership of the bridge passed to the City of Chesapeake after the bridge commission's indebtedness was finally satisfied in 1977.

The Jordan Bridge has been struck by ships many times. On June 2, 1939, the oil tanker Rhode Island *struck it, and the east tower and lift span collapsed into the river, injuring two bridge employees, closing it for six months. Another major collision occurred on June 13, 1943, when the freighter* John M. Morehead *struck the bridge. Both vessels had failed to successfully navigate the sharp thirty-degree turn four hundred feet south of the Jordan. The Jordan Bridge remains Virginia's oldest drawbridge.*

River had its debut on May 23, 1952, and soon thereafter the ferries that had carried people over the water for more than two centuries were retired. A new Berkley Bridge that linked the tunnel to Norfolk was completed at the same time and the old bridge was torn down. The *Virginian-Pilot* reported in its February 13 and 26, 1960 editions that the ease of communication afforded by the new tunnel increased traffic so quickly that revenue predicted for 1970 had nearly been achieved by 1959, eleven years ahead of schedule. Cars jammed the underwater highway, nearly bumper to bumper, and demand soon arose for another tunnel. Engineers picked a route for the second tunnel from Pinner's Point in Portsmouth to the foot of Hampton Boulevard in Norfolk, declaring that this location was the most economically practicable. The success of the Norfolk-Portsmouth Bridge-Tunnel, popularly known as the Downtown Tunnel, led to a successful bond issue in February 1960, which guaranteed construction of the new tunnel. The Midtown Tunnel opened on September 6, 1962, nearly four months ahead of schedule. Tunnels, expansive highways and the advent of containerized shipping removed people from a direct, daily association with the Elizabeth River. Containerized shipping, which emerged as the preferred mode of moving cargo by the mid-twentieth century, required larger facilities and Norfolk's and Portsmouth's waterfront wharves and piers were quickly rendered obsolete for this purpose. Facilities such as Norfolk Tidewater Terminals, later Norfolk International Terminals, and Portsmouth Marine Terminal soon took their place. Lack of close contact and visibility cost people their intimacy with the Elizabeth that would not return for decades to come. The waterway of opportunity became a lonesome lady, starved for attention and well on her way to ruination had four concerned citizens not gathered around a kitchen table—the genesis of what would be The Elizabeth River Project—in 1991 to flesh out her fate.

CHAPTER EIGHT
THE MARRIAGE OF WATER AND RAIL

Transportation prior to the arrival of the railroad was confined almost entirely to water routes, save what little overland traffic there was by freight wagons for goods and stagecoaches for passengers. The easiest means of travel was by water. For the area encompassed by the Elizabeth River, honeycombed by tributaries, creeks and marshes, there were few places from which a water lane could not be reached. Where there had been no water route, in fact, a man-made one was dug—the Dismal Swamp Canal—to join the Elizabeth River with the rivers and sounds of North Carolina. Ferries and steamers, discussed earlier, remained the preferred mode of moving goods and passengers from one point to another. The emergence of steam power in navigation set the stage for development of steam engines in the railroad industry.

The railroads had not been successfully routed to Portsmouth in the early 1800s until a number of the town's citizens gathered sufficient subscribers together to get one started. Portsmouth became the pioneer of railroad building among the communities abutting the Elizabeth. In March 1832 the Portsmouth and Roanoke Railroad Company (also called the Portsmouth and Weldon Railroad) was incorporated by act of the Virginia General Assembly; Captain Arthur Emmerson was its first president and Colonel Claudius Crozet, an engineer with an international reputation, its chief consultant. Norfolk interests subscribed heavily to the Portsmouth line. Captain Emmerson, the son of Reverend Arthur Emmerson, the third rector of Trinity Episcopal Church, had defended Norfolk and Portsmouth with his artillery at the battle of Craney Island in the War of 1812; he also inherited the home built by his father on High Street opposite the courthouse in 1784. Emmerson's descendants lived in the High Street residence until about 1930, when it was subsequently torn down to make room for business purposes.

The first American to operate a locomotive was a Portsmouth man, Edward E.G. Young, who made the trip between Frenchtown and Newcastle, Delaware, on November 26, 1832.

Contracts were given out for the Portsmouth and Roanoke Railroad shortly after its incorporation and building operations commenced immediately. The newspapers carried an advertisement for two hundred laborers for work on the railroad. It was plainly stated that the wages would be ten dollars a month and, moreover, they must have a spade or be responsible for the one lent to them by the company. Work continued but the project proved difficult for Portsmouth's small, but enterprising, businessmen. The company appealed to the Virginia legislature for financial aid from the state. There was much debate in the assembly through the end of 1832. On January 19, 1833, the Portsmouth and Roanoke Railroad Bill passed the Virginia Senate. News reached Portsmouth via a special messenger. Cannon had been placed at intervals on the road to Suffolk so that the news would reach there quickly. Rockets were shot across the Elizabeth River and for two hours cheerful pandemonium reigned in Portsmouth.

Building a railroad in Portsmouth turned out to be an engineering feat—and all the rails had to be made in England. In spite of setbacks and much wrangling, the track reached Suffolk by July 1834 and on the twenty-ninth the train was set to make its first trip from Portsmouth to Suffolk. Train schedules were advertised; there were two trips a day to each place at a cost of $1.50 for the round trip. The depot or passenger station at that time was located at the junction of High and Chestnut Streets, placed there, in such a remote place, as the "old inhabitants" later recounted, so that horses would not be frightened by the locomotive, and children would be less likely to be injured by the train. The Chestnut Street station was known as the "upper depot" when the tracks were afterward extended to the ferry at the foot of High Street in 1835, connecting the rail to the water. The ferry landing move from North Street to the foot of High Street was for the convenience of Norfolk, that city having invested in Portsmouth's railroad if that condition were met.

The twenty-ninth of July 1834 went by, but still no engine had made its appearance on the track. Despite the potential of the railroad, horses still satisfied the transportation needs of many Portsmouth residents. While the railroad's supporters were sorely disappointed that no engine had yet been seen on the track, others were content to continue the mode of transportation with which they had long been comfortable. The railroad company, to keep the train visible to the public, sent it out to Suffolk drawn by horses in the absence of an engine. The trip was made twice a day from each town according to the schedule, until October 11, 1834, when the engines, made in England, were put into service. One of the engines delivered to Portsmouth was a Watt engine named *John Barnett*; the other has little information known about it. On that October day the train made its first trip to Suffolk in due form, drawn by its new engine,

and filled with invited guests. It left town, wrote one chronicler, with flags flying and band playing. No sooner had Portsmouth initiated its railroad service, than Norfolk declared it was not satisfied with the deal in an attempt to force the Portsmouth and Roanoke Railroad Company to make its terminus Norfolk. In 1835 Norfolk's representatives petitioned the legislature to make the town on the Elizabeth's east bank the rail's terminus. The argument that ensued between Norfolk and Portsmouth was heated. The representatives in both houses of the General Assembly were from Portsmouth at that time—Colonel James Langhorne and Captain Samuel Watts. Both men delivered eloquent speeches against the bill, denying the claim that the railroad company had promised to make Norfolk its terminus. Records showing that it had agreed to bring the tracks to the foot of High Street and to move the ferry to the same location were provided. The measure by Norfolk was defeated. The charter of the railroad made Portsmouth the terminus and that instrument was upheld. Having failed to sway the assembly, Norfolk immediately turned to the line at the other end of the Portsmouth and Roanoke Railroad's track, at Margaretsville, North Carolina, which had been reached by the tracks of the railroad. The objective of the railroad in extending its track line to the west and below the North Carolina–Virginia state line was to bring commodities to market, much of which would be loaded on merchant vessels in the Norfolk harbor and sent to the North.

Norfolk was not the Portsmouth railroad's only trouble in the 1830s. On August 7, 1836, the railroad had its first accident. Upon the return of an excursion train to Suffolk there was a collision with a heavily loaded freight train from McClenny's Station. The excursion train carried about

This locomotive and passenger car were used by the Portsmouth and Roanoke Railroad in 1834. The sketch was first published by the Seaboard Air Line Railroad News Bureau. *Courtesy of the author.*

The last of Town Back Creek, which at one time extended nearly all the way to Church Street, today known as Saint Paul's Boulevard, was first platted in 1680. By 1880 the name City Hall Avenue was given to land that had been filled-in marsh land. The last of the creek in this photograph extended from Granby Street to what is today Boush Street. This picture was taken from the Norfolk and Western Railway trestle visible in the accompanying image of McCullough's Wharf. The last of Town Back Creek was filled in by 1905 and Boush Street extended to Main Street. The buildings in the picture include the Market and Armory Buildings (left) constructed in 1892; the city courthouse (center) built in 1850; and the Haddington Building (right) completed in 1893. The Haddington Building was considered Norfolk's first skyscraper. *Courtesy of the author.*

two hundred passengers; forty of them were injured and four killed. The dead were all women, all of Suffolk. The accident occurred just outside of Suffolk, and doctors from both Portsmouth and Suffolk responded to help the injured. The naval hospital sent a medical team, and Richard Godwin, who owned a large home near the track, turned it over as a temporary hospital. The accidents were not over that day. The engine that carried the naval hospital's medical staff returned that night in a blinding storm and two men walking on the track unaware of the train's approach were run over and killed. This terrible sequence of events stirred the community deeply. The Portsmouth town council ordered an investigation, appointing Samuel Watts, Richard Blow and Robert Taylor to a committee of inquiry. Their report exonerated the conductor of the excursion train, placing blame for the accident squarely on the shoulders of the freight train's conductor. The latter left town before he could be punished for his negligence.

The Portsmouth and Roanoke would not remain the only railroad for very long. The Petersburg and Weldon Railroad, with which the Portsmouth and Roanoke had conflicting interest, made several attempts to put the latter out of business by what one observer described as "devious means." Officers of the Petersburg and Weldon succeeded in enticing the owner of property in Southampton County, through which the Portsmouth and Roanoke had right of way, to permit a work party to wreck the tracks on his land. The matter was taken to court and the Petersburg and Weldon was ordered to re-lay the tracks without delay. Except for financial difficulties experienced periodically, the railroad continued its services without significant problems, but in the 1850s the Portsmouth and Roanoke's stockholders were in need of more capital to extend and improve the railroad. Dr. William Collins of Portsmouth was then the railroad's president. Collins had represented Portsmouth in the Virginia Legislature, and in 1844 had been appointed by President John Tyler as first auditor of the United States Treasury. Washington, D.C., became his home until the end of President James Polk's administration in 1850. With the exception of his six years in Washington, Collins lived in an old brick home at the corner of Crawford and Queen Streets, which he had inherited from his father. Under Collins's presidency Portsmouth's first railroad investors were taken over by Philadelphia capitalists. The railroad was then almost entirely rebuilt and new tracks laid; these rails, too, were made in Newport, England. Two new engines were purchased, the *Romulus* and the *Remus*. A printed schedule of the Seaboard and Roanoke Railroad, as the Portsmouth line was then called, made out by O.D. Ball, master of transportation in 1859, indicated the speed at which trains were expected to travel. The speed of trains was not to exceed twenty-five miles an hour for express trains; accommodation and

Charles J. Colonna designed and built his Colonna Marine Railway in 1875 on the west side of Herbertsville's (now Berkley's) Main Street where the north end of the street terminated at the water's edge; there was no bridge there at the time. The railway had a fifty-ton lifting capacity; the four-inch-wide iron track was fitted with four-inch-diameter iron rollers that carried the hauling chain inshore. This was commonly called a floored railway because of its foundation construction, which rested on a mat of flat boards laid over a graded, inclined mud bottom. Horses were used as needed, depending on what kind of vessel was being dry-docked.

freight twelve miles an hour; and in passing over bridges, over trestles and through towns six miles an hour.

After the railroad's reorganization in the 1850s, much progress was made. Warehouses were constructed along the waterfront on Portsmouth's Water Street, which had been gradually acquired, and an outlet was required from the upper depot at Chestnut Street to the new wharves to reach from London to Glasgow Streets. Right of way was granted and a track was laid on London Street as far as Middle and there branched diagonally through the block to Crawford Street, and the river. In order to reach the waterfront, the historic old house, later 213 Middle Street, was moved from its original location on Crawford. Another house on London Street just beyond Middle was also altered to accommodate the railroad. About 1870 a room in the house abutted on the line of the rail track. The room was cut also diagonally across, giving it a half-square shape.

The Crawford Street tracks were not laid until 1890, nor were they laid without considerable, violent protest by many property owners on

McCullough's Wharf, also called McCullough's Dock, was located at the terminus of City Hall Avenue and Boush Street. The picture was taken about 1895. The boat slip in the foreground is all that was left of Town Back Creek. To the left was the building supply company of Gammage and Waller and at lower right is the McCullough Lumber Company. The trestle bridge connected Boush Street to Newton Street, later Boush Street extended. Railway docks and warehouses are also visible in this photograph. *Courtesy of the author.*

the street. Threats were made and excitement ran high in Portsmouth. A temporary injunction was issued by the court, but it expired on a Friday night, leaving petitioners to wait until Monday, when court convened, to request a permanent one. The railroad took this opportunity to put a train on the track, for it was believed that if the track were used it would be too late to obtain a permanent injunction. Saturday morning Crawford Street was alive with workers by daybreak. They busily laid track from one end of Crawford Street to the other, and the train soon passed over it. The issue was not resolved, despite the railroad's taking advantage of the situation, for many months. Property owners received damages, with the exception of two, who happened to be the two who had protested most vehemently against the laying of the tracks. The railroad made certain that the tracks curved around their properties just a few feet beyond the legal limit. The new tracks did away with the need for those on London Street, which proved an opportune moment for the Portsmouth Street Railway, which purchased them for the new railroad being built to Port Norfolk. One railway train a day passed over these tracks in order that the railroad could keep its right of way.

The Seaboard Market and Armory, with its castellated towers, was completed in 1893 at the northwest corner of Crawford and South Streets in Portsmouth. The building was torn down in 1945. This picture was taken about two years after the market and armory was built. *Courtesy of the author.*

SEABOARD MARKET AND ARMORY—Portsmouth.

When the Norfolk and Western Railway found the draft on the Eastern Branch insufficient to build collier piers, the railroad carried its track in a wide sweep around the city of Norfolk to Lambert's Point, where the water was 26 feet deep, and built a great pier out over the water, 894 feet long, 60 feet wide and 48 feet high. From this point coal deliveries were 504,153 tons in 1886, and over a million tons in 1889. In all 3,821 vessels took on coal at Lambert's Point in those four years.

The Portsmouth and Roanoke Railroad was one of the oldest in the South in 1832, eventually to become the Seaboard Air Line Railroad, serving a large area in the South and East. But before the railroads the people of Norfolk and Portsmouth of the eighteenth century had regular lines of sailing ships for passengers from this port to New York and Philadelphia as well as to Charleston and other Southern cities. These ships had regular days for sailing and advertised to carry the mail. The beginning of the nineteenth century saw a steamboat line established here. On May 23, 1815, the steamboat *Washington* arrived in Norfolk en route to Washington, D.C. The following day, the *Norfolk Gazette and Publick Ledger* reported that the citizens of Norfolk and Portsmouth, few of whom had ever seen a steamboat, had been highly gratified with the performance of the sidewheeler *Washington*—the first steamboat the citizens of Norfolk and Portsmouth had seen on the Elizabeth. Just a few weeks later, on June 19, the steamboat *Eagle*, under the command of Captain Moses Rogers, made the voyage from the capes of Delaware Bay, arriving in Norfolk in twenty-nine hours. The 110-foot, wooden-hulled paddle-wheeler's arrival inaugurated the first steamboat service between Norfolk and Baltimore, but the *Eagle* was also the first to make the journey from Norfolk up the James River to Richmond. She became a regular workhorse of the Chesapeake Bay. The *Eagle*, built in Philadelphia in 1813, had been bought by a company made up of men from Norfolk and Portsmouth in New York, but after she was acquired by a company from Alexandria, the *Eagle* changed routes, working between Portsmouth and points far closer than Baltimore.

In 1816 the steamboat *Powhatan* began working the route from Norfolk's harbor to Richmond. After the *Powhatan*'s trial trip, her proprietors announced that they could determine a departure and arrival schedule with some accuracy by places en route. When steamboats could capture a regular schedule, they appealed to a better class of passenger and freight, but also mail, which was described as "packets." Only the difficulty of procuring fuel slowed down a steamboat's schedule in the early years of their use. On March 18, 1817, when the *Powhatan* was within eight miles of Richmond, her engineer had to depart the steamboat and go ashore in search of fuel. During his absence there was no one onboard capable of managing the machinery; the steam greatly increased and the boiler burst. In addition to the loss of the vessel, a number of people were killed. The *Powhatan*'s successor was built in Norfolk at William F. Hunter's shipyard at the foot of Newcastle Street. This steamboat was christened *Richmond*, and remained in service for many years.

On the front page of the morning edition of the Friday, September 6, 1839 *American Beacon* ran an advertisement for the Maryland and Virginia Steamboat Company, which plied the waters between Norfolk,

Portsmouth and Baltimore with the steamboats *Alabama*, *Kentucky* and *Jewess*. The company's steamboats left Hunter's Wharf daily at three o'clock in the afternoon, running, too, a connection with the Portsmouth and Roanoke Railroad, and the Richmond boats *Patrick Henry* and *Thomas Jefferson*, and, from the middle of September, the Charleston boats *South Carolina* and *Georgia*. The *Beacon*'s front page carried several steamboat company advertisements, including a notice dated January 22, 1838, the year prior, stating that on that date the Portsmouth and Roanoke Railroad was informing the public that it was prepared to regularly carry any amount of produce that might be ordered. Beginning with the first parties of pleasure embarked on the *Washington*, residents on the banks of the Elizabeth continued to enjoy the pleasures of the many steamboats that plied the river, taking them to and from destinations up and down the Chesapeake Bay. In an interesting advertisement, on the third page of the *Beacon*'s September 6, 1839 edition was an article about yet another pleasure trip, this one to commemorate the anniversary of the battle of North Point, Baltimore. "The swift and commodious steamer *Alabama*, Captain Thomas Sutton, will make her last pleasure trip for the season to Baltimore, on Tuesday, the 10th of September, leaving Norfolk at the usual hour, three o'clock, and Portsmouth at half past three." Tickets there and back were five dollars; meals fifty cents.

Harry C. Mann took this picture of the cotton wharf on Front Street about 1910. Norfolk was the fourth cotton port established in the United States. *Courtesy of the author.*

275

The Old Dominion Line's docks and warehouses at the foot of Norfolk's Church and East Main Streets were photographed by Harry C. Mann about 1912. Small work boats loaded with produce and assorted goods from nearby farms along the rivers and waterways in the area—some from as far away as Northeastern North Carolina—came to Old Dominion Line's docks to load steamers bound for New York City. The turnaround time for fresh produce delivery from Norfolk to New York was one day. The steamship company maintained daily service to

New York except Sunday. The docks were destroyed by fire on June 7, 1931, and never rebuilt. The service was continued from the old extension of Boissevain Avenue in West Ghent, where Old Dominion Steamship Company had built new piers and warehouses. The company's ships were taken over by the United States government during World War II; some were sunk. The line never resumed service when the war ended. *Courtesy of the author.*

At the beginning of the twentieth century the coal trade out of Norfolk had grown so rapidly that H.H. Rogers, one of America's great capitalists, was inspired to construct a new railroad from the coalfields to Norfolk—the Virginian Railway. Norfolk Mayor Barton Myers and others secured an appropriation of $95,000 to purchase the right of way, and got an option on five hundred acres at Seawell's Point. They then went to New York and sealed the deal with Rogers. The Virginian, which ran from Deepwater, West Virginia, to Seawell's Point, a distance of 442 miles, opened for business on April 1, 1909.

Tickets could be purchased at French's and Exchange Hotels as well as the office of the steamboat company, Norfolk, Hygeia Hotel, Old Point Comfort and at the post office and railroad ticket office in Portsmouth, until the day of departure.

By the mid-nineteenth century Norfolk was Virginia's principal seaport town, situated strategically in what was then the northern part of Norfolk County, on the north side of the Elizabeth River, at the mouth of its Eastern Branch and immediately opposite Portsmouth and the confluence of the Southern Branch. The city of Norfolk at that time was situated on a small, level peninsula, or neck of land, of approximately eight hundred acres, with the wide, blue river on the south and southwest, Smith's Creek on the northwest and Newton's Creek on the east. Norfolk is near the southeasternmost extremity of the commonwealth of Virginia at latitude 36°50'50"; longitude, west from Greenwich, 76°42'43", first calculated from the Farmers' Bank, corner of Main and Bank Streets.

For the purpose of trade and commerce, both foreign and domestic, the ports of Norfolk and Portsmouth stood out, even then, as virtually unrivalled, situated in the middle of the Atlantic seaboard, the nearest and most convenient location for the shipment of the goods, particularly the crops, of Virginia and North Carolina as well as a significant portion of the great West. But the railway situation had remained essentially unfavorable to Norfolk in the years preceding the Civil War. The City of Norfolk made a concerted effort in 1851 to secure a railway to Petersburg that would link with the Southside Railway that connected with the Virginia and Tennessee at Lynchburg, which, in turn, linked up at Bristol with the railway system of Tennessee. Norfolk merchants needed a means of linking freight trains to their wharves, thus enabling them to ship grain from the Cumberland Valley or cotton from the Deep South. The charter for the Norfolk and Petersburg Railway was secured but the project stalled, mired in financial wrangling in the Virginia House of Delegates. The railroad that Norfolk interests desperately wanted to come to fruition had already been partly surveyed. After further negotiation the Commonwealth of Virginia and City of Norfolk subscribed to the stock of the Norfolk and Petersburg, ensuring that it would be pushed forward. William Mahone led the charge.

Beginning in Norfolk at the east end of Main Street, the track made a wide circle over the Eastern and Southern Branches of the Elizabeth River, and sliced through the Dismal Swamp to Suffolk, where it then swung northwest in nearly a straight line to Petersburg. An article in the April 5, 1855 *American Beacon* later observed that Mahone had done the railroad and Norfolk a great service by insisting that the roadbed for the railway, the bridges, rails and rolling stock be of the latest and most substantive type, that the grades be easy, the ditching deep, the curves

OLD DOMINION STEAMSHIP JAMESTOWN AT WHARF IN PORTSMOUTH.

few. Much had been learned about railway construction since the days of the Portsmouth and Weldon. By July 1858 trains were running. The transferring of goods from freight cars to wharves was made easy by the laying down of track along Norfolk's Water Street from the station to Town Point. Unfortunately, the Norfolk and Petersburg had not had time to build up paying traffic before the advent of the Civil War. Tonnage carried on Norfolk and Petersburg freight cars in 1860 was only 7,502 as compared with 32,660 by the Seaboard. But its connection to the southwest had been achieved, and had there been more time before the war, with the Southside, and the Virginia and Tennessee, the Norfolk and Petersburg would have become a great conduit of trade. The Norfolk and Western, into which these railway lines would eventually merge, was later to achieve what they could not and Norfolk would flourish as a result.

After the Civil War, railroads had much work to do to repair their lines and restore services. By early 1866 trains moved over both Norfolk and Petersburg and Seaboard and Roanoke lines, the Norfolk and Petersburg in February and the Seaboard and Roanoke in April. Due to these

The Old Dominion steamship *Jamestown* is shown at a wharf in Portsmouth about 1895. The *Jamestown* provided passenger service between Norfolk and New York. *Courtesy of the author.*

279

Frank J. Conway took this panoramic photograph of the Norfolk and Western Railway coal yards at Lambert's Point in 1915. *Courtesy of the author.*

connections, Norfolk began to emerge as—as one observer wrote more than half century ago—"a great cotton port." The Norfolk and Petersburg merged with the Southside Railroad, which ran the route from Petersburg to Lynchburg, and the East Tennessee and Virginia that connected Lynchburg to Bristol under the title Atlantic, Mississippi and Ohio with William Mahone as its president. In 1873 Mahone's consolidated railroad suffered the setback of financial instability, which swept through the industry, eventually forcing the reorganization of the Atlantic, Mississippi and Ohio three years later under the more familiar name Norfolk and Western. With the emergence of the Norfolk and Western a new era began for Norfolk's port. Connections were established, by 1883, with the rich Pocahontas coal region of southwest Virginia and West Virginia, the first coal car arriving here that year. The Eastern Branch terminal was quickly determined to be too small to accommodate the number of coal cars, thus three years later new piers were built at Lambert's Point to handle the steady flow of coal to ships. In 1887 the Norfolk and Western expanded farther to the west from Bristol through Kentucky to Ohio and on to Columbus, tapping the important western grain belt.

The Norfolk and Western was not the only railroad line snaking its way to port terminals along the Elizabeth River. The Elizabeth City and Norfolk Railroad, which had been chartered in 1870, began operating in 1881; it extended from Edenton and was eventually consolidated with the Albemarle and Pantego in 1891 to form the core of the Norfolk and Southern Railway, which largely superseded the canals between Virginia and North Carolina, evident on maps by the end of the nineteenth century. Going back to 1867 a line extended from Norfolk to Danville and in 1882 the Atlantic and Danville was chartered. The line to Danville was finished eight years later, in 1890, and nearly a decade would pass before

the railroad was leased, in 1899, for fifty years to the Southern Railway, which through this deal gained deep-water access at Pinner's Point, across the river from Norfolk. Another company was also looking for deepwater terminal space. In 1886 the Western Branch Belt Line, which ran to Suffolk, the Tunis and Serpell Lumber Company narrow gauge and the Chowan and Southern that ran to Tarboro, North Carolina, merged into the Norfolk and Carolina as part of the Atlantic Coast Line system, also with terminal space at Pinner's Point. The railroads that extended to the Elizabeth River had sculpted access to all geographic points except north, largely due to bodies of water that then limited routes for rail lines. This problem did not last long. By 1883 the New York, Philadelphia and Norfolk Railroad, called the NYP&N, was built, due largely to strong financial input from its Pennsylvania investors. Starting in Pocomoke City, Maryland, the sixty-four miles of Eastern Shore track terminated at Cape Charles, Virginia, where passengers and freight were ferried to Norfolk by steamer and car barge. Fifteen years later, in 1898, management of the NYP&N took the lead in establishing the Norfolk and Portsmouth Belt Line Railroad, which was jointly owned and managed by all the railway companies vested in port facilities along the Elizabeth River, a move to better facilitate the distribution and transfer of freight to terminals hugging the river's waterfront.

Railroads continued to be formed in the early twentieth century. The Virginian Railway, sponsored by H.H. Rogers of New York, was planned, according to historical records, as early as 1905, but not put into operation until four years later. The Virginian connected the West Virginia coalfields near Deepwater on the Kanawha River with a deep-water terminal at Seawell's Point. The Virginian also took freight and passengers, but had been created largely to handle coal. By the mid-twentieth century, the

The Norfolk and Portsmouth Belt Line Railroad Main Line Bridge over the Southern Branch of the Elizabeth River sits at mile 2.6 on the Atlantic Intracoastal Waterway at the cities of Portsmouth and Chesapeake. The bridge, as currently configured, was completed in 1958, with additional modernization in the decades since to ensure safe passage of larger ships. The railroad bridge is nearly side by side with the Jordan Bridge, a vehicular bridge at mile 2.8 on the Intracoastal—a difference between the bridges of only 1,350 feet.

combined coal offloaded by the Virginian at Seawell's Point and the
Norfolk and Western at Lambert's Point, since 1886, and the Chesapeake
and Ohio at Newport News, since 1883, had already made the Port of
Virginia the world's greatest coal port.

With the railroads came great change to the river's edge. One of the
best examples of this came with the transformation of Town Back Creek.
A.A. McCullough was among Norfolk's most prominent businessmen
of the nineteenth century. He was in the lumber business at the foot of
Church Street, but in the 1870 time frame relocated his business to the
northwest corner of Granby Street and Town Back Creek, later City Hall
Avenue, where the Royster Building was subsequently constructed. A
stone bridge connected the north and south ends of Granby Street. While
much of the creek had been filled in beyond Bank Street, the waterway
was still open, though marshy, between Bank and the bridge. The stone
bridge and low-lying marsh precluded sailing craft from entering this part
of the creek, though they could go around the west side of it, which had
not been filled in to Boush Street until 1905. McCullough constructed a
bulkhead around his property on the north side of the creek, as well as
a substantial dock that became known among mariners as McCullough's
Wharf or McCullough's Dock.

The Norfolk and Western Railway coal piers at Lambert's Point are shown here ca. 1920. *Courtesy of the author.*

A considerable portion of the area west of Boush Street, including most of the area to Southgate Terminal, had been marshland that gave off an incredible stench during the summer months and was full of mosquitoes. A.A. McCullough reclaimed roughly sixty-five acres of this marshland, some of it later sold to the NYP&N Railroad, later the Pennsylvania Railroad; the Chesapeake and Ohio Railroad; and the Anheuser-Busch Brewing Company. In the early 1880s the railroad companies built piers and warehouses on their land and Anheuser-Busch built a building on the southwest corner of Boush Street and Brooke Avenue. Norfolk and Western Railroad constructed a connector from Water Street over the creek into this reclaimed area.

McCullough's reclaimed marsh area became particularly important post-1900, when Thomas S. Southgate, a well-known food broker, proposed that Norfolk's wholesale and manufacturing businesses, largely the grocers, which had been located on Water Street and its cross streets, would be able to operate more efficiently and at higher profit margins if they were moved into warehouses serviced by the Chesapeake and Ohio Railroad. Southgate found McCullough's reclaimed marsh area ideally suited to this purpose. The Chesapeake and Ohio Railroad partnered with Southgate, forming the Southgate Terminal Corporation. By 1914 Southgate's company was building its first warehouses on the south side of Tazewell Street between Duke and Dunmore Street; they were completed in 1915. A short time later another group of warehouses went up on the west side of Dunmore Street, terminating at College Place, and a third

By 1926 Norfolk Tidewater Terminals, then situated between the U.S. Army and Navy bases off Hampton Boulevard, handled 507 steamers at its piers; in 1927, this number was no fewer than 632. The cargo tonnage in 1927 was 543,579, of which almost half was for exportation, according to the January 3, 1928 Virginian-Pilot.

Harry C. Mann photographed Norfolk and Western Railway coal cars at Lambert's Point in 1920. *Courtesy of the author.*

section, a two-story warehouse, was built at the foot of Tazewell Street that extended several hundred feet beyond the shoreline, over the river.

While Norfolk was the first coal port, the first tobacco port and the fourth cotton port in America, by the turn of the twentieth century, the city was also recognized as the second-largest fertilizer manufacturing and distribution center, and one of the most significant fuel oil ports in the world. The Standard, Sinclair, Mexican Petroleum, American and Texas Oil Companies did business through the port of Norfolk. Their combined fuel oil facilities at the port were in excess of thirty-four million gallons by 1926, when Norfolk's harbor was being touted as the finest harbor on the Atlantic Coast. "It is free from ice all year 'round" proclaimed advertisements from the Norfolk Advertising Board, though this had not always been true. The port also offered "anchorage to an unlimited number of vessels," according to another marketing piece, which also noted that there was a tidal range of only two and a half feet, and a depth ranging from thirty feet upward.

Eighty years ago the channels to Norfolk and Portsmouth had been improved to a depth of 40 feet, mean low tide, 750 feet wide. The amazing increase in Norfolk's and Portsmouth's foreign commerce during the ten

News that Henry Ford had chosen Norfolk as the site for the largest automobile assembling and distribution plant on the Atlantic Coast was first announced on December 7, 1921, on the front page of the Norfolk newspapers. The Ford Motor Company, Norfolk Assembly Plant, was constructed on a fifty-one-acre tract in Newton Park beginning in 1924. This is a ca. 1925 photograph of the plant; the Eastern Branch of the Elizabeth River is on the left. *Courtesy of the author*.

years from 1914 to 1924 was an indication of the possibilities of the Elizabeth's harbor as an Atlantic gateway. Exports in 1914 amounted to $9.5 million. In 1924 this figure had grown to $150 million, an increase of 1,474 percent. Imports in the same period grew from $3.1 million to $9.4 million, an increase of 201 percent. By the mid-1920s Norfolk enjoyed ocean rates to foreign destinations that had only previously been available to ports to the north, and lower, generally, than rates applied from South Atlantic and Gulf ports. Norfolk's inland rates by rail to and from the great manufacturing and production centers lying north of the Ohio River, east of the Mississippi and west of a line from Sandusky through Columbus, Ohio, were the same as those for the port of Baltimore and lower than rates to and from Boston, New York, Philadelphia or the South Atlantic and Gulf ports.

When the Norfolk Advertising Board published data for the Norfolk port in 1926, there were eight trunk line railroads that entered the Elizabeth's harbor from the north, west and south, and a belt-line railway, one of the finest in the world, that linked all of these railroads with the water transportation system through steamship wharves and the Municipal Union Terminal, where steamships from all over the world could receive and discharge their cargoes directly from and to freight cars of all these railroads. The railroads at that time included the Atlantic Coast Line, Chesapeake and Ohio, Norfolk Southern, Norfolk and Western, Pennsylvania, Seaboard Air Line, Southern, Virginian and the Norfolk and Portsmouth Belt Line.

More than a dozen coastal steamship lines provided rapid and convenient freight and passenger transportation between Norfolk and points north, east and south by the mid-twenties. Thirty or more foreign steamship lines connected the port with ports of Europe, the Far East and South America. Service between Norfolk and Pacific Coast points by way of the Panama Canal was being rapidly extended. Lines of operation some eighty years ago included Baltimore Steam Packet Company—the Old Bay Line—from Baltimore; Baltimore and Virginia Steamboat Company—the Weems Line—from Baltimore; Bennett's North Carolina Lines; Buxton Line, which went to Richmond, Petersburg and James River landings; Chesapeake Steamship Lines— the Old Dominion Line—from New York; Elizabeth City Boat Line from North Carolina points; Hampton Roads Transportation Company from Willoughby and Old Point Comfort; and Merchants' and Miners' Transportation Company from Boston and Providence. There were also services via the Norfolk, Baltimore and Carolina Line, Baltimore to points in North Carolina via Norfolk; Norfolk and Mobjack Bay Steamboat Company from Mathews and Gloucester County; Norfolk-Carolina Line, from North Carolina; Norfolk and Washington Steamboat Company that ran from the nation's capital; Philadelphia and Norfolk Steamship Company, from Philadelphia; and Smithfield,

Located at a site between the United States Army and Navy bases off Hampton Boulevard, the Norfolk Tidewater Terminals were among the most modern in the United States when this aerial photograph was taken in 1925. The first pier built at this site was 1,250 feet long and 494 feet wide, and was equipped with tractors, trailers, electric and gravity conveyors, lifting devices, cranes, winches and portable scales. On each side of the pier were built concrete warehouses 100 feet wide and 1,175 feet long. Along with other then-equally modern export and import piers and terminals at Norfolk, the Norfolk Tidewater Terminals and these key port facilities provided a total of 10 million square feet of covered warehouse space in addition to berthing for more than fifty oceangoing ships and trackage space for more than five thousand freight cars. These terminals were the beginning of what is today the Norfolk International Terminals. *Courtesy of the author.*

Newport News and Norfolk Steamship Company from Newport News, Battery Park and Smithfield.

The municipal piers and covered warehouse space at the United States Army Supply Base were operated by the Norfolk Tidewater Terminals for the City of Norfolk. These terminals were so connected by the Norfolk and Portsmouth Belt Line that they were really union terminals. Arrangements had been made whereby all freight, when properly routed, came into Norfolk for export, or in moving out from these terminals, could be handled on one bill of lading, the switching charge via the Belt Line absorbed in the Norfolk rate. The Belt Line was the connecting link between the Norfolk Municipal Terminals and the previously mentioned eight trunk line railroads entering Norfolk and Portsmouth. In those days, two modern piers of reinforced concrete and steel were operated in conjunction with the terminals. Each pier was 1,328 feet long and 300 feet wide, with berthing space alongside with a depth of 35 feet. Tractor conveyors, tiered and lifting devices, locomotive and mobile cranes, cargo masts and electric and steam winches composed the handling equipment

Brand-new 1926 Fords, assembled at Norfolk, were being loaded aboard the oceangoing merchant ship *Commercial Pathfinder* at Norfolk Tidewater Terminals when this picture was taken. *Courtesy of the author.*

This five-masted schooner, berthed at Norfolk Tidewater Terminals, was being loaded with brick for delivery to a U.S. Army base in Florida when this picture was taken ca. 1925. Schooners were often interspersed among large oceangoing vessels at this time. When the Norfolk Port Commission was organized, with E.E. Palen as its chairman, Arthur Godwin King became its first port director on March 23, 1920. Later, in 1925, when the city-owned shipping berths were leased to Norfolk Tidewater Terminals, King also became manager of these facilities. *Courtesy of the author.*

designed to expedite the movement of export and import traffic, and to minimize costs. Norfolk was rapidly developing as a grain port in 1926 due largely to its facilities and direct rail services to important Western grain districts. The Norfolk Municipal Grain Elevator had storage capacity of 800,000 bushels. There were two receiving legs and three shipping legs, each with a 30,000-bushel-per-hour capacity, the largest ever placed in an elevator at that time. There were eight unloading pits, each equipped with power shovels and pneumatic grain door removers. The elevator was served by a concrete wharf, 1,400 feet long, that could accommodate three vessels. To handle general cargoes that supplemented grain movement, the City of Norfolk built a concrete pier adjoining its municipal grain elevator. This solid-fill, concrete pier was 1,210 feet long and 500 feet wide. On each side were one-story warehouses.

Down the Elizabeth at Lambert's Point the Norfolk and Western Railway operated three large coal piers and adjacent terminals for general merchandise. The Virginian Railway also had large coal terminals at Seawell's Point, a short distance from the city's municipal grain facilities. Extensive terminal facilities were also maintained by the Atlantic Coast Line, the Chesapeake and Ohio, the Norfolk Southern, the Pennsylvania, the Seaboard Air Line and the Southern. The Pennsylvania Railroad was three years away from constructing an extensive terminal at Little Creek in 1926, a facility that would measurably shorten the ferrying time from Cape Charles, Virginia, into the city of Norfolk. A large waterfront site

and right-of-way into Norfolk had already been purchased. Among the private firms operating terminals along the Elizabeth's shoreline were the Southgate Terminal Corporation, the Security Storage and Safe Deposit Company, Jones and Company and the Norfolk Warehouse Corporation. The Norfolk harbor's anchorage facilities were a magnet to the combined naval and commercial fleets of all nations, most of which could find safe haven in its protected waters at one time. The Elizabeth's piers and terminals were accessible, as they are today, to this anchorage by deep and wide channels, today far wider and deeper than those of eighty years ago.

Interestingly, there were other developments in rail service to the port that are also worth note. The Southern Railway's fifty-year lease, initiated in 1899, of the Atlantic and Danville track ended in 1949. By this time the Atlantic and Danville was being actively managed again. Both lines thereafter maintained their freight connection to Norfolk over the Atlantic Coast Line tracks to Pinner's Point and then by barge and sometimes lighter. The NYP&N lost its identity to the Pennsylvania Railroad system, but this was largely a change in name, not service. A new freight terminal was built at Little Creek, where freight cars were ferried from Cape Charles. The Chesapeake and Ohio maintained a car ferry terminal from Newport News to downtown Norfolk, with offices at Boush Street and Brooke Avenue. Norfolk was thus served by nine trunk lines, three by land: the Norfolk and Western, Norfolk and Southern and Virginian; six by ferry: Pennsylvania, Chesapeake and Ohio, Seaboard Airline, Atlantic Coast Line, Southern and Atlantic and Danville; and the Norfolk and

The Virginia Portland Cement Corporation loaded its first shipment of cement from Norfolk to Uruguay aboard the *Angeles* on April 19, 1926. H.E. Hilts, the company's Norfolk general manager, noted in correspondence accompanying this photograph that it showed the end of the marl storage shed, which at that time had storage for approximately 18,000 cubic yards of marl and 2,200 tons of clay. The shipment was bound for Montevideo, Uruguay. *Courtesy of the author.*

A photographer for the Virginia Department of Agriculture took this photograph of iron rails, the "modern" trail through the Dismal Swamp, ca. 1930. It was observed all those years ago that these rails were somewhat disillusioning to youthful imagination of gloom, dread and dark mystery that had always been closely associated with the Great Dismal. But pathless jungles were then still in the swamp, and vast morasses of trees and underbrush remained. Even today, at the swamp's center, Lake Drummond, this place remains as beautiful as when Sir Thomas Moore, the Irish poet, found inspiration to sing of the "lover and maid so true," crossing by "firefly lamp" in "white canoe." *Courtesy of the author.*

Portsmouth Belt Line that encircled two cities and connected the others with waterfront facilities. There were also six primary steamship lines that formerly served Norfolk, two to Baltimore, the Washington Line, the Old Dominion Line to New York, the Merchants' and Miners' to Boston, the Clyde Line to Philadelphia and the Baltimore Steam Packet Company—the Old Bay Line—that alternated between Baltimore and Washington. The Old Dominion Line was the post–Civil War successor of the earlier New York and Virginia Steamship Company, which had been founded in 1850, and derived its name from Virginia's nickname—the Old

Dominion—a reference to the colony's loyalty to the Stuarts during the English Commonwealth period. After 1923, the Old Dominion Line was a subsidiary of the Eastern Steamship Company. It is important to note, also, that starting in 1866 with the first steamship service to Liverpool, Colonel William Lamb, agent, Norfolk was connected by direct ocean freight service, including limited passenger service, to the rest of the world.

The Norfolk Port and Industrial Authority was established by the City of Norfolk in 1948, largely to highlight the port's strengths and expand business. While Hampton Roads's port facilities had consistently led all North Atlantic ports in export tonnage, observed Marvin Schlegel in 1962, most of this tonnage was in coal and other bulk-loaded cargo, which brought scant revenue to the port. The port saw little exported or imported general cargo, which is more profitable for port operators. The authority's primary job was to sell shippers on the advantages of Norfolk and, importantly, Schlegel noted, to sell Norfolk on the advantages of shipping. The popular slogan at that time was apropos: "Bring the world to Norfolk, and bring Norfolk to the world." The port's newest advocate advertised Norfolk at home and abroad, publishing a monthly magazine, *World Trade*, and made calls on individual shippers to encourage them to use the port to ship their general cargo. The port authority was successful, so much so that it also acquired operation of the municipal airport two years later, in 1950, and took on the responsibility of increasing air service to the city. Today, a separate authority operates what later became Norfolk International Airport.

In 1952 the Virginia State Port Authority was established as a political subdivision of the commonwealth of Virginia for the purpose of stimulating commerce of the ports of the state, promoting the shipment of goods and cargoes through the ports, improving the navigable tidal waters within Hampton Roads and in general performing any act or function that may be useful in developing, improving or increasing the commerce of the ports of the commonwealth. At that time an engineering survey indicated to officials of the state and city port authorities that there were fourteen general cargo terminals in three Hampton Roads cities, but the lion's share of business was being handled by only four of them, and only one met modern standards. The port's general cargo facilities, which had been touted as among the most modern only a quarter-century before, had not kept up with competitors. All of these pier facilities belonged to the railroads, which operated them at a loss; the railroads, as a result, could not afford to construct new buildings to serve highway trucks, viewed as an improvement that negatively influenced the railroads' bottom line. The state agency promulgated a plan to improve the piers and lease them back to the railroads to operate them day to day. The legislation to carry through this plan was passed in the 1960 Virginia General Assembly. The

By the early twentieth century the three great coal carrying railroads—the Norfolk and Western, the Chesapeake and Ohio and the Virginian—made Hampton Roads the greatest coal port in the world. There was a constant stream of trains from West Virginia to Lambert's Point, Seawell's Point and Newport News, where ocean liners, bay steamers, tramps and coasting vessels waited for cargo or bunker coal. As early as 1911 the coal requirement for New England alone took nearly four million tons from Hampton Roads. By 1926 the port delivered no fewer than twenty-seven million tons.

Norfolk and Western
Railway's Lambert's
Point coal piers and
rail yard is shown as
it appeared in 1933.
Courtesy of the author.

*The Gilmerton Bridge
is a double-leaf
bascule structure
constructed in 1938
for highway service.
It was billed as a
toll-free highway. The
Gilmerton bridges the
Southern Branch of
the Elizabeth River
at mile 5.8 on the
Atlantic Intracoastal
Waterway.*

state port authority later dropped the word "state" from its title, becoming the Virginia Port Authority.

City officials on both sides of the Elizabeth River would find it easier to determine who owned pier facilities than the river itself when a dispute erupted between Norfolk City Attorney Philip R. Trapani and Chesapeake Commissioner of the Revenue Robert H. Waldo over ownership of the tip of Pier 6 at Lambert's Point, which revived a question that had occupied local geographers, surveyors and lawyers on occasion since the first settlers made their homes along the Elizabeth's banks. This time, in the mid-1970s, the controversy grew heated. Waldo contended the pier, a modern coal dock jutting 1,600 feet into the Elizabeth River, had 900 outer feet that was in Chesapeake and should be paying taxes to that community. The tip of the pier, he claimed, contained about $10 million worth of cranes and loading equipment, which could provide

The Norfolk and Western Number 611 was coming into Norfolk when this picture was taken by Carroll H. Walker in 1983. *Courtesy of the author.*

Chesapeake about $50,000 a year in corporate taxes. Trapani told Waldo he would have to prove his claim in court. Waldo's claim was based on the laws of inheritance. In theory the city of Chesapeake, formed from the consolidation of Norfolk County and the city of South Norfolk, inherited all that was in Norfolk County at the time of consolidation: January 1, 1963. Norfolk County, according to theory, owned everything on the south side of Hampton Roads that had not been legally assigned to what are today the cities of Norfolk, Portsmouth, Virginia Beach and Suffolk—all of which are offspring of Norfolk County. Waterfront lines, drawn largely by annexation courts, varied greatly. Some were predicated on the low water lines, some on the center lines of rivers, creeks and channels and some on what are called port warden lines. In years past Virginia had port wardens whose duties were similar to those of modern harbormasters. England still has port wardens who inspect cargo and stowage and have charge of channels and traffic and port facilities. But it has never been certain what role Virginia port wardens played. One function is apparent: they drew lines. These lines seemed to follow the waterfront pier lines, but little else is known. The port warden lines were still there when Waldo questioned ownership of Pier 6 at Lambert's Point.

According to Waldo's argument, one of the port warden lines skirted the ends of the shorter piers at Lambert's Point, chopped off the tips of a couple of longer ones and finally slashed through the middle of the longest one—Pier 6. According to evidence presented to a three-judge tribunal sitting for the last Portsmouth-Chesapeake annexation case, decided at the end of 1966, by Merrick I. Campbell, a Norfolk lawyer who specialized in real estate law, Norfolk ownership of its waterfront varies according to definition. Along Ocean View and Willoughby Spit, it extends to the

The Dominion Boulevard Steel Bridge, called by locals "the Steel Bridge," is a double-leaf bascule, two-lane drawbridge that spans the Southern Branch of the Elizabeth River in Chesapeake. It carries U.S. Route 17, finished in 1925, which is also called Dominion Boulevard, formerly identified as VA Route 104, as it crosses the bridge. The Steel Bridge was built in 1962 and is operated by the City of Chesapeake. It is located at mile 8.8 on the Intracoastal Waterway.

The High Rise Bridge is a bascule drawbridge that carries a portion of the Hampton Roads Beltway designated as Interstate 64 across the Southern Branch of the Elizabeth in Chesapeake. The twin span's concrete and steel structure was completed in 1972, and is owned by the Virginia Department of Transportation.

low water line. Across Willoughby Bay, past Norfolk Naval Station, past Lambert's Point and on to Smith's Creek (now The Hague), it extends to the port warden line. From The Hague to about the Campostella Bridge it pulls back to the low water line, and then it re-expands to the port warden line from the bridge to the mouth of Indian River. And after that, it follows the center of the Eastern Branch of the Elizabeth River on to the city limits at Newtown Road. One oddity of all this, Campbell would point out, is that Berkley was left surrounded by Chesapeake and connects to Norfolk only by bridges across Chesapeake waters. Campbell explained to the court that he had originally presented his boundary theory at the behest of the City of Portsmouth, which would have liked to have obtained a ruling on whether it adjoined Norfolk in the middle of the Elizabeth River or whether the Chesapeake flowed between them. The judges did not rule on Campbell's request for the line of demarcation. One of the reasons they did not rule was that the boundary line dispute rested on the question of inheritance and Norfolk County's origins are obscure in that respect.

Despite such boundary disputes, there were positive steps forward for the port. Former Norfolk Mayor Roy B. Martin Jr. observed later that the creation of the Virginia Port Authority was one of the best outcomes of his period in office, which was lengthy, beginning in 1959 and ending

This photograph of Norfolk's World Trade Center was taken ca. 1995. Groundbreaking ceremonies for the center occurred in the spring of 1982. The events surrounding the building's beginnings refocused international attention on Norfolk as a major player in the ports and maritime industry. Norfolk was granted its world trade center charter of operation in 1979. The 367,000-square-foot facility, designed by Skidmore, Owings and Merrill's Chicago office (Phase I) and Smallwood Reynolds of Atlanta (Phase II), was built for nearly $40 million and is nine stories high. The trade center was constructed in two phases, the first finished in 1983 and the second in 1986. The site on which it was built originally had Fayette Street on the east, but the center's expansion eliminated this street. *Courtesy of the author.*

in 1974. While the Norfolk Port and Industrial Authority had been proactive in the development of the old United States Army Intermediate Depot off Hampton Boulevard, converting it to the Norfolk Tidewater Terminals, it had no control over similar activities in Portsmouth and Newport News. Shipping terminals in Norfolk, Portsmouth and Newport News competed against one another for business. During a speech to the Virginia Conference on World Trade on October 19, 1967, Martin stated that he thought there should be one body in control of port terminals in Hampton Roads. At that time the Virginia Port Authority had no power over the Norfolk Port and Industrial Authority, the Portsmouth Port and Industrial Commission and the Peninsula Ports Authority of Virginia, the agencies charged with responsibility for port development within their own communities without regard to what the other cities were doing to increase their share of the export and import market. Martin's public call for unification of the ports in Hampton Roads was the first by any city official in the region. A proposal from the cities asking for state unification soon followed. The Commonwealth of Virginia would eventually purchase the cities' terminals under the auspices of the Virginia Port Authority.

According to the Virginia Maritime Association, the Port of Virginia, the heart of which resides along the banks of the Elizabeth River, has grown from its early founding at Jamestown, cited as "America's first port," through the era of the great clipper ships to the present-day sophistication of computerized intermodal technology, to put Virginia at the forefront of every major change in the shipping industry. Today, more than 95 percent of the world's largest shipping lines link Virginia's sheltered, now ice-free harbor on the Elizabeth River to destinations around the world. Within Hampton Roads there are twenty-five square miles of readily accessible waterways and a prime location, just eighteen miles from open sea, proffering ships with the heaviest cargoes the convenience of steaming in and out of fifty-foot-deep, obstruction-free channels. Just as it did more than a half-century ago, the Port of Virginia continues to set records and benchmarks. The port ranks as one of the leading ports in the United States in total foreign waterborne commerce. In general cargo, containerized and break bulk cargo, it is the second largest port on the United States East Coast, just behind New York/New Jersey. Between 1982 and 2001, general cargo tonnage at Virginia's state-owned port facilities increased from $2\frac{1}{2}$ million tons in 1982 to $11\frac{1}{2}$ million tons in 2001, an unmatched growth record among United States ports. In terms of total cargo, which includes container, break bulk and bulk cargo, the port handled over 37 million short tons. The port's phenomenal growth is due, in large measure, to the unification of the ports of Hampton Roads, including key facilities at Norfolk International Terminals and Portsmouth Marine Terminal on the Elizabeth River. In 1981 the Virginia General

The Norfolk Port Authority was established by the city in 1948. The objective of this organization was to "bring the world to Norfolk, and bring Norfolk to the world."

Assembly passed landmark legislation designed to bring the ports under a single agency, the Virginia Port Authority, with a new, single operating company, Virginia International Terminals. Also managed by Virginia International Terminals are the Newport News Marine Terminals and the Virginia Inland Port, located at Front Royal, Virginia.

CHAPTER NINE
CENTURIES OF ABUNDANT BIODIVERSITY

The first explorers and settlers in this virgin land were more than interested in its natural resources, and their early reports are full of descriptions of the flora and fauna of the region encompassed by the Elizabeth River and its branches, Tanner's Creek and the Great Dismal Swamp. As early as 1529 it was noted that Indians of the Atlantic Coast lived on maize, fish and game, which they had in great abundance, and dressed in wolf and fox skins, per the Diego Ribeiro map. Arthur Barlowe, who wrote about the first Roanoke expedition in 1584, mentioned seeing white cranes, bucks, conies or hares and various varieties of fish, as well as fruits, melons, walnuts, cucumbers, gourds and peas. "Our pease," he wrote, referring to what had been brought over from England, "grew fourteen inches in ten days." Barlowe, however, had not reached as far north as the Chesapeake Bay, and Ralph Lane, who followed him in 1585–86, visited Lower Tidewater but did not report on it in any detail. Lane mentioned "multitudes of beare, being an excellent victual and great woodes of sassafras and walnut-trees" but nothing else. When Captain John Smith explored the Elizabeth River in 1608, he wrote later that he saw the greatest pine and fir trees he had encountered in Virginia; since the fir does not occur naturally this far south, he must have been referring to the cedar. John Smith's *Generall Historie of Virginia*, published in 1624, provided a lengthy description of abundant natural resources in the colony:

> *Virginia doth afford many excellent vegetables, and liuing* [sic]
> *Creatures, yet grasse there is little or none, but what groweth in*
> *low Marishes: for all the Countrey is overgrowne with trees,*
> *whose droppings continually turneth their grasse to weeds, by*
> *reason of the rancknes of the ground, which would soone be*
> *amended by good husbandry. The wood that is most common is*

Paul D. Camp, whose Camp Manufacturing Company owned vast acreage of the Dismal Swamp, had his own sawmill in 1876, producing 6,000 feet of lumber daily. His brother, James L. Camp, engaged independently in the same field. The brothers later joined together and extended their operations to North Carolina. A third brother, Robert J. Camp, joined to found what became the Franklin, Virginia, Brothers' Camp Manufacturing Company in 1887. Activities gradually extended to include pulp and paper operations, and in 1936 the Chesapeake-Camp Corporation was formed to handle additional lumbering operations. The company eventually built up its output to 100,000 feet of lumber. The Camp Company merged in May 1956 with Union Bag and Paper Company to form Union Camp Corporation. In 1999 the Union Camp Corporation was acquired by International Paper.

Oke and Walnut, many of their Okes are so tall & straight, that they will beare two foote and a halfe square of good timber for 20 yards long; Of this wood there is two or three severall kinds. The Acornes of one kinde, whose barke is more white then the other, & somewhat sweetish, which being boyled, at last affords a sweet oyle, that they keepe in gourds to annoint their heads and ioynts [sic]. The fruit they eate made in bread or otherwise. There is also some Elme, some blacke Walnut tree, and some Ash: of Ash and Elme they make sope Ashes. If the trees be very great, the Ashes will be good, and melt to hard lumps, but if they be small, it will be but powder, and not so good as the other. Of walnuts there is 2 or 3 kindes; there is a kinde of wood we called Cypres, because both the wood, the fruit, and leafe did most resemble it, and of those trees there are some neare three fadome about at the foot, very straight, and 50, 60, or 80 foot without a branch. By the dwelling of the Salvages [sic] are some great Mulbery trees, and in some parts of the Countrey, they are found growing naturally in prettie groues. There was an assay made to make silke, and surely the wormes prospered excellent well, till the master workeman fell sicke. During which time they were eaten with Rats.

Smith wrote, too, of the many animals that had been observed:

Of beasts the chiefe are Deere, nothing differing from ours. In the deserts towards the heads of the rivers, there are many, but amongst the rivers few. There is a beast they call Aroughcun, much like a badger, but vseth to liue on trees as Squirrels doe. Their Squirrels some are neare as great as our smallest sort of wilde Rabbets, some blackish or blacke and white, but the most are gray…Their Beares are very little in comparison of those of Muscovia and Tartaria. The Beaver is as big as an ordinary water dog, but his legs exceeding short. His forefeete like a dogs, his hinder feet like a Swans. His taile somewhat like the forme of a Racket, bare without haire, which to eat the Salvages esteeme a great delicate. They haue many Otters, which as the Beavers they take with snares, and esteeme the skins great ornaments, and of all those beasts they vse to feed when they catch them. An Vtchunquoyes is like a wilde Cat. Their Foxes are like our silver haired Conies, of a small proportion, and not smelling like those in England. Their Dogges of that Country are like their Wooalues, and cannot barke but howle, and the Wooalues not much bigger then our English Foxes. Martins, Powlecats, Weesels, and

Minkes we know they haue, because we haue seene many of their skinnes, though very seldome any of them aliue. But one thing is strange, that we could never perceive their Vermine destroy our Hennes, Egges, nor Chickens, nor doe any hurt nor their flyes nor serpents any way pernicious, where in the South parts of America they are alwayes dangerous, and often deadly.

And he described innumerable birds, many species of which still occupy habitats in the Elizabeth River watershed and the Great Dismal Swamp:

Of Birds the Eagle is the greatest devourer. Hawkes there be of divers sorts, as our Falconers called them: Sparrow-hawkes, Lanarets, Goshawkes, Falcons and Osperayes, but they all prey most vpon fish. Their Partridges are little bigger then our Quailes. Wilde Turkies are as bigge as our tame. There are Woosels or Blackbirds with red shoulders, Thrushes and divers sorts of small Birds, some red, some blew, scarce so bigge as a Wrenne, but few in Sommer. In Winter there are great plentie

Bald cypress trees and knees, characteristic of the Great Dismal Swamp, are shown in this photograph, taken about 1900 and part of a Norfolk folio produced by the Department of the Interior, United States Geological Survey two years later. *Courtesy of the author.*

of Swans, Cranes, gray and white with blacke wings, Herons, Geese, Brants, Ducke, Wigeon, Dotterell Oxeies, Parrats, and Pigeons. Of all those sorts great abundance, and some other strange kinds, to vs vnknowne by name. But in Sommer not any, or a very few to be seene.

In addition to Smith's observations, Robert Beverley had written in 1703 a comprehensive list of the birds and animals most familiar to Virginia colonists of the seventeenth century, including deer, rabbits, foxes, raccoons (which Williams Strachey had called "apes" in his account of 1616), squirrels, opossums, beavers, otters, muskrats and minks; swans, geese and many species of duck; cranes, curlews, herons, sandpipers, pheasants, partridges, pigeons, turkeys and larks. He mentions, too, the "mock-bird," which he remarked so loved society that it would always make its home near the habitation of man, and "sing the sweetest wild Airs in the world." There are a few birds that can readily be added to this list: cardinal, blue jay, robin, song sparrow, catbird, thrasher, woodpecker, sparrow, starling, ruby-throated hummingbird, crow, eastern turkey vulture, gull, white heron, great blue heron, osprey, marsh hawk and bald eagle. There is, too, the purple or bee martin. Beverley also wrote of edible fruits known today as huckleberries, cranberries, cherries, plums, persimmons, raspberries, strawberries, varieties of grapes, watermelons and cantaloupe.

Early records of the towns of Norfolk and Portsmouth make it clear that the people living there had an entirely different economy from that of the river plantations. The basic difference was the sandy soil of the coastal counties that yielded a much poorer grade of tobacco, which was the "brown gold" of the inland communities. While it is true that Norfolk and Princess Anne planters cultivated fields of tobacco along with their maize or Indian corn, beans, potatoes, strawberries, pumpkins and other staple food crops, they also recognized from the beginning that the trees of this area were an invaluable source of income and economic self-sufficiency. This independence was found close at hand in the untouched forests of pines, oaks, junipers, cedars and cypresses that choke swampland along the river's edge and throughout its watershed, importantly including the expansive acreage of the Dismal Swamp. With a population that was increasing daily, there was a sharp demand for timber to build houses and the ships that carried precious commodities. As early as 1620 a shipbuilder applied for land on the Elizabeth River because of the abundant supply of timber for building and water for launching ships. Beverley, too, had mentioned the importance of naval stores. The people of Norfolk, from the colonial period on, found economic salvation in the trade of pine tar, pitch and turpentine, oak barrel staves, planks and sills, juniper, cedar and

cypress shingles. A prosperous merchant class grew from Norfolk's early population boom; this merchant class became the underpinning of the town, those who took the ship stores and building materials from suppliers, who got European goods in return, which the people plying their trade on the Elizabeth wanted.

One of the best sources of information on trees in the Elizabeth River watershed is found in the land grants and deeds of sale in the seventeenth century and later. In the process of the metes and bounds of a piece of land, surveyors customarily cited marked trees at corners rather than driving a stake or setting a stone. Some of the trees mentioned in these early survey documents include pine, white oak, cedar, gum, holly, dogwood, mulberry and chinquapin. Beverley's list of trees was far more extensive: oak, poplar, pine, cedar, cypress, sweet gum, holly, sweet myrtle, live oak, mulberry, chestnut, hickory and black walnut. The sweet myrtle, observed Beverley, yields a grayish berry, which when cooked, makes sweet-smelling green wax that is much favored for candles; this tree and berry are also called the bayberry. Another source of information on trees are wills and family papers. A Norfolk County gentleman of the eighteenth century bequeathed to one of his heirs a chair made of "black wornot."

One of the most important natural resources within the bounds of the Elizabeth River watershed is the abundance of fish and other seafood in

A group of excursionists spent the day picnicking and taking walks in the Dismal Swamp, ca. 1900. Despite the heat, insects and snakes, these visitors appear to have enjoyed their day. *Courtesy of the Museum of the Albemarle.*

The Dismal Swamp's Jericho Ditch was overgrown by woods and canebrake, the vegetation in the foreground, ca. 1900. *Courtesy of the author*.

its waters. The *Ostrea virginica*—the oyster—was enjoyed by Indians long before it became known to English settlers who came to live on the banks of the Elizabeth. These earliest residents knew of mussels, sturgeon and other fish. Smith furnished, in fact, a long list of fish in these waters: sturgeon, porpoise, stingray, mullet, white salmon, eel, catfish, perch, crab, toadfish, herring, shad, rock, trout, flounder, bass and sheep's head. Smith knew of stingrays; he was seriously wounded by one during his explorations. Later, in the seventeenth century, there are accounts of drum, croaker and bluefish. The early eighteenth century is the first time that spot are mentioned, called "old wife." The alewife was not the "old wife" fish; alewives are a small shad, often called mooneyes. Smith observed that the toadfish "will swell till it be like to brust [*sic*] when it cometh into aire." Interestingly, the Atlantic right whale was killed in large number off the coast in the colonial era. By 1698 Virginia's crown governor, Edmund Andros, was petitioned to prohibit the killing and stripping of whales in the bay because of the pollution of the waters. Beverley mentioned substantive exports of sperm oil, blubber and whale bone from Virginia to England. He noted, too, the shad coming up the rivers to spawn. In 1796 a visitor to Norfolk remarked on the abundance of blue crabs. Freshwater

fish, fewer in number than saltwater species, belong to four families: bass, perch, pike and sunfish. Large- and small-mouth bass; yellow, speckled and bluenose perch; pickerel and muskellunge pike; and bream and robin, of the sunfish family, are readily found within the river's watershed.

While terribly difficult to imagine today, it is also true that the Elizabeth River froze over completely; in fact, there are several notable occurrences that are worth mention. The first occurred over the winter of 1779–80, at which time the river froze solid for many weeks. William S. Forrest wrote that this particular winter was one of extraordinary severity. "The harbor was frozen entirely across to Portsmouth, admitting a free and an uninterrupted communication between the two towns, on the ice, for several weeks," he observed. The Atlantic Ocean was frozen far out from shore to a depth of forty fathoms. The Chesapeake Bay, Forrest would report, was so thickly frozen that teams of horses crossed for some time from shore to shore as far down as the Virginia Capes. The ice was piled up along Virginia's shore, at some places twenty feet high, with large quantities still observable in the middle of May 1780. The Norfolk harbor could not be entered, a remarkable circumstance for the river's latitude. Two small schooners, returning to Norfolk from the West Indies in the

Bald cypress trees growing in Lake Drummond, at the heart of the Dismal Swamp, are shown in this picture, taken about 1900. *Courtesy of the author.*

The title of this 1910-era postcard is "Lady of the Lake," otherwise known as Cap'n Jack's wife, who played hostess to many travelers who ventured into the Dismal Swamp. Cap'n Jack was keeper of the locks at Lake Drummond. *Courtesy of the author.*

latter part of that February, were forced to land their cargoes several miles south of Cape Henry—a temporary harbor having been made by the melting and removal of ice in some places between the shore and the icebergs—which were then conveyed to Norfolk by carts, in which return cargoes were also sent down. The river was frozen over in 1815 and again in 1836; however, the greatest freeze occurred in 1857. Up to the seventeenth of January the winter had been an average one, but about that date extreme cold set in and by the nineteenth the snow was six feet deep, reaching to the awnings of stores in Norfolk, Portsmouth and all of the communities that dotted the Elizabeth River and its tributaries. Snowdrifts went as high as twenty feet. In the back streets and lanes, particularly in those near the Portsmouth Naval Hospital and adjacent cemetery, the cows walked over the lines of the fences on the frozen snow. On the twenty-third it was noted that several people had been stranded on Craney Island; they walked, with a woman amongst them, for some distance until the lady was put on a sled and pulled from Craney Island to a hostelry in Portsmouth. Extreme cold and blocked roads and waterways soon led to the exhaustion of the meal supply in Portsmouth. W.G. Maupin went over in a sled and brought a thousand bushels of supplies. This was the beginning of a sled ferry. In the extreme cold of that winter, the river was a gorgeous sight as the sun went down and the moon came out over Craney Island. The *Southern Argus* reported on the twenty-sixth of January that the harbor had been converted to a brilliant promenade; belles, beaux, husbands, wives and children thronged the thoroughfare between the two cities. A booth was actually built midway across the river, catering to thirsty patrons making the trek over the frozen Elizabeth River. Many even walked to Hampton Roads and the Norfolk harbor was actually measured by a tapeline. An amusing incident occurred when a young lady and gentleman tried to cross the ice and came to what appeared to be a weak spot. They hesitated. Starting again, they stepped back; ultimately the lady walked ahead and when she was safely over the young man followed. On the first of February the steamer *Georgia* got as far as Old Point Comfort and three days later boats once again plied the waters of the Elizabeth River, bringing in supplies from the outside world. In front of the Waverly Apartments on Portsmouth's Court Street, the tide left a large unfrozen place and it was there that vast numbers of wild ducks and other birds congregated and were killed by the hundreds. Interestingly, this bout of extreme cold was followed less than two weeks later by very warm weather; the temperatures rose to seventy-nine degrees. The next "great freeze" did not occur until the winter of 1917–18, when the harbor again froze solid between Norfolk and Portsmouth.

The southern end of the Elizabeth River watershed is defined by 3,108-acre Lake Drummond at the heart of the Great Dismal Swamp. The swamp was formed as the result of the gradual emersion of land originally composing the flat ocean bottom. Millions of years ago a sandy ridge called the Suffolk Escarpment, a sharply delineated Pleistocene shore line, bound the swamp on the west, marking the original coastline when centuries ago the surface of the continent was twenty-eight feet below its present level. A north-south linear high, and Fentress Rise, composed of interglacial marine and barrier sediments, marks the swamp's eastern boundary. On the north the swamp is bound by the urbanized Churchland Flat; on the south by the Pasquotank River. A swamp formed when normal drainage

On September 18, 2003, Hurricane Isabel came through Hampton Roads. Defense Fuel Support Point Craney Island absorbed a major hit from the storm. During the storm's tidal surge, the waters of the Elizabeth River completely flooded the southeast portion of the terminal. The waters rose to a level of over five feet and did extensive damage to the facilities. A half-mile of the main access road onto Craney Island was washed away, limiting access to the terminal. The most intense damage was done to Pier D, the main fuel pier. All facilities and services have since been restored.

This photograph of a flooded downtown Norfolk was taken on April 3, 1915, during a northeast gale. The view is looking west toward Granby Street from City Hall Avenue. The Royster Building in the center of the picture was completed in 1912. The Monticello Hotel is on the right. This area was a creek bed when Norfolk was platted in 1680. Until construction of Norfolk's floodwall at the end of City Hall Avenue, this low-lying area flooded frequently. *Courtesy of the author.*

was impeded by the flatness of the elevated land and, oddly enough, the Dismal Swamp today exists at a greater elevation than the dry land that surrounds it on three sides, and five bodies of water: the Southern Branch of the Elizabeth River, the Southern Branch of the Nansemond River, North Run, Northwest River and Pergamon River. There have been a number of explanations as to exactly how the Dismal Swamp was formed. Some scientists have suggested the swamp might have been created by a meteorite that struck the earth, creating a crater-like indenture around which displaced earth was embanked. This is a plausible explanation because the earth around Lake Drummond, at the swamp's heart, is among the highest land masses in Lower Tidewater, being some twenty feet above sea level. George Washington was one of the first to observe that areas of the Dismal Swamp are actually a hillside, sloping gradually toward the sea. Along the Suffolk Escarpment, on the western side of the Great Dismal Swamp, elevations rise and relief is variable. Traveling eastward across the refuge from the Suffolk Escarpment, elevation drops at a rate of one foot per mile to the Deep Creek Swale (east of the Dismal Swamp Canal). In the Virginia portion of today's refuge, elevations range from fifteen to twenty-five feet; in Pasquotank County, North Carolina, elevations range from ten to twenty feet; Camden County, twenty-one feet or lower. The topography exhibits a gentle west to east slope imposed on an even gentler north to south slope. The normal surface elevation of Lake Drummond is a little over eighteen feet.

In ancient times the Dismal Swamp actually covered as much as two thousand square miles; today it is down to about six hundred square miles. Estimates of the swamp's original acreage range anywhere from five hundred thousand to two million acres. Its ten-mile-wide center runs parallel to the Atlantic Coast for forty miles, from the Elizabeth River in the city of Chesapeake to the Pasquotank River in North Carolina. Roughly 40 percent of the present swamp is in Virginia, largely in the cities of Chesapeake and Suffolk. Geologically and biologically the Dismal Swamp is not a "normal" swamp. Most swamps are formed by rivers flowing into land basins, but in the case of the Dismal Swamp, seven bodies of water flow out from the higher lands at its center, which are covered with such trees as fir, gum and mulberry, not generally found in swamplands. While it is true that the moisture, darkness and heat that contribute to the decay of vegetable and animal matter normally abundant in swamps are found in areas of the Dismal Swamp, unlike other swamps, the Dismal has few deposits of bacterial decay. Juniper and bald cypress juices make the swamp waters too acidic for bacterial growth to develop. Thus, the Dismal Swamp is really a thick deposit of dead organic matter that is slowly building up one of the few major beds of peat still being naturally formed in the United States.

The swamp's ecosystem is predicated on its water resources, native vegetative communities and diverse wildlife species. The Dismal Swamp's ecological significance, coupled with its rich history and folklore, has made it one of the last great wild areas that remain in an increasingly urbanized American East Coast. Though the Dismal Swamp is not located in the Deep South, it is draped, nonetheless, with Spanish moss like that found in many Southern swamps, particularly in South Carolina and Florida, and it is also inhabited by *Agkistrodon piscivorus*—the cottonmouth water moccasin—which is never found north of Virginia's James River. But unlike many of her swampy neighbors to the south, the Dismal Swamp has animal life such as bats and rodents usually found much farther north. In the winter months, it is not unusual to see marsh grasses glazed in delicate frost, and during the summer months, the swamp is surpassingly rich and luxuriant. "The yellow jessamine [*sic*], the laurel, the myrtle, and evergreen bay are the most striking," wrote *Harper's Weekly* artist and reporter David Hunter Strother, who, under the pseudonym Porte Crayon, made important observations of the Dismal Swamp during his visit there in March 1856. He also documented the reptiles and insects present in every quarter of the swamp he ventured through.

Strother found bear, deer, otter, raccoons, opossums, pheasants, partridges and wild ducks. "The waters also abound," wrote Strother, "in fine freshwater fish, the esteemed of which are the speckled perch. There are also a number of wild cattle that subsist upon the leaves and shoots of the reed." He observed that the Dismal Swamp was rarely entered except by the "most resolute and experienced swampers," thus the "wild beasts" roamed for the most part undisturbed. Strother was in the swamp during March, where he saw for himself a frosty, brisk and bright morning in the Great Dismal. The lake was entirely hidden by a thick coverlet of white mist, which lay upon its surface almost as palpable, he remarked, as if it had been a light cotton comforter.

Many of the swamp's most inspired legends concern its plants and animals. An oft-told tale is about the Deer Tree of Lake Drummond. As the story goes there was once a mischievous old witch who bedeviled hunters by running their dogs until they were lost in the swamp. For years the witch played her tricks on hunters by changing into a deer to draw out the hounds until they were deep in a morass of vines and briars. The witch-turned-deer would then turn into a tree and cackle at the dogs' confusion. One day, though, she ran into the lake before she was able to turn into a tree; hunters later found their dogs at Lake Drummond's shore barking at an old bald cypress stump. The legend goes that when the dogs had come too close, the witch had become a tree to save herself, but then, once in the lake, she could not again become a witch. For many years hunters told of a bald cypress tree, in the shape of a deer; it actually existed as an oft-visited destination point at Lake Drummond.

Human occupation of the Dismal Swamp began nearly thirteen thousand years ago. Five thousand years ago the swamp was the hunting grounds of native peoples whose trading network reached as far as the Ohio Valley, and it is from them that the name Dismal Swamp might have come. Legend has it that the name is a translation of an Indian word that means "swamp" or "dismal." Dennis Blanton, director of the Center for Archaeological Research at the College of William and Mary, has studied many bolas found there, long tethers weighted with round stones that were flung to entangle prey, noted John Tidwell in the April/May 2002 edition of *American Heritage Magazine*. By 1650 few Native Americans remained in the area, and European settlers had shown little interest in it until William Drummond discovered the lake in 1665. After William Byrd II's survey of the North Carolina–Virginia border in 1728, his survey of the Dismal Swamp and exploitation of the region's wealth of flora and fauna was soon to follow. Of Norfolk, Byrd observed on March 1 of that year, "This place is the mart for most of the commodities produced in the adjacent parts of North Carolina. They have a pretty deal of lumber from the borders of the Dismal, who make bold with the King's land thereabouts without the least ceremony. They not only maintain their stock upon it," he continued, "but get boards, shingles and other lumber out of it in great abundance." Byrd later observed that the margins of the swamp were being ebbed away by settlers who increasingly encroached on it for timber. Predictably, as settlers went deeper into the swamp, the more man and nature did battle. Bringing timber out of deep woods required the construction of corrugated or corduroy roads, trails forged with beds of transverse-laid logs. In addition to the roads, swallowed deep in the swamp's ancient forests were woodcutters' and shingle makers' temporary huts and settlements, one of which was located on White Marsh Road in proximity of Suffolk; it bore an adequate descriptor—Dismal Town.

When Suffolk resident Robert Arnold published his early recollections of the Dismal Swamp in 1888, he observed that railroader and former United States Senator William Mahone of Virginia was, by then, the swamp's largest shareholder. The swamp had also been leased for several years to John L. Roper, of Norfolk, who employed a large number of workers to cut away valuable timber, further degrading the dense forests of the Great Dismal. But Arnold also offered a more amusing picture of pleasure

Hopkins Fish and Oyster Company, founded by William C. Hopkins in 1895, was engaged in the production, packing and shipping of fish and oysters. Hopkins started out in the oyster packing business in 1891 with Alfred A. Jordan at Ludlow's Wharf. The firm was called Hopkins and Jordan. Four years later, Hopkins established his own enterprise and in 1907 was joined by his son, William Jr. The company was located on Southampton Avenue in Norfolk's Atlantic City when this picture of William Hopkins, company founder, was taken in his office, ca. 1915. *Courtesy of the author.*

The shucking department of Hopkins Fish and Oyster Company, ca. 1915, was where the oysters were opened, graded into classes according to size and placed in strainers. Fresh water was run over the oysters and a paddle used to swish them around to remove foreign matter. Cans of oysters were packed in crushed ice in barrels and boxes shipped to all parts of the United States and Canada. *Courtesy of the author.*

parties to the swamp. In getting up a party to visit Lake Drummond, "you will always find more or less of the party who are afraid of snakes," he wrote. On one occasion, the party consisted of only three—Smith, Jones and Brown—all citizens of Suffolk. They prepared themselves with the necessary gear and started out for the Dismal Swamp Canal. Their boat, ready when they arrived, embarked and they were soon on their way down the waterway. Smith took the wheel, Brown placed himself at the bow to ward off approaching danger and Jones, the most timid in the party, was put amidships, with his back to Brown. The men had not yet passed "the great terror to all who go to the lake"—Paradise Old Field—where "things of unquestionable shapes have been seen by persons passing it." No one had ever given any account of the history of this place, which was passed on the way to Lake Drummond, but many of the stories associated with Paradise Old Field have to do with snakes. "Some have argued," wrote Arnold, "that the Field was at one time filled with grottos, and that the fairies of Lake Drummond would leave their realm and by a subterranean passage into it to bask in the beauties which surrounded it." But this had little to do with the snake story that Arnold told. "A snake is a wonderful reptile," he observed. "It is not necessary for one to be seen that one should be frightened. The very mention, in some instances, is sufficient to scare those who are the least timid," and so it went with Jones. He was afraid of snakes. Smith and Brown knew it and they determined to have a little sport at Jones's expense. Jones was delighted with the swamp's scenery as they passed down the canal, expatiating upon the wonders of nature. Smith was charmed with Jones's romantic effusions, and paid no attention to Brown, who was sitting at the bow of the boat, when Smith suddenly noticed Brown intently searching for something; he asked what was wrong. Brown answered that a snake was in the boat and he was trying to find it. Jones began to twist and squirm. "Hallo!" Jones exclaimed as he sprang into the canal. He made several lunges toward shore that looked as if he was walking on water. Smith added more steam to the boat and Jones was taken back aboard, very frightened. They had not gone very far when Brown started in again, "I believe that snake is in the boat yet," throwing a piece of rattan at Jones that looked like a snake. Jones jumped out of the boat a second time, only to be retrieved once more by his friends. Brown and Smith never had the heart to tell Jones that the rattan was not a real snake. Years would pass and the story endured.

But Arnold had other observations of the Dismal Swamp that are worth knowing today. He recalled George Washington's farm, owned in the late nineteenth century by the widow of John Trotman, who had in her possession the original title deeds of every person who had owned the place at various times, from Washington down to the last purchaser, who was Burrell Brothers, Esquire, of Gates County, North Carolina, and her uncle. At his death it fell to his widow, who gave it to Trotman. "I have visited the place several times," wrote Arnold, "and the cellars can now be seen where stood the first house. It is very certain that it was settled many years ago, from the fact that I saw a tombstone of a doctor from Waterbury, Connecticut, who died there in 1800." The headstone had been seen by many persons. There was also another place that adjoined the Washington farm known as Hamburg Ditch, a cross canal. At this place a ditch or canal was dug, running east to the northwest lock of the Dismal Swamp Canal, through which a vast quantity of grain and other produce raised by the farmers of Gates County, North Carolina, was shipped to Norfolk. An extensive mercantile business was carried on at Hamburg Ditch by Colonel T.W. Smith, who eventually moved his home to Suffolk. It was at Hamburg Ditch that so many refugees ran the blockade during the Civil War from Norfolk and other places, and a number of incidents occurred in which persons sought out Hamburg Ditch to pass in and out of the Confederate lines. The ditch at Hamburg was later described as a beautiful place, which must have known human occupation that predated the Revolutionary War, as many arrow points and tomahawks had been ploughed up on the place.

The Great Dismal Swamp had always been somewhat of a mystery and legends abounded, particularly in the nineteenth and into the twentieth

Six bascule bridges are currently in highway service on Virginia's Southside, all built after 1932. The only single-leaf bascule is the Deep Creek Bridge in the city of Chesapeake, built in 1934 over the Dismal Swamp Canal. The double-leaf bascules, all in Chesapeake with the exception of one, are the Gilmerton Bridge, built in 1938 over the Southern Branch connecting U.S. Route 13 to U.S. Route 460; the Dominion Boulevard Steel Bridge, built in 1962, also over the Southern Branch; the Great Bridge Bridge, rebuilt in 2004 over the Intracoastal Waterway; the High Rise Bridge, constructed in 1972 over the Southern Branch; and Norfolk's Berkley Bridge, constructed in 1990 over the Eastern Branch.

THE ELIZABETH RIVER

The Elizabeth River was frozen over completely when this photograph was taken on January 5, 1918. Merchant seamen crossed the waterway from ship to ship with ease. During the first week of January, waterborne traffic in the tributaries, rivers and the Chesapeake Bay was at a standstill with the exception of the ferries and some tugs that plodded slowly across Norfolk waters. Seagoing vessels had suspended operations. *Courtesy of the author.*

centuries. In May 1888 two sunburned travelers named John Boyle O'Reilly and Edward A. Moseley set off from Norfolk aboard a tug bound for the swamp. As they drew closer to the swamp, a deckhand on the tug pointed to the river, which had grown dark like the stream from a dye-works, and said to them, "See, that is the juniper water of the Dismal Swamp." O'Reilly remarked that it was singular that neither the captain of the tug nor his men could tell them anything about the swamp itself. Their knowledge ended at the lock. This was, in their experience, characteristic of the whole neighboring population. "Richmond knows as little about the swamp as Boston," he observed, "even Norfolk and Suffolk know little more." "All I know," said the captain to O'Reilly, "is that there are lots of snakes in there." "And bears," said another. "And panthers," said a third crewman, and so on, and so on, while each one gave a friendly hand to launch their canoes as they closed to a wharf near the lock, where about thirty black men were loading a schooner with lumber and bundled shingles of juniper and cypress. As a parting word of warning, the tug's second hand cautioned O'Reilly and Moseley to keep their Smith and Wessons handy, but before they could ask why, the sturdy little steamer that had brought them to the lock had backed out and was headed back to the Elizabeth River.

O'Reilly and Moseley paddled to Roper's sawmill at Deep Creek in about an hour. By the time they arrived at Roper's there was no one there who could tell them anything about the swamp, so they paddled on to the village of Deep Creek, but before reaching it, passed through another lock. Here the Dismal Swamp proper was said to begin. At this lock the two men were again raised several feet so that they were about sixteen feet above sea level, although only a few miles from tidal water. "The whole Southern coast is margined by swamp lands, but the Dismal Swamp is not of them," O'Reilly wrote later. "It is high land instead of low land."

Colonel William H. Stewart of Portsmouth, a Confederate veteran who lived in the Dismal Swamp as a boy and man, later became an invaluable "human document" concerning it. He wrote a description of the swamp for the *Old Jamestown Digest* in his later years in which he called the swamp "one of those wonderful, mysterious, never-to-be-visited places, as inaccessible almost as the North Pole, and where abound alligators, reptiles, tarantula, and other deadly animals. As one's horizon enlarges with age," he continued, "the Dismal Swamp appears to be just as inaccessible as ever." While some of the reptiles, arachnids and animals Stewart referenced were a far cry from what was actually found in the swamp, such descriptive accounts helped perpetuate the swamp's air of mystery. Stewart painted a familiar picture when he wrote that when leaves are falling on frosted nights, black bear come out from the thick reeds and rush up great gum trees to sup on gum berries, straddling strong limbs to draw in switches laden with fruit.

Little had changed when another observer plied the waters of the swamp in 1910. Passing through the locks of the Dismal Swamp Canal at Deep Creek, Walter Prichard Eaton observed two schooners coming out, loaded almost to the waterline with clean-smelling cypress shingles. As water foamed through the gates, it shone in the sun with every shade of burnt sienna, amber and brown—the strange, dark water of the Dismal Swamp, colored by the juniper and cypress roots. As he traveled deeper into the swamp, Eaton noticed that the banks of the canal were so high and so overgrown with verdure that from the upper deck of the steamer passengers could not see over them. To the east telegraph poles bespoke a road, and occasionally the roof of a house was visible, or the face of a black child peering through the bushes. Every mile or so along the canal Eaton's steamer stopped at an opening in the bank and slung out freight to waiting black handlers, who put the cargo on a two-wheeled mule cart, by then a century-old custom in the swamp. Through the gaps were farms that stretched out, level as a Western prairie, reclaimed from dense forest. But on the western bank there was no break, nor over it any cessation in the steady, monotonous march of vine-draped gums and cypresses or the darker ranks of pines.

Having traveled some twenty-four miles from Norfolk, Eaton's steamer ultimately reached the home of Captain John C. Wallace, "Cap'n Wallace's place," where they dropped off Wallace's mail. Eaton called Captain Wallace the "squire of the swamp." Years before the Wallace family had

The Great Bridge Bridge in Chesapeake, which carries VA Route 168 over the Albemarle and Chesapeake Canal, was designed and rebuilt in 2004 by the U.S. Army Corps of Engineers, Norfolk District, as a double-leaf bascule, fast-acting hydraulic, five-lane vehicular bridge—the first of its kind in Virginia. The bridge it replaced had been built 1943, and was declared obsolete as it was carrying double its design load and had structural problems that required weight restrictions to be strictly enforced. The bridge's mechanical and electrical equipment also needed updating. The National Highway Systems Designation Act of 1995 authorized the corps's project, sponsored by the City of Chesapeake, which today operates the bridge.

Two hundred thousand bushels of oyster shells are shown on this divided-back Chessler Company postcard, mailed from Norfolk, Virginia, on July 15, 1921. This mountain of shells adjoined one of Norfolk's large oyster packing plants. *Courtesy of the author.*

reclaimed a square mile on the west bank by sinking a drain under the canal to carry off the water eastward around Dover Farm, which provided them with a large and prosperous corn and hay plantation, dotted with black farm workers' cabins. A mile beyond the Wallace homestead at Glencoe was Lynch's Landing, where lumber was loaded on schooners. Eaton stayed overnight in the village of Wallaceton, little more than a lumber camp surrounding a large sawmill, where he ate at a hotel where lumbermen were fed. Wallaceton had a store, a church and a school. Wallaceton was really in the swamp, on reclaimed land, far removed from the conveniences of Norfolk and Portsmouth. No one kept a cow at Wallaceton. "You drink condensed milk in your coffee," he wrote, "and on your cereal." But this truly dismal feature was forgotten the next morning, when Eaton and his party rose into a new-washed world, shipped their stores to a motorboat and turned out of the main canal into the feeder ditch that came down from Lake Drummond. Eaton observed that when Strother entered the swamp in 1856, he had come in from Suffolk, on the other side. The Washington Ditch was much narrower than the feeder, so that the trees often met above it; and Strother's motive power was provided by two black boat handlers, on a towpath of logs, while Eaton's had been furnished by gasoline. Otherwise, Strother's description of the swamp written fifty-four years before fit perfectly to what Eaton saw on his own trip. The same great turkey buzzard sailed languidly overhead. The same tall, slender reeds made a feathery hedge along the bank. The same wild profusion of myrtle, greenbrier, bay and juniper hung over the black, narrow canal. The same hushed stillness, broken only by the calls of birds and the steady chug of his boat's engine, stole over the senses and seemed to blot out all memory of the outer world. Eaton described a beautiful, glorious morning. In the black stream that lay ahead the great trees were mirrored so clearly that image and object were of almost equal distinctness, and the perspective of the canal was like a long tube. "We saw little into the swamp," he noted, "for the flowering jungle on the banks. But over the jungle rose the gums and cypresses and pines and oaks and maples, twined with enormous creepers and bearing their pendant vines like hair. Across our path ahead flashed the red of a cardinal bird." He saw a flicker tapping off to the left. A water thrush greeted him from the bank. The Carolina wren uttered a pleasant call and the whole forest seemed to come alive with music. Penetrating this magical waterway but four miles, Eaton's party disembarked in shoal water at a rough landing, climbed the bank and tugged their baggage along a path through high reeds a few hundred yards, coming out into a small clearing. In the clearing was an unpainted, two-story cottage, a shed, a vegetable garden with fruit trees and grapes, the locks that regulated the outflow from Lake Drummond and a military tent. Sitting on the lock gate, clad in the shirt and trousers of the United States Navy was a young sailor shooting little mud turtles with a Krag-Jörgensen rifle, which took Eaton aback, as the rifle was sighted for two thousand yards and would kill at three miles; there was something incongruous in the sailor's appearance. The cottage was occupied by "Cap'n Jack," keeper of the locks, who belonged to what Eaton called the "swamp folk." He was born on the margin of the swamp, at Deep Creek, and had always lived in its shadow. Before the Civil War, when Cap'n Jack was a small boy, he could remember dark nights when his father, a strong Union sympathizer, stole into the swamp with provisions for fugitive slaves. Cap'n Jack himself wanted, when the war came, to go with other young boys, to the front, but his family would not let him. Union troops would eventually ride into his yard one day and take the gun he had concealed.

At Cap'n Jack's, Eaton discovered that the military tent propped in the cottage yard belonged to a party of young sailors on shore leave from the Norfolk Navy Yard in Portsmouth. With no available place to put up their tents, Cap'n Jack offered Eaton's party sleeping quarters in an upper room of his house, where a feather bed, long unused, spread a dusty and dubious welcome. Aunt Jane, Cap'n Jack's old housekeeper, could not keep up cooking for all their guests, but they were offered use of her kitchen to make their meals. The captain kept several flatboats and a long canoe dug out of cypress log, which he rented to hunters and fishermen. Half an hour after their arrival Eaton and his group were paddling up the canal,

Non-military industrial activities along the Southern Branch of the Elizabeth River have had a long history of contributing to its degradation. Evidence of the river's degraded quality, according to a 1983 Virginia State Water Control Board report, has been officially dated to at least 1925, when shellfish consumption from the Elizabeth River was first banned. Documentation revealed that in 1983, forty-eight industrial and fifteen domestic point discharges existed within the Elizabeth River system.

under the dark shadows of overhanging trees. After about an eighth of a mile he observed open water. The boat shot over the black, silent ditch, suddenly emerging from the wall of the forest into the lake of the Dismal Swamp. "In silence, in astonishment, even in awe," he wrote later, "we gazed at the scene before us, at the realization of our dream." This portal to the Dismal Swamp was like nothing else he had ever seen. Into this body of water, undisturbed by any boat, ringed only by the eternal silences of the wilderness, what looked like bleached mastodons' bones rose out of the water, a hundred feet from shore, like twin lighthouses marking the channel; it was a stand of two bald cypresses, their gray, quick-tapering trunks rearing on a wicker island of roots, their crooked limbs flaunting a shred of green, delicate foliage.

As Eaton's party rowed out into the lake, they could see huge cypress ruins growing in the water all along the shores of the lake, some of them quite dead, some of them still bearing umbrellas of delicate foliage. On the shore itself were the trunks of many more, some felled by the wind, but the majority by the axes of lumbermen perhaps a century before. The entire shore, extending well out into the shallow water, was gray with the bleached cypress knees, looking as if it were strewn with the bones and tusks of prehistoric animals. The knees of the cypress were about two to four feet long, he noted, growing up from the roots above the surface of the water to secure air for the tree. Landing on the lake's shore, Eaton and his group squeezed through a hedge of ten-foot-tall reeds and under the shadows of huge black gum trees. Finding no snakes and the land dry, they forged a path through blackberry vines covered in white blooms and blocked by fallen tree trunks. The density of the swamp's foliage soon made Eaton and the others realize why slaves had fled to it before the Civil War, often eluding capture for years, even raising families in its jungled maze. He had heard the stories, too, that the swamp held wild cattle, strayed from domestic herds on the borders of the Great Dismal. Captain Wallace had told him that he had heard the bulls fighting with bears at night, and once at least the body of a bull and the body of a bear were found lying side by side. Rowing across the lake, the group came upon another dugout canoe occupied by boys fishing for black bass. Behind the fishermen's canoe the shore attained an astonishing elevation of three feet, crowned with pines and two hunters' camps, roughly built and hidden in the dense foliage. Between the camps a brook trickled down. "We walked up this brook a few hundred feet, and came upon a merry picnic party of men, women and children," he wrote, "and a rough shack owned by a 'swamp man,' who housed his guests for twenty-five cents a day." The shack was at the locks that marked the end of the Washington Ditch. A second canal, known as the Jericho Ditch, also ended there. It, too, he noticed, ran northwest to Suffolk, but was by then impassable. The picnic party had come in from Suffolk by rowboat, up the Washington Ditch, a favorite outing for the inhabitants of that town. In a Virginia gazetteer published in Charleston, South Carolina, in 1856, it was recorded that the Lake Drummond Hotel, "a favorite public house," occupied this site. The shack that Eaton encountered bore little resemblance to "a favorite public house" but afforded shelter and during the spring and fall was frequently occupied by hunters and campers.

Making their way back to Cap'n Jack's, Eaton and his group once again found sailors busy fishing or out tending their traps. Now and then

Five thousand Virginians and North Carolinians celebrated the formal opening of the George Washington Highway at Wallaceton, four miles from the North Carolina–Virginia state line, on July 17, 1925. The George Washington Highway is also U.S. Route 17 South. This was the first hard-surfaced road to the North Carolina border through Virginia. As originally constructed, the highway hugged the banks of the Dismal Swamp Canal through the swamp for fifteen miles to the state line after leaving the village of Deep Creek. Prominent speakers at the ceremony included Virginia Governor E. Lee Trinkle (1922–26); General J.P. Jervey, city manager, city of Portsmouth; Hugh Johnston, commissioner, Norfolk County, who presided over the day's events; Colonel George C. Cabell; W.A. Hart, North Carolina district road commissioner; H.G. Shirley, chairman, Virginia State Highway Commission; and R.J. Job, secretary, Elizabeth City Chamber of Commerce. Speakers delivered their speeches from a platform erected on the verandah of the historic Wallace plantation, and included Senator Harry Flood Byrd, a Virginia gubernatorial candidate; Rear Admiral Roger Welles, and several other high-ranking naval officers; Virginia Lieutenant Governor Junius E. West; and I. Walke Truxtun. Governor Trinkle is sixth from the left, standing on the verandah in this Charles S. Borjes photograph. *Courtesy of the Sargeant Memorial Room, Norfolk Public Library.*

he recorded the crack of a rifle. The sailors had captured alive, too, two raccoons and an opossum, which they had caged up to carry back to the fleet. Like so many campers, they had wantonly killed innumerable birds and squirrels as well, and tacked the wings and tails over their tent door. They had also shot several cottonmouth water moccasins, the most deadly snake in the swamp, though Cap'n Jack swore to his guests that the viper avoided people whenever possible. Leaving the sailors to their activity, Eaton and the few men accompanying him plunged into the woods, beating down a path to a huge maple tree, where a bunch of mistletoe as large as a bushel basket was growing far up, and he managed to climb high enough to cut it down. The swamp abounded in mistletoe and holly, though the task of getting it down was not easy. In the rich green gloom of the woods birds kept them company. Eaton's party counted more than twenty varieties, including the rare water thrush, the beautiful cardinal and the humble chickadee. Returning to Cap'n Jack's, Eaton listened most of the evening to his stories of the past, to the days when bloodhounds would follow escaped slaves into the swamp.

Eaton disagreed with the findings of Dr. N.S. Shaler, published in 1888–89 for the United States Geological Survey, in which Shaler advocated lowering the locks of the Dismal Swamp Canal and cutting transverse ditches to drain the swamp for agricultural use, which the professor reported could yield $16 million in produce per year. The lumber yield, Shaler had declared, was only worth $100,000 a year. "But there are thousands upon thousands of square miles in the South still uncultivated which do not require costly drainage," wrote Eaton, "and there is only one Dismal Swamp." A delegation of the Virginia Legislature had toured the swamp ahead of Eaton in consideration of a plan to set apart at least so much of the swamp as it immediately surrounded the lake as a state reservation. Charles Frederick Stansbury's *The Lake of the Great Dismal*, published in 1924, fifteen years after Eaton's adventure in the swamp and two years after Stansbury's death, told of a bill before the United States Congress intended to complete draining of the swamp with the notion of transforming it into farmland. "This I believe to be a great error which might afterwards be fraught with serious consequences—namely the substitution of drought and disastrous fires in a wide region now blessed by rain and the beneficent dampness of the swamp." With the swamp drained and turned into farmland, Stansbury observed, "we know not what climatic changes would take place, but a lessening of rainfall would necessarily follow. When Professor Shaler, the geologist, advocated the draining of the swamp in a report published some years ago, there was seemingly but one side to the question. Now, however, thoughtful and intelligent men who have studied the subject, doubt the advisability of such draining, and regard the swamp as it is, as of great and

The pilot of this Lewis and Voight VE-7SF, Bureau Number A5937, landed his aircraft on the waters of the Dismal Swamp Canal on July 17, 1925, as part of day-long events celebrating the opening of George Washington Highway, which winds its way parallel to the canal. The airplane was attached to the USS *Arkansas* as part of Observation Squadron Six (VO-6), Aircraft Squadrons, Scouting Fleet. Charles S. Borjes took the photograph shown here. *Courtesy of the Sargeant Memorial Room, Norfolk Public Library.*

lasting value to agriculture." Captain William F. Wise, a prominent truck farmer of Norfolk County, vigorously protested against the draining of the Dismal Swamp. He sent a statement of the theory to Washington, D.C., long ago advocated by Commodore James Barron and Captain Samuel Watts, that the Dismal Swamp protected the rich agricultural territory of Southeastern Virginia from droughts. In this theory, Captain Wise was supported by a remarkable daily record of the weather in the area; this record had been kept without interruption for seventy-four years, first by Captain Wise's father and then by himself. The crux of Captain Wise's statement concluded that Lake Drummond had a decided effect on local rainfall at Norfolk. When the water in Lake Drummond was lowered, for example, by improvements in the canal just years before, it resulted in the first loss of a cucumber crop since the Civil War.

During a visit into the swamp that started on September 9, 1906, Charles Stansbury headed to Deep Creek. "The canal may be said to begin at Gilmerton," he wrote. He reached it by trolley from Portsmouth, the run taking thirty minutes. As the trolley terminated there, he found it necessary to walk to Deep Creek about three miles farther on; the road that he took followed the bank of the canal, the waters of which were a dark reddish-brown color. During the 1906 season rainfall had been unprecedented, he recalled; the Dismal Swamp gave forth such a quantity of water as never was known before. So great was the volume of it that it washed away the lock in the feeder, leading to Lake Drummond, and poured for many weeks an enormous stream of dark water into the canal from whence it found its way into the Elizabeth River and Hampton Roads. So enormous was the volume that it colored the channel for many miles and was distinctly traceable to the waters of the Chesapeake Bay. Until the lock was repaired, much commerce came to a standstill. The lock keeper at Deep Creek explained to Stansbury that a small steamboat left Norfolk on Tuesday and Friday each week, going through the canal to Elizabeth City, North Carolina. One of his duties was to collect the toll on vessels less than thirty tons, which was five dollars, the larger vessels and lumber barges paying at the rate of so much per ton gross. To illustrate how busy the keeper's job could be, Stansbury took a random day's shipping report from the April 21, 1906 *Virginian-Pilot*. The shipping report for the Dismal Swamp Canal, published by Hudson and Brother, agents, Sanford Building, read as follows: Northbound: tug *John Taxis*, Whitehurst, North Carolina, to Norfolk; schooner *Ida G. Farron*, Bloodgood, North Carolina, to Norfolk, lumber; schooner *William Young*, Russell, North Carolina, to Norfolk; schooner *R.T. Ellyson*, Watkins, North Carolina, to Norfolk, oysters; tug *Helen*, Goodwin, North Carolina, to Philadelphia; barge *W.B. Blades*, North Carolina to Philadelphia, lumber; barge *E.E.*

The hurricane that struck Norfolk on August 22, 1933, paralyzed the city as floodwaters rose nine feet above mean low tide. Norfolk saw winds of seventy miles per hour and the streets were littered with broken plate glass, awnings and signs from storefronts. The Virginia Electric and Power Company plant on Reeves Avenue was flooded and all current shut down, leaving the city in darkness. Life in downtown Norfolk before the floodwall meant City Hall Avenue and the lower end of Granby Street were left with water at least four feet deep, flooding many stores. Floodwaters even reached the intersection of Granby and Freemason Streets, a part of the city that had never recorded flooding. The nearby Norva Theater was flooded up to the top of its orchestra seats. The old Navy Young Men's Christian Association (YMCA) on Brooke Avenue had ten feet of water in the basement. This Charles S. Borjes photograph was taken the day after the storm blew through, on August 23, 1933. *Courtesy of the Sargeant Memorial Room, Norfolk Public Library.*

Dale, North Carolina to Philadelphia, lumber; barge *J.W. Jannings*, North Carolina to Philadelphia, lumber; tug *Cyrene*, Eure, North Carolina, to Norfolk; barge *John Quinn*, North Carolina to Norfolk, juniper logs; barge *Vanslyck*, North Carolina to Norfolk, juniper logs; tug *W.W. Graham*, Morrissette, North Carolina, to Norfolk; schooner *Freddie Hamblin*, Burriss, North Carolina, to Washington, D.C., shingles; schooner *Maggie Davis*, Truitt, North Carolina, to Norfolk, oysters; schooner *Pearl Cullen*, Buzzy, North Carolina, to Norfolk, oysters; schooner *Edna A. Brown*, Carpenter, North Carolina, to Norfolk, oysters; schooner *M.J. Delan*, Munford, North Carolina, to Norfolk, oysters; schooner *Thomas E. Taylor*, Sterling, North Carolina, to Norfolk, oysters. Southbound: steamer *Nina Overton*, Norfolk to North Carolina, general cargo; tug *Frank K. Eskerick*, Dryden Norfolk to North Carolina; barge *Tioga*, Norfolk to North Carolina, fertilizer; barge *Agnes McNally*, Philadelphia to North Carolina; tug *Cyrene*, Eure, Norfolk to North Carolina; barge *Bear*, Norfolk to North Carolina; barges *Number 1* and *2*, Norfolk to North Carolina; tug *John Taxis*, Whitehurst, Norfolk to North Carolina; schooner *Mary Gaylord*, Midgett, Norfolk to North Carolina, general cargo; schooner *James L. Milford*, Jones, Norfolk to North Carolina; schooner *John D. Robbins*, Norfolk to North Carolina; sloop *Annie Hill*, Norfolk to North Carolina; schooner *Daniel Bell*, Ways, Norfolk to North Carolina; schooner *Topaz*, Williams, Norfolk to North Carolina; steamer *Thomas Newton*, Cahoon, Norfolk to North Carolina, general cargo. The volume of traffic varied each day in accordance with the time of the year.

Stansbury returned to the Dismal Swamp on the fourteenth of September, this time in a small gasoline-powered launch belonging to Captain N.B. Ransom of Norfolk. Accompanied by a photographer, their destination was Lake Drummond and the intent of the visit was to obtain good pictures of the Dismal Swamp. As they sped down the Southern Branch of the Elizabeth River, keeping the red buoys on the starboard and the black ones to the port, the wind and tide remained in their favor. As Stansbury's party passed the navy yard they observed the dismantled USS *Olympia* (C-6), famous as Commodore George Dewey's flagship at Manila, the grim old battleship USS *Texas* and a fleet of torpedo boats and destroyers. The water in the river, heavily tinctured with the juniper water of the swamp, became deeper in color as they progressed until their wake began to resemble port wine in a violent state of agitation. Stansbury overshot the entrance to Deep Creek about a mile and then, by the direction of some black pile drivers, retraced the course until it was discovered. It was marked by a large sign on the shore on which in white letters on a black background was the legend, "Entrance, Dismal." Deep Creek, he wrote, was a tortuous tidewater estuary with pleasant-looking banks of low pine and sedge. Upon reaching Captain Wallace's Glencoe,

Field studies have established that the eastern side of the Campostella dump received municipal solid waste until the early 1980s. The landfill's northeast section was closed before Resource Conservation and Recovery Act regulations were established in December 1988. Reports indicate that up to thirty feet of dredge material was placed on top of municipal solid waste before this closure. To the west, construction and demolition debris was accepted from 1983 until about 1992, when the landfill was closed. Filling in of the dump began in its southeast corner and progressed to the northeast. The Ingram Auto Mall property was filled in between 1963 and 1980, both by the City of Norfolk and the property owner.

During the fierce snowstorms of February 1937, working boats sought refuge at piers within the protected waters of Atlantic City. The boats shown here were tied to piers adjacent to E.R. Clark and Company, located at the foot of Botetourt Street. *Courtesy of the Sargeant Memorial Room, Norfolk Public Library.*

lake almost the entire swamp area lay bare below them. As they spiraled down toward Lake Drummond, Hamilton shot pictures as the flying boat descended, the time seeming longer than it was. Water from Washington Ditch was pouring into the lake, seething with glistening foam. The mouth of Jericho Ditch was clearly outlined, as was the narrow ribbon that he knew to be a feeder, which took the overflow from the lake and poured it into the canal. Below them they saw a dun hut—a shack—on shore at the mouth of Washington's canal and some dark figures rowing a shadowy boat through opaque wavelets.

As Miller settled the flying boat on the lake's surface, the winter sun hid behind a silver-tinged cloud and the dark, mysterious and forbidding forest encircled and enfolded the plane and its passengers. The water was the color of blood. Later, on January 17, in Norfolk a noted newspaper editor told Stansbury that he was in more danger than he knew that day on the lake: "I doubt if you know the greatest peril that confronted you when your seaplane rested on Lake Drummond in the heart of the Swamp." Not understanding what he meant, Stansbury asked the editor to explain. "The danger of being shot," was the reply. "The Great Dismal swarms with moonshiners. They are not society people; they certainly do not relish sudden visits from strange gentlemen from the sky. Perhaps you were out of range; but, for the sake of your friends, please don't go out there that way again." Stansbury wrote later that while resting on Lake Drummond, they must have been entertaining an angel unawares. As they rose from the lake, headed skyward, a magnificent bald eagle swept up with them. At times he came close to the flying boat, his altitude one of anger, curiosity, aggression. Lake Drummond, Stansbury observed, was never without its solitary bald eagle. "I have never visited the lake without seeing one," he jotted in his journal. To Stansbury the keynote of Lake Drummond was desolation. Despite the beauty of its densely wooded shores where wild elm, cypress, juniper and gum struggled for supremacy, the general effect of the lake was depressing. As he looked on it from a frail bateau, no sail broke the monotony of its dark waters or the somber hue of burnt umber. No sign of life disturbed its solitude but an isolated eagle sailing high in majestically graceful circles near its edge.

Within the Dismal Swamp that Stansbury and other chroniclers like him had known, four species of trees—juniper (*Juniperus virginiana*, commonly called Eastern red cedar, though not a true cedar), gum, bald cypress and Atlantic white cedar (actually *Chamaecyparis thyoides* sub. *thyoides*, the Atlantic white cypress, popularly called the Atlantic white cedar, though also not a cedar)—had long tolerated the marshland swamp, their roots running deep into the fertile earth below. Pine tree stands are still found largely on the ridges that are situated along the swamp's margins. Juniper and Atlantic white cedar can sustain even dry, hot summers, and both gum and bald cypress trees can thrive where the entire area is covered by water during the growing season. Bald cypress is the most water-tolerant of the trees in the Dismal Swamp, but both cypress and gum generally have root systems that provide ready access to air. Cypress knees develop only when the roots on which they rest are beneath the water's surface during the growing season. These knees are ancient in some trees. Gum tree roots arch up near the bole until they get air, and these protruding arches become covered with annual plants. If the arch is small, the tree is actually stunted. The body of a cypress tree is twice, often three times, as large at the base, as it is ten feet above the ground. Cedar-laden swamps stabilize water flow, temporarily storing floodwaters and mitigating the effects of droughts. Cedars filter and purify water as it flows through them. Soils are a telling element of the swamp's environment. "For the first three and a half centuries after settlement, people were interested in cedar swamps mainly for the fragrant, rot-resistant wood which could be harvested from them," wrote John E. Kuser, associate professor, Department of Natural Resources, Cook College, Rutgers University, in his 1995 study of the restoration of the Atlantic white cedar.

Trees and plant life are tell-tale signs as to what kinds of soils are present in the area. Juniper thrives in light swampland, usually composed of pure peat—or close to it—made up of a brown mass of vegetable matter deriving from juniper or white cedar, which was frequently mistaken for juniper as it

The mid-Atlantic and Chesapeake Bay states alone, in 1850, recorded a catch of 145 million pounds of oyster meat, shells excluded. This declined to 111 million in 1901 and to 45 million in 1935, 28 million in 1960 and 26 million in 1970. These numbers worked out, by the 1850 catch, for example, to 6 pounds, 6 ounces of oysters per every man, woman and child living within the reaches of the Chesapeake Bay, including the Elizabeth River watershed. By 1977 the catch amounted to only 6 ounces per person.

Students from
Norfolk's Northside
Middle School seed
an oyster reef on the
Western Branch of
the Elizabeth River,
ca. 1998. *Courtesy of
the National Oceanic
and Atmospheric
Administration.*

was being harvested from the swamp. The thickness of these peat deposits often varies from eight to ten feet. About 75 to 90 percent of this is organic matter. Soil such as this, once cleared and drained, has little agricultural use. The peat hardens and becomes caked like charred wood, and thus loses its value for agricultural purposes. Nearly one-third of the Dismal Swamp consists of this type of light swampland.

The juniper districts within the Dismal Swamp make up the nursery for timber trees. Juniper reproduces quickly; cypress very slowly. Cypress wood increases no more than roughly one inch per year, and there are about three cuttings of marketable lumber every twenty years. Dark swampland normally bears cypress, black gum and red maple, and is far richer for agricultural use. There is considerable organic substance found in the upper portions of dark swampland, but this diminishes with proper drainage. After fifty years of cultivation, the soil still remained black for the first farmers who worked fields from this reclaimed land. The use of lime kept the soil from becoming too acidic. This land, when reclaimed, is very fertile and capable of yielding a higher volume of vegetables. One observer wrote that from eighty to one hundred bushels of corn per acre could be harvested from this dark, rich soil. Potatoes, however, flourish in the light soil near the coastal areas and sometimes heavier soil at the Dismal Swamp's eastern border. The average potato yield by the late nineteenth century was roughly eighty barrels per acre; twentieth-century farmers would later cultivate celery on reclaimed black gum land. From a climatic standpoint, the Dismal Swamp is on the isothermal line, which means that the climates of north and south meet, in years past often making the year seem like every day was May. There was a time when there were no extremes of hot and cold within the bounds of the swamp.

Nature staved off development in the swamp that threatened to take increasingly larger portions of swamp acreage for industrial development. Virginia's State Corporation Commission issued a charter to the Dismal Swamp Industrial Committee in 1959, with the intent of evaluating the swamp as a site for future industrial uses. An increasing number of commercial activities rapidly began to disrupt the environmental balance of the Dismal Swamp. Union Camp Corporation owned fifty thousand acres to grow and harvest timber, but its engineers experimented with the raising and lowering of the swamp's water levels, impounding water in certain locations by constructing gates along some of the waterways and creating reservoirs. Experimental plantings were also made. About nineteen hunt clubs also made use of the Union Camp property, over which roads and bridges were constructed. Other land companies drained and developed acreage for farms, recreation and housing projects. Efforts to drain the swamp for wholesale development ultimately failed, but logging of the Dismal Swamp's juniper, bald cypress, Atlantic white cedar and gum, as well as additional tree species, continued until 1976. The United States Fish and Wildlife Service has documented that the entire Dismal Swamp has been logged at least once, and many areas have been burned by periodic wildfires.

Before the Great Dismal Swamp National Wildlife Refuge was established, over 140 miles of roads were constructed to provide access to lucrative timber. These roads severely disrupted the swamp's natural hydrology, as the ditches that were dug to provide soil for the roadbeds drained water from the swamp. Roads also impeded the flow of water across the swamp's surface, bathing some areas of the swamp in stagnant, putrid water.

The least tern (*Sterna antillarum*), shown here, and countless other shore birds are known to nest on man-made habitats at Craney Island. *Courtesy of the National Aeronautic and Space Administration.*

Logging operations removed natural stands of bald cypress and Atlantic white cedar that were replaced by other forest types, especially red maple. A drier swamp and the suppression of wildfires, which once cleared land for seed germination, created environmental conditions that proved less favorable to the survival of bald cypress and cedar stands. As a direct result of degradation of the swamp's hydrologic system, plant and animal diversity decreased.

By the mid-twentieth century conservationists began to raise red flags about the Dismal Swamp's degraded state, calling for America to demand something be done to preserve what was left of the Great Dismal Swamp that had left so many early settlers in awe of its natural beauty and mysterious, secret places that lay undiscovered. In 1973 the Union Camp Company of Franklin, Virginia, which had owned extensive tracts of the swamp since the beginning of the twentieth century, donated just over forty-nine thousand acres of its holdings to The Nature Conservancy, which transferred the property the following year to the United States Fish and Wildlife Service as a refuge. The refuge was officially established by the United States Congress through the Dismal Swamp Act of 1974. With help from The Nature Conservancy and The Conservation Fund, it is anticipated over time that the refuge will continue to acquire land. The Great Dismal Swamp National Wildlife Refuge is the largest intact remnant of a vast habitat that once covered more than one million acres of Southeastern Virginia and Northeastern North Carolina.

The primary purpose of the refuge's resource management programs is to restore and maintain the natural biological diversity that existed prior to human-induced alterations. The goal is restoration of the aforementioned essential elements of the swamp ecosystem—water resources, native vegetation communities and diverse wildlife species. Water is conserved and managed by placing water control structures in the ditches. Plant community diversity is being restored and maintained through forest management activities that simulate the ecological effects of wildfires. Today's swamp has evolved to five major forest types and three non-forested types of plant communities that compose swamp vegetation. The forested types include pine, Atlantic white cedar, maple and black gum, water tupelo and bald cypress, sweet gum, oak and poplar. The non-forested types include a remnant marsh, a sphagnum bog and an evergreen shrub community. Currently red maple is the most abundant and widely distributed plant community, as it expands into other communities due to the lingering effects of past forest cutting, extensive draining and the exclusion of forest fires. Water tupelo, bald cypress and Atlantic white cedar, formerly predominant forest types in the swamp, today account for less than 20 percent of the total cover. Three species of plants deserving special mention are the dwarf trillium, silky camellia and log fern. The dwarf trillium is located in the northwestern section of the swamp and blooms briefly each year for a two-week period in March. Silky camellia is found on the hardwood ridges and in the northwestern corner of the refuge. The log fern, one of the rarest of American ferns, is more common in the Great Dismal Swamp than anywhere else.

The Great Dismal Swamp National Wildlife Refuge straddles two states and two ecological systems—the Roanoke-Tar-Neuse-Cape Fear watershed and the Chesapeake Bay-Susquehanna River watershed, of which the Elizabeth River and the swamp are an integral part (and interdependent on one another)—allowing for a broad range of plant and animal species. Wildlife is currently managed by ensuring the presence of required habitats, with hunting used only to balance specific animal populations with available food supplies. Many animal species, including black bear, bobcat, otter and weasel along with over seventy species of reptiles and amphibians, call the Dismal Swamp home. More than two hundred bird species can be seen at the swamp year round, and an additional ninety-six of those species are known to nest on the refuge.

CHAPTER TEN
PROMULGATING A
HEALTHY ELIZABETH

One Sunday afternoon Marjorie Mayfield Jackson and her dog sat at the edge of a concrete culvert watching a narrow reach of the river framed with wetlands. "We were very still and the water was very clear and suddenly," she observed, "a large rock rose up from the shallow river bottom and moved through the water toward us." It was not a rock at all, of course; as it passed just below her dangling feet and through the culvert, Jackson could see that the "rock" was an enormous turtle, its back camouflaged with mossy growth. Its head was larger than Jackson's hand and its shell must have been, by her estimate, three feet long. Turtles live a long time, she noted later; maybe longer than any other animal. This one looked to Jackson like the grandmother of the Elizabeth, perhaps alive since before the turn of the twentieth century, when man began in earnest to pollute the river from businesses, industries and homes. Jackson thinks about that turtle often in her work as executive director of The Elizabeth River Project, the nonprofit organization tasked with the river's restoration, realizing that such a creature has survived the worst abuses of man. "The wonder and the challenge of the Elizabeth River," she wrote in the summer 2006 edition of the project's newsletter, *Mudflats*, "is that it is possible, no, imperative, to foster a living, breathing river that is also a great port. It requires of us an uncommon stewardship."

Thirty years ago, an article in the *Ledger-Star* on September 1, 1977, was far less assuring that the Elizabeth had a future. In "Elizabeth River wounded, dirty lady in need of help," writer Jack Dorsey called her the "wounded lady, not quite dead." He wondered if she would ever recover from her assailants' daily attacks. He asked if she was nothing more than an industrial sewer, so filled with chemicals, metals and other pollution that she might not be worth saving. A spokesman for the Virginia State Water Control Board told Dorsey, "It is questionable whether or not this body of water can be restored." Despite these grim predilections,

$63 million were being spent to upgrade sewage treatment plants and millions more on studies, tests and ways of saving the elderly lady, once elegant princess, from the indignities heaped on her by man for centuries. A quarter-century before Dorsey penned his article it was observed that no one thought twice about swimming in the Elizabeth or eating fish and shellfish caught from her banks. People once fished for Atlantic croaker, spot, flounder, sand sharks, rays, bluefish, trout and puppy drum, caught crabs by the bushel and, on a rare day, could catch a glimpse of a school of bottlenose dolphins. The Elizabeth River, which divides the South Hampton Roads like a large three-pronged fork, was here long before the white man, long before settlers built homes, established mercantile houses and constructed wharves and piers to accommodate prosperous waterborne trade.

"The joys of remembering the Elizabeth," wrote Dorsey, "are more pleasant than the reality of inspecting her today." Still beautiful, at least on the surface, the Elizabeth offered spot and croaker to be fished, as well as crabs, trout and an infrequent bluefish; however, none could be kept legally or consumed because the pesticide Kepone was discovered in the James River in 1975. Thirty years ago health officials would not permit fish to be eaten that were caught in any portion of the James River Basin because Kepone is a toxic chemical when consumed in large quantities. The James River Basin, which includes the most important fluvial system

The Norfolk waterfront is pictured as it appeared in 1945. *Courtesy of Norfolk Redevelopment and Housing Authority.*

331

THE ELIZABETH RIVER

This aerial photograph was taken June 27, 1960, looking west toward the mouth of the Elizabeth River. The focus of this photograph was the United States Naval Air Station, Norfolk, Virginia (center) but other important landmarks are captured in the image, including Mason's Creek, the body of water snaking its way below the air station runway. Norfolk Naval Station, above the air station, is located on the historic Seawell's Point peninsula. Across the Elizabeth River from the naval station is the Craney Island Dredged Material Management Area. Other landmarks include Tanner's Point, marking the entrance to Tanner's Creek (now the Lafayette River), upper left in the picture. *Courtesy of the author.*

in the commonwealth of Virginia, flows four hundred and fifty miles from its central-western Virginia headwaters to the Chesapeake Bay. Of Virginia's total land area of forty thousand square miles, the James River Basin contains over ten thousand square miles, just over a fourth of the state's surface area. The Elizabeth River is one of the basin's many tributaries and enters the James just above its confluence with the Chesapeake Bay, draining Norfolk, Chesapeake and Portsmouth of their runoff water. The Elizabeth begins in the Dismal Swamp, where the water is brackish—dark and acidic. But as the river winds its way from Chesapeake toward the Chesapeake Bay, the Elizabeth loses her swampy character. Strong lunar tides turn the river's waters from brackish to salty and from brown to nearly blue. The tides invigorate and purge the river twice daily and remove small amounts of the Elizabeth's pollution.

The Elizabeth River remains, even today, one of the world's busiest commercial roads for the shipping industry. It is a strategic link in the military's defense program due to the Norfolk Naval Shipyard and related ship repair facilities on her shores. Her harbor is vital to the import-export trade. Communities on the Elizabeth's shores have used the river to survive, prosper and sustain themselves, observed Dorsey. While some people then noted that the Elizabeth was no worse than any other major waterway that runs through cities where a half-million people or more live, the Elizabeth River was called one of the worst water pollution problems in Virginia in a water quality inventory report published by the State Water Control Board in 1976 for the Environmental Protection Agency (EPA) administrator and United States Congress under federally mandated reporting requirements. The river contained high bacterial counts, heavy metal concentrations, oil, creosote, untreated excrement, sulfur concentrations and chemical nutrients that were not supposed to be there, all resting in the mud and clay bottom, or suspended in salty brine, stirred by the propeller wash of ships plying her waters. Over a quarter-century ago, there were more than a dozen known polluters on the Elizabeth, including cities, the State, the military and private industrial firms. None polluted intentionally; pollution occurred under cover of progress, industrialization and war. The State Water Control Board knew who the polluters were, even then, and most of the river's worst polluters had federal licenses to dump wastes into her muddy tidal waters, creating toxic goo. By the mid-seventies polluters were dumping an estimated seventy thousand pounds of chemical waste a day into the river and its tributaries. The cities of Norfolk, Portsmouth and Chesapeake, with populations far smaller than they are today, contributed more than sixty million gallons a day of treated domestic wastewater. These numbers did not include accidental pollution from the shipping industry, from storm sewers that carry insect-killing pesticides into the river or the hundreds of nonpoint sources of pollution. Occasionally, even Mother Nature has polluted the river. When the Dismal Swamp's Lake Drummond experiences periods of drought, it allows oozing sediments to enter the Elizabeth, destabilizing the river's life chain.

The State Water Control Board's 1976 report pointed to the fact that the Elizabeth River received wastewater generated by the United States Navy activities in the watershed and the heavy industrial complex in the surrounding land area. The lowermost part of the James River estuary, including the Elizabeth River watershed, was then receiving in excess of one hundred million gallons daily of treated domestic wastewater. State officials noted that there was increasing evidence that the chlorination of these wastewaters caused toxic, chlorine-related compounds in the river to build up to a level detrimental to seed oyster beds and to certain species of migratory fish. The condition was marked by massive fish kills in the springs of 1973 and 1975. Chlorination—the disinfection of domestic wastewater—is important to treating wastewater. At that time, though studies were undertaken to find alternative methods of treating wastewater, none had then been found. More than $300 million in improvements had been undertaken by the Hampton Roads Sanitation District to upgrade its sewage treatment plants. All were designed to clean wastewater in a primary stage and a secondary stage, but little progress was made for

*Eastern (also called American) oysters (*Crassostrea virginica*) are essential to the health of the Chesapeake Bay and the highly urbanized Elizabeth River. In Southern Virginia dense reefs can be found in the Chesapeake Bay's intertidal areas surrounding the edges of marshes and rivers along the bay. These living siphons have the ability to filter sixty gallons of water a day, which reduces sediments and pollutants in the water. Oyster reefs also form three-dimensional structures offering homes for over three hundred different species. Some animals living on oyster reefs include crabs, gobies, blennies and toadfish. In fact, the spot fish that anglers seek uses these reefs for shelter, feeding and breeding.*

economic reasons. Seven major sources of wastewater discharge on the Elizabeth were identified and scheduled for upgrading—the sewage treatment plants at Western Branch, Lambert's Point, the former army terminals off Hampton Boulevard, Pinner's Point, Washington and Deep Creek plants, in addition to the Norfolk Naval Station. The United States Navy, which the water control board cited for heavy concentrations of waste disposal from its ships, introduced a $50 million pollution abatement program to stop existing water pollution problems. Under

The city of Norfolk's landfill at Campostella is a fifty-acre tract that operated as Norfolk's municipal dump from 1944 to 1992. The landfill is located north of the Norfolk-Chesapeake city line, and 2,500 feet south of the Eastern Branch of the Elizabeth River. This view, photographed in July 1969, is looking from shore toward the river. The site is bordered to the east by Ingram Auto Mall, an active automobile junkyard; Norfolk Southern Railroad has a right-of-way to the south. A tidal marsh tributary and properties that have been used for industrial and commercial uses, largely automobile junkyards, are located north of the landfill. Prior to its use as a city dump, the eastern side of the site was low-lying, undeveloped land with a third tributary of Steamboat Creek running through its center. There is a World War II housing development known as Anderson Park to the site's west. *Courtesy of the United States Army Corps of Engineers, Norfolk District.*

construction at Norfolk Naval Station and Norfolk Naval Shipyard, both on the Elizabeth, were industrial treatment plants. A state-of-the-art oily waste reclamation plant was also under construction at the navy's Craney Island fuel depot. The USS *Nimitz* (CVN-68) was the first aircraft carrier to pump sewage into a pierside collection system. This event, which took place on June 22, 1976, was the beginning of the end of one of the navy's oldest environmental problems. More than $12 million in pipelines were completed, or being constructed, at the Norfolk Naval Shipyard, Norfolk Naval Station and Little Creek Amphibious Base to meet a federally imposed deadline, set for 1981, to eliminate overboard discharge of sewage. By the mid-seventies the navy no longer operated any large sewage treatment plants in Hampton Roads; the Hampton Roads Sanitation District or the cities in which the United States Navy maintains a substantive presence, such as Portsmouth, took charge of former military systems.

As state and federal regulators began taking a harder look at the Elizabeth River's problems, her polluters became clear. Virginia Chemicals, Inc., was a major polluter of the river, according to the State Water Control Board's report, although its report credited the company with upgrading its sewage treatment plant. Additionally, Carolanne Farms sewage treatment plant, owned by Kempsville Utilities, contributed to the problems of the river. The Campostella Heights neighborhood and, to a smaller degree, nearby Newton Park discharged raw sewage into Steamboat Creek, just east of the Campostella Bridge. Ten homes in old Newton Park had sewage lines tied directly to an outfall into the river. Oil spillage from ships passing down the river had also been reported as problematic; the United States Coast Guard had reported that in 1974 oil spills totaled 40,729 gallons for the Elizabeth River alone. Oozings from the city of Norfolk's landfill at Campostella presented another serious set of problems—but there were no immediate solutions offered when they were identified in the mid-seventies.

Creosote was yet another longtime river contaminate, as was Virginia Electric and Power Company's (now Virginia Power's) power generating plant on the Southern Branch of the river near the Gilmerton Bridge, which discharged large amounts of water used for cooling condensers, as well as chlorinated water, that adversely affected aquatic life. Another significant problem in the river at that time was zinc and large quantities of metals from ship refitting work in which paint spills and ship hull scrapings were dumped. Virginia Chemicals, then a manufacturer of textile chemicals and components for the refrigeration industry, had been located on the western bank of the river for nearly seventy years, since the turn of the twentieth century, when textile mills also dotted the Elizabeth's waterfront in Berkley, South Norfolk, Tanner's Creek and Portsmouth.

There were reasons other than gluttony and pollution that depleted Crassostrea virginica—*the American oyster. At the time of the Civil War, 650,000 bushels of seed oysters were carried annually from Maryland and Virginia to the North in attempts to replenish oyster beds. But in addition to this practice, Northerners also ate transplanted three- and four-year-old oysterlings before the* C. virginicas *were able to reproduce themselves. Oyster beds in the North never recovered.*

The 1,100-acre Craney Island Fuel Terminal is the U.S. Navy's largest fuel facility in the country. The facility was first opened in 1918.

The Norfolk floodwall pumping station and a portion of the wall were under construction in this picture, taken in 1968. The large building on the right is the Boush Cold Storage facility and the structure to the immediate right of the pumping station is occupied by Southern Sanitary Company. The Boush Cold Storage building was converted to condominiums in the 1980s. *Courtesy of the United States Army Corps of Engineers, Norfolk District.*

The State Water Control Board estimated that the firm had dumped 3½ pounds of zinc a day into the river, plus 2,100 pounds a day of sulfites and 303 pounds a day of ammonia. Unfortunately, the EPA, which issued the company's water discharge permit, also allowed the firm to dump a maximum of 7 pounds of zinc a day into the river. Virginia Chemicals, Virginia Electric and Power Company, Gulf Oil Company and the Hampton Roads Sanitation District had been cited in 1976 for separate violations of their discharge permits.

Interestingly, Tanner's Creek (popularly known as the Lafayette River) had gotten a worse report than the Elizabeth River from the State Water Control Board. The water quality of Tanner's Creek was considered poor, particularly with respect to fecal coliforms, noted the state report. Such water degradation came from a small amount of freshwater inflow, urban runoff, boating and marina activities and the influx of wastewater from area sewage treatment facilities. Tidal flushing at the mouth of Tanner's Creek was relatively poor. Effluents from Lambert's Point and the sewage treatment plant near the Norfolk International Terminals mixed with the river and remained for many tidal cycles. As a result, nutrients concentrated in the water and sediments, subsequently resulting in nuisance growths of sea lettuce (*Ulva lactuca*) that had plagued portions of the Elizabeth in the decade before the water control board's report in the mid-seventies. Sea lettuce, an abnormal algae growth, is considered by some marine scientists

Sailboats gathered for Harborfest, Norfolk's annual waterfront festival held at Town Point Park, in 1979. *Courtesy of Norfolk Harborfest.*

The maximum concentration of total PAH recognized in the entire Elizabeth River system was obtained proximal to the Norfolk Naval Shipyard, according to SPAWAR's 2003 study, whose authors suggest "shipbuilding and repair operations and the associated shipping/anchorage activities are the most likely source of PAH in the river." Lower concentrations of PAH were found proximal to the Atlantic Wood Industries and Eppinger and Russell properties. These concentrations were suggested to be the result of "creosote spills and runoff."

to be more threatening than bacteria to aquatic life because it saps oxygen content from the water. The upper reaches of Tanner's Creek, east of the Granby Street Bridge, were responsible for most of the contamination. The Lafayette Park Zoo (now the Virginia Zoo) had also been cited for contributing pollutants into the creek.

There were few optimists when the state issued its water quality assessment in 1976. Dr. Bruce Neilson, of the Virginia Institute of Marine Science (VIMS) and a registered engineer who had studied the river system since 1973, was one of these optimists. Neilson produced another study of the river that analyzed sewage treatment plant operations along the river's shores. His conclusion: the Elizabeth River was not an industrial sewer. "I think it's better than that," he told the *Ledger-Star*'s Jack Dorsey. "At least it has the potential to come back." Neilson's report, published in 1975, demonstrated numerous violations of the dissolved oxygen standards over several miles of the river. Dissolved oxygen is the term used to determine the amount of oxygen required in the water to support aquatic life. An overabundance of certain chemicals causes plant life to thrive beyond normal capacities, thus robbing the environment of the oxygen needed to sustain fish and shellfish. Neilson's study also pinpointed heavy concentrations of metals, including copper, zinc, mercury and lead. The heaviest concentrations of metals were found near industrial centers collocated with the Norfolk Naval Shipyard in Portsmouth, the Smith-Douglass Plant and the Virginia Electric and Power Company generating plant near the Gilmerton Bridge and the Washington Sewage Treatment Plant near the High Rise Bridge that carries Interstate 64 over the Southern Branch of the Elizabeth River.

A *Virginian-Pilot* editorial on August 1, 1985, observed that the notoriety gained by Cleveland, Ohio's Cuyahoga River, which once caught on fire, might be eclipsed. "More than a hundred years of sludge, trash, chemicals and raw sewage entitles Hampton Roads' Elizabeth River to high standing on the country's list of filthiest tributaries," wrote the

Waterside Festival Marketplace, Phase I, shown here in 1985, opened in 1983 and was a key development in the revitalization of downtown Norfolk's waterfront. When first opened it contained over one hundred specialty shops, kiosks and restaurants. The marketplace, even today, is considered a fine example of urban waterfront retail development in the United States. Phase II opened in 1990. Its location overlooking the Elizabeth River is one of the most pleasing vistas in the city. Waterside Associates Limited Partnership, an affiliate of the Enterprise Development Company of Columbia, Maryland, developed it as well as similar facilities in a host of other cities across the country. The Enterprise Development Company was founded by James W. Rouse, founder and former chief executive of the Rouse Company. *Courtesy of Norfolk Harborfest.*

Pilot's editors. Then-Virginia Governor Charles Robb called the Elizabeth River's pollution "clearly the worst of the worst." Handwringing over the Elizabeth River's polluted condition came easily, they said; finding solutions was a bit trickier. A summary of headlines from Elizabeth River news stories published in the *Virginian-Pilot* between 1975 and 1985 only proved their point:

> *"Elizabeth River polluted beyond early recovery?"—May 17, 1975*
> *"Dirty, abused Elizabeth River needs help"—September 1, 1977*
> *"Dirty river may worsen"—June 19, 1980*
> *"Hope fades for cleaner Elizabeth"—November 11, 1980*
> *"Carcinogens pollute Elizabeth River"—May 19, 1983*
> *"Elizabeth River awash in sewage"—April 15, 1984*

Little had changed since the State Water Control Board report in 1976 that had drawn so much attention to the plight of the river. When the board issued its bad news on the river's health, included in an assessment completed in January 1984, the report indicated that concentrations of toxic metals, including mercury, chromium, cadmium, zinc and copper, in the Elizabeth River had reached up to ninety-seven times the amount considered hazardous by the EPA. Pollution from nickel was recorded as fifteen times greater than the level that has chronic harmful effects on aquatic life. In 1972 the EPA reported that mercury levels in the Elizabeth River were three times the level of safety. There was little doubt that the river's condition was growing worse. At the end of July 1985 the EPA reported that it was considering placing Atlantic Wood Industries, a wood treatment plant situated near the Jordan Bridge, on the Superfund list of sites with major hazardous waste problems. The firm, according to the EPA, had caused severe creosote pollution. Superfund listing gives the EPA authority to take owners of hazardous waste sites to court to force a cleanup.

"The metals, the creosote, the sewage and who knows what else that lies in the Elizabeth pose no threat to human health," continued the *Pilot*'s editors, "that is, so long as people do not drink or swim in the water or eat fish caught there. But the precise effects of pollutants on river life remain unknown. Neither is there an abundance of knowledge on the dynamics of water movement—and the pollution contained there—within the Chesapeake Bay and its tributaries, of which the Elizabeth River is one."

The brown pelican is the symbol of The Elizabeth River Project (ERP) because the large bird was down to fewer than two hundred on the East Coast before dichloro diphenyl trichloroethane (DDT) was banned. Now the intrepid brown pelican has returned in plentiful numbers—symbolic of the hope for river recovery. There were no brown pelicans seen on the Elizabeth River until the 1980s. The original drawing of the brown pelican was wrought by artist Steve Sierigk; an update of the logo was completed by marketing professional Tammy Deane and debuted in the summer of 2006. *Courtesy of The Elizabeth River Project.*

THE ELIZABETH RIVER

Money Point was named, as local folklore goes, for treasure the pirate Blackbeard buried off of its shores. Others paint a different picture of a place where people could make a dollar. Many residents along the river's Southern Branch historically made their living through industries located at Money Point, which included fertilizer plants, plastic and leather shops or creosote plants, but they were also employed elsewhere along the branch, typically at textile and lumber mills.

The Chesapeake Bay is a single, migratory system, according to marine scientists. During periods of high water, a storm or a disturbance of the river bottom caused by dredging, the pollution lying in the Elizabeth River becomes suspended in the water and can move. While boards and agencies hoped to have plans to clean up the Elizabeth River, many formed committees and commissions with advisory groups, such as the United States Navy, but none, largely due to budgetary constraints, did much to turn the river's poor condition around. "The Elizabeth River, it should be recalled, was once a pristine stream flowing from the tall pines and cypresses of the Dismal Swamp to the Chesapeake Bay," concluded the *Pilot*'s editorial. "Now it's an ugly mess, made so by man. Man must set it right."

Early efforts to mitigate pollution and revive decaying waterfronts in Norfolk and Portsmouth varied in their success. Bill Geroux, a writer for the *Richmond Times-Dispatch*, observed dorsal fins cutting the surface of the water directly over the Midtown Tunnel. Three young bottlenose dolphins wheeled gracefully out of the water and then dove. They were feeding, Robin Bedenbaugh, a researcher at Old Dominion University, told Geroux, as he angled his johnboat in for a closer look. To Geroux, whose article appeared in the *Times-Dispatch* on July 21, 1991, the grimy Elizabeth seemed an unlikely place to watch dolphins play. The river is so sick in parts, he wrote, that scientists use it as a laboratory to study pollution. Cleanup strategies that had helped other rivers barely seemed to scrape the Elizabeth's crust of pollution. But for all of its problems, the Elizabeth remains a living, working part of the bay system, he observed. A decade and a half ago the river that Geroux came to write about had teemed with crabs and eels and served as a nursery for migratory fish and birds. "It's disgusting," Jolene Chinchilli of the Chesapeake Bay Foundation said of the river, "but it's not dead." To those looking to mitigate the river's problems, consideration had to be given to the Elizabeth's changing shape. Constant dredging and filling to keep channels open for ship traffic has left the Elizabeth twice as deep and two-thirds as wide as it was during colonial times. Unlike other rivers of the lower bay—the Potomac, James, York and Rappahannock—the Elizabeth receives little fresh water from its tributaries, but it also spills little into the Chesapeake Bay. "Generally, what goes into the Elizabeth tends to stay in there a long time," Dr. Raymond Alden Jr., a pollution specialist at Old Dominion University's Applied Marine Research Laboratory, told the *Times-Dispatch* in July 1991. What goes in is a "witches' brew" of potential contaminants. The brew includes heavy metals, many already mentioned, and organic compounds such as polychlorinated biphenyls (PCBs), pentachlorophenols (PCPs) and polycyclic aromatic hydrocarbons (PAHs) that are known to cause cancer.

Restoration A Reality

The Craney Island Dredged Material Management Area (CIDMMA) has grown to a 2,500-acre man-made confined dredged material disposal site located near the mouth of the Elizabeth opposite Lambert's Point. The area is divided into three cells. One cell is always being pumped into while the other two are drying out. A weir across the stream controls the flow of water out of one area into another. The weirs on Craney Island separate dredged material settling to the bottom from clear water on the surface, thus permitting clear water to flow back into the harbor. Plans for the site developed in the early 1940s to provide a long-term disposal area for material dredged from the channels and ports of Hampton Roads, largely the Elizabeth River. The amount of dredge material deposited there has increased with nearly every dredge project that has taken place in Hampton Roads since World War II. Hampton Roads is generally recognized as the southernmost boundary of the Boston-New York-Washington industrial, commercial, residential and recreational complex. Commercial, agricultural and industrial development in the Elizabeth River watershed, in particular, is largely dependent on maintaining project depths in the Hampton Roads channels. Prior to and during World War II dredged material removed from the channels was primarily disposed of in open water sites. As open water sites neared capacity at war's end, Congress authorized a study to determine a more permanent and lasting means for disposing of dredged material from the Hampton Roads area. As a result, development of the Craney Island disposal area was recommended and approved by Congress under the River and Harbor

In 1998 the Cities of Chesapeake, Norfolk, Portsmouth and Virginia Beach, the Commonwealth of Virginia and the United States government signed a historic agreement "for the river's rebirth"—agreeing to cost-share a $2.4 million feasibility study by the U.S. Army Corps of Engineers, Norfolk District, for the cleanup of Scuffletown Creek and restoration of twenty-two acres of wetlands. *Courtesy of The Elizabeth River Project.*

The Elizabeth River

In 1963 huge tanks caught fire at the former Eppinger and Russell wood treatment plant; eighteen firemen were injured and at least forty thousand gallons of raw creosote, the tar used to treat telephone poles, escaped toward the Elizabeth River at Money Point.

Act of 1946. Actual construction of the first phase of the Craney Island dredge area was completed in 1957. Since that time this site has received maintenance and private and permit dredged material from numerous dredging projects in the Hampton Roads area.

Within the Craney Island dredge area natural growth of marsh and upland vegetation has created an important wildlife habitat and is a stopover point for many species of birds on the Atlantic Flyway. The United States Army Corps of Engineers Norfolk District's Craney Island Dredged Material Area staff received the Virginia Society of Ornithology Jack M. Abbott Conservation Award for 1996. The award was presented for the corps' contributions and assistance in the creation, protection and preservation of critical habitat for beach nesting birds. The management of these nesting areas and protection of these sites have resulted in the increased population of the piping plover and the least tern. The bird protection project first became formal in 1984 under a cooperative agreement with the College of William and Mary and the Virginia Department of Game and Inland Fisheries.

Pollution and dredging have exacted a heavy price on aquatic life

NOVA Chemicals, a Model Level River Star, was the first industry on the Elizabeth River to achieve a large voluntary habitat restoration with the planting of eleven acres of native trees and shrubs for migratory songbirds on the river's Southern Branch. The project received recognition in the *Wall Street Journal*. This picture was taken by Van White on September 30, 2006, at dusk looking across Mains Creek. Mains Creek flows to the left into the Elizabeth River's Southern Branch. *Courtesy of Van H. White, www. VansPhotos.com.*

from the bottom of the food chain up. The Elizabeth's communities of plankton and bottom-dwelling aqua life have been ebbed down to a few more resilient species. Over fifteen years ago, when VIMS caught fish in the river for toxicology studies, they found species with cancer of the liver and other organs, with cataracts, rotted fins, lesions and tumors. Scientists wrote then that constant exposure to the river's poisons weakened the fishes' immune systems and left them vulnerable to bacteria they might otherwise be able to fight off. Every year, even today, young spot and mullet continue to swim into the Elizabeth's upper reaches, past known hot spots of pollution, to seek food and protected waters. Dolphins and other predators follow them into the river. There have been no restrictions on fishing and crabbing in the Elizabeth and no fishing advisory is in effect for the river or its tributaries. Like many rivers in Virginia, the Elizabeth feeds a number of subsistence fishermen and their families. In the 1990s crabbers harvested between 150,000 and 250,000 pounds of crab from the river every year and sold them to seafood houses in South Hampton Roads. Despite being the most industrial tributary of the Elizabeth, the Southern Branch of the river also offers commercial and recreational fishing and crabbing. Particularly abundant seasonal fish include bluefish, spot and Atlantic croaker. American eel and striped bass, particularly juveniles, are also common, according to a 1999 National Oceanic and Atmospheric Administration report. A variety of shellfish species can also be found in the Southern Branch, including crabs and hard clams (Northern quahogs, sp. *Mercenaria mercenaria*); however, since 1925 the Virginia Department of Health (VDH) has prohibited harvesting of most

Then-Environmental
Protection Agency
(EPA) Administrator
Christine Todd
Whitman visited
The Elizabeth River
Project in August
2002 commensurate
with EPA funding
for the Paradise
Creek restoration.
She observed then,
"If you're looking
for an example
of the success of
partnerships, The
Elizabeth River
Project is the model."
*Courtesy of The
Elizabeth River Project.*

*Stormwater education
received a long-term
boost when cities
and counties of the
Hampton Roads
Planning District
helped The Elizabeth
River Project establish
a permanent exhibit
on the topic at
NAUTICUS, the
National Maritime
Center.*

shellfish (species other than crabs, including oysters, clams and mussels) from the Elizabeth River and its tributaries. According to VDH, this prohibition is based on elevated levels of bacteriologic contamination in the Elizabeth's waterways.

The river's Western Branch and the upper part of its Eastern Branch remain relatively clean, its shores lined with wetlands and residences, but the main stem, Southern Branch and part of the Eastern Branch are of greatest concern. Even after the Clean Water Act of 1972, which required action to make waterways fishable and swimmable, cleanup of the Elizabeth lagged far behind that of other rivers for years. The United States Navy and local industries were loath to surrender control of the river. The public had much of their access to it curtailed over the years, and it would take some time for a "friends of the Elizabeth" organization to spring to action. There were important initiatives, nonetheless, to revive downtown waterfronts that had slipped into decay in the years following World War II. The 1983 opening of the Waterside Festival Marketplace on the Norfolk waterfront brought many local people to the river's edge for the first time, while others returned after decades of having avoided a depressed downtown. An earlier effort, designed to draw public interest to the water's edge and back to the city center in larger number, had nothing to do with buildings but everything to do with sculpting a new image for the Norfolk waterfront. During the summer of 1975 the Norwegian sail training ship *Christian Radich* visited Norfolk's harbor; thousands of people turned out to see her. By July 4, 1976, the city was preparing for the arrival of tall ships from New York City that had just taken part in Operation Sail, a national event. Ships from four countries came to Norfolk as part of what became Norfolk's Op Sail '76. As preparation for the event, the City of Norfolk dredged Otter Berth and constructed a pier. Last-minute preparations were still ongoing as tall ships made their way up the Elizabeth River toward Town Point. More than fifty thousand people visited the ships while in port; this was the beginning of Norfolk's annual Harborfest, an annual event that inspired the return of investment in downtown Norfolk. Waterside Festival Marketplace came to fruition as those drawn by Harborfest proved that people would come back to the city center.

While Harborfest was the brainchild of Norfolk civic leaders Timothy Jones and John R. Sears Jr., it was also the vision of Charles A. Miller, Donald W. Mathias, Lane A. Briggs, Dennis Richardson, Shields Parsons and many others who had in common a group known as Nautical Adventures. There were about ten individuals who formed the heart and soul of Harborfest and held leadership positions in Nautical Adventures, founded in 1977 to preserve the maritime heritage and promote waterfront development in Norfolk. In its second year, 1977, Harborfest featured the *Pride of Baltimore*, a 136-foot two-masted schooner owned by the City of Baltimore. The presence of this 1812 period replica vessel drove festival attendance higher than Op Sail '76. Attendance would increase exponentially with the coming year, as anticipation of tall ships, music and merriment on the downtown Norfolk waterfront spread across Hampton Roads. Visitation rose from 80,000 in 1977 to in excess of 150,000 in 1978. But in the years to come, participants in Harborfest water events would realize that the Elizabeth was no playground. During the 1991 event VIMS researcher Jon A. Lucy scraped his knee while paddling in a boating competition. The following day his leg was infected and swollen.

The 1978 Harborfest event was the year that Allegheny Beverage Corporation of Baltimore gave the historic Chesapeake Bay skipjack, one of the remaining few, to the City of Norfolk. Dating to 1900, she was built at Deal Island, Maryland, and originally christened the *George W. Collier*. She was restored in 1970 at Deagle's Boat Yard in Deltaville, Virginia, and rechristened the *Allegheny*. In 1978, after Allegheny Beverage gifted the boat to the city, she was christened *Norfolk* and underwent initial restoration under a maritime preservation grant awarded by the National Trust for Historic Preservation. This wooden skipjack was designed for working Chesapeake Bay oyster beds in heavy winds. It has a raked mast, low profile and shallow draft. It measures fifty-one feet four inches from stem to rudder and seventy-one feet from the bowsprit to the end of the boom. The mast is fifty-seven feet high and the main mast and jib have

The highest concentrations of total PAH in the entire Elizabeth River system were recorded just downstream from the former Eppinger and Russell property. There were two reported releases of thousands of gallons of creosote, what some reports indicate was a mix of creosote and coal tar mix, from the Eppinger and Russell property in 1960 and 1963, recorded as the likely source of elevated PAH observed just downstream. According to a September 2003 SPAWAR Systems Center San Diego study addressing sources of PAH in sediments in the vicinity of the Norfolk Naval Shipyard, no chemical fingerprinting evidence was provided to support this contention.

The Elizabeth River Project moved to Portsmouth's downtown waterfront in 2003. Held at Admiral's Landing next to the ferry dock on the Elizabeth River, the ribbon cutting was attended by (left to right) Marjorie Mayfield Jackson, executive director, The Elizabeth River Project; Richard S. Bray Jr., president, Beasley Foundation; Guy M. Aydlett, director of Water Quality, Hampton Roads Sanitation District (HRSD); R. Scott Morgan, former chair, Portsmouth Redevelopment and Housing Authority (PRHA); Angelica D. Light, president, Norfolk Foundation; Dr. James W. Holley III, mayor, city of Portsmouth; Paul D. Fraim, mayor, city of Norfolk; and Meyera E. Oberndorf, mayor, city of Virginia Beach. *Courtesy of the Hampton Roads Sanitation District.*

a total sail area of eighteen hundred square feet. This ten-ton boat has a draft of three to seven feet. The skipjack *Norfolk* was for many years a goodwill ambassador for the city of Norfolk and a training ship for Sea Scout Explorer Troop VI, sponsored by Nautical Adventures. On November 24, 2004, the skipjack was moved to Cobb's Marina at Ocean View. The *Norfolk* is one of the last authentic skipjacks in existence—and the second oldest. As such, she is an artifact from a bygone era of the Chesapeake Bay. She symbolizes the days when oyster boats raced one another to port, with the first boat at dockside gaining the highest price for prime oysters. The skipjack had been long outmoded by higher-powered vessels and restrictions on oyster dredging in the bay.

The fate of skipjacks followed that of the oyster. Over the past century the oyster population in the Chesapeake Bay and the Elizabeth River has been reduced by as much as 99 percent. Environmental stressors that spurred this decline included over harvesting, disease and pollution. Past harvesting techniques flattened reefs, resulting in less-than-optimal population levels for reproduction. Two introduced parasites, MSX and Dermo, have further taken their toll on oyster populations. Development and urbanization throughout the bay and Elizabeth River has resulted in increased sediment and contaminant loading that also has detrimental effects on oyster populations. While these factors still plague oyster populations, results seen in the Elizabeth River show that large-scale restoration is effective in jump-starting a local population of oysters. Today, the Elizabeth River has one of the highest number of sanctuary oyster reefs anywhere in the Chesapeake Bay, rivaled only by the much larger

Elizabeth River Project member Chris Daniel took this photograph of a dead bird recently found on the river's edge. Severe habitat loss is one of the greatest stressors on the river's ecosystem. The watershed, however, still provides a viable— and improving— habitat for migratory songbirds making their way along the Atlantic Flyway. *Courtesy of The Elizabeth River Project.*

The Elizabeth River Project and the City of Norfolk won the international Clearwater Award in 1997 for Birdsong Wetland. The success inspired the restoration of Pescara Creek Wetland in Norfolk in 1999 and the creation of Oscar's Landing Wetland in Chesapeake in 2002. Virginia Beach set aside $50 million for land acquisition and conservation and began a scenic greenway on the Eastern Branch.

Rappahannock River. Because of its restored reefs, the Elizabeth is one of the areas in which native oysters are recovering. Oysters are now seen growing on every piling, where ten years ago one would be hard pressed to find any growing throughout the river, according to 2006 information.

The State Water Control Board undertook the Elizabeth River Initiative, a series of measures designed to prioritize the river's problems and find solutions, in 1988. The coordinator of this effort was Debra Trent. Trent's first step was to "turn off the valves" of the industries crowding the riverbank that had been spilling toxic substances into the Elizabeth for decades with little interference. But there were many "valves" to shut off and some industrial polluters, such as the Norfolk Naval Station and Norfolk Naval Shipyard, had been operating for decades by their own rules, exempt from state regulations. The navy had already become largely cooperative, but the task of stemming pollution from the hundreds

Mummichogs (*Fundulus heteroclitus*) are small fish—reaching only four to six inches in length—that are plentiful along the bottom of the Elizabeth River. Unlike many fish that migrate great distances, the mummichog travels only about fifty yards in its lifetime, making it an ideal measure of the health of its immediate environment. On the Elizabeth's Southern Branch, the mummichogs have exhibited cancer and precancerous lesions at a rate as high as 90 percent, due largely to creosote contamination from old wood treatment plants along the Southern Branch. The mummichog is an important food source for better-known species such as striped bass, bluefish, red drum and trout, as well as wading birds such as egrets and herons. *Courtesy of Bill Tiernan and the* Virginian-Pilot.

of pipes in its huge, aging facilities had become overwhelming. During Trent's tenure, no one had figured out what to do with the Elizabeth's underwater toxic goo. Leaving those sediments alone in anticipation of cleaner sediments burying the bad was considered, but as long as dredging continues in the river, toxic substances are unlikely to remain buried.

Marjorie Mayfield Jackson saw a different Elizabeth River. In the late 1980s she had moved into an idyllic home on Portsmouth's Scott's Creek, though she has since moved to Tanner's Creek. The former *Virginian-Pilot* reporter observed that she would walk out on the dock behind the house and see the fish jumping, the night herons roosting in her mulberry tree or stalking in the shallows. "It was a very beautiful, special place to me," she said later. But her sheltered, quieted piece of the river was also deceiving. "There was all this beauty," she continued, "yet the headlines were quoting scientific reports about the fish having cancer. It made me sad. I would enjoy the sunset and try not to look down. I would feel guilty, sick for our community, that the health of our river was so poor." Jackson did not ignore her feelings for the river, realizing that there was still an opportunity to make a significant impact on the health of the Elizabeth. In late 1991 Jackson and three other concerned citizens—Sharon Quillen Adams, Michael Kensler and Robert Dean—met around a kitchen table to discuss the river's condition. Adams had been active with the Women's League of Voters and had been part of a citizens' roundtable that established the Chesapeake Bay Act to protect the buffer along Virginia's waterfront. Kensler, at that time, was manager of the Hampton Roads office of the Chesapeake Bay Foundation (he has since moved to Maryland with the Foundation). Dean was founder of Clean the Bay Day, a volunteer group that had begun an annual cleanup

of the bay shores. "At the time," noted Jackson in a later interview, "a lot of people thought that the river was dead. I could see it wasn't, with all that life in my protected little corner. The four of us wondered whether there would be an interest among the citizens of the area to try and bring back the health of our home river. We didn't know the answer at that time." Within a year of their meeting Jackson had resigned from the *Virginian-Pilot* to begin building The Elizabeth River Project, an independent, grass-roots nonprofit that has served since its founding as a catalyst—and advocate—for cleaning up the river. Their premise: the river's large problems could not be solved by government alone, but by a new level of community stewardship. In the first year of the Project's existence, Jackson worked as a freelance writer and waited tables to supplement her thirty-three-dollar-a-week salary. In 1993 The Elizabeth River Project incorporated, and the following year had secured a grant from the Environmental Protection Agency for a comparative risk planning project. Jackson used the grant to poll sixty people from all walks of life to identify problems with the river and suggest solutions. She found that various interests were alienated, most seeing nothing in common with one another. But they all agreed, she concluded, that the river was the lifeblood of the local economy.

Jackson's canvas of the river's users and abusers also revealed that for river restoration to be truly successful, involvement had to take place at every level. One of the most crucial plans, observed Jackson,

Then-Virginia Governor Mark Warner visited The Elizabeth River Project in 2004 to announce a trust fund for cleaning up the river's sediments. Warner is shown on the Elizabeth River Ferry discussing his environmental views with student participants from River Star schools. *Courtesy of The Elizabeth River Project.*

The Virginia Port Authority (VPA) created Plum Point Park in 2004 on five acres of waterfront formed from the dredge spoils of the Midtown Tunnel. The port authority is a Model Level River Star, recognized widely for its progress in implementing pollution prevention and habitat projects. *Courtesy of the Virginia Port Authority.*

Paradise Creek presents a microcosm of the Elizabeth River—its challenges and its promise. Reaching 2.6 miles into Portsmouth from the Southern Branch of the Elizabeth, the creek is lined with industrial facilities to the north and the Cradock community to the south. Open spaces harbor surprising levels of wildlife.

was for the United States Army Corps of Engineers to remove badly contaminated sediment from the river bottom. Participating industries now follow the Project's "clean fourteen"—a fourteen-step watershed action plan first debuted on June 20, 1996. The Elizabeth River Project remains unique in its nonconfrontational approach to currying participation from industrial and residential partners. To avoid the inevitable finger-pointing among the river's polluters, The Elizabeth River Project has galvanized diverse interests to clean it up. After four centuries as a world center of maritime commerce and

naval power, few rivers are more intensely industrialized, and few are more important to American security and economic vitality, than the Elizabeth in Lower Tidewater. Millions of dollars in voluntary environmental improvements are being spent by all major sectors of the Elizabeth's great harbor—interests that in 1991 seemed hopelessly opposed to working together. Until The Elizabeth River Project introduced its first watershed action plan, much of the surrounding community believed the river was dead. Today, all four river cities, the state and the federal government are proactively working together to clean the river bottom, having funded a multi-million-dollar project developed by the United States Army Corps of Engineers to clean the toxic river bottom and restore nine wetland sites. Leaders of the four cities bordering the Elizabeth, as well as industry leaders and state officials, had signed a historic agreement on October 5, 2000. The joint signing was a victory for the river and The Elizabeth River Project. The corps' cleanup of the river bottom started with Scuffletown Creek, which flows beside Elizabeth River Park near the Chesapeake end of the Jordan Bridge. The creek is loaded with tar-like creosote, chemicals and heavy metals including lead, zinc and chromium.

This white egret is juxtaposed against trash at the water's edge in this Van H. White photograph. *Courtesy of Van H. White, www. VansPhotos.com.*

A survey by The Elizabeth River Project found that many people still consume fish from the Elizabeth River despite the EPA's contamination study of the river's fish tissue that warned eating as much as two fish per month increases the risk of cancer. This picture was taken by Jacqueline Murphy Miller. *Courtesy of The Elizabeth River Project.*

The River Star program is the grass-roots Elizabeth River Project's way of involving the business sector in a community-wide initiative to restore the environmental health of the Elizabeth River. When people shop for services today, they look for evidence of environmental stewardship. River Star's participation means you care.

Creosote, black sticky goo used as a sealant for telephone poles, pilings and bulkheads, is the most powerful of the pollutants and is suspected of causing cancer. The Chesapeake Health Department recommends against swimming or fishing in Scuffletown Creek and other waters on the Southern Branch. In addition to dredging toxins from the bottom of Scuffletown Creek, nine wetland restoration projects were included in the 2000 agreement: Scuffletown Creek itself, Carolanne Farms, Northwest Jordan Bridge, Crawford Bay, Woodstock Park, Lancelot Drive, Grandy Village, Old Dominion University Drainage Canal and Portsmouth City Park.

The number one priority in the Elizabeth River watershed action plan is to remove contamination from the river bottom, documented at as high as 463 times the average for the Chesapeake Bay for polycyclic aromatic hydrocarbons (PAH). The motto of this effort is "the goo must go." *Courtesy of The Elizabeth River Project.*

The Learning Barge was designed by University of Virginia architectural professor Phoebe Crisman and her graduate architecture students as a community outreach project in support of The Elizabeth River Project. Design features include a wetland nursery on board, an "artifacts wall," enclosed classroom space and open decks. The barge was also designed as a field station for The Elizabeth River Project's "one creek at a time" initiative.

The Elizabeth River has shown some of the most significant improvements in water quality of any tributary of the Chesapeake Bay since 1992. In a period of human history in which mankind has trashed much of its habitat, environmental progress on the Elizabeth has been a hopeful sign that those who have abused Mother Nature can also show her great kindnesses. The Elizabeth River Project's partnership approach has drawn substantial interest from national environmental groups. "If you're looking for an example of the success of partnerships," said then-EPA Administrator Christine Todd Whitman, "The Elizabeth River Project is the model." She visited The Elizabeth River Project on July 29,

Marjorie Mayfield Jackson helped found The Elizabeth River Project in November 1991 as one of four citizens around a kitchen table who sculpted this critical effort to save the river. By 2006 the project had grown to an operating budget of $2.8 million, eight employees, fifty-five River Star industries, fifty-nine River Star schools and federal, state and local partners engaged in hundreds of projects. Jackson is The Elizabeth River Project's first and only executive director. This photograph of Jackson in hip boots was taken by *Virginian-Pilot* photographer Bill Tiernan for an April 2006 feature story in the newspaper. *Courtesy of Bill Tiernan and the* Virginian-Pilot.

2002, to present a $100,000 check for the restoration of Paradise Creek as a model for the Chesapeake Bay. The EPA's recognition came on the heels of a study commissioned by The Elizabeth River Project, which had hired a North Carolina State University environmental innovator, Dr. Bill Hunt, to conduct an analysis of thirty sites for runoff improvements and recommend unique solutions. One recommendation was floating wetlands on barges. Floodwaters would be pumped to the barges and used to nurture flowering gardens and grasses, noted Jackson. Today, Hunt's vision for such a barge has been developed as a collaborative project between The Elizabeth River Project and the University of Virginia School of Architecture. This innovative and self-sustaining floating environmental education field station, called the Learning Barge, is designed to move between ongoing restoration sites, serving as an operational headquarters and providing meaningful, hands-on kindergarten through twelfth grade and public environmental education about how the river and humans are inextricably interconnected.

Since The Elizabeth River Project's incorporation in 1993, the Project and its partner agencies have completed hundreds of environmental improvement projects. These efforts have been scattered across the Elizabeth River's urban watershed, where a diverse array of restoration and conservation methods have achieved award-winning wetland restorations, stormwater innovations and public education, wildlife habitat and pollution prevention advances with industrial partners and the initiation of the aforementioned demonstration effort by the United States Army Corps of Engineers to clean the toxic river bottom. On August 1, 2003, the Project introduced a plan to restore Paradise Creek as a model for how to restore the Elizabeth River and the Chesapeake Bay—"one creek at a time." Paradise Creek presents a microcosm of the Elizabeth River—its challenges and its promise. Reaching 2.6 miles into Portsmouth from the Southern Branch of the Elizabeth, the creek is lined with industrial facilities to the north and the Cradock community to the south. Paradise Creek regularly receives large, potentially polluted volumes of fresh water—not from a spring, not from industrial wastewater, but in the runoff from each rain. In urban cities such as Portsmouth, stormwater runoff typically contains sediments, nutrients, bacteria, oil, grease and heavy metals. Built before runoff pollution was identified as a concern, the city's aging stormwater pipes are designed to send the runoff directly to the creek as quickly as possible, with no treatment except in isolated instances. Paradise Creek's stormwater pipes, emptying into the creek at thirty-two different points, drain as much as a third of the city of Portsmouth. The creek's open spaces, however, harbor surprising levels of wildlife. While old navy landfills on the shores of Paradise Creek exemplify past abuses, actually making the National Priorities/Superfund listing for the urgency of the contamination, the United States Navy, its industrial, municipal and residential neighbors became zealous partners in its restoration plan. "Restoring an urban river is a long and daunting task," said Marjorie Mayfield Jackson of the project. "Through this planning process, we have found a Paradise Creek that lives up to its name: holding forth our highest hopes for our river's future."

Environmental stewardship of the Elizabeth has led to precedent-setting collaborations, among them an initiative to restore oyster reefs to the river's most polluted tributaries. Restored reefs are created by placing multiple piles of old oyster shells on hard bottom areas of the river, allowing young oysters to settle, grow and reproduce. In the summer of 2004, The Elizabeth River Project created three new native oyster reefs in the Southern Branch of the Elizabeth River, the most impacted part of the river. One reef was restored at the mouth of Paradise Creek, a Portsmouth sub-watershed that is undergoing intense restoration activities. A second reef was constructed near the Jordan Bridge and a third adjacent to Norfolk Shipbuilding and Drydock Company (NORSHIPCO) near the mouth of the Southern Branch. Those who funded the reefs included Chesapeake Bay Small Watershed Grant Program; United States Environmental Protection Agency, Chesapeake Bay Program; National Fish and Wildlife Foundation; National Oceanic and Atmospheric Administration; and Fish America. Major partners in the project were the Chesapeake Bay Foundation, Virginia Marine Resources Commission, Virginia Department of Environmental Quality, Oyster Reef Keepers, Giant Cement of Virginia and NORSHIPCO. These bring the number of reefs restored in the Elizabeth to eleven since 1998, when the first was built in the Western Branch. As a result, one of the highest settlements of new

Seven thousand square feet of degraded wetland adjoining Scott's Creek have a new lease on life thanks to the Naval Medical Center Portsmouth, one of The Elizabeth River Project's Model Level River Stars. The center's employees cleaned out several decades' worth of debris and weeds from the area, graded it and added a layer of sand. Next they installed a low-crested rock sill to minimize erosion and keep out new debris brought in by high tides. The pièce de résistance: two thousand sprigs of native wetland grasses protected from hungry Canada geese by a formidable maze of low posts strung with goose-deterring ribbon.

Elizabeth River Project volunteers add native plants to a "rain garden" to absorb stormwater runoff on Portsmouth's Paradise Creek in the spring of 2006, part of twenty projects to restore the creek as a model for river restoration—"one creek at a time." Pictured are Jim Lang and his daughter, Laura. *Courtesy of David Louria.*

oysters on reefs was recorded in 2002 on the Elizabeth compared to other areas of the Chesapeake Bay. The eleven reef sites include the Hampton Boulevard Bridge and Tanner's Point on Tanner's Creek; Craney Island Creek and Portsmouth Marine Terminal on the Elizabeth River's main stem; the West Norfolk Bridge, on the Western Branch; Ford Motor Company, Norfolk Plant, on the Eastern Branch; and NORSHIPCO, Jordan Bridge, Paradise Creek, Gilmerton Bridge and High Rise Bridge on the Southern Branch. Importantly, too, there was another initiative just as vital to the Elizabeth River's long-term health—the Living River Restoration Trust.

The Living River Restoration Trust, a brainchild of sister organization The Elizabeth River Project, was established in 2004 when the Norfolk District of the United States Army Corps of Engineers, the Virginia Department of Environmental Quality and the Trust's independent board reached agreement on operating guidelines. APM Terminals made the first payment, $5.3 million, that year, to offset ten million cubic yards of dredging for a port terminal, thus helping clean up thirty-five acres of severe contamination off Money Point on the Southern Branch of the Elizabeth River. Today the Living River Restoration Trust meets the needs of developers seeking a win-win approach to offset environmental impacts to the river's watershed, particularly to life along the river bottom, which represents the foundation of the food chain for the Elizabeth River.

Sixteen percent of all life occurs along the bottom of waterways. Striped bass, spot and blue crabs are examples of commercial and recreational fisheries dependent on a healthy river bottom. The Living River Restoration Trust replaces lost habitat for these and other species of this critical link in a healthy ecosystem for Hampton Roads. The Trust is the first mitigation tool of its kind in the United States to be approved by the federal government for compensation of negative impacts to the bottom of a waterway.

A little over three years after initiation of the Paradise Creek restoration project, in October 2006, The Elizabeth River Project, working with the University of Virginia School of Architecture's Institute for Environmental Negotiation, introduced its plan for Money Point's revitalization. For decades the Elizabeth River off Money Point has been a thirty-five-acre biological dead zone. Little can survive along the river bottom, laced with some of the highest concentrations of cancer-causing PAHs in the world. Liver cancer, deformities, cataracts and lesions are found in the fish. Until 2005 the river bottom at Money Point, almost a mile of prominent waterfront on the Southern Branch at the gateway of the city of Chesapeake, was considered a lost cause. No one imagined it was possible to clean it up. In a recent experiment, the popular sport fish, spot, survived for only two hours after being exposed in an aquarium to contaminated sediments removed from the Elizabeth River bottom at Money Point. This

The Elizabeth River is a vibrant working river, home to one of the busiest ports on the East Coast. *Courtesy of the Virginia Port Authority.*

research by the Virginia Institute of Marine Science is only one of a series of studies documenting the effects of severe contamination in this stretch of waterway, intensely industrialized since the early nineteenth century. The plan was born when The Elizabeth River Project was contracted to oversee a sediment cleanup project at Money Point by the Living River Restoration Trust. It calls for cleanup of the largest problem area at Money Point, offshore of the notorious former Eppinger and Russell wood treatment facility, followed thereafter by another offshore of another such facility, Republic Creosoting. Cleanup of these sites, well underway, promises to alleviate some of the Chesapeake Bay's highest levels of PAHs. High levels of this contaminant have been correlated with elevated cancer in an indicator species, the bottom-dwelling mummichog. The health of the mummichog will be tracked to judge the success of cleanup efforts in reviving the bottom-dwelling community of the river.

Efforts to breathe health into the river are working. Marjorie Mayfield Jackson wrote in the fall 2006 *Mudflats* that she had been surprised by yet another magnificent presence in the Elizabeth. It was not the turtle she reported in the summer newsletter; this creature was different. This time Jackson and her sister were about to swim in Tanner's Creek, behind Jackson's house. "Yes," she admitted. "I do occasionally swim in the Lafayette, its water quality having improved markedly in recent years." She noted that the creek's water tastes sweet if it gets in your mouth, and the powdery silt of the bottom is like walking on grainy clouds. Sediment quality is another story, particularly in the Southern Branch, where it remains inadvisable to wade or swim. But behind her home, as she looked down, scouting for jellyfish, Jackson caught a glimpse of large spots gently undulating at the surface of the river. Her first thought was that it was a weird snake, but on closer inspection, the creature had a long, narrow snout, more like a seahorse, and penny-sized spots all the way to its tail fins, which stuck out of the water a full three feet from its head. Jackson started yelling for her husband and sister to come see her discovery. This big fish, gently nosing along the marsh grasses, was a longnose gar, a survivor of an ancient and primitive group of aquatic life that flourished during the age of the dinosaur, before most fish had evolved, and which appeared in John White's paintings and Theodor de Bry's engravings published in 1590, shown in this volume. No one Jackson spoke to had seen such a large longnose gar on the Elizabeth River. When she looked on websites, she found that the longnose gar she had seen was about the size of those posted as records around the country. "Ya'll must be doing your job," Jackson's sister, from out of town, said later. Indeed they must be. The same week Jackson saw the longnose gar, Portsmouth City Attorney G. Timothy Oksman called her from City Hall, which overlooks the Elizabeth River a block from The Elizabeth River Project's waterfront

office. "I have something important to tell you," he said. Jackson braced for Oksman's call to be another legal issue pertaining to the Project's planned waterfront park. "Look out your window," Oksman told Jackson. "A school of about twenty dolphins is going by."

As Charles Kuralt envisaged and this picture of young Landon Cofer confirms, "When the forest returns to the shore, when healthy fish and clams and oysters find a home in the Southern reaches of the river again, and the sun rises off the Atlantic in the morning to reflect itself in the serene, pure waters of the Elizabeth River, our children and grandchildren will know that we had them in mind." *Courtesy of Bill Cofer.*

BIBLIOGRAPHY

PRIMARY SOURCES

Abraham Lincoln Papers. Library of Congress. Manuscripts Division. Transcribed and annotated by the Lincoln Studies Center, Knox College, Galesburg, IL. Specific writings, largely correspondence, are cited in the text.

Annals of Congress. Senate. 10th Congress, 1st session, Volume 1 (through page 920, covering Dismal Swamp Company's survey of 40,000 acres). Library of Congress, U.S. Congressional Documents and Debates, 1774–1875.

City of Chesapeake, Virginia. Department of Public Works. *The Bridges of Chesapeake, Virginia*. Brochure, n.d.

City of Virginia Beach. Department of City Planning. "Elizabeth River Watershed." http://www. vbgov.com/

Department of Agriculture and Immigration, Commonwealth of Virginia. *Virginia—Yorktown Sesquicentennial Issue*. Richmond: Division of Purchase and Printing, 1931.

The Diaries of George Washington, Vol. I. Donald Jackson, editor; Dorothy Twohig, associate editor. Library of Congress. Manuscript Division.

George Washington Papers. Library of Congress. Manuscript Division. Specific writings, largely correspondence, cited in the text were compiled for the period 1741–1799. Information was derived from original images of the correspondence and translations provided by collection editor John C. Fitzpatrick.

James Madison Papers. Library of Congress. Manuscript Division. Specific writings, largely correspondence, cited in the text were compiled for the period 1723–1836. Information was derived from original images of the correspondence and translations provided by collection editor John C.A. Stagg.

Kuralt, Charles. Elizabeth River Project watershed action plan announcement. Keynote address, June 20, 1996.

———."The goodliest land." Address delivered at Scenic America's National Conference, Baltimore, MD, May 12, 1997.

Letters of Delegates to Congress, Vol. 17, March 1, 1781–August 31, 1781. Library of Congress, U.S. Congressional Documents and Debates, 1774–1875. Specific writings, largely correspondence, are cited in the text.

———, Vol. 22, November 1, 1784–November 6, 1785. Library of Congress, U.S. Congressional Documents and Debates, 1774–1875.

Library of Congress. "The Capital and the Bay: Narratives of Washington and the Chesapeake Bay Region, circa 1600–1925." Lake of the Great Dismal: Human Documents Relating to the Dismal Swamp.

Mendenhall, Thomas Corwin. Norfolk Harbor and Vicinity, chart number 404. United States Coast and Geodetic Survey. Washington, D.C.: Government Printing Office, 1891.

National Oceanic and Atmospheric Administration. Coastal Protection and Restoration Division. "Elizabeth River Watershed Contaminant Conceptual Model Project." http://mapping.orr.noaa. gov/website/portal/elizriver/

———. National Weather Service. Hydrometeorological Prediction Center. "Early Nineteenth Century." http://www.hpc.ncep.noaa.gov/research/roth/vaerly19hur.htm

Sanborn fire insurance maps for Norfolk, Virginia.

Slaves and Courts, 1740–1860. Proceedings of the citizens of the Borough of Norfolk, on the Boston outrage, in the case of the runaway slave George Latimer, published in Norfolk by T.G. Broughton and Son, printers, 1843, and all collection documents related to the same. Library of Congress.

Thomas Jefferson Papers. Library of Congress. Manuscript Division. 12 vols., federal edition. Specific writings, largely correspondence, are cited in the text. Information was derived from original images of the correspondence and translations provided for select works by collection editor Paul Leicester Ford.

Three Centuries of Broadsides and Other Printed Ephemera Collection. To the enemies of Jefferson and Madison in the district, Norfolk, April 22, 1809, from the original document. Library of Congress.

U.S. Army Corps of Engineers. Norfolk District. *Cruising into History*, brochure, n.d.

———. *Elizabeth River Basin Restoration*, n.d.

U.S. Congress. House. Committee on Rivers and Harbors. *Inland Waterway from Norfolk, Virginia, to Beaufort Inlet, North Carolina: Letter from the Chief of Engineers, United States Army Transmitting the Report of the Board of Engineers for Rivers and Harbors on the Advisability of Acquiring the Lake Drummond (Dismal Swamp) Canal*. 67th Congress, 2nd session, 1922.

Bibliography

U.S. Congress. *House Journal*, 1st Congress, 2nd session, August 3, 1790. Library of Congress, U.S. Congressional Documents and Debates, 1774–1875. Specific writings, largely correspondence, are cited in the text.

———. 8th Congress, 2nd session, February 19, 1805. Library of Congress, U.S. Congressional Documents and Debates, 1774–1875. Specific writings, largely correspondence, are cited in the text.

———. 10th Congress, 1st session, February 11, 1808. Library of Congress, U.S. Congressional Documents and Debates, 1774–1875. Specific writings, largely correspondence, are cited in the text.

———. 43rd Congress, 1st session, May 9, 1874. Library of Congress, U.S. Congressional Documents and Debates, 1774–1875. Specific writings, largely correspondence, are cited in the text.

U.S. Congress. *Senate Journal*. 14th, 1st session, March 30, 1816. Library of Congress, U.S. Congressional Documents and Debates, 1774–1875. Specific writings, largely correspondence, are cited in the text.

U.S. Department of Health and Human Services. Agency for Toxic Substances and Disease Registry. Public Health Assessment: Atlantic Wood Industries Incorporated, Portsmouth, Virginia. http://www.atsdr.cdc.gov/HAC/pha/atlanticwood/awi_toc.html

U.S. Department of the Interior. National Park Service. National Register of Historic Places. Drydock Number One, Norfolk Naval Shipyard, nomination form, February 26, 1970.

U.S. Environmental Protection Agency. Mid-Atlantic Superfund Office. Atlantic Wood Industries, Inc., Virginia Superfund. http://epa.gov/reg3hwmd/npl/VAD990710410.htm (updated August 7, 2006).

U.S. Fish & Wildlife Service. Great Dismal Swamp National Wildlife Refuge. "The Great Dismal Swamp and the Underground Railroad." http://www.fws.gov/northeast/greatdismalswamp/pdf%20files/UR%20reference%20facts.pdf

Virginia Department of Conservation and Development. *State Historical Markers of Virginia*. 6th ed. Richmond: Division of Publicity and Advertising, 1948.

———. Virginia Division of Forestry. *Forest Trees of Virginia*. Charlottesville: Virginia Division of Forestry, 1969.

Virginia Department of Environmental Quality/Water Quality Standards. Office of Water Quality Programs. Fish Tissue and Sediment Monitoring Plan. March 19, 2001.

BOOKS

Abbott, William W. *A Virginia Chronology 1585–1783*. Williamsburg: The Virginia 350th Anniversary Celebration Corporation, 1957.

Armstrong, George D. *The Summer of Pestilence: A History of the Ravages of the Yellow Fever in Norfolk, Virginia, A.D. 1855*. Philadelphia: J.R. Lippincott & Company, 1856.

Arnold, Robert. *The Dismal Swamp and Lake Drummond*. Norfolk: Green, Burke and Gregory, 1888.

Art Works of Norfolk, Virginia, and Vicinity. Chicago: W. Kennicott and Company, Publishers, 1895, 1902.

Brown, Alexander Crosby. *The Dismal Swamp Canal*. Chesapeake, Virginia: Norfolk County Historical Society, 1967.

————. *Juniper Waterway: A History of the Albemarle and Chesapeake Canal*. Charlottesville: University Press of Virginia, for The Mariner's Museum and Norfolk County Historical Society, 1981.

Butt, Marshall W. *Portsmouth Under Four Flags*. Portsmouth, VA: Portsmouth Historical Association, 1961.

Cobb, Elijah. *A Cape Cod Skipper*. New Haven: Yale University Press, 1925.

Cross, Charles B., Jr. *A Navy for Virginia: A Colony's Fleet in the Revolution*. Yorktown: The Virginia Independence Bicentennial Commission, 1981.

Cross, Charles B., Jr., and Eleanor Cross. *Chesapeake: A Pictorial History*. Virginia Beach: Walsworth, 1985.

De Costa, B.F. *The Pre-Columbian Discovery of America by Northmen, with Translations from the Icelandic Sagas*. Albany, NY: Joel Munsell's Sons, Publishers, 1890.

Drake, Samuel Adams. *The Making of Virginia and the Middle Colonies*. New York: Charles Scribner's Sons, 1893.

Elizabeth River Project. *Wildlife Habitat Guide for Restoration and Landscaping in the Elizabeth River Watershed*. Portsmouth, VA: The Elizabeth River Project, 1999.

Emmerson, John C., Jr. *The Steamboat Comes to Norfolk Harbor and the Log of the First Ten Years*. Ann Arbor, MI: Edwards Brothers, Inc., 1949.

Forrest, William S. *Historical and Descriptive Sketches of Norfolk and Vicinity*. Philadelphia: Lindsay and Blakiston, 1853.

Foss, William O. *The United States Navy in Hampton Roads*. Virginia Beach: The Donning Company Publishers, 1984.

Goldenberg, Joseph A. *Shipbuilding in Colonial America*. Charlottesville: University Press of Virginia, 1976.

BIBLIOGRAPHY

Greeley, Horace, et al. *The Great Industries of the United States*. Hartford, CT: J.B. Burr and Hyde, 1873.

Hagemann, James A. *The Heritage of Virginia*. Norfolk: The Donning Company Publishers, 1986.

Haile, Edward Wright, ed. *Jamestown Narratives: Eyewitness Accounts of the Virginia Colony*. Champlain, VA: Roundhouse, 1998.

Hakluyt, Richard. *The Principal Navigations, Voyages, Traffiques &Discoveries of the English Nation, Made by Sea or Over-Land to the Remote and Farthest Distant Quarters of the Earth at Any Time within the Compasse of these 1600 Yeeres*. Glasgow, Scotland: J. MacLehose and Sons, 1903–05. Reprint, New York: A.M. Kelley, 1969.

Hallahan, John M. *The Battle of Craney Island: A Matter of Credit*. Portsmouth, VA: Saint Michael's Press, 1986.

La Rochefoucauld-Liancourt, François-Alexandre-Frédéric, duc de. *Voyage dans les États-Unis d'Amérique, fait en 1795, 1796 et 1797*. Paris: DuPont, 1799.

Lamb, Robert W., ed. *Our Twin Cities of the Nineteenth Century: Norfolk and Portsmouth—Their Past, Present and Future*. Norfolk: Barcroft, Publisher, 1887–88.

Lossing, Benson J. *Pictorial Field-Book of the War of 1812*. New York: Harper, 1868.

Loth, Calder, ed. *The Virginia Landmarks Register*. Charlottesville: University Press of Virginia, 1987.

Mapp, Alford J., and Ramona H. Mapp. *Portsmouth—A Pictorial History*. Virginia Beach: The Donning Company Publishers, 1989.

Martin-Perdue, Nancy J., and Charles L. Perdue Jr., eds. *Talk About Trouble: A New Deal Portrait of Virginians in the Great Depression*. Chapel Hill: The University of North Carolina Press, 1996.

McDonald, Jerry N., and Susan L. Woodward. *Indian Mounds of the Atlantic Coast*. Newark, OH: The McDonald and Woodward Publishing Company, 1987.

Moomaw, W. Hugh. *Virginia's Belt Line Railroad: The Norfolk and Portsmouth, 1898–1997*. Gloucester Point, VA: Hallmark Publishing Company, 1998.

O'Reilly, John Boyle. "Canoeing Sketches," in *Athletics and Manly Sport*. Boston: Pilot Publishing Company, 1890.

Peterson, Norma Lois, ed. *The Defence of Norfolk in 1807 as told by William Tatham to Thomas Jefferson*. Chesapeake, VA: Norfolk County Historical Society, 1970.

Powell, William H. *Officers of the Regular Army and Navy Who Served in the Civil War*. Philadelphia: L.R. Hamersly and Company, 1892.

————. *Officers of the Volunteer Army and Navy Who Served in the Civil War*. Philadelphia: L.R. Hamersly and Company, 1893.

Pugh, Jesse F., and Frank T. Williams. *The Hotel in the Great Dismal Swamp and Contemporary Events Thereabouts*. Richmond, VA: Garrett and Massie, 1964.

Sellers, John R., comp. *Civil War Manuscripts: A Guide to the Collection in the Library of Congress*. Washington, D.C.: Superintendent of Documents, 1986.

Smith, John. *The Generall Historie of Virginia, New England and the Summer Isles, Together with the True Travels, Adventures and Observations*. London: Michael Sparks, 1624. Available from the Library of Congress.

Stansbury, Charles Frederick. *The Lake of the Great Dismal*. New York: A. and C. Boni, 1925.

Swem, Earl Gregg, ed. *Description of the Dismal Swamp and a Proposal to Drain the Swamp*. Metuchen, NJ: C.F. Heartman, 1922.

Tazewell, William L. *Norfolk's Waters: An Illustrated Maritime History of Hampton Roads*. Woodland Hills, California: Windsor Publications, 1982.

Tucker, George Holbert. *Norfolk Highlights 1584–1881*. Portsmouth, VA: Printcraft Press, 1972.

Walker, Carroll H. *Carroll Walker's Norfolk: A Tricentennial History*. Virginia Beach: The Donning Company Publishers, 1981.

————. *Norfolk: A Pictorial History*. Virginia Beach: The Donning Company Publishers, 1975.

Wertenbaker, Thomas J. *Norfolk: Historic Southern Port*. Durham: Duke University Press, 1931.

Whichard, Rogers Dey. *The History of Lower Tidewater Virginia*. 3 vols. New York: Lewis Historical Publishing Company, 1959.

Wingo, Elizabeth. *The Battle of Great Bridge*. Chesapeake, VA: Norfolk County Historical Society, 1964.

Yarborough, Betty Hathaway, and Jayne Cosby Wilkinson. *The Great Dismal*. Chesapeake, VA: Norfolk County Historical Society, 1965.

Yarsinske, Amy Waters. *Ghent: John Graham's Dream, Norfolk, Virginia's Treasure*. Charleston, SC: The History Press, 2006.

————. *The Jamestown Exposition: American Imperialism on Parade*. 2 vols. Charleston, SC: Arcadia Publishing, 1999.

————. *The Martin Years: Norfolk Will Always Remember Roy*. Gloucester Point, VA: Hallmark Publishing Company, 2001.

————. *Norfolk, Virginia: The Sunrise City By the Sea*. Virginia Beach: The Donning Company Publishers, 1994.

BIBLIOGRAPHY

————. *Norfolk's Church Street: Between Memory and Reality*. Charleston, SC: Arcadia Publishing, 1999.

————. *Ocean View*. Charleston, SC: Arcadia Publishing, 1998.

————. *Summer on the Southside*. Charleston, SC: Arcadia Publishing, 1998.

————. *Wings of Valor, Wings of Gold: An Illustrated History of U.S. Naval Aviation*. Stratford, CT: Flying Machines Press, 1998.

————. *Winter Comes to Norfolk*. Charleston, SC: Arcadia Publishing, 1997.

ARTICLES, ORAL HISTORIES, PAMPHLETS, PAPERS, REPORTS AND SPEECHES

There were numerous articles, brochures, pamphlets, meeting minutes and organization papers and broadsides that informed the author; some were dated, some not, while others had been carefully cut out and slipped into the vertical files of research libraries, including the Sargeant Memorial Room, Norfolk Public Library. As many as possible are listed below while others are sporadically included as textual references.

Barbachem, M.J. "Toxics management in the Elizabeth River watershed: A Chesapeake Bay region of concern," paper delivered October 8, 1996, Surface Water Quality and Ecology Symposia: Watershed Management.

Barrow, Mary Reid. "Our 'hidden' river." *Virginia Beach Beacon*, June 23, 1996.

Blair, John L. "Excavations at Burnt House field site." *Quarterly Bulletin of the Archeological Society of Virginia* 24, no. 1 (September 1969).

Clancy, Paul. "Leaders unite to pursue cleanup." *Virginian-Pilot*, October 6, 2000.

Colonna, William Willoughby, Jr. "Captain Will Colonna's Blackwater 1940s–1997." Privately printed, 1997.

————. "Colonna houseboat built 1927." Privately printed, May 1996.

————. "The history of Charles J. Colonna 1849–1920." Privately printed, May 1996.

————."W.W. Colonna residence." Privately printed, 1997.

Colonna, William Willoughby, Jr., and Benjamin O. Colonna Jr. "The mystery of John Wilkins Colonna 1877–1899." Privately printed, 1996.

Colonna, William Willoughby, Jr., Benjamin O. Colonna Jr. and Nicholas W. Paxson. "Colonna Marine Railway 1875." Privately printed, 1989.

Conlin, Joseph. "Consider the oyster." *American Heritage* 31, no. 2 (February/March 1980).

Cross, Charles B., Jr., ed. "An address embracing a historical sketch of Norfolk County, Virginia, delivered at Berkley, July 4, 1876, by request of the board of supervisors, by the Honorable Legh R. Watts, judge of the County Court of Norfolk County." Norfolk County Historical Society, 1964.

Dorsey, Catherine. "River of hope." *Southern Home and Garden*, n.d.

Dorsey, Jack. "Elizabeth River wounded, dirty lady in need of help." *Ledger-Star*, September 1, 1977.

Eaton, Walter Prichard. "The real Dismal Swamp." *Harper's*, December 1910.

Elizabeth River Project. "Elizabeth River restoration and conservation: A watershed action plan," June 20, 1996.

———. "Elizabeth River restoration and conservation: A watershed action plan," September 8, 2002.

———. *Mudflats*, Fall 2006.

———. *Mudflats*, Summer 2006.

———. "Paradise found: Paradise Creek restoration plan," August 1, 2003.

——— "Paradise found," www.elizabethriver.org/Archives/Paradise.htm

———. "River Stars," pamphlet.

———. "Superfund sites on the Elizabeth River." http://www.elizabethriver.org/Superfund/Superfund.htm

Elizabeth River Project and University of Virginia Institute for Environmental Negotiation. "Rediscover the treasure: Money Point revitalization," October 2006.

Elizabeth River Project and Virginia Department of Environmental Quality. "State of the river 2003," 2003.

Elizabeth River Restoration Trust. Annual report, October 31, 2005.

Etheridge, Ruby F. "Freezing wintertime? Norfolk had its share." *Norfolk Virginian-Pilot*, March 11, 1951.

Flanders, Alan. "Freedmen began trek to Africa at Portsmouth; newspapers tell us how many left on each voyage and who the sponsors were." *Portsmouth Currents*, February 16, 1996.

Friddell, Guy. "Elizabeth River runs through memories of old-timer." *Virginian-Pilot*, September 6, 1993.

Garden Club of Virginia. Historic Garden Week in Virginia, program excerpts. April 22–30, 1978.

Geroux, Bill. "Dirty but not dead, river throbs with both marine, industrial life." *Richmond Times-Dispatch*, July 21, 1991.

Hampton Roads Sanitation District. "Penalty fund boosts Elizabeth River education, Mattaponi River shad." *WaterWays* 15, no. 2 (2003).

Harper, Scott. "Elizabeth River Project draws attention on a national scale." *Virginian-Pilot*, February 20, 2002.

————."Elizabeth River troubles ebbing." *Virginian-Pilot*, November 20, 1999.

Holladay, Mildred M. "A history of Portsmouth." *Portsmouth Star*, January 19, 1936.

Houston, Charles W. "Virginia oyster, queen of seafoods, once more graces the festive board." *Virginian-Pilot and Norfolk Landmark*, September 5, 1926.

Jones, Rebecca Burcher. "Old-growth forest lives on near Courtland." *Virginian-Pilot*, December 3, 2006.

Kruser, John E., and George Zimmermann. "Restoring Atlantic white cedar swamps: A review of techniques for propagation and establishment." *Tree Planters Notes* 46, no. 3 (Summer 1995).

Lake, Marvin Leon. "Lakewood Bridge action delayed." *Virginian-Pilot*, February 11, 1981.

Lane, Ralph. "An account of the particularities of the imployments of the English men left in Virginia by Sir Richard Greeneuill vnder the charge of Master Ralfe Lane of the same, from the 17 of August 1585, vntill the 18 of June 1586, at which they departed the Countrie: sent, and directed to Sir Walter Raleigh." In *The Principall Navigations, Voiages and Discoveries of the English nation, made by Sea or ouer Land, to the most remote and farthest distant Quarters of the earth at any time within the compasse of these 1500 yeeres*, edited by Richard Hakluyt. London: George Bishop and Ralph Newberie, 1589. (Provided in multiple forms by several research institutions.)

————. "An account of the particularities of the imployments of the English men left in Virginia by Sir Richard Greeneuill vnder the charge of Master Ralfe Lane of the same, from the 17 of August 1585, vntill the 18 of June 1586, at which they departed the Countrie: sent, and directed to Sir Walter Raleigh." In *The Roanoke Voyages 1584–1590: Documents to Illustrate the English Voyages to North America Under the Patent Granted to Sir Walter Raleigh in 1584*, edited by David Beers Quinn. 2 vols, Hakluyt Society, second series 104, 1955. New York: Dover, 1991.

Ledger-Star. "Elizabeth River polluted beyond early recovery?" May 17, 1975.

Living River Restoration Trust, United States Army Corps of Engineers, Norfolk District and Virginia Department of Environmental Quality, pamphlet.

MacCord, Howard A. "Camden: A post contact Indian site in Caroline County." *Quarterly Bulletin of the Archeological Society of Virginia* 24, no. 1 (September 1969).

Matteson, Keith, Kevin Kluzak and Dean Starook. "Creative containment." *Waste Age*, March 1, 2004.

McPherson, Elizabeth Gregory, ed. "Letter of William Tatham." *William and Mary Quarterly* 16, no. 2, Second Series (April 1936).

Miller, Ann B., and Kenneth M. Clark. "A survey of movable span bridges in Virginia," final report. Study sponsored jointly by the Virginia Department of Transportation and the University of Virginia. Published in Charlottesville, February 1998.

Mook, Maurice A. "Algonkian ethnohistory of the Carolina Sound." *Journal of the Washington Academy of Sciences* 34 (July 15, 1944).

Norfolk Ledger. Editorial, June 24, 1807.

Norfolk-Portsmouth Chamber of Commerce. "Norfolk-Portsmouth: A busy port, a thriving metropolis, an all-year playground." Published as an advertising piece, circa 1926.

Seltzer, Craig. "Selling environmental restoration projects." *Geo-Strata*, January 2003.

Southern Argus. "Local intelligence." June 10, 1854.

Spong, William B., Jr. "What the Elizabeth has given the nation," excerpted remarks. The Elizabeth River Project, October 22, 1993.

Stanus, Joan. "Saving the river." *Norfolk Compass*, October 8, 1998.

Stout, S.A., J.M. Leather and W.E. Corl III. "A user's guide for determining the sources of contaminants in sediments: A demonstration study: Sources of PAH in sediments in the vicinity of the Norfolk Naval Shipyard, Elizabeth River, Norfolk, Virginia." Technical Report 1907, Department of the Navy, SPAWAR Systems Center, San Diego, September 2003.

Strother, David Hunter. "The Dismal Swamp." *Harper's Weekly* 13, no. 76 (September 1856).

Tidwell, John. "The Great Dismal Swamp." *American Heritage* 53, no. 2 (April/May 2002).

Tucker, George Holbert. "Little-known Elizabeth inspired our river's name." *Virginian-Pilot*, May 26, 1997.

———."The Norfolk visit of Thomas Moore." *Virginian-Pilot*, September 17, 1933.

———. "The river ripples her name." *Virginian-Pilot*, April 17, 1971.

———. Untitled column. *Virginian-Pilot*, June 7, 1969.

Verrazano, Giovanni da, to Francis I, King of France, July 8, 1524, conveying record of Verrazano's voyage of 1524. In *The Voyages of Giovanni da Verrazano, 1524–1528*, edited by Lawrence C. Wroth. New Haven: Yale, 1970.

BIBLIOGRAPHY

Virginia Maritime Association, synopsis of Port of Virginia. http://hrma.portofhamptonroads. com/about/History/index_html/?searchterm=port%20of%20virginia

Virginian-Pilot. "The Elizabeth improves." Editorial, November 26, 1999.

———. "Elizabeth's friends." Editorial, October 23, 1998.

———. "Merrimac anchor found in harbor." April 19, 1911.

———."Oyster, queen of seafoods, more graces the festive board." September 5, 1926.

———. "Worst of the worst." Editorial, August 1, 1985.

Virginian-Pilot and Norfolk Landmark. "Another avenue to Lakewood section." January 1, 1931.

Watts, Legh R. "An address embracing a historical sketch of Norfolk County, Virginia," delivered at Berkley, July 4, 1876.

Wharton, Tony. "Relics from the mud." *Virginian-Pilot,* February 27, 1997.

Wilkins, Guy. "Poplar Hall displays gracious living of ages." *Norfolk Virginian-Pilot and Portsmouth Star,* April 17, 1955.

Women's Propeller Club of the United States. "Mary Ann Brown Patten—Valiant Woman." http:// www.propellerclubhq.com/wpc/mary.html

INDEX

INDEX

ABOUT THE AUTHOR

A nationally known author of narrative nonfiction, Amy Waters Yarsinske received her bachelor of arts degrees in economics and English from Randolph-Macon Woman's College in Lynchburg, Virginia, and her master of planning degree from the University of Virginia School of Architecture, where she was a DuPont Fellow. Yarsinske is also a 1998 graduate of the prestigious CIVIC Leadership Institute, a member of Investigative Reporters and Editors (IRE), Authors Guild and is involved in a wide range of current community-based organizations and committees, public and private sector projects. She is the author of over forty books, including *Wings of Valor, Wings of Gold: An Illustrated History of U.S. Naval Aviation* (Flying Machines Press, 1998), *Mud Flat to Master Jet Base: Fifty Years at NAS Oceana* (Hallmark, 2001), "Memories and Memorials" in *Naval Aviation* (Hugh Lauter Levin Associates, 2001), *Forward for Freedom: The Story of Battleship Wisconsin* (BB-64) (Donning, 2001), *No One Left Behind: The Lt. Comdr. Michael Scott Speicher Story* (Dutton, 2002), *Rendezvous with Destiny: The FDR Legacy* (Donning, 2003), *Ghent: John Graham's Dream, Norfolk, Virginia's Treasure* (The History Press, 2006) and *125 Years of the Actors Fund* (Donning for the Actors Fund, 2007).

Yarsinske lives in Norfolk, Virginia, with her husband and three children.

Visit us at
www.historypress.net